101 Outstanding Wooden Toy and Children's Furniture Projects

No. 3058
$24.95

101 Outstanding
Wooden Toy and Children's Furniture Projects

Wayne L. Kadar

TAB BOOKS Inc.
Blue Ridge Summit, PA

FIRST EDITION
FIRST PRINTING

Copyright © 1989 by TAB BOOKS Inc.
Printed in the United States of America

Reproduction or publication of the content in any manner, without express permission of the publisher, is prohibited. No liability is assumed with respect to the use of the information herein.

Library of Congress Cataloging-in-Publication Data

Kadar, Wayne Louis.
101 outstanding wooden toy and children's furniture projects / by Wayne L. Kadar.
p. cm.
Includes index.
ISBN 0-8306-9558-3   ISBN 0-8306-9358-0 (pbk.)
1. Wooden toy making. 2. Children's furniture. I. Title.
TT174.5.W6K33 1988
684'.08–dc 19   88-24967
                              CIP

TAB BOOKS Inc. offers software for sale. For information and a catalog, please contact TAB Software Department, Blue Ridge Summit, PA 17294-0850.

Questions regarding the content of this book should be addressed to:

Reader Inquiry Branch
TAB BOOKS Inc.
Blue Ridge Summit, PA 17294-0214

Manuscript prepared by Lori L. Grezeszak
Edited by Joanne M. Slike

Contents

	Acknowledgments	*vii*
	Introduction	*viii*
Section I	**ABOUT TOY MAKING**	**1**
1	**Necessary Tools** Safety • Saws • Shaping Tools • Drilling Tools • Clamps • Abrasives	3
2	**Tips on Toys** Wheels • Axles • Methods of Assembly • Finishing Materials	6
Section II	**THE FLEET**	**15**
3	**Light Trucks** Pickup Truck • Mini Motor Home • Delivery Van	17
4	**Cars** Wagon, Sportscar, Sedan, and Import • Indy-Style Racer	26
5	**Large Trucks** The Cab • The Hood • Flatbed Truck • Log Hauler • Lumber Truck • Dump Truck • Semitruck • Semitruck Trailers • Gas/Milk Hauler • Cement Mixer	36
6	**Construction Vehicles** The Creeper Unit • The Bulldozer • The Creeper Shovel • Pay Loader • Grader • Truck Mounted Shovel	61

Section III	**TOY BOX STUFFERS**	***87***
7	*Quick Cutouts*	***89***
8	*Things That Fly* Piper Cub Airplane • Helicopter • Interstellar Fighter • The Orican Shuttle • Personnel Transporter • Planetary Landing Vessel • Planetary Mobile Unit (P.M.U.) • Venusian Star Cruiser	***110***
9	*Project Potpourri* Doll Cradle • The Creature Keeper • 35mm Camera • Krayon Keeper • Clipboards and Lap Boards • Doll Bed • "Old 99" Toy Train • Name Train • Tictactoe • Stilts • Doll High Chair • Hydroplane • Bass Boat • Great Lakes Freighter	***151***
10	*For the Little Ones* Shape Box • Toolbox and Tools • Building Blocks • Simple Pull Toys • Jumping and Profile Bears • Clown Doll • Sandwich Stacking Toy • Toothbrush Tugboat • Shape Puzzle • Passenger Ship	***199***
Section IV	**KIDS' FURNITURE**	***251***
11	*Room Organizers* Child-Size Clothes Pole • Personalized Coatracks • Wall Shelf Unit • Corner Shelf • Baseball Bat Coatrack • Baseball Equipment Rack	***253***
12	*More For the Kids' Rooms* Toy Box • Painting Easel • Child-Size Workbench • Balance Beam • Child's Stool	***273***
	Appendix: Toy Making Suppliers	***291***
	Index	***303***

Acknowledgments

This book has long been in the making. I started it by searching through toy books for that "special" gift for my nephew. Upon not finding the special gift, I made a personal design. I continued this book of toys through the births of my own three children and two more nephews. Wood toys were a natural pursuit for a woodworking teacher with children. For this reason I thank Brandon, Kasie, Grant, Scott, Derek, and Ramie for giving me the reason to design and build the toys found here. I dedicate this book to them.

Others who have been of assistance in one way or another include my wife Karen, whose confident prodding kept the book going when the writing bogged down. Many woodworking students of Harbor Beach High School helped build several of the projects, including Brent Kramer, Bruce and Pat Holdwick, and Jeff Lieberskind. The woodworking abilities of these people proved to be a valuable contribution. Thanks also to the Harbor Beach Community Schools who permitted the use of the high school industrial education laboratories for some construction.

The developing and printing of photographs was handled by the capable people of Oltz Studios in Bad Axe, Michigan. The typing and initial editing was done by Lori L. Grezeszak. Finally, I would like to thank Sandi Skinner for being the back-up typist and coming through when I needed her.

Introduction

In all known civilizations, relics have been found which archeologists have determined to be children's toys. They might be as simple as sticks tied together with reed or as elaborate as miniature birch bark canoes. Although toys for children have been around for quite some time, they have changed over the centuries. Handmade toys have been replaced by those that are commercially mass-produced. Wood and cast metal, the traditional materials for toys, have given way to plastic. Despite their functionality, the plastic mass-produced toys (produced by the millions) are missing one important feature: the toymakers' love for the craft. The toy-making craftsperson, who creates a child's toy, one piece at a time, adds a little bit of love in each step along the way. Similar to Gepetto's love as he worked on his toy puppet, Pinnochio.

In this book, I have tried to bridge the gap between the mass-produced commercial toys that fill the shelves of most stores, and the toys made by the hands of the craftsperson. These toys have been designed to be built with the most popular of the traditional materials: wood. Wood allows the craftsperson to shape each piece, adding a little of themselves as they go. Yet, many of the toys have been designed to allow the craftsperson to utilize some mass-production techniques in order to speed production, especially if the toys are being made in multiples for gift-giving or resale.

Some of the toys are also of modern design. The chapter on airplanes and other flying things contains instructions on building several spacecraft.

If you are building for resale, there are several projects that include hints on how the projects can be built quickly and efficiently, yet still retain their one-of-a-kind look. In fact, there is a whole section of vehicles that can be built using mass-production techniques. Each toy in the section is designed to approximately the same scale, so the cars and trucks form a fleet of vehicles.

Cars, trucks, and spacecraft are not the only types of toys that can be built. There is also a chapter that includes a wide variety of projects such as a doll cradle, 35mm camera, and a creature keeper.

Because not all toys are right for all children, one chapter includes toys especially designed for youngsters. Younger children do not have the muscle control required to operate some toys. Therefore, many of the toys in that chapter are designed to allow a child to have fun while teaching such things as hand-eye coordination, balance, and muscle control.

Also, there is a section that has instructions for several projects for use in the toyroom, play house, bedroom or outdoors. Some of the projects are shelf units. Shelves will be needed for the child's room just to store all of the toys that have been built by the craftsperson. Other projects include coatracks, equipment racks, and other items to help keep the child's room neat.

In addition, to aid you in selecting the wood and other items, I have provided a list of required materials at the end of each chapter that gives dimensions and the quantity of each piece needed. This way you can be certain you have everything before you begin a project.

Finally in the Appendix, I have included a list of Toy Making Suppliers who sell plans, kits, tools, parts, and so on.

Section I

About Toy Making

Having the desire to build children's toys is often not all that is required. There are many factors that must be taken into consideration; among them are tools and their uses, materials available to the toy-making craftsperson, hints on how to build toys easily, and most importantly, safety. The next two chapters address these concerns.

1
CHAPTER

Necessary Tools

This chapter describes some of the tools you can use when building the toys in this book. The description of each concentrates on the safe use of the tool and how it is used in toy construction. The information is brief. If you require more information, there are fine books available that deal exclusively with tools.

The tools have been grouped into categories based on the function they perform. The categories are listed in the approximate order in which they might be used in toy construction.

SAFETY

Any tool used in toy making, whether hand- or power-operated, has the potential to harm its operator and those nearby. With this in mind, you must approach each tool with an eye toward safety. Remember that wood is much harder than flesh. A tool that is designed to cut, shave, or shape wood, will most definitely have little problem causing injury.

Another characteristic of wood that requires special attention is that when cut, splinters have a tendency to fly away from the surface. The operator should *always wear eye protection* while working.

SAWS

Saws can be divided into three subcategories: handsaws, portable power saws, and stationary power saws. The most common types of handsaws are *crosscut* saws and *ripsaws*. You use the crosscut saw, as the name indicates, to cut across the grain of the wood. When you are cutting in the same direction of the grain, you should use a ripsaw.

The crosscut saws and ripsaws can only make straight cuts. In order to cut curves in wood, you should use a *coping saw*. The coping saw has a U-shaped frame and a thin, reducible blade that allows the craftsperson to cut irregular shapes.

Over the years, portable power saws have been developed that operate in the same manner as hand-operated saws. The portable electric circular saw is used to cut wood with and against the grain, the same as handsaws, but much faster.

The *scroll saw,* or jigsaw, is a portable power saw which, like the coping saw, is designed for cutting curves. The scroll saw has a small blade that functions in an up-and-down cutting motion. The small blade allows it to cut tight curves into wood.

The portable circular saw, equipped with a 7½-inch-diameter blade, can make most cuts that are done with both a hand-powered crosscut saw and a ripsaw. The circular saw can operate much faster than its hand-powered counterparts; but you must remember to use much care and caution while operating the fast-turning blade.

The next kind of saws are stationary power machines. These machines are capable of much more accurate work than is possible with the other cutting tools.

The *radial-arm,* or *cutoff saw* is designed to function primarily in a crosscutting capacity. Because crosscutting is not the only operation necessary in most toy making, the saw is also capable of ripping, cutting miters and compound miters, rabbeting, and dadoing.

While the primary function of the radial-arm saw is crosscutting, the table saw has been designed to function as a ripsaw, cutting with the grain. Nevertheless, this saw can also perform all of the same functions as the radial-arm saw.

The *band saw* is capable of cutting curves in any thickness of wood. While it cannot cut as tight as the thin-bladed jigsaw, it can be used for most irregularly shaped cutting operations.

SHAPING TOOLS

A *rasp* is an extremely coarse file that is used to remove large amounts of material quickly. A rasp is strictly a shaping tool; it is not a smoothing tool. It leaves a very rough surface that requires further refining.

Once the initial shaping has been done with a rasp, the rough surface must be worked with a series of wood files. The coarse ones are used first, since they remove a lot of material at once. The finer files are used next to remove very little material. They are capable of producing a smoother surface.

DRILLING TOOLS

Toy construction requires many holes to be drilled. They can be holes to hold the axle onto a car, or dowel holes used to strengthen a glued joint. Whatever the purpose of the drilled hole, there are two methods by which they can be made. They can either be made manually or with a power tool.

The brace and bit, although no longer found in commercial production use, is still a handy tool when used on soft woods. The drill bits used with a brace are required to have an enlarged square shank. These drill bits should not be used in any other type of drill bit because they also have a screw point. If the screw point is turned too fast, as is possible with a power tool, the bit will draw itself into the wood too quickly, possibly damaging the bit, if not the wood. The hand drill is a helpful tool for drilling holes in wood. Any bit except the brace bit can be used, providing it fits into the chuck.

If there are many holes that must be drilled (as in the example of the "Old 99" toy train, where there are at least five holes in each car), using the bit-and-brace and handdrill will become quite tiring and time-consuming. An electric drill will make the job much easier. A portable electric drill can be purchased at any hardware, discount, or department store. The price of a hand-held electric drill can be as low as $20 or as high as several hundred dollars, for a heavy-duty commercial model. The size of the portable electric drill is determined by the largest-size drill bit that will fit into the chuck. Common sizes are ¼ inch, ⅜ inch, and ½ inch. Larger sizes are available, but in more expensive professional models.

There are several types of drill bits that you can purchase for use with electric drills. The twist drill is the most common type of drill bit and is used in both metal and woodworking. The bits are available is sizes from ¹⁄₁₆ inch to over an inch in diameter. If the drill motor being used can only handle bits of ⅜ inch, for example, the chuck of the drill motor will only open to allow a drill bit shank with a diameter of ⅜ inch. If a larger-size hole is necessary, a specialty bit is required. These bits are sold with a shank, the portion of the bit held in the drill, which is sized to fit the drill motor chuck; but the twisting and cutting part of the bit can be much larger than the shank. The drill can cut holes up to ¾ inch in diameter.

CLAMPS

Most woodworkers will have access to either spring, hand-screw, or bar clamps. The spring clamp is the most handy of these. You only need to squeeze the handles, put them in place, and release the pressure. Though easy to use, these clamps should be avoided when a lot of pressure is required.

The hand-screw clamp is most commonly used in woodshops. It is a good clamp that is adjustable to various thicknesses. The amount of pressure it exerts is only limited by the strength of the craftsperson. This type of clamp is relatively inexpensive.

If the hand-screw will not open large enough for the wood to be clamped, then bar clamps are necessary. Bar clamps are available in sizes ranging from 24 to 48 inches long and longer.This type of clamp is adjustable for use from a few inches to several feet, thus making it very useful for the home shop.

An alternative for a woodworker who is on a budget are pipe clamps. These are the two ends of the clamp that are sold without the bar. You can then purchase pipe, available at most hardware and plumbing stores, to form the bar portion. The pipe may be any length to accommodate even the longest jobs.

ABRASIVES

The use of sandpaper in smoothing a wood project is often looked upon as a necessary evil. It is a job that needs to be done to produce a smooth, defect-free surface. However, this is a job that is time-consuming and tedious.

Sandpaper is available in many grades, ranging from coarse to very fine. To standardize the grading of sandpaper, a numerical system has been developed by the industry that applies a large number to fine paper, and progressively lower numbers as the papers become more coarse. An 80-grit paper is a coarse paper that cuts through wood faster than a finer abrasive paper. After the wood has been ridded of major defects, then a 120- to 150- grit should be used. A fine paper will have a grit number within the range of 220 to 400.

The tools that have been described in this chapter are part of the craftsperson's heritage. Learn to use your tools, care for them, and respect them. They can be old friends or deadly enemies.

2
CHAPTER

Tips on Toys

To some, a homemade toy can be a block of wood with four hand-cut wood wheels held in place with large-head nails. While it is undoubtedly true that this will entertain a child, it is not a safe toy. I have written this chapter to assist the toymaker in making wise decisions concerning each project's safety. It includes some points which are "musts" for toys, while others are only suggestions. The craftsperson should read this chapter and apply the processes when necessary to produce the best and safest toys possible.

WHEELS

Many of the toys described in this book have wheels of one kind or another. The cars, trucks, and construction vehicles, of course, require wheels. But some of the other toys also have wheels as part of their design.

The toys in this book, for the most part, have been designed to use precut hardwood wheels. You can purchase wheels from many of the fine mail-order supply companies, listed in the Appendix. The wheels, axle pegs, slotted dowels, and many other materials used throughout this book have been supplied by the Toymakers' Supply Company of Tahoe City, California. (Their address and additional information can be found in the alphabetical listing of suppliers.) The wood wheels are sold in a wide range of diameters, from ¾ inch to 4¾ inches. The wheels are shaped to resemble a tire mounted on a hub, with an axle hole predrilled in the center.

Precut wood wheels, although easy to use, are usually more expensive than other types of wheels. These hardwood wheels are of a higher quality, which results in a professional appearance of the finished product.

Hardwood wheels are not the only wheels available to the toymaker. Three other types can be used. The first is hard rubber wheels. These wheels have been molded to resemble the shape and tread of real tires. A few of the toy-making supply companies sell hard rubber tires. The hard rubber tires are best held in place on the toy with an axle peg or a dowel axle with end caps. Both of these axles are described in detail later in this section.

Homemade wooden wheels and plastic or rubber wheels salvaged from broken toys are an inexpensive alternative to new, premade wheels.

Wooden wheels can be cut from solid lumber in one of three ways. The first method is to draw out the proper diameter wheel on the wood with a compass (Fig. 2-1), drill out the axle hole and cut out the wheel. (Cutting can be done with a coping saw, saber saw, or jigsaw.) Then file and sand round and smooth.

The second method, used to cut wooden wheels from solid lumber, is to use a circle cutter or fly cutter mounted in a drill press (Fig. 2-2). This method is especially good for cutting large wheels. The attachment will drill the axle hole and cut the wheel diameter in one operation. If you have access to a drill press, this is a quick and easy way to cut wheels. However, two notes of caution must be followed: (1) *Do not use a circle cutter in a hand-held portable drill.* The vibrations produced when the cutter is spinning are too great to be safely controlled in a hand-drilling operation; and, (2) *Be sure to securely tighten and double-check all adjustments on the circle cutter.* If they are loose when the cutter begins to spin, the parts might separate and fly apart with a force similar to that of a bullet. Also, do not use this without first securely clamping the board to the drill press table. Attempting to use a circle cutter while holding onto the wood might result in skinned and broken fingers.

Another method that can be employed to cut small wheels is with a hole cutter (Fig. 2-3). Once the hole is drilled, what remains is a circular piece of wood with a ¼-inch hole drilled through the center, perfect for use as a wheel! There are some drawbacks to this method, though. The wheels are usually quite rough and will require filing and/or

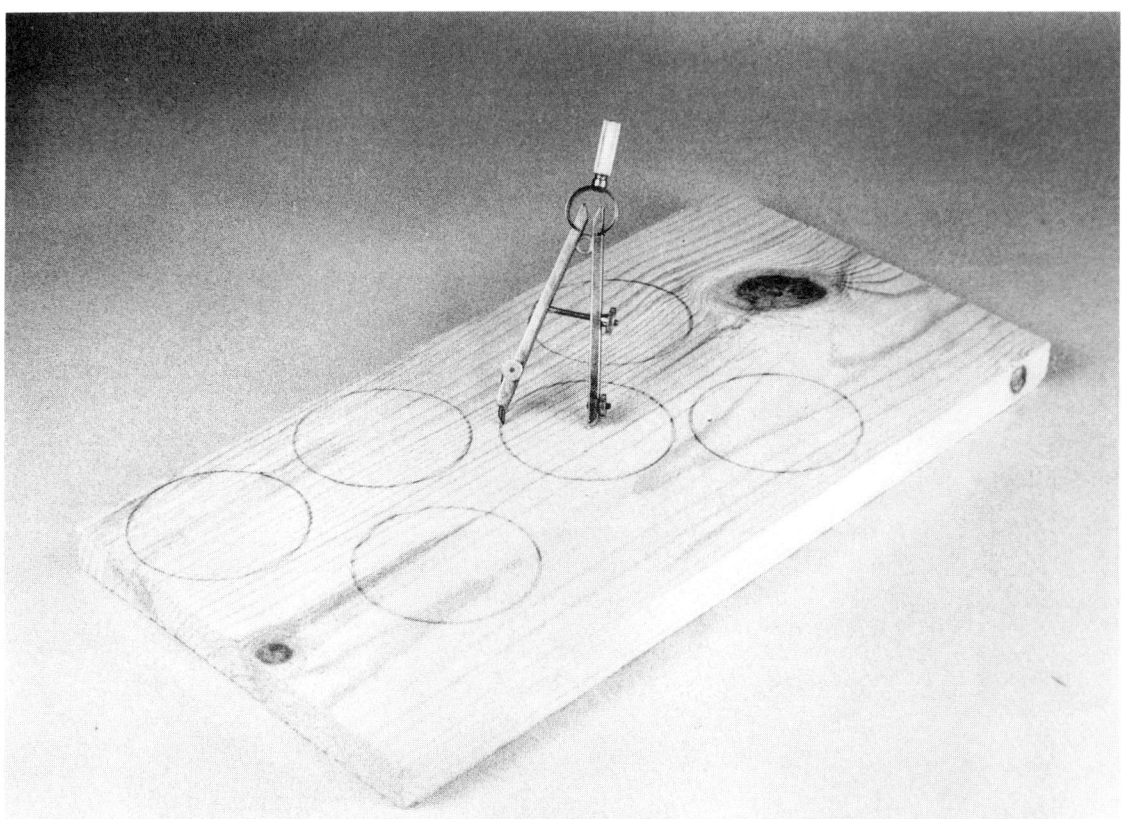

Fig. 2-1. *Wood wheels can be drawn on a piece of wood by using a compass, then be cut out and sanded.*

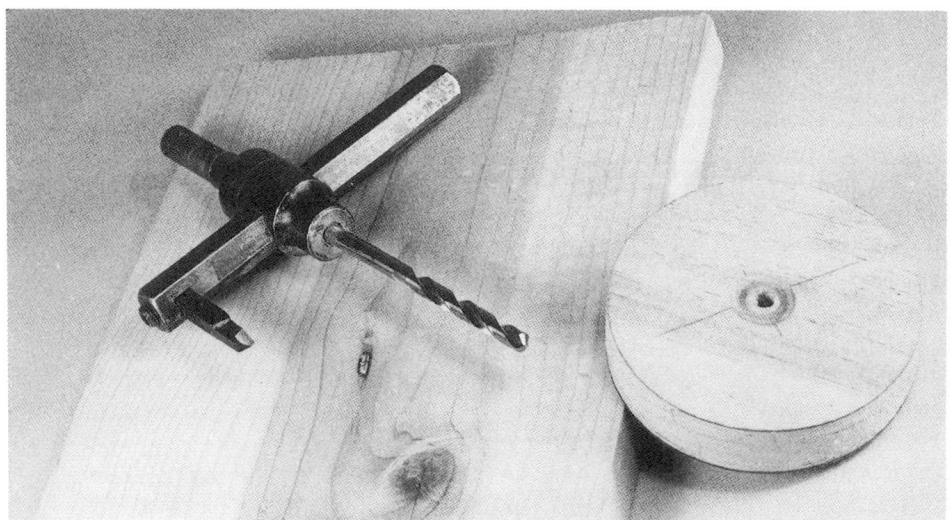

Fig. 2-2. *A circle cutter or fly cutter may be used to cut large circles, but be sure to refer to the safety cautions in the text prior to use.*

sanding. Care must be taken to make sure that all wheels used on a project are sanded to the same diameter. Another disadvantage of the hole cutter is that the thickest wheel that can be cut is ¾ inch. If thicker wheels are needed, you must drill partway, turn the board over, and drill the rest of the way through. It can be done, but you must be sure that the center drill is lined up perfectly, or it will be cut a bit lopsided.

Fig. 2-3. *Hole cutters are designed to be used with a drill press or at slow speeds in a hand-held drill. The hole cutter will cut both the outside diameter and the axle hole.*

AXLES

The next major point to consider is how to attach the wheels to the body of the vehicle. This can usually be accomplished *safely* in only two ways: wood dowels used as axles, or commercially produced wood axle pegs.

These two methods have been selected as the only two ways to attach wheels to vehicle bodies. Other methods that may be used cannot be considered safe. Although often used, screws and nails are *not* recommended methods. Screws turn in and they just as easily turn out. Once out, they are dangerous objects in the hands (or mouths) of children. Screws must not be used in any phase of toy making when the toy will be used by children under 5 years old.

Axle pegs can be purchased from several of the mail-order supply companies listed in the Appendix. The axle pegs are a very good way to hold the wheels in place. They are inserted through the axle hole in the wood or rubber wheel, and the peg is then glued into the wood body of the vehicle (Fig. 2-4). Axle pegs are available in three sizes, according to the diameter of the axle hole in the wheel (Fig. 2-5). The axle pegs will require a hole the same size or no more than $\frac{1}{16}$-inch larger than the diameter of the peg where each wheel is to be installed. Another safe method to affix wheels is with wood dowels. *Dowels* are wooden rods, usually of maple or birch, and are available at most hardware stores and lumber yards. They are sold in 3-foot lengths, with diameters ranging from $\frac{1}{8}$ to 1 inch.

When using the dowel method, you must first select a dowel equal to, or slightly less than, the diameter of the axle hole in the wheel. The hole drilled in the body of the wood vehicle must then be drilled large enough so that the wood dowel turns freely in it. The wood wheels are glued to the dowel. Be careful not to allow glue to leak into the hole drilled into the body, otherwise the axle will not spin freely.

Fig. 2-4. Commercially produced axle pegs are used to hold wood or rubber wheels permanently to a vehicle body.

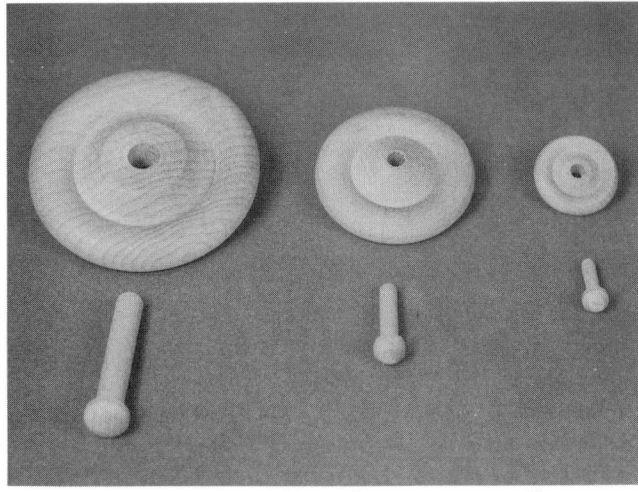

Fig. 2-5. *Three sizes of axle pegs are available.* (Courtesy of Toymakers Supply Company).

A new development in the wood dowel axles is the grooved dowel (Fig. 2-6). This type of dowel is superior to common dowels because the grooves provide a better gripping surface and more glueing area. The axle is force-fitted into the axle hole. The glue in the grooves not only adheres to the wheels, but also causes the dowel to swell slightly, making an even tighter fit.

Grooved dowels are currently available from a few of the mail-order toymaker suppliers. Although these dowels are more expensive than conventional dowels, the superior wheel adhesion is well worth the added cost.

Plastic wheels that are permanently mounted on a metal axle, which have been salvaged from discarded toys, should be avoided in homemade wooden vehicles. There is no practical, safe method to attach the wheel and axle assembly to the wooden vehicle.

METHODS OF ASSEMBLY

When assembling a project a very important point to consider is how to apply the adhesive. Always read and carefully follow the instructions on the glue container. Some adhesives require you to apply two layers of glue, a thin layer on each piece, while other types might give other specific instructions concerning the amount of clamping pressure

Fig. 2-6. *Grooved dowels work well as wood toy axles. They are superior to conventional dowels.*

or clamp time. Yet another brand of glue might require a specific "open time" (i.e., the time between when the glue is applied and when it is clamped). There are, however, only a few adhesives suitable for use in children's toys: liquid hide glue, resorcinol waterproof glue, and white glue.

Liquid hide glue, made from the hides of animals, is usually light brown in color and produces a very strong wood joint. The glue requires a clamp time of 2 to 3 hours before the glue will set. Liquid hide glue is not a waterproof glue and should be avoided on products that will be subjected to water or used out-of-doors.

Resorcinol waterproof glue comes as a two-part compound: One part liquid, the other a dry powder. The two need to be mixed each time the glue is used, because once mixed, the compound has a very short shelf-life. The mixed glue must be used within 8 hours. The glued joint will be very strong, dark brown in color, and completely waterproof. You should use this type of glue on projects that will be used outdoors or where moisture will be a problem. If it is not necessary that the wood joint be waterproof, you should avoid this type of glue, as it is expensive, causes a dark color of the glued joint, and requires a 16-hour clamping time.

The third type of glue is white glue. This glue is sold ready-for-use, is fast setting, strong enough for most applications, and has a short clamp time. However, white glue does not offer any resistance to moisture and should not be used where water might be a problem.

Some types of white glue that have been recently developed are specifically formulated for use on wood. The wood glues are sometimes yellowish in color, but this discoloration is more than made up for by very short clamp times, some as little as 1 hour.

Even with the development of very strong adhesives, often the glue alone is not enough to create a secure wood joint. One safe way to make a stronger joint is to use dowels glued between two boards.

Also available to the craftsperson are dowel pins, which are short dowels (2½ to 3 inches) with a groove cut spiraling along the surface. The spiral cut allows the glue to seep along the length of the dowel and provide better adhesion between the dowel and wood.

The illustration in Fig. 2-7 shows the method of installing a dowel to securely hold two boards together. Begin by clamping the boards in position where they will ultimately be glued and doweled together. With a twist bit, drill a hole through both boards that is ¹⁄₁₆-inch larger than the diameter of the dowel you are using. Apply a small amount of glue in the holes, making sure the glue coats the inside surfaces of the drilled holes. Then insert the wood dowels into the holes.

When the glue has had an opportunity to set, the dowel and boards will be permanently assembled. All that remains is to cut off the excess amount of dowel and sand the dowel flush with the surface.

Another type of dowel joint that can be used in toy making is the blind dowel. The *blind dowel* is a dowel that does not travel through both boards, but through one board and only partially into the next (Fig. 2-8). When using this method, be sure not to get large amounts of glue in the second hole. Otherwise the dowel will not be able to fill the drilled hole adequately because the excess glue will prohibit the dowel from sitting properly.

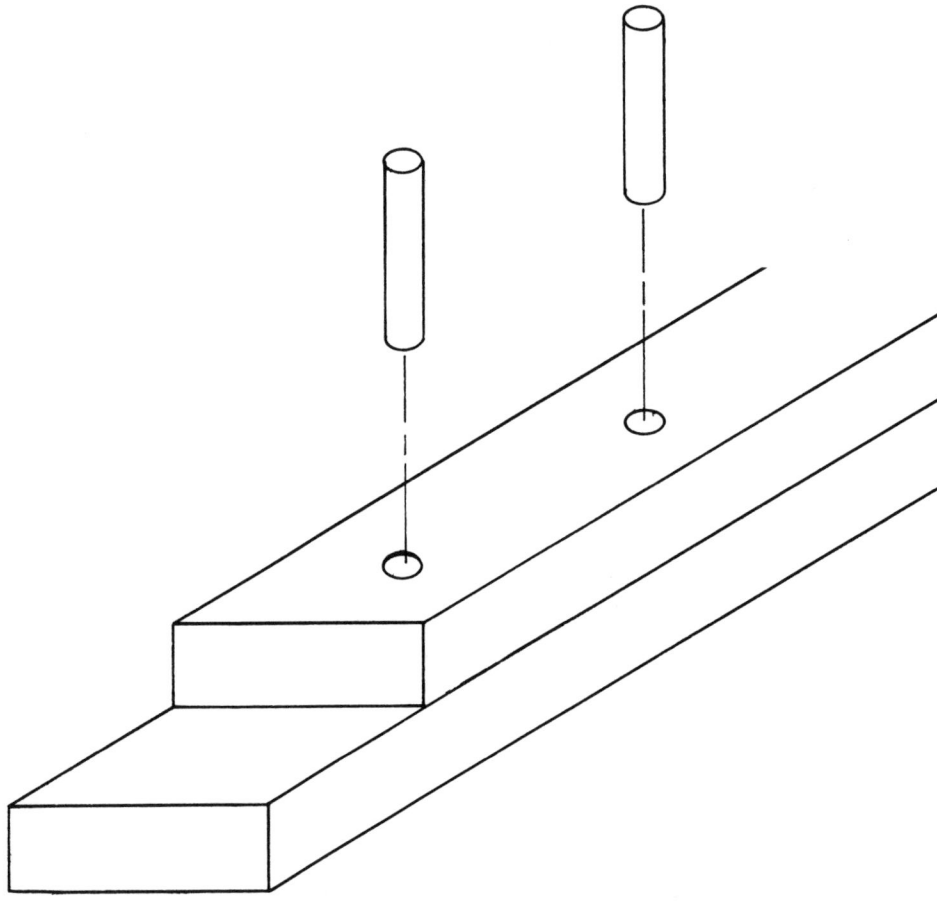

Fig. 2-7. *This is how two boards are doweled together.*

FINISHING MATERIALS

Finishing materials are applied to the surfaces of the project to protect and enhance the beauty of the wood. There are many types of finishing materials, but I will discuss only the most general types.

One of the oldest types of finishing materials is paint. Some craftspeople feel that a colored surface greatly improves the appearance of a toy and that an unpainted toy has the appearance of not being finished. You will have to decide what kind of look you prefer.

If you decide to paint your wooden toy, you should first consider the chemical makeup of the paint. First and foremost, the paint should not contain lead, as it is very harmful if ingested by a growing child. Other paints that should be avoided include any paints with labels that indicate they should not be used for toys or other child-related uses. Some paints to watch for are special-purpose paints such as those chemically formulated to be used on leaky basement walls or formulated to retard growth or mildew. Another kind to avoid are paints containing insecticides—once used as an aid to control household

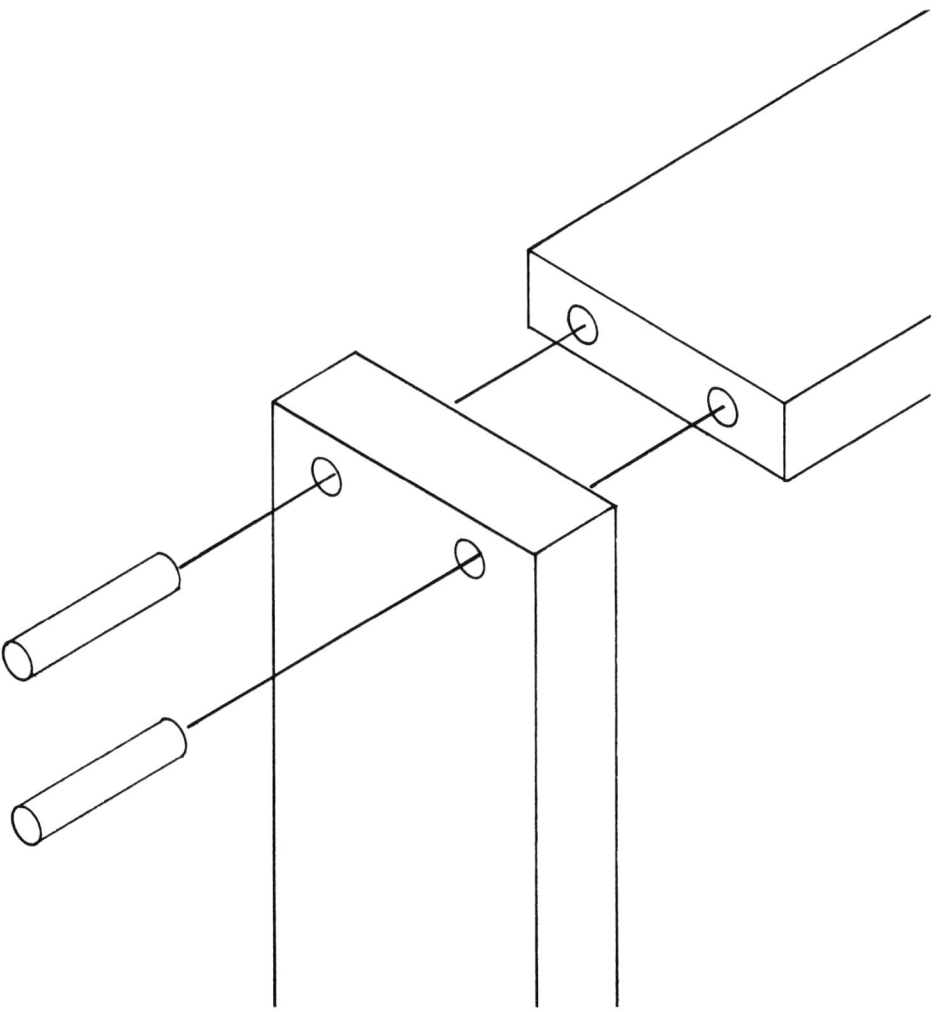

Fig. 2-8. *Often in woodworking a dowel hole cannot be drilled through both boards being joined together. When this situation occurs, use a blind joint.*

fly, insect, spider, and termite problems. Also, some porch and floor paints contain undesirable compounds, as do some paints developed to fight off rust on metal.

Stain is another finishing material. Stain is only used as a method of altering the color of the wood. It will not provide a protective coating. Stain is available commercially in two basic forms, water-base and oil-base.

One advantage of water-based paints is its easy clean-up. Simply washing with soap and water will clean the stain off hands or spill spots. However, this same advantage can also work against you. On some woods, usually softwoods, the water base will cause the grain of the wood to slightly swell and raise. When this happens, you will quickly notice that the smooth sanded surface of the project is now somewhat rougher, almost as if it weren't sanded.

On the other hand, oil-base stain is not as susceptible to grain-raising problems as water-base stains. However, it does have other disadvantages. One disadvantage is clean-up problems. Brushes, clothes, spills, and hands must be cleaned up with a special solvent, paint thinner, turpentine, or mineral spirits. Be sure to check the stain instructions to determine which type of solvent is best used with that particular stain.

Since the stains are only used as a coloration for wood, the wood must be protected in some manner. Varnish is an excellent method. The varnishes available on the market today are compounds of plasticized resins that dry to a very hard, resilient protective surface. These types hold up well to the heavy use and abuse a child's toy might be subjected to. The only caution is that you read the instructions on the can to ensure there is no health threat to youngsters. Also be sure to allow more than ample time for the varnish to dry prior to the child playing with the toy. Often harmful fumes or chemicals are present as the varnish is drying that are not present after it dries.

A final type of finish that can be applied to wood toys are penetrating oil finishes. These are oily substances that are absorbed into the pores of the wood and solidify to protect the wood. Check the individual brand of penetrating oils for its recommended use. Many can be safely used for such projects as bread boards, fruit bowls, and other projects meant to be in contact with food.

If you use penetrating oils, be sure to allow the project to sit for 30 days after the oil has been applied, to allow total solidification of the oils in the wood pores. After this length of time, the chemicals in penetrating oils should be nontoxic.

Whether the toy built by the craftsperson is finished with paint, varnish, stain and varnish, or penetrating oils, the finish is just as much part of the project as is the design and wood itself. Plan the finish carefully. A finish that is ideal for one particular project might be totally wrong for another. It is up to you to make professional decisions about what type of finish to apply to each individual project.

Section II

The Fleet

The fleet is a series of vehicles built to approximately the same scale, in an effort to produce a uniform collection of play vehicles. An interesting feature of the fleet is that many of the vehicles are built using mass-production techniques to simplify construction and speed production time. But remember: though the vehicles have been designed with mass production in mind, they can also be built one at a time. Do not ignore this section simply because you do not intend to build *all* of the vehicles. Select any individual cars, trucks, and construction vehicles you wish.

3
CHAPTER

Light Trucks

This chapter contains complete plans for the Pickup Truck with camper, Local Delivery Van, and Mini Motor Home (Fig. 3-1). The vehicles, while individual in appearance, are built using many of the same parts. For example, the frame and hood used for all three of the vehicles is the same. This is important, because it cuts production time. This is especially important for those of you who build for resale. Because less time is spent building a quality project, there is a higher profit margin per unit. (See Table 3-1 for a list of required materials for each vehicle.)

PICKUP TRUCK

Many of the steps used for the Pickup Truck are repeated when constructing the other vehicles. The frame for all three vehicles is a 1⅝-inch-wide, 6-inch-long section of ½-inch-thick wood.

On the edges of the frame, measure back from the front edge ⅞ inch and draw a line across the edge. From that line, measure back 3⅜ inches and draw another line. At the lines, measure down ¼ inch and draw a cross line, as shown in Fig. 3-2. Repeat the measuring and marking process on the other side of the frame, as this is where the four wheels attach to the frame. If you are going to use axle pegs, as in this example, drill a 5/32-inch-diameter hole approximately ½ inch deep. However, if you intend to use another means of wheel attachment, such as dowels (no screws!), you will need to drill the proper-size hole entirely through the frame.

Whichever method you use, the wheels can now be permanently affixed to the frame. Be careful not to get glue in any spots where it will interfere with the free spinning of the wheels when dry. After completion, set the assembly aside to dry. Occasionally take a moment to run the frame and wheel assembly on a surface to ensure that the wheels will spin freely.

The hood used on these three vehicles is the same as those used on the larger trucks and construction vehicles described in Chapters 5 and 6. If you also intend to build all or several of the larger trucks, you should construct several hoods for future use. This also holds true for the cabs on the other vehicles.

The following instructions will direct you to build three hoods at one time. If you need more hoods for future use, you will have to adapt the instructions accordingly.

Begin by obtaining a piece of wood 1 inch thick, 1⅛ inches wide, and 5 inches long. On the end of the block, measure ¼ inch in from the sides toward the center. Along

Fig. 3-1. *The Light Trucks: Pickup Truck, Local Delivery Van, and Mini Motor Home.*

the top surface, draw the ¼-inch lines down the length of the block, as shown in Fig. 3-3A.

Next, measure up from the bottom ⅜ inch and draw a line the length of the block on both sides (Fig. 3-3B). The wood area between the ¼-inch lines on the top and the ⅜-inch lines on the sides (the shaded area in the illustration in Fig. 3-3B), needs to be removed. You can do this by setting the blade of a table saw at an angle or by filing and sanding.

Once the initial shaping of the hood has been completed, you need to cut the block into individual hood lengths (Fig. 3-3C). Measure 1½ inches in from one end and cut off the hood unit. Measure and cut the second, then the third, hood unit. There will be a little extra hood material left over from the block once the three hoods have been cut away. This should be discarded.

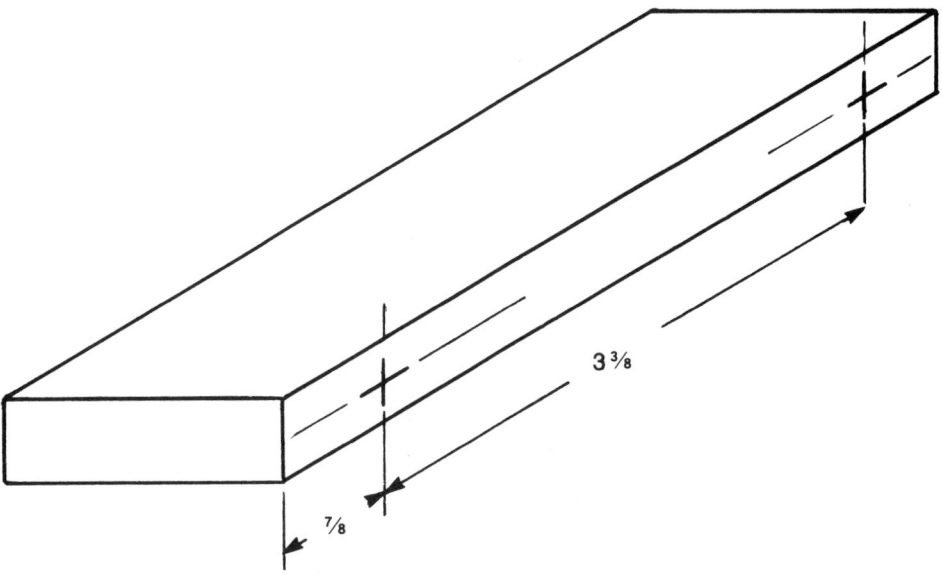

Fig. 3-2. *Drill the axle holes into the sides of the frame.*

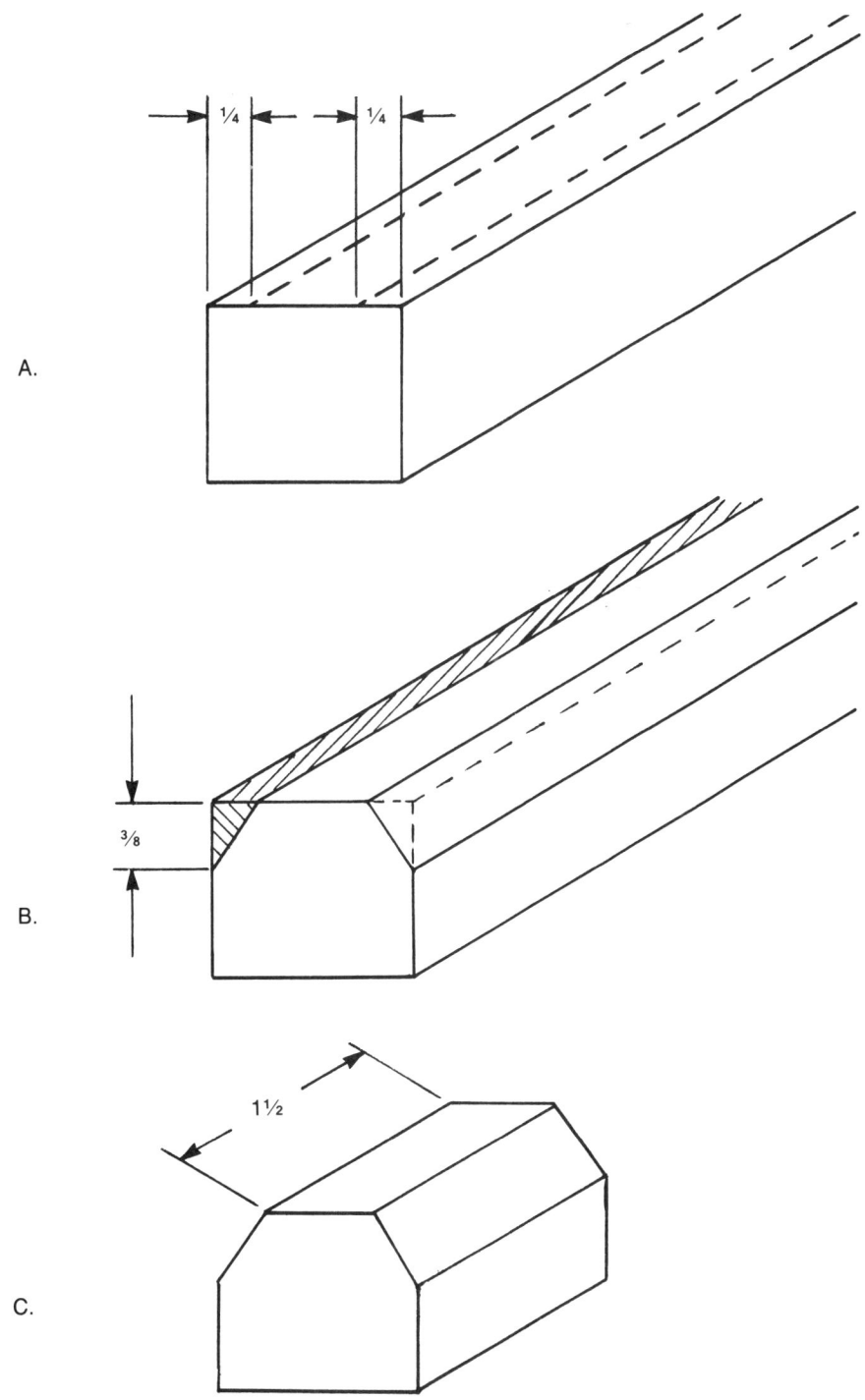

Fig. 3-3. *Laying out, cutting, and shaping the hood.*

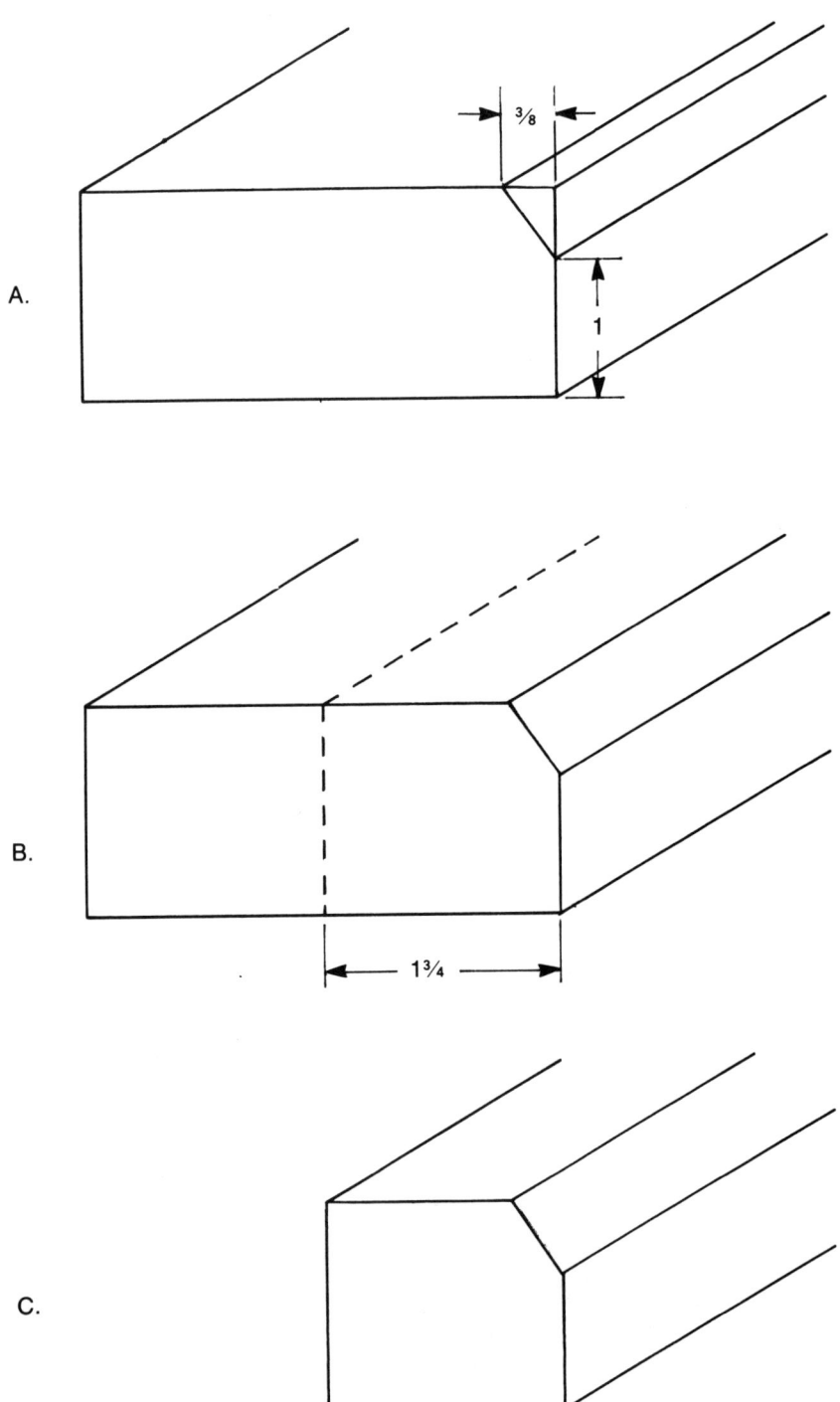

Fig. 3-4. *Making the cab for the light trucks.*

The next part to be cut is the cab. The cab is used on the Pickup Truck and Mini Camper, but not on the Local Delivery Van. As with the hood, the cab is made from a 2-by-4-inch piece of lumber. The length of the 2 by 4 depends on the quantity of cabs needed. (Remember, the same cab is used on the trucks and construction vehicles.) Begin by drawing a line along the top surface 3/8 inch from the edge. Draw another line on the edge 1 inch up from the bottom (Fig. 3-4A). Remove the material between the two lines, as shown in Fig. 3-4B. Next, measure 1 3/4 inches in from the edge and cut the cab from the rest of the 2 by 4. Finally, cut the cab into the proper 1 1/4-inch lengths (Fig. 3-4C).

The next procedure is glueing the hood and cab onto the frame and wheel assembly. Glue the hood onto the frame 1/4 inch back from the front end. (The center of the wheel is 7/8 inch from the front end of the frame.) The hood must be centered between the sides of the frame. Next, glue the cab in place. You should glue the front of the cab so that it is situated next to the hood and is centered between the frame sides (Fig. 3-5). This procedure is also used for the Mini Motor Home.

All that remains to complete the pickup truck is to cut the bed sides. These are made from two pieces of wood, each 1/4 inch thick, 3/4 inch wide, and 2 5/8 inches long. The bed sides are glued to the frame, then butted and glued to the cab (Fig. 3-6).

An optional feature to build for the Pickup Truck is the Pickup Camper. The camper is built from a 2-by-4-inch piece of wood that is 4 3/8 inches long, and another piece of wood which is 3/4 inch thick, 3 1/2 inches wide, and 4 3/8 inches long. Begin construction by glueing these two pieces of wood together surface to surface (Fig. 3-7A). When the glue has had sufficient time to dry, draw out the design of the camper on the wood block. The exact dimensions of the camper are shown in the illustration in Fig. 3-7B. (*Note*: The sharp corners of the camper have been rounded to eliminate edges that might cause injury to children.)

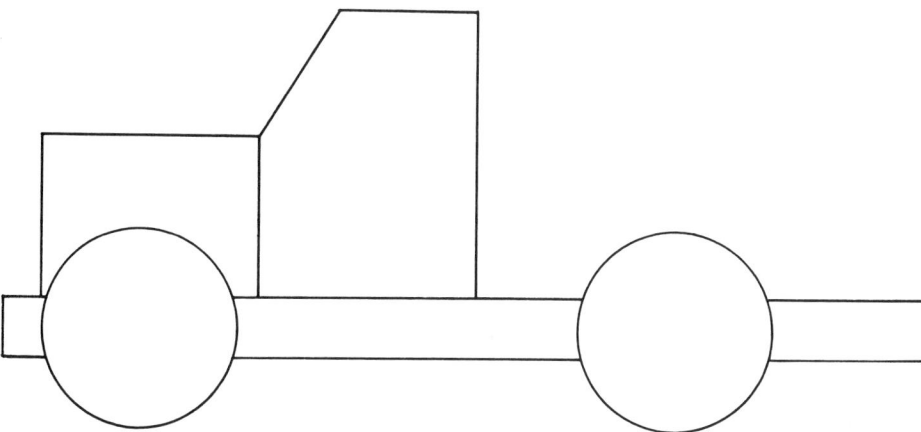

Fig. 3-5. *Glue the hood onto the frame 1/4 inch back from the front of the frame. Just behind the hood, glue the cab into place.*

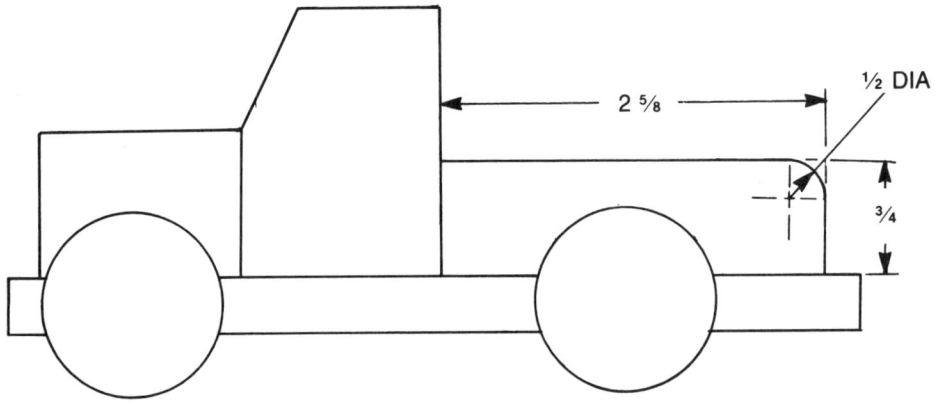

Fig. 3-6. Glue the pickup bed sides onto the frame, butted against the rear of the cab.

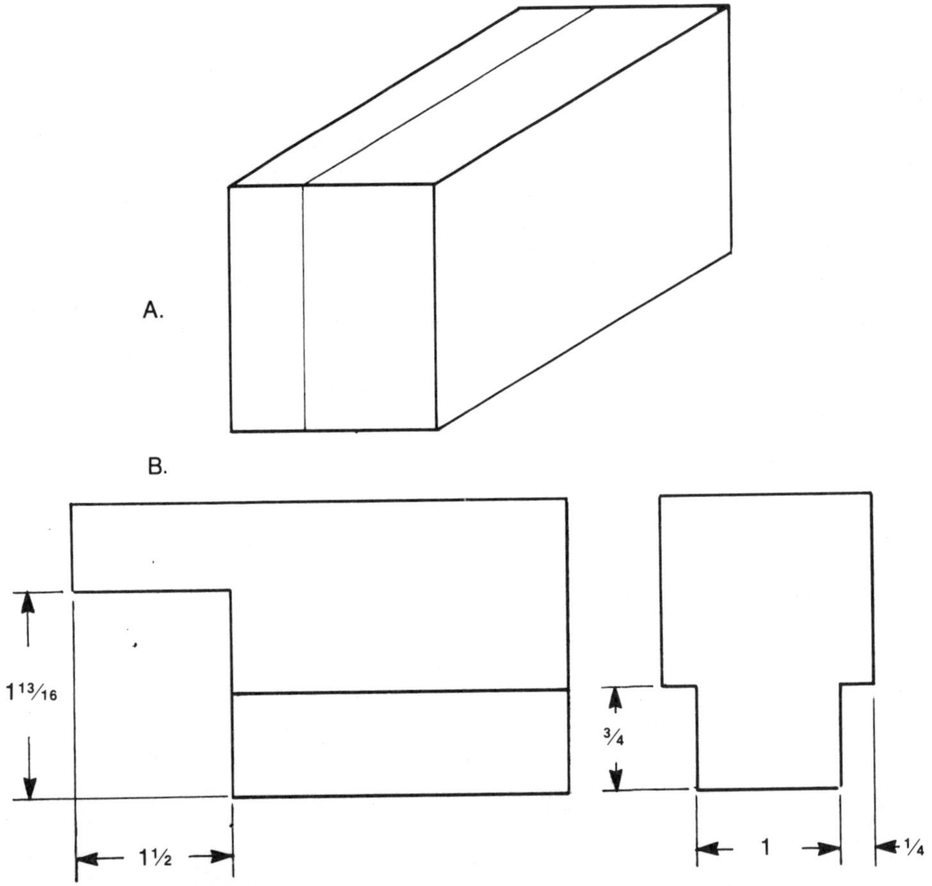

Fig. 3-7. The wood needed to build the Pickup Camper must be 2¼ inches wide. (A) To obtain this thickness, glue a ¾-inch-thick board to a 1½-inch thick board. (B) How to cut the camper block.

Fig. 3-8. The Mini Motor Home is built using the same frame, hood, and cab as the Pickup.

MINI MOTOR HOME

The Mini Motor Home (Fig. 3-8) is built on the same frame as the Pickup Truck, with hood and cab mounted to the frame as it is on the pickup. The difference is that the Motor Home has living quarters mounted to the frame.

The living quarters is cut from a piece of 2-by-4-inch lumber, 3¾-inches long. All you need to do to construct the living quarters is to cut a 1 13/16-inch-by-1½-inch recess

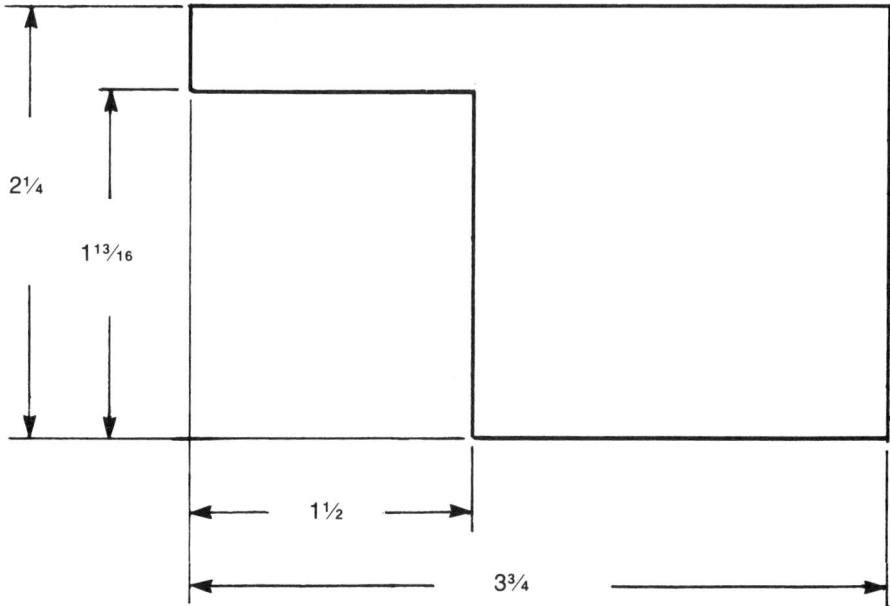

Fig. 3-9. The living quarters of the Mini Motor Home is made from a 3¾-inch length of 2-by-4 stock.

Fig. 3-10. The Local Delivery Van is used for light-duty deliveries around town.

from the 2-by-4 block (Fig. 3-9), to cut down the width to 2¼ inches.

If you intend to build both the Mini Motor Home and the Local Delivery Van, keep in mind that the living quarters and the cargo compartment of the van are the same piece. When building one, it is just as easy to build the other. To complete the Mini Motor Home, all you have to do is glue the living quarters onto the frame assembly.

DELIVERY VAN

The Delivery Van (Fig. 3-10) is built on the frame assembly just as the Pickup and Mini Motor Home, with the hood glued in the same position. Another similarity is that

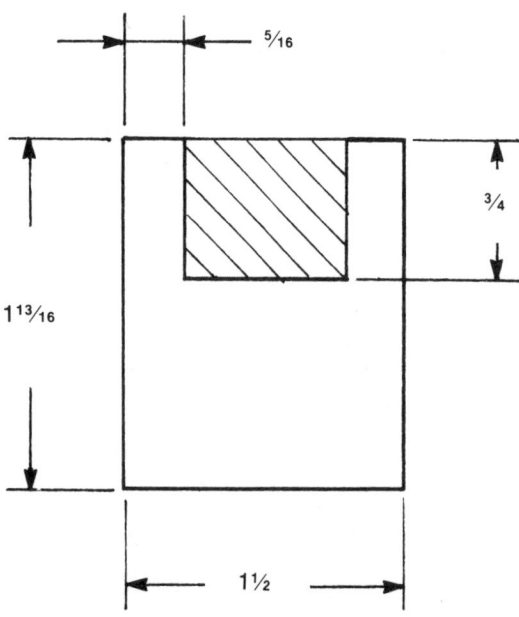

Fig. 3-11. Cut the windshield of the Local Delivery Van to the size shown here. Remove the shaded area.

the cargo compartment of the Delivery Van is the same as the living quarters of the Mini Motor Home. The only different feature is the windshield and seat.

The windshield is made from a piece of wood ½ inch thick, 1½ inches wide, and 1¹³⁄₁₆ inches long. Draw and cut out the opening, as illustrated in Fig. 3-11. Then, glue the windshield to the rear of the hood and the frame. You can now glue the cargo compartment onto the frame. Glue it so that the front edge slightly overlaps the front of the windshield. Center the rest of the cargo compartment between the sides of the frame.

Next, glue a small seat in place inside the driver's compartment. The seat measures ½ inch thick, ⅝ inch wide, and 1⅛ inches long. A good idea is to round the front edge of the seat slightly so that the seat will appear more realistic.

The light trucks described in this section are fun and easy to build. These vehicles are a perfect project to be built for resale since their cost is low, the production time is short, and the finished products are attractive and great fun.

LIST 3-1. REQUIRED MATERIALS

Pickup Truck

1	-	Frame	- ½ × 1⅝ × 6
4	-	Wheels	- 1¼-inch diameter
4	-	Axle Pegs (if used)	
1	-	Hood	- 1 × 1⅛ × 1½
1	-	Cab	- 1½ × 1¾ × 1¼
2	-	Bed Sides	- ¼ × ¾ × 2⅝
1	-	Camper Body	- ¾ × 3½ × 4⅜
1	-	Camper Body	- 1½ × 3½ × 4

Mini Motor Home

1	-	Frame	- ½ × 1⅝ × 6
4	-	Wheels	- 1¼-inch diameter
4	-	Axle Pegs (if used)	
1	-	Hood	- 1 × 1⅛ × 1½
1	-	Cab	- 1½ × 1¾ × 1¼
1	-	Living Quarters	- 1½ × 3½ × 3¾

Delivery Van

1	-	Frame	- ½ × 1⅝ × 6
4	-	Wheels	- 1¼-inch diameter
4	-	Axle Pegs	
1	-	Hood	- 1 × 1⅛ × 1½
1	-	Windshield	- ½ × 1½ × 1¹³⁄₁₆
1	-	Cargo Compartment	- 1½ × 3½ × 3¾
1	-	Seat	- ½ × ⅝ × 1⅛

4
CHAPTER

Cars

In every village, town, or city, there are cars of every size, shape, and color. It's an American way of life. This section provides instructions for five vehicles: the Wagon, Sports Car, Sedan, Import, and Indy Racer (See Fig. 4-1). These cars are each made from common 2-by-4 lumber that can be purchased from any local lumberyard. Since the wood required for each car is only 5¼-inches long, (except a piece 6 inches long for the Indy Racer), you should be very selective when choosing the wood. It should be free from loose, or large knots, and certainly should not have cracks or any other defects that might cause injury to youngsters.

WAGON, SPORTS CAR, SEDAN, AND IMPORT

The following directions are provided to build the Wagon, Sportscar, Sedan, and the Import—one of each design. (If more or less are desired, you will need to adjust the directions accordingly.

Begin with two lengths of 2-by-4-inch lumber, each 12-inches long. The pieces must be both ripped, and cut along the grain, to a width of 2 inches (Fig. 4-2A). The boards, now measuring 1½ inches thick, 2 inches wide, and 12 inches long, will require a 60-degree chamfer (a beveled edge) to be cut on both edges. To accomplish this, measure down from the top 9/16 inch on both edges and draw a 60-degree line up from that point. Cut the 60-degree chamfer as shown in Fig. 4-2B.

Fig. 4-1. *The instructions in this chapter provide step by step instructions for the Wagon, Sports Car, Sedan, Import, and Indy racer.*

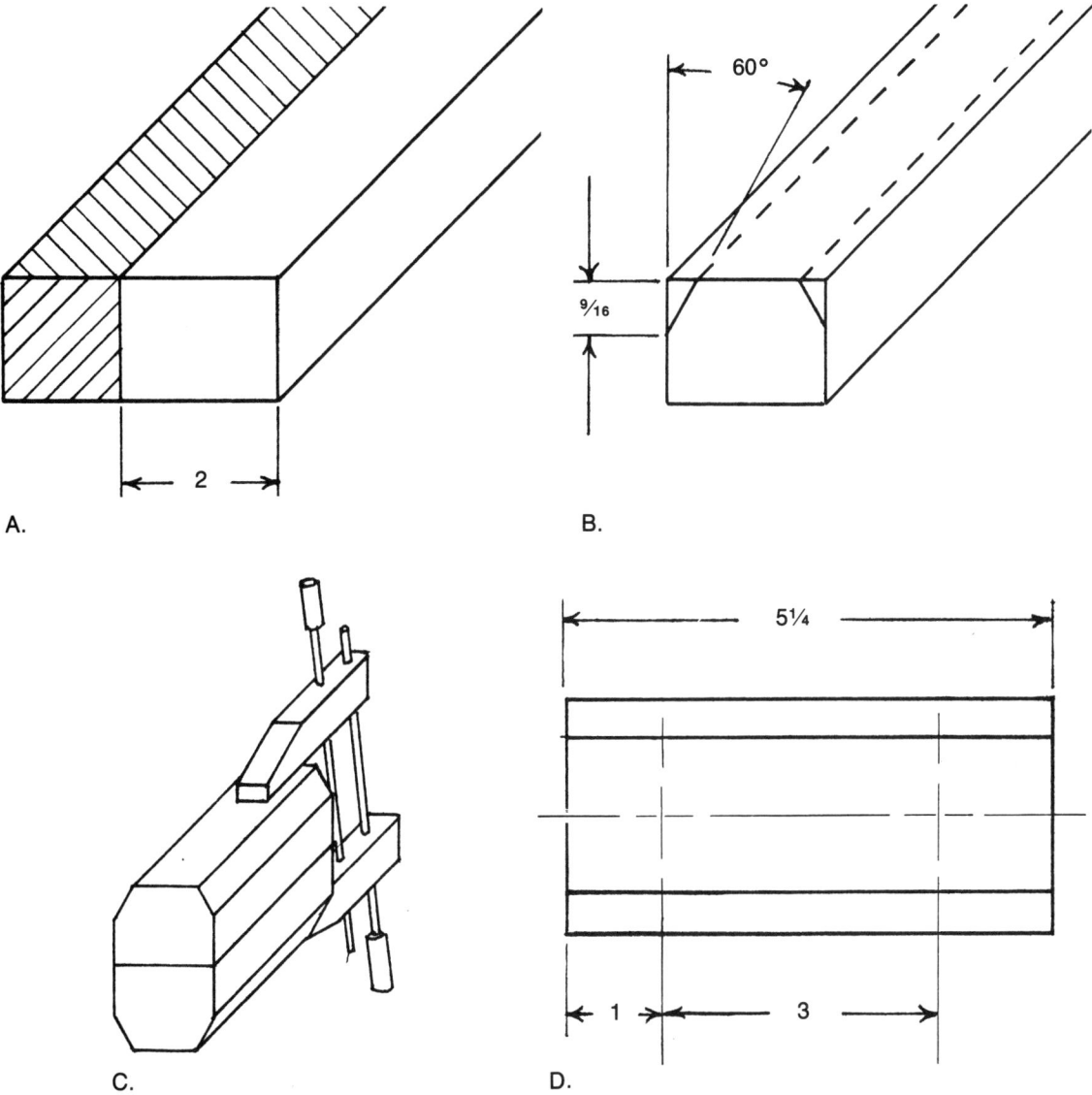

Fig. 4-2. *This series of drawings graphically illustrates the steps in building the cars. (A) Cut the basic shape of the cars from a length of 2-by-4 lumber. (B) Cut a 60-degree chamfer on the edges of the car. (C) After cutting to length, clamp the car stock together, bottom to bottom. (D) Drill the 1⅜-inch-diameter holes 1 inch in from one end, and 3 inches back from the 1-inch mark.*

The two 12-inch pieces are now crosscut into four 5¼-inch-long pieces. Next, clamp two of the 5¼-inch blocks together, base to base, with the 60-degree chamfered edge of one on the top and another on the bottom (Fig. 4-2C). On the side of the two blocks, measure in from the left end 1 inch. Make a mark at the point where the two boards meet. Next, measure in from the first mark 3 inches, and again make a mark.

27

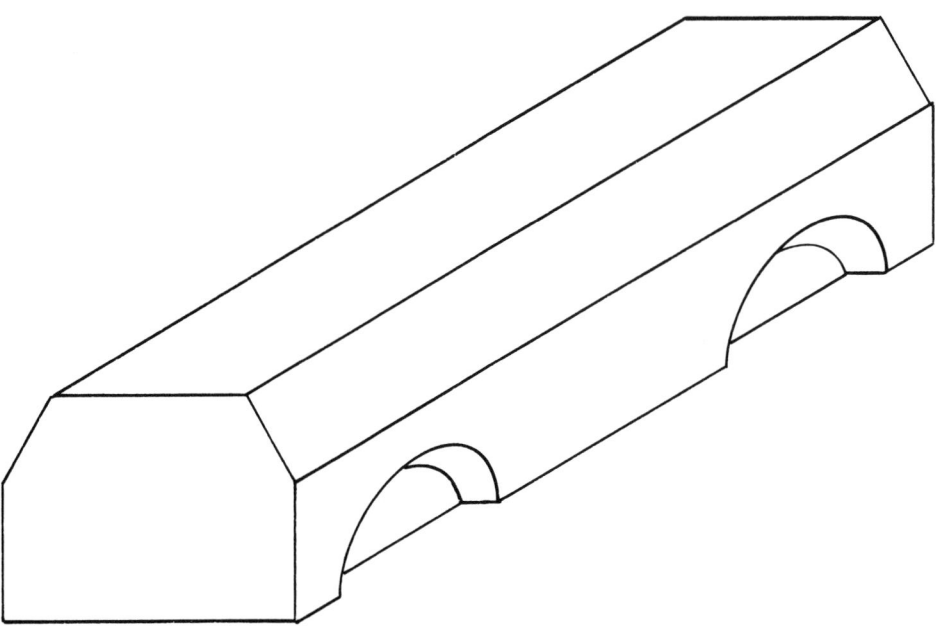

Fig. 4-3. *This is how the wood car stock should look after the wheel wells have been drilled and the two blocks separated.*

Repeat these measurements on the reverse side of the two boards. At the marks, drill a 1⅜-inch-diameter hole to a depth of ⅜ inch (Fig. 4-2D). These holes are best drilled with a spade bit. Repeat the drilling operation on the other side and the other 5¼-inch blocks.

These ⅜-inch-deep holes form the wheel wells for the vehicles. Once drilled on both sides, the two blocks can be separated. The result is four wood blocks that look like the illustration in Fig. 4-3.

Set the wood aside for a while. It's now time to draw the cars out on paper. The drawings in Figs. 4-4 through 4-7 are drawn on a ½-inch grid pattern. Draw the ½-inch

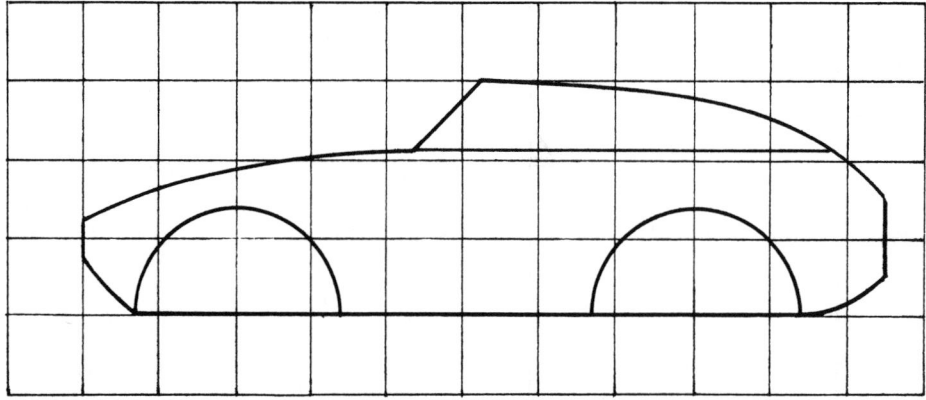

Fig. 4-4. *The Sports Car drawn on a ½-inch-square grid pattern.*

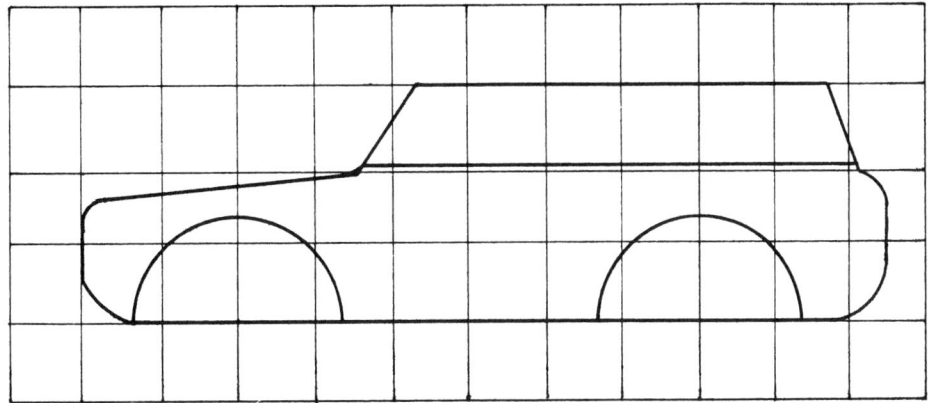

Fig. 4-5. *The Station Wagon drawn on a ½-inch-square-grid pattern.*

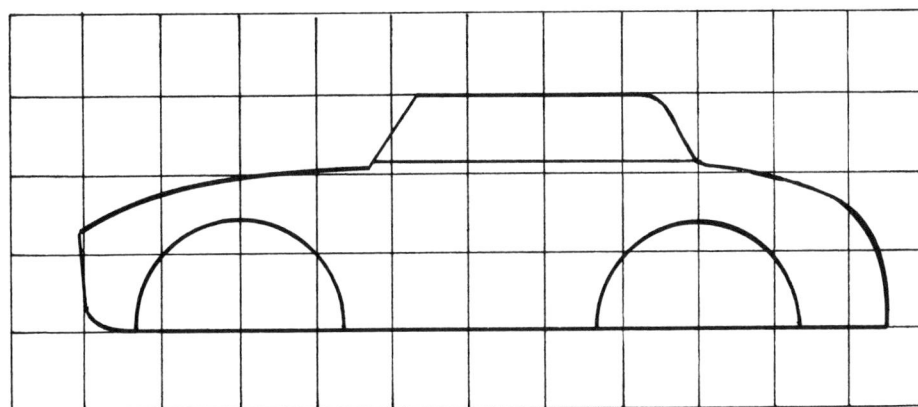

Fig. 4-6. *The Sedan drawn on a ½-inch-square grid pattern.*

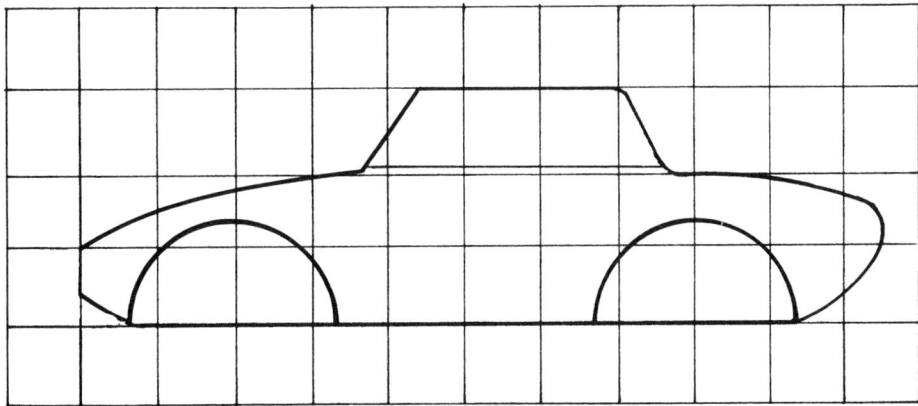

Fig. 4-7. *The Import Car drawn on a ½-inch-square grid pattern.*

grid pattern on a sheet of paper, then sketch the outline of the car onto the pattern.

Next, cut out the outline of the automobiles and trace them onto the wood blocks. (*Hint*: If many cars are to be made, the paper templet should be made from cardboard, hardboard, sheet metal, or some other material that is more durable than paper and that will hold up to many tracings.)

Using a band saw, preferably (or, if necessary, any other saw that is capable), cut the outline of the automobiles out of the wood blocks. The cuts should be made outside of the outline so the automobile can be filed and sanded down to the drawn line.

Next, glue two wood blocks, each ¼ inch thick, ¾ inch wide, and 1¼ inch long, on the bottom of each automobile, centering them in the wheel wells. Clamp these blocks in position until the glue sets. Once dried, drill a 5/32-inch-diameter hole to ½ inch deep. The holes are drilled at the same location as the center of the 1⅜-inch wheel well holes previously drilled. Repeat this process on each of the cars.

The wheels are held in place using small axle pegs that are 13/16 inch long with a 5/32-inch-shaft diameter. When installing the wheels, be careful to get a small amount of glue in the hole drilled into the car, then slide the peg through the wheel into the hole. Be sure no glue gets into the hole in the wheel, or they will not spin properly.

The cars, which have been designed approximately to the same scale as the rest of the fleet, are now completed, short of a final sanding and a paint, varnish, or oil finish. The cars must be thoroughly sanded, including rounding all sharp edges and corners to prevent injuries. The cars can be painted to resemble your own car or one you dream of owning. Varnish can be used to retain the natural wood look, or the entire car can be emersed in an oil, such as Watco oil, for an alternative finish that allows the natural grain of the wood to show through.

Whichever finish is selected, the cars are a quick project, easily adapted to mass production, and a welcome addition to complement the fleet of other vehicles described in this section.

INDY-STYLE RACER

The cars that drive at the Indianapolis 500 Speedway are a breed apart from any other vehicle (Fig. 4-8). They are specially designed, custom-built cars created for high speeds and endurance. The fleet of vehicles described in this section would not be complete without the inclusion of an Indy-Style Racer.

The Indy-Style Racer is built from a single piece of wood. A 2-by-4-inch board 6 inches long will do the job. The forming of the car body can be accomplished by simply cutting the straight lines of the car with a saw. A band saw is probably the easiest saw to use, but almost any saw that can cut a straight line can be used.

The first step in construction of the Indy Racer is to cut the 1½-inch-thick, 3½-inch-wide, 6-inch-long board (actual size of a 2 by 4) to a width of 2½ inches. On one side of the board, draw the basic outline of the racer. The size and shape of the car profile is shown in Fig. 4-9A. Then cut out the basic racer shape.

Next, draw and cut out the design along the top surface (Fig. 4-9B). Toward the front of the vehicle, measure back ⅜ inch, and draw a pencil line across the vehicle body. Then draw another line, 1¼ inches from the first line. The rear end of the vehicle also requires a line across the body section, 1¾ inches from the back.

Fig. 4-8. Built of inexpensive materials, the Indy Racer is a car that is sure to be a favorite.

The next two lines to be drawn are located on the front of the vehicle, between the ⅜- and 1¼-inch lines. The line is ½ inch in from the sides (Fig. 4-9C). Also draw two lines from the rear end to the 1¾-inch line previously drawn. Be sure to draw these lines ⅜ inch in from the sides.

Cut along the lines just drawn to create a ⅜-inch-thick by 1¾-inch-long wheel well opening at the rear, also shown in Fig. 4-9C. Repeat this operation for the other rear wheel well. Next cut the front wheel wells by removing the material between the ⅜-inch line and the 1¼-inch line, ½ inch back from the edges.

The rear of the Indy-Style Racer is cut into an airfoil for a streamline design. This will require only two straight cuts, one horizontally, and one at a slight diagonal, as shown in Fig. 4-10.

Next, the car needs to be shaped by filing and sanding. A saw will not be needed. Begin shaping on the two outboard fuel tanks, located between the front and rear wheel wells. Lay out a line ¼ inch from the top and bottom edge of the fuel tanks (Fig. 4-11). Remove the material between the line on the top surface to produce an inclined, more streamlined surface. Repeat this process on the bottom of the outboard tanks.

Along the top surface of the Indy Racer body, draw a line that begins ¼ inch in from the sides on the front edge and ends at the outside rear corner of the outboard fuel tanks (Fig. 4-12). Sand away the material outside the previously drawn line to provide the car with a more aerodynamic shape. Also, lay out and shape the front of the outboard fuel tanks by marking a line ¼ inch up from the front edge of the fuel tanks and then drawing a line from that point to the inside front edge of the tank.

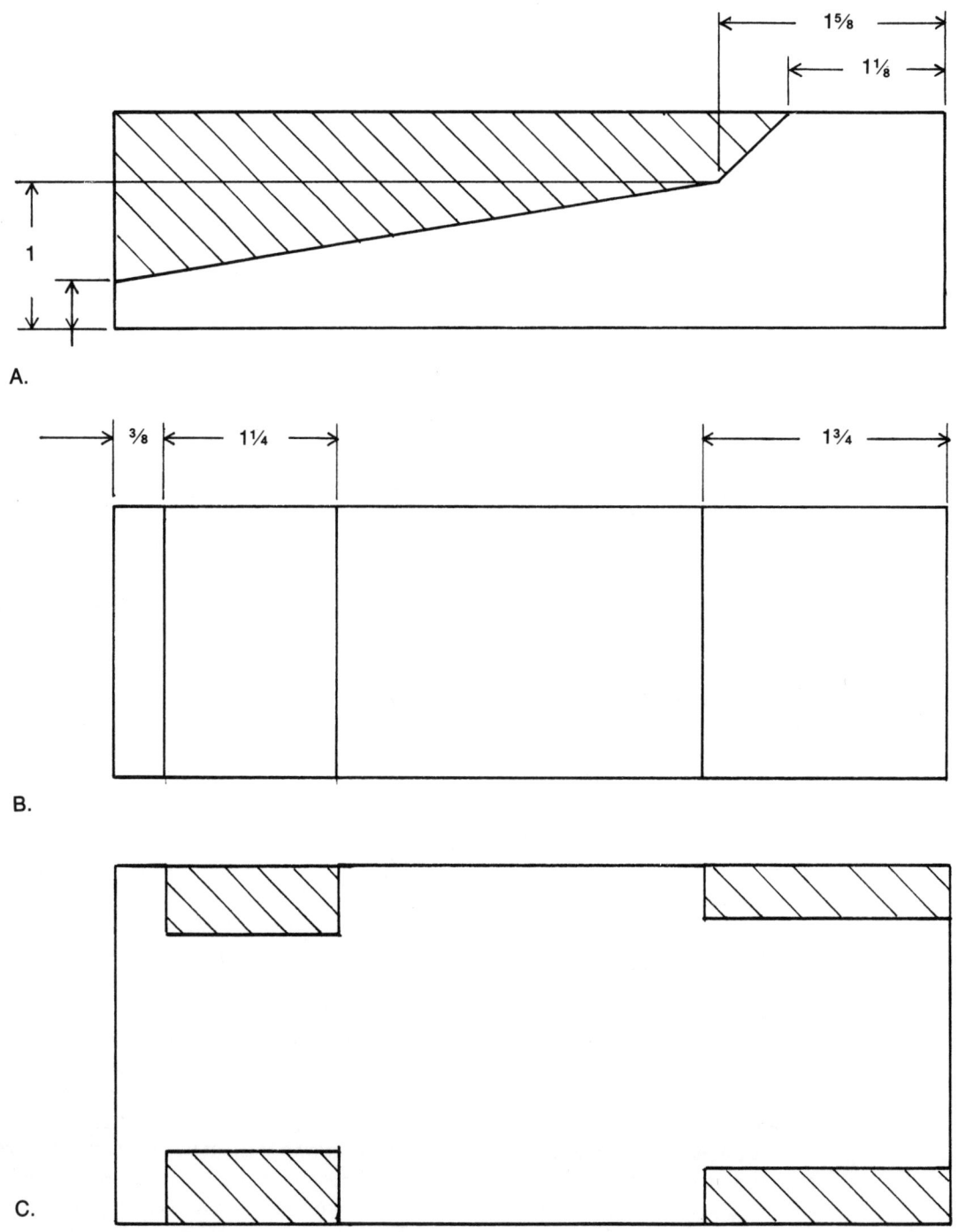

Fig. 4-9. This series of drawings illustrates: (A) The profile; (B) The top; (C) The top with the wheel wells cut. (The shaded material is to be removed.)

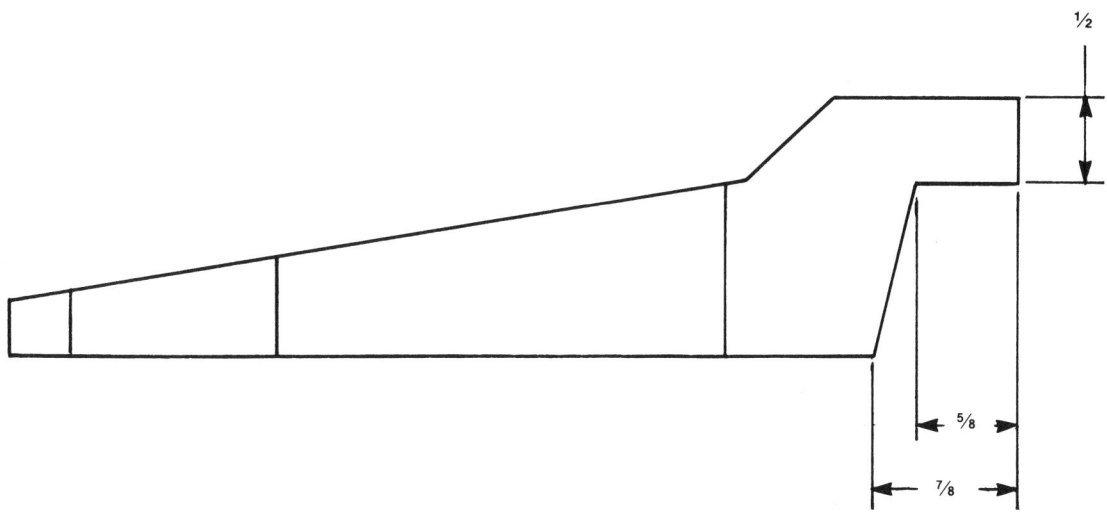

Fig. 4-10. *Cut the rear of the Indy Racer to a streamline airfoil.*

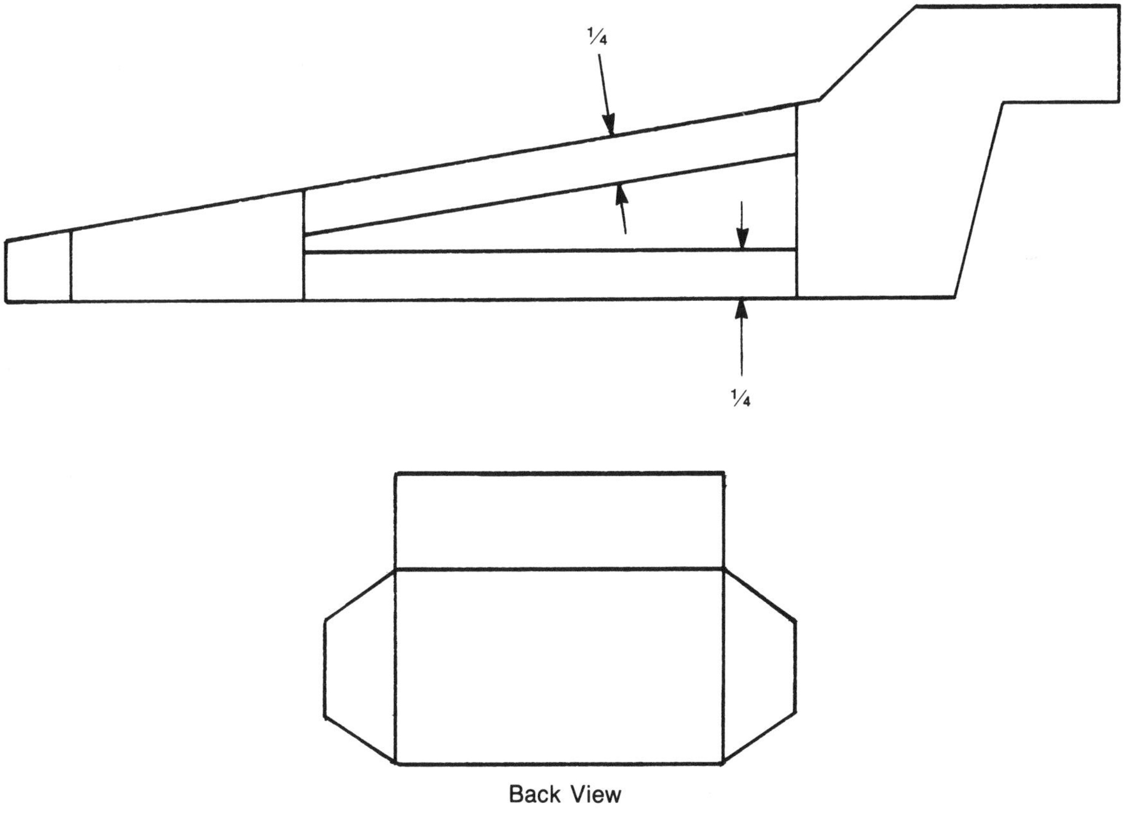

Fig. 4-11. *Shape the outboard tanks of the Indy Racer to a slight incline.*

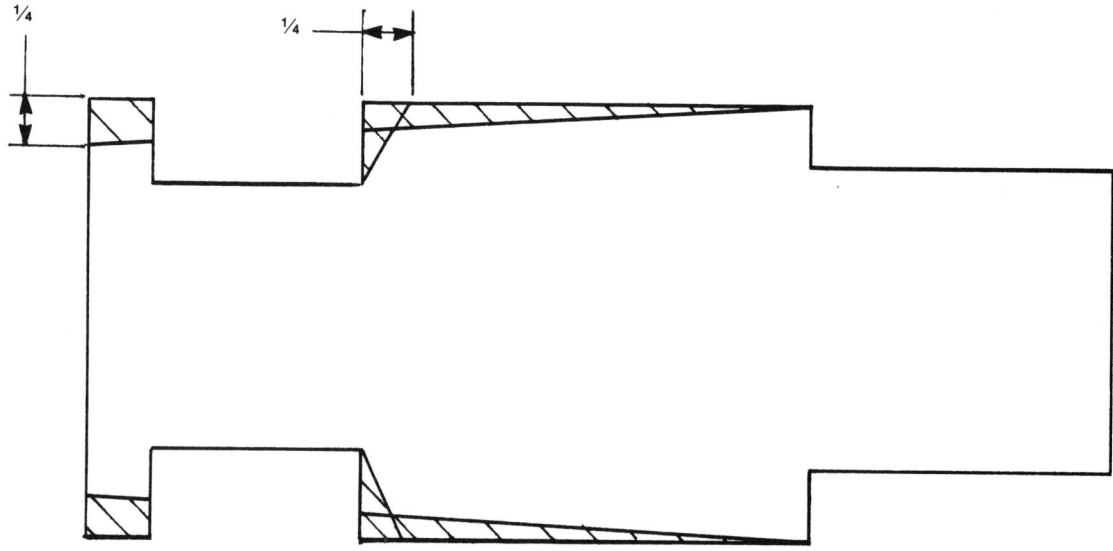

Fig. 4-12. *Looking down onto the top of the Indy racer, cut the front of the outboard tanks back at an angle and angle the entire side back slightly.*

At this point, all the cutting and initial shaping has been completed. What follows is a thorough sanding of the entire project. Sanding and filing are an important step in this project. If it is not done correctly, the race car will not be as pleasing to the young eyes. The car should also be sanded for safety reasons.

Drill the axle holes along the side of the racer, in the wheel wells. These holes are 5/32 inch in diameter and located 1/4 inch in from the racer end, and 1 1/8 inch in from the front end. Then drill holes 1/4 inch from the bottom edge of the racer (Fig. 4-13).

Fast cars have always been a favorite of youngsters. The Indy-Style Racers are not only fast—their sleek one-of-a-kind bodies create an appeal for both young and old alike. This replica is no different. You will especially enjoy its low cost and ease of construction. The lucky recipient of the car will spend hours lying on the floor, racing around the "old brickyard."

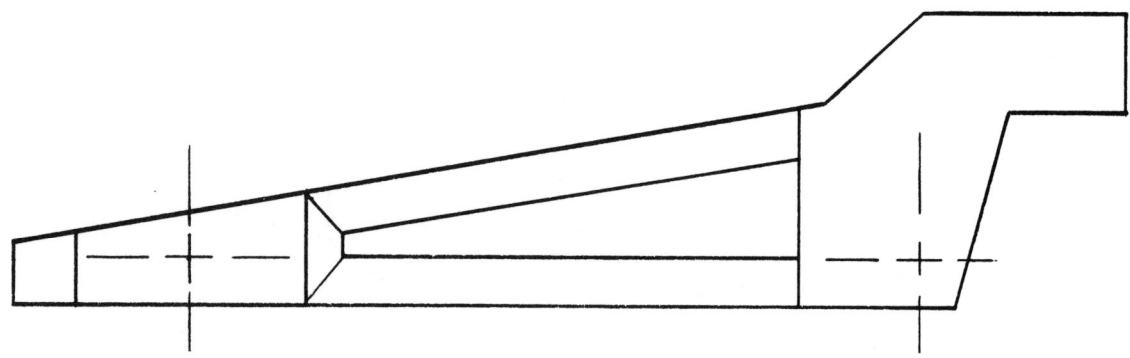

Fig. 4-13. *The location of the axle holes.*

LIST 4-1. REQUIRED MATERIALS

Station Wagon, Sedan, Sports Car, Import

(Each car is made from the same-size materials.)

1 – Car Body   – 1½ × 3½ × 5½
4 – Axle Pegs
4 – Wheels   – 1-inch diameter
2 – Axle Supports   – ¼ × ¾ × 1¼

Indy Racer

1 – Body   – 1½ × 3½ × 6
4 – Axle Pegs
4 – Wheels   – 1-inch diameter

5
CHAPTER

Large Trucks

The instructions for the fleet continues with a discussion of the basic truck component, then follows up with instructions and designs for the specific trucks, such as the Log or Lumber Truck, Dump Truck, or Cement Mixer (Fig. 5-1).

The trucks bear a close resemblance to one another, and, therefore, are good candidates for mass production techniques. The hood, cab, frame, and front and rear axle support can all be produced in mass, saving time and effort. Once these parts have been assembled, each rear section of the truck chassis receives special treatment. The Flatbed receives the bed, the Cement Mixer receives the rotating drum, the Gas Tanker its tank, and so on.

If you intend to build several or all of the trucks, you would be wise to borrow some mass-production techniques from industry. For example, rip a long length of ½-inch-thick wood to a 1½-inch width. Then cut the long length into individual 7¼-inch pieces, thus producing several truck frames in not much more time required to make one. This technique can also be used to make the hood, cab, and front- and rear-axle supports.

In addition, many of the construction vehicles that I describe in the next chapter use the same hood and cab as the ones found on these trucks. If you intend to build the construction vehicles in Chapter 6, prepare by cutting their cabs and hoods while working on the trucks in this chapter.

THE CAB

The cab used in many of the projects found in this section is a solid piece of wood that measures 1¾ inches tall, 1¼ inches wide, and 1½ inches long. In the following instructions, I will describe the method for making ten cabs. If more or fewer cabs are desired, alter the directions accordingly.

First, obtain a piece of wood thick enough for the cab. A 2 by 4 (actual measurement: 1½ by 3½ inch) is ideal because it is already of the correct thickness, 1½ inches. The length of the board for 10 cabs should be 14 inches long. This allows enough wood for 10 cabs and an additional 1½ inches for cutting. (Each cut made reduces the length somewhat, usually about ⅛ inch.) The 14-inch piece is a good length to work with, as it is long enough to be safely worked on with power tools. (Using power tools, such as a table saw on pieces less than 10 inches is dangerous and should be avoided.) The series of drawings shown in Fig. 5-2 illustrate the steps involved in making the cab.

Fig. 5-1. *This fleet includes the Log Hauler, the Lumber Truck, the Dump Truck, the Semitruck, and the Cement Mixer.*

On the end of the 2-by-4 board, draw the diagonal line that will eventually form the windshield of the cab. The corner of the board is easiest removed with a table saw. Tilt the blade to the same angle drawn on the end of the board. Then hold the board against the rip fence and cut the diagonal "windshield." In the event that a table saw is not available, you can make the diagonal cut with suitable portable power tools or a hand plane.

The next step is to cut the 2-by-4-inch board to the proper 1½-inch length. Again, if a table saw is available, you can easily rip the board using the rip fence, but a hand saw, band saw, or almost any saw that is capable of cutting a straight line may be used.

The last illustration in the series of drawings demonstrates the cutting of the individual cabs from the long length of stock. These, again, can be cut with any saw capable of the operation, but use a fine-tooth backsaw (or miter saw) to produce a smoother cut.

The final step in producing the cab is to sand each surface smooth, then lightly sand the top corners to remove their sharpness. Once sanded, set the cabs aside until they are needed.

THE HOOD

The hood used on most of the vehicles in this chapter can also be mass-produced. The following hood instructions will produce enough material for 10 hoods. If more hoods are needed, the length of the board will have to be increased.

Begin with a board that is 1 inch thick, 1⅛ inches wide, and 16½ inches long. A 2-by-4-inch board can be used, but you will need to reduce the width and thickness.

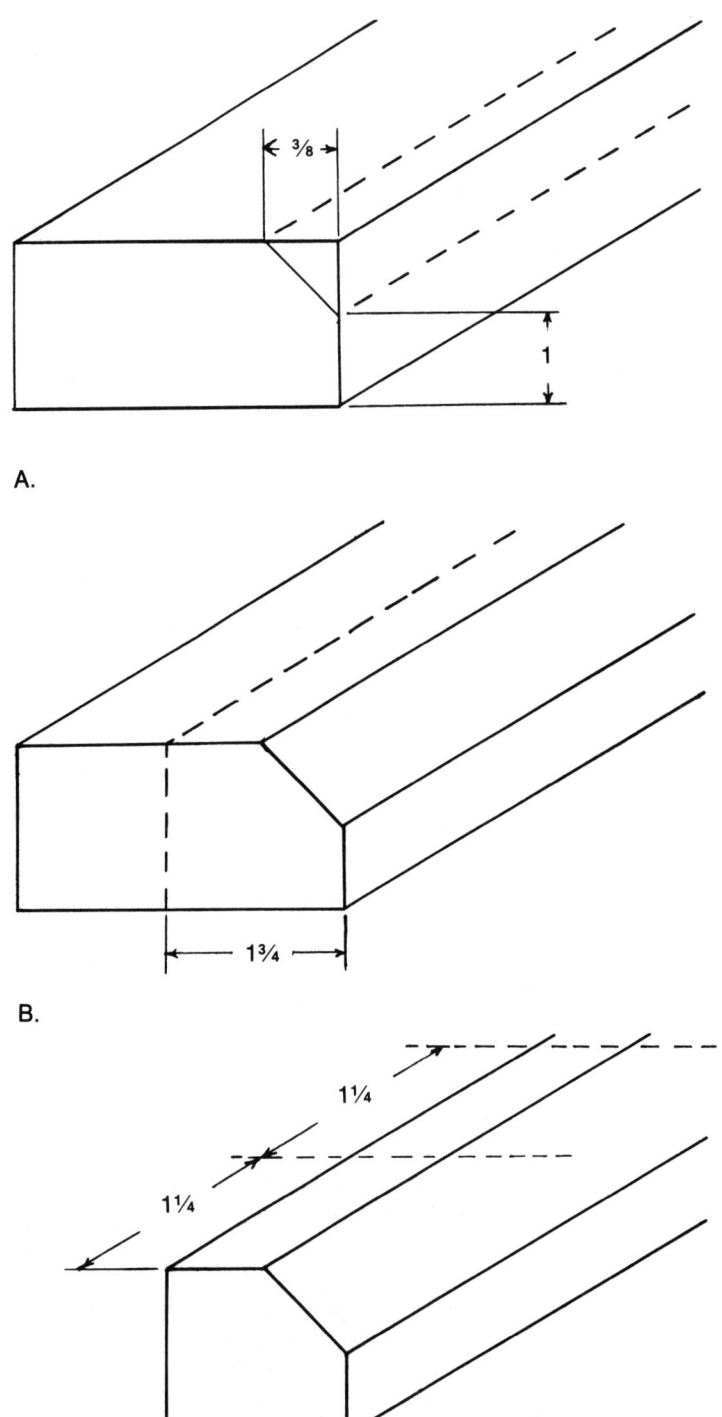

Fig. 5-2. Constructing the truck cab.

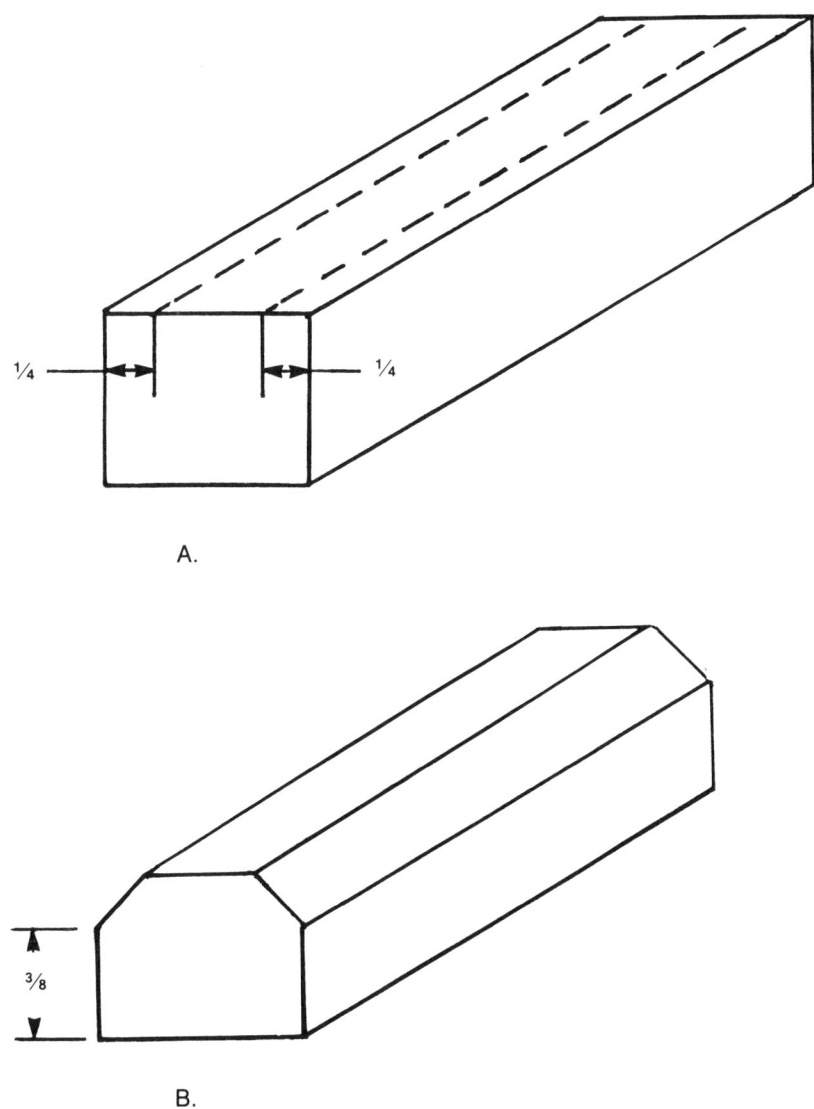

Fig. 5-3. *Making the hood.*

Now draw two ¼-inch lines along the top surface of the 1-by-1⅛-inch board (Fig. 5-3A). Measure up from the bottom ⅜ inch on both sides and draw the lines. Next, draw a diagonal line on the end between the ¼- and ⅜-inch line, as shown in Fig. 5-3B. Either a table saw set to the same approximate angle as the diagonal line or a hand plane can be used to cut the hood shape. The result will be a board 1 inch thick and 16½ inches long, cut to the shape of the hood. Next, cut the 16½-inch board into 1½-inch lengths.

Glue two axle supports to the bottom of the chassis. The front axle support measures ⅜ inch thick, 1⅝ inches wide, and 1 inch long. On both ends of the axle support, drill a 5/32-inch-diameter hole (Fig. 5-4) for the axle pegs. (If you use another method of

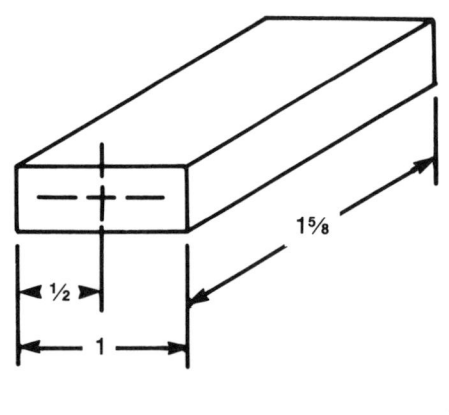

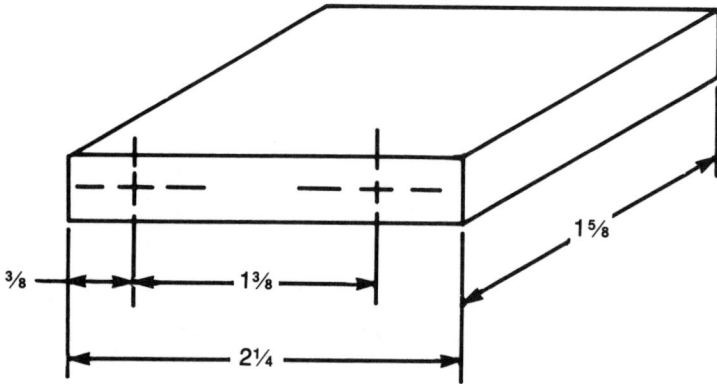

Fig. 5-4. Drill axle peg holes in the front and rear axle supports.

attaching the wheels, like dowels, other measures will need to be taken.) The rear axle support, which is also ⅜ inch thick and 1⅝ inches wide, is 2¼ inches long.

On both sides of the axle support, drill two ⁵⁄₃₂-inch-diameter holes. Center the holes ⅜ in from one end and 1⅜ inches in from the first mark, as shown in Fig. 5-4. If you are making several vehicles, the axle supports can also be made in volume by cutting

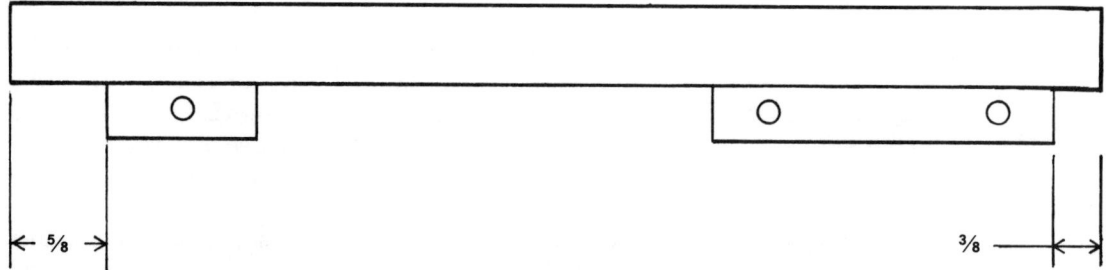

Fig. 5-5. Glue the axle supports into position on the truck chassis.

a long length of ⅜-inch-thick, 1⅝-inch-wide material. It should then be cut to the lengths required.

Figure 5-5 shows the position of the front and rear axle supports. Mount them on the chassis with a good-quality glue that has been formulated specifically to bond wood to wood. Apply pressure to the chassis and axle supports with clamps or a heavy weight until the glue dries.

After the chassis and axle-support assembly has had sufficient time to set, you should glue the hood into place. Glue the front end of the hood ¼ inch in from the front end of the chassis and center within its width (Fig. 5-6A).

Next, glue the cab—already produced in mass—to the chassis assembly. Position the cab directly behind the hood, centering between the chassis edges. Apply glue not

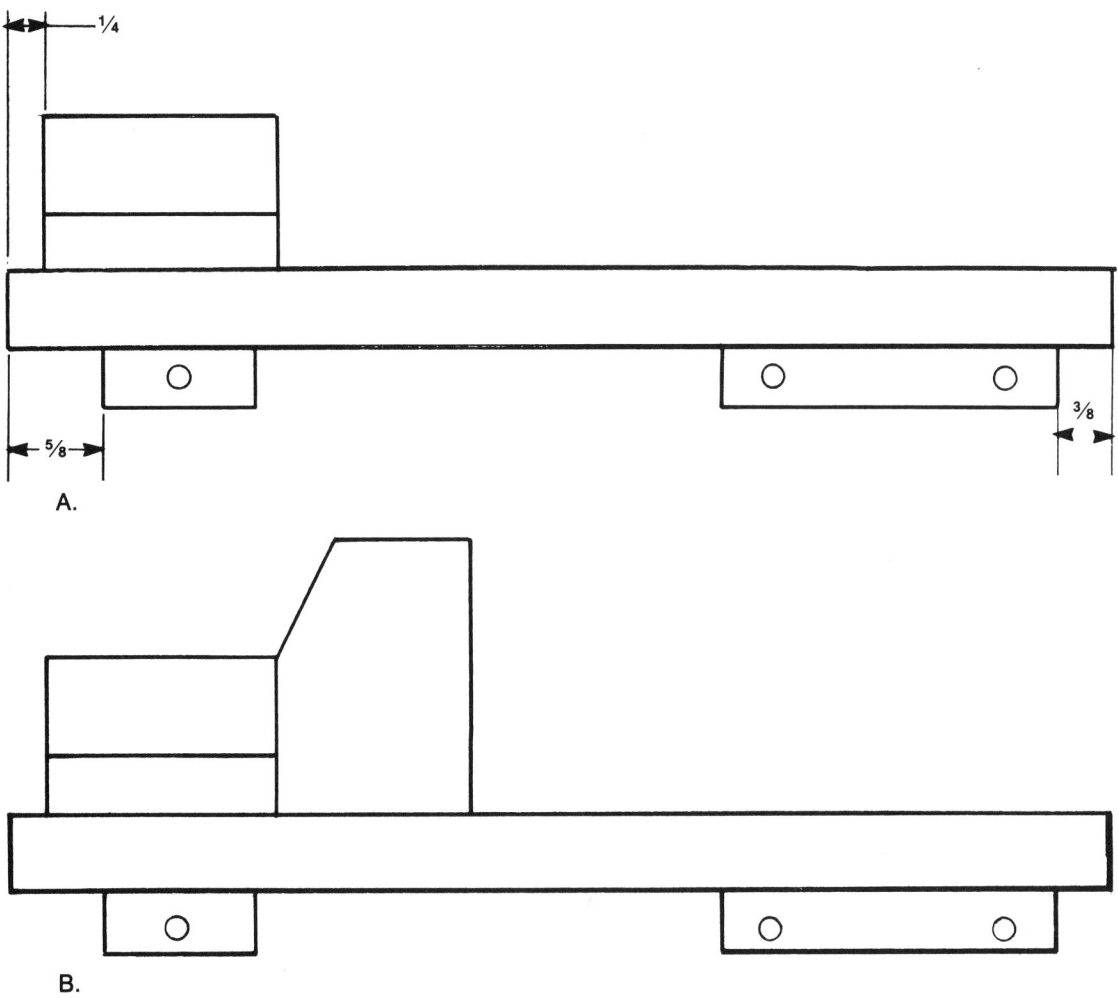

Fig. 5-6. *(A) Glue the hood of the truck onto the truck chassis ¼ inch back from the front end. (B) Glue the truck cab onto the chassis as shown.*

only to the base of the cab, but also to the rear end of the hood, so that it will adhere to the cab as well (Fig. 5-6B).

With the basic assembly all but complete, you can now install the wheels and axles by whatever method you choose. I have given instructions here for the axle peg method.

A final sanding to remove any sharp edges, ends, or corners, and the basic truck unit is ready for customizing into one of the many designs that follow.

FLATBED TRUCK

The Flatbed Truck is one of the backbones of the world's transportation industry. Versatility is the largest advantage of this vehicle. Almost any size and shape load can be carried and off-loaded with ease. The Flatbed Truck has the task of carrying the heaviest loads a child can conjure up.

The foundation for the Flatbed Truck is the basic truck component already described. The remainder of the flatbed consists of an upright cab protector and an enlarged bed. The cab protector is made from a piece of wood that measures ⅜ inch thick, 2¼ inches wide, and 2¼ inches long (Fig. 5-7).

Along the top end of the cab protector, cut off two corners at a 45-degree angle to prevent any injuries that might be caused by the sharp corners. The cab protector is glued onto the rear of the cab, centered on the frame.

The enlarged truck bed is made from a piece of wood that is the same thickness and width as the cab protector, ⅜ inch and 2¼ inches, respectively; but the length is 4¼ inches. Again, be sure to cut off the corners at a 45-degree angle, as shown in Fig. 5-8. Glue the truck bed onto the frame of the basic truck component. Make certain the

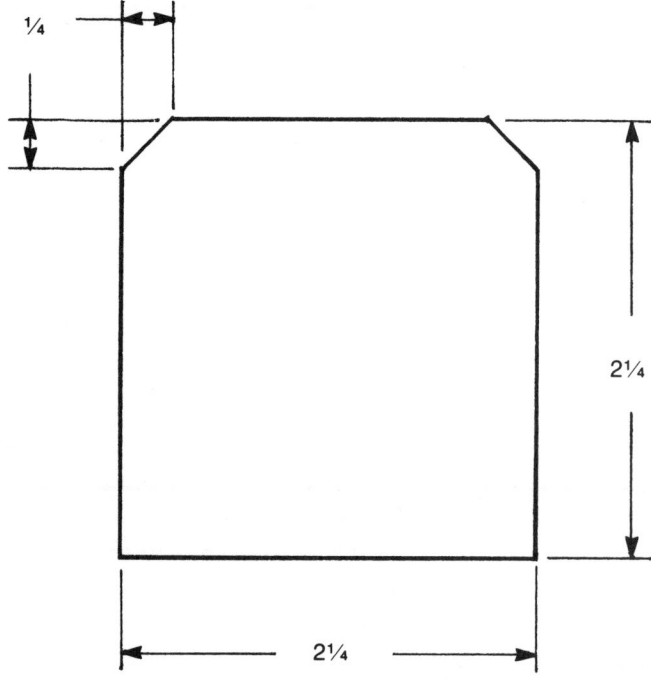

Fig. 5-7. Cut the upright cab protector from a 2½-inch-wide by 2¼-inch-long piece of ⅜-inch-thick wood.

Fig. 5-8. Make the bed of the Flatbed Truck from a 3/8-inch-thick, 2 1/4-inch-wide, 4 1/4-inch-long piece of wood. On one end of the bed, cut the corners to a 45-degree angle.

truck bed is centered on the frame and even with the cab protector.

That's it! That is all that's needed to adapt the basic truck component to the flatbed truck. The flatbed truck can carry any load the young driver gives it, but the flatbed can also be transformed into either a log hauler or lumber truck.

Log Hauler

The Log Hauler (Fig. 5-9) is a basic flatbed truck that has the ''logs'' glued into on the bed. The truck shown in the illustration is carrying five 5/8-inch-diameter logs each 4 1/4 inches long. The logs are cut from tree branches, then glued permanently in place on the truck bed.

Lumber Truck

The Log Trucks haul the raw material to the sawmill, and the Lumber Trucks carry

Fig. 5-9. *The Flatbed Truck can be converted into a Log Hauler by glueing a load of logs onto the bed.*

the finished product to the consumer. The Lumber Truck is a variation of the flatbed, with a load of lumber glued into place on the bed.

The lumber consists of several boards at random lengths that measure 1/8 inch thick and vary from 1/4 inch to 1/2 inch wide. The pieces can be glued together and then glued onto the flatbed, or left as individual pieces. If the pieces are left individually, the load tends to shift and fall off the truck. This problem can be eliminated by holding the load on with small rubber bands around the lumber and truck bed. The rubber bands look and even act as the banding straps used on real trucks.

If you are building the trucks for resale at craft shops, flea markets, etc., consider this: the trucks that have a load, whether logs or lumber, seem to sell better than the basic Flatbed Truck. The customer feels he or she is buying a completed project. Another advantage is that you can create three distinct vehicles with very little additional work.

DUMP TRUCK

The dump box described here is designed to be installed on the basic truck component, with some modification of the frame. The rear end of the frame has a 1/2-by-7/8-inch recess cut out (Fig. 5-11). The dump pivot will fit into this recess. On the sides of the frame, drill a 5/32-inch-diameter hole. The location of the holes can be determined by the drawing in Fig. 5-12A. The last change that you must make to the basic truck component is to slightly round the top edge of the frame where the recess has been cut (Fig. 5-12B).

Five pieces of 3/8-inch-thick wood will be needed to make the dump box. Glue the two sides (1 7/8 inches wide by 4 5/8 inches long) to the floor of the box, which is 2 3/8 inches

Fig. 5-10. The Dump Truck is a favorite with children. The Fleet would be incomplete without it.

wide by 4⅝ inches long. Also glue in place the front of the box, which measures 1⅝ inches wide by 1⅞ inches long. The rear of the box is the same size as the front, but it is *not* glued in place. It remains free so it will swing open when the dump box rises. However, it might be necessary to put the rear part in place to hold the sides correctly while they are being glued to the box floor.

After the glue has set, drill a ⁵⁄₃₂-inch hole through the side walls into the rear of the box (Fig. 5-13). Through these holes, insert two wood pins through the side walls

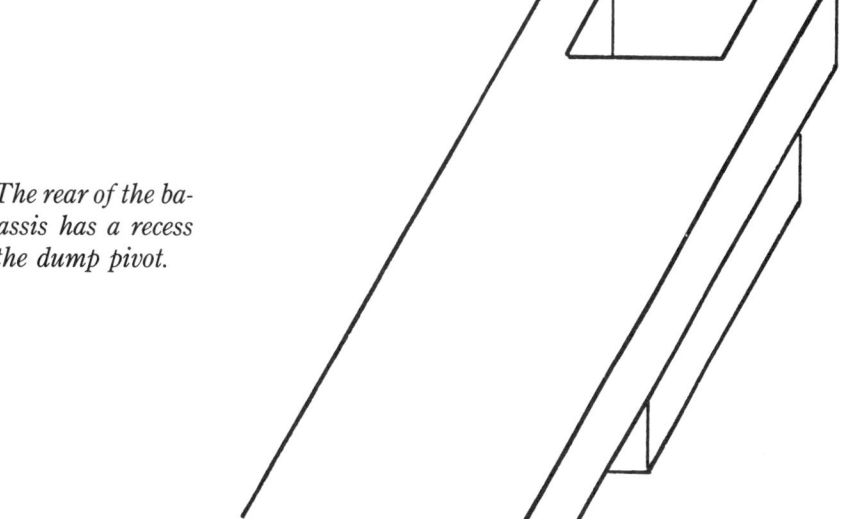

Fig. 5-11. The rear of the basic truck chassis has a recess cut into it, the dump pivot.

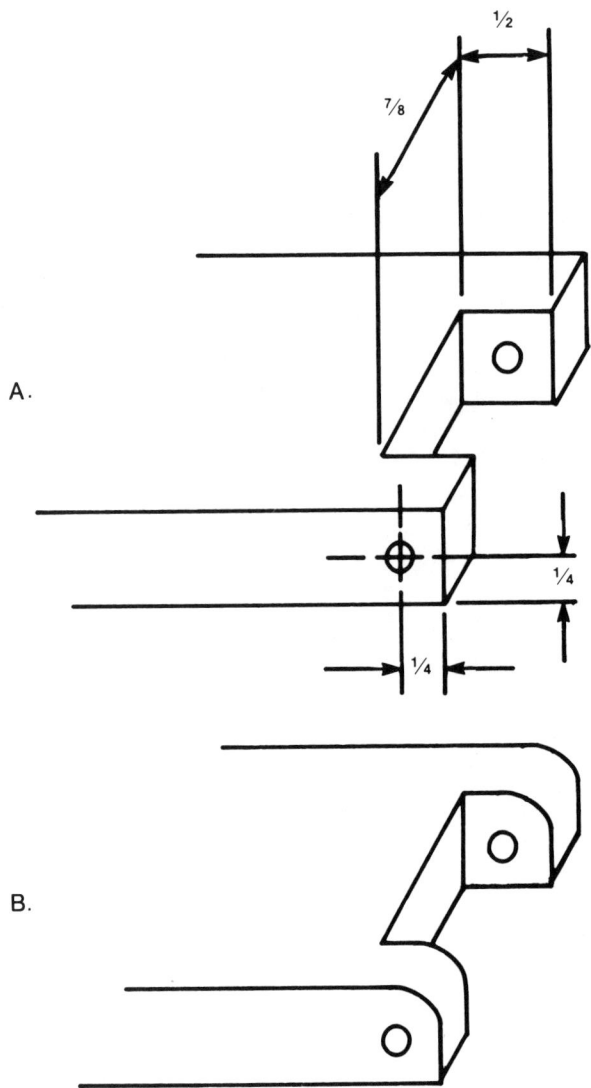

Fig. 5-12. *(A) Drill two 5/32-inch-diameter holes into the rear end of the Dump Truck basic component, from the outside edges into the dump pivot recess. (B) Round the top edge of the Dump Truck chassis so that the dump box will easily tilt.*

into the edge of the rear wall. These pins will serve as the pivot point for the rear gate.

Drill a 5/32-inch-diameter hole through the bottom of the dump box, 13/16 inch from either side, and ½ inch in from the back (Fig. 5-14A). The dump pivot is made of a 3/8-inch-thick piece of wood, ½ inch wide and 7/8 inch long. Drill a 5/32-inch hole 7/16 inch from the end of the pivot (Fig. 5-14B). After the hole has been drilled, round one bottom edge.

Insert the dump pivot block into the recess previously cut in the truck frame. It should fit snugly in the recess. If the parts fit properly, drill through the two holes in the side of the frame and into the ends of the pivot block. These holes should be 5/32 of an inch in diameter. Trial-fit a wood pin through the sides into the pivot block. The pivot block, when pinned, should *not* be lower than the frame. In fact, if it is 1/16 inch higher than the frame, the dump action of the truck will operate smoothly.

46

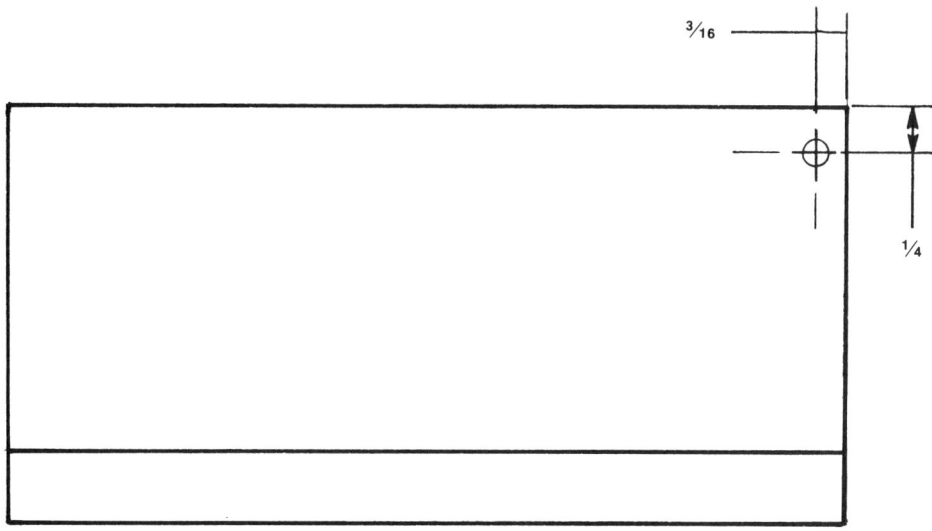

Fig. 5-13. Drill two holes through the sides into the top of the rear gate. Insert two small axle pegs through the sides into the rear so that the gate will swing open as the box tilts.

Insert another wood pin in the hole drilled through the floor of the dump box. Then glue the pin into the hole in the pivot block (Fig. 5-15). Coat the top surface of the pivot block with glue, in order to permanently affix the dump box to the truck frame. When the glue has set, test the action of the box, making sure that the rear gate swings open as the box is raised.

The Dump Truck can be built to carry marbles, blocks, or anything else the youngsters wish, and will supply the child with the basic ingredients needed for hours of imaginative play.

SEMITRUCK

When a person thinks of the trucking industry, generally the large semitrucks come to mind. The long-haul trucker, the "King of the Road," is often thought of as the workhorse of the industrialized world (Fig. 5-16).

Sleeping Cab

The Semitruck begins with the basic truck component described in the beginning of this chapter. The first part you must make for the Semitruck is the sleeping cab. The sleeping cab is made from a piece of 1-inch-thick wood that is 1½ inches wide and 2 inches tall. (Be sure to round all corners to prevent accidents.) Glue the sleeping cab in place behind the truck cab, centering on the truck frame (Fig. 5-17).

Fuel Tanks

Long-haul truckers make money by being on the road, piling up the miles. When

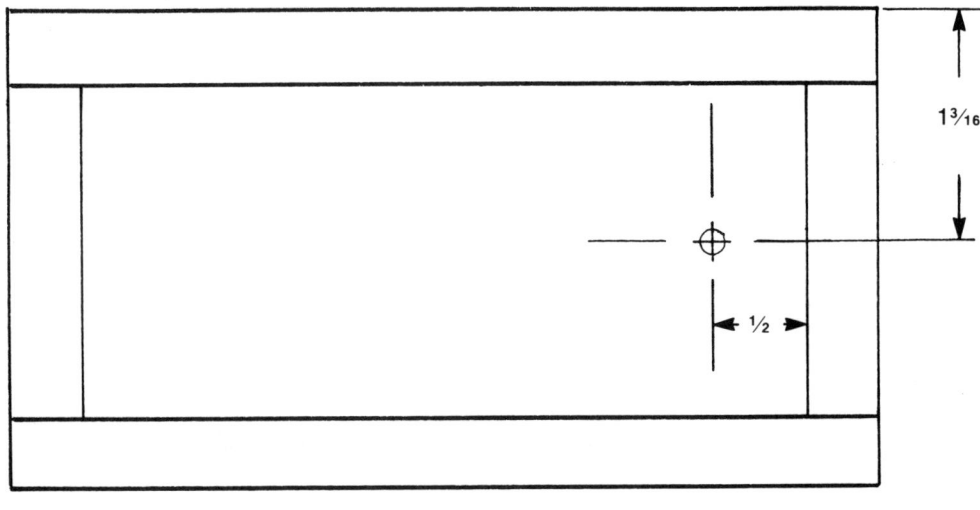

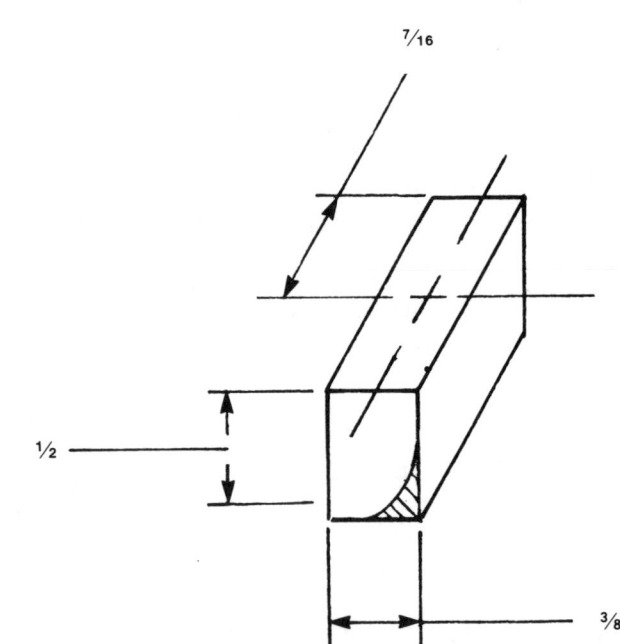

Fig. 5-14. *(A) Drill a hole through the bottom of the dump box. (B) Also, drill a hole through the center of the dump pivot and round one corner.*

the truck must stop for fuel, this decreases the profitability of the run. Therefore, long-haul trucks are equipped with large fuel tanks. The tanks are usually cylindrical tanks mounted on the frame. In order to be truly authentic, I have included these outboard tanks on the toy.

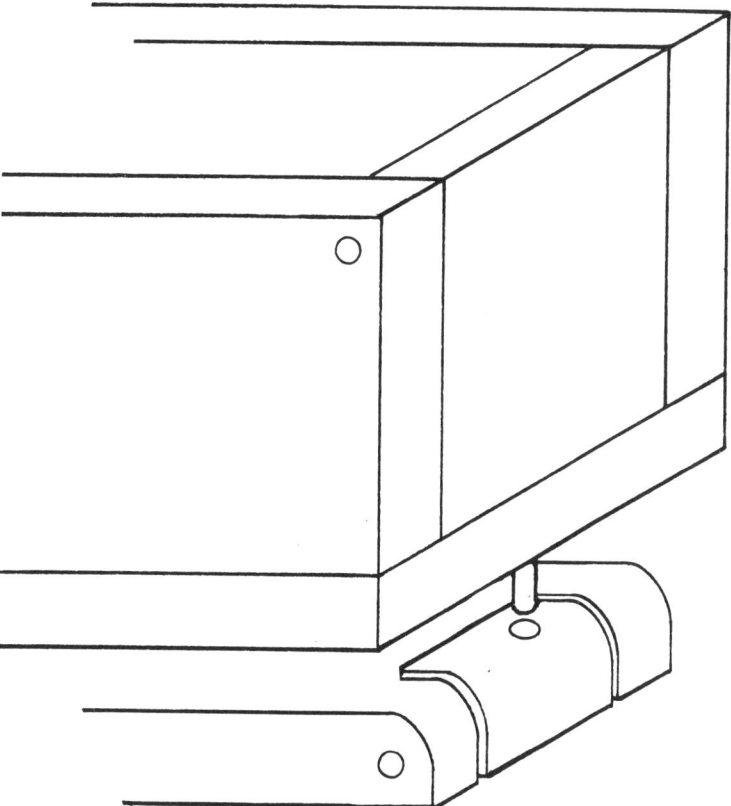

Fig. 5-15. *Place an axle peg through the floor of the dump box into the pivot, then glue the box onto the pivot. The axle peg acts as a dowel, adding strength to the glued joint.*

Cut the tanks from a piece of ½-inch-diameter dowel rod. The tanks, one on each side of the truck, should be 1¼ inches long. Glue onto the frame 2⅝ inches back from the front end of the truck frame (Fig. 5-18).

Semitruck Trailers

The last operation that must be done to the basic truck component is that a 5/32-inch hole must be drilled into the truck frame. This is where the trailer will attach to the

Fig. 5-16. *The large Semitruck can be seen on every highway or expressway across the nation.*

Fig. 5-17. *Glue the Semitruck sleeping quarters onto the basic truck component, behind the truck cab.*

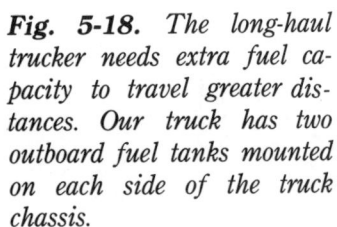

Fig. 5-18. *The long-haul trucker needs extra fuel capacity to travel greater distances. Our truck has two outboard fuel tanks mounted on each side of the truck chassis.*

Fig. 5-19. *There are two types of trailers that can be built for the Semitruck, (A) the Flatbed and (B) the Box Trailer.*

truck. Drill the hole 1⅝ inches in from the rear end of the frame; centering between the sides.

The next feature to build is the trailer. There are two common types of trailers found on semitrucks. The first is the flat trailer (Fig. 5-19A), which is used to haul a wide variety of loads that don't need to be confined in trailer walls. The second trailer is the box trailer (Fig. 5-19B), which is used to carry loads of grain, fill dirt, or coal.

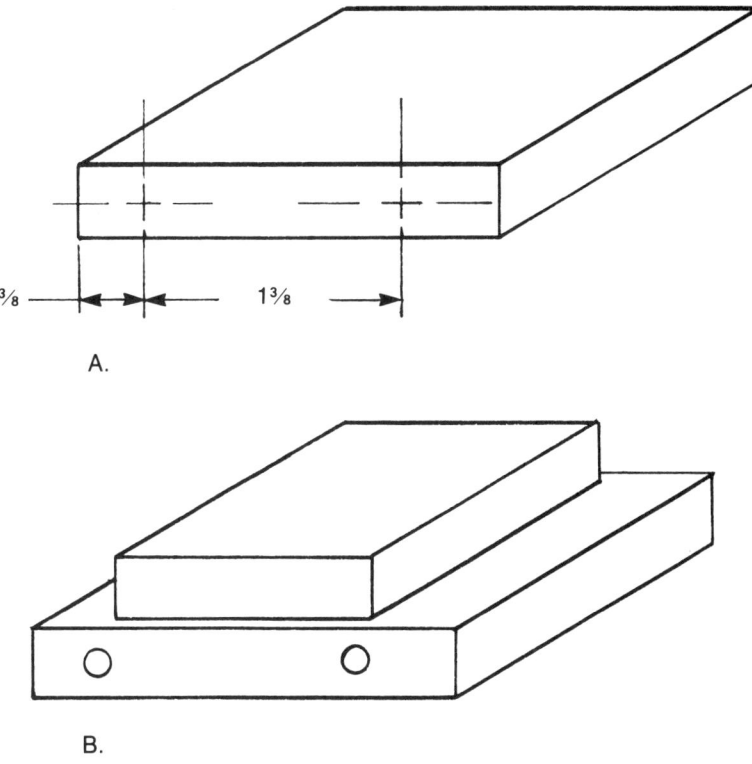

Fig. 5-20. *(A) Drill four 5/32-inch-diameter holes into the rear axle. (B) Glue the axle extender centered into the axle support.*

Flat Trailer. The Flat Trailer consists of one long, flat trailer bed that measures ⅜ of an inch thick, 2½ inches wide, and 8½ inches long. Sand the bed to smooth all edges, ends, and surfaces. The rear axle is the same as that used on the basic truck component. It measures ⅜ inch thick, 1⅝ inches wide, and 2¼ inches long. Drill four 5/32-inch-diameter holes, ½-inch deep into the rear axle, as shown in Fig. 5-20A.

The next part to make, the axle extender, is ⅜ inch thick, 1½ inches wide, and 2⅜ inches long. This piece is necessary to raise the rear of the trailer bed to a height equal to that of the front. Glue the axle extender to the top of the rear axle, centering within its area (Fig. 5-20B).

Next, glue the rear-axle assembly, with the axle extender, onto the bottom of the trailer bed. Position the assembly so that it is centered between the sides of the trailer bed and is 1⅜ inches from the rear end (Fig. 5-21).

Then drill an axle peg hole into the front of the trailer bed, ⅝ inch in from the front end and 1¼ inches from the side. It must correspond to the hole previously drilled in the truck frame.

The trailer is attached to the semitruck by inserting a peg through the trailer into the truck frame. If the trailer is to be removed from the semitruck, the peg should be glued into the trailer portion, but not into the truck frame. This procedure will allow the trailer to swivel behind the semitruck.

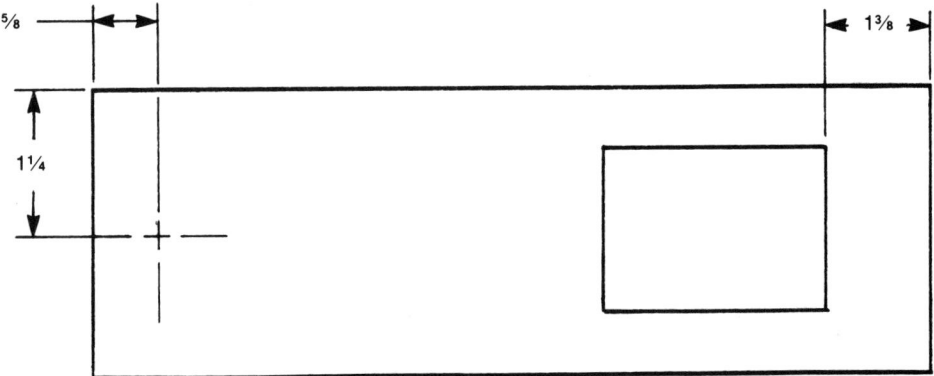

Fig. 5-21. Glue the axle support on the bottom of the Flatbed and Box Trailers, and drill an axle peg hole into the front end.

Many craftspersons prefer the trailer to be permanently mounted to the semitruck. If this is the case, it is necessary to insert the peg through the trailer and glue the peg into the truck frame only. This will permit the trailer to swivel, yet still be permanently attached to the truck.

Box Trailer. All of the pieces of the trailer box, the bed, sides, and end, are cut from 3/8-inch-thick wood. Begin by cutting out the bed, which measures 1¾ inches wide and 8½ inches long, again, making sure the sharp corners of the bed are slightly rounded to prevent accidents. Next, glue the sides, which are 2 by 8½ inches to the edges of the trailer bed, keeping the ends of the sides even with the end of the bed.

The next two pieces to be cut are the ends, which are 3/8 inch thick, 1¾ inches wide,

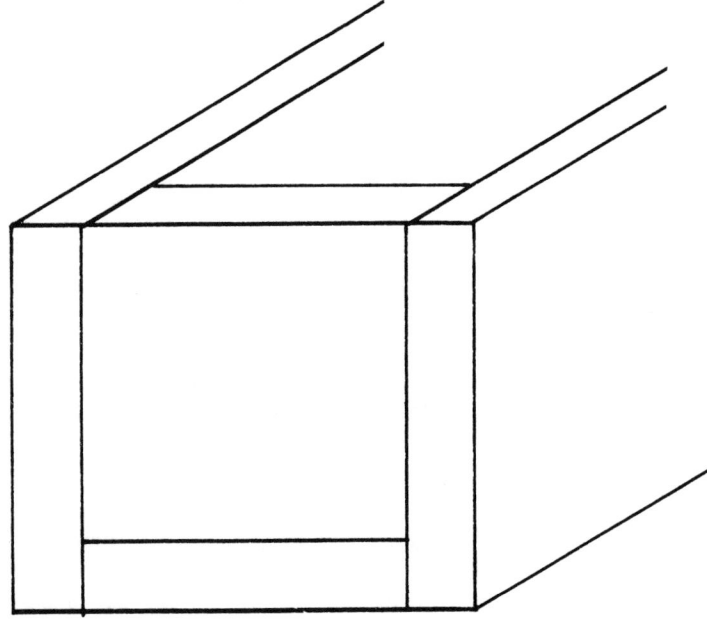

Fig. 5-22. Glue the ends of the Box Trailer between the sides. Make sure the ends are flush with the ends of the side pieces.

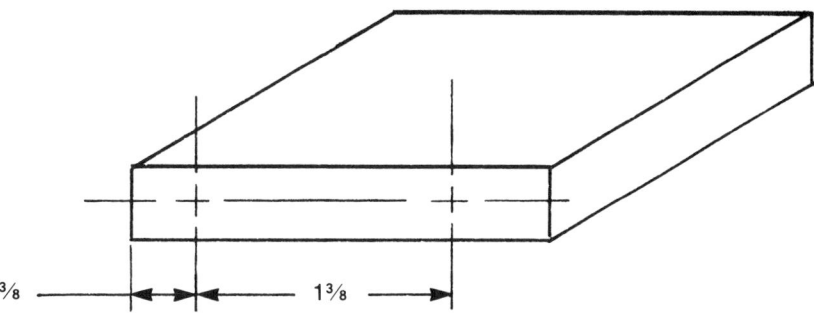

Fig. 5-23. Raise the rear wheels of the trailer box to the required height by glueing a rear axle support to the bottom of the trailer.

and 2 inches long. Glue the ends between the sides of the box, making sure that all ends are flush (Fig. 5-22).

Until the wheels are added, the trailer box is just a wooden box. To make the box into a trailer, you need two pieces of wood. The larger of the two is the rear axle. This is the same rear-axle support as the one on the basic truck component. It measures 3/8 inch thick, 1 5/8 inches wide, and 2 1/4 inches long. Drill four 5/32-inch-diameter holes in this piece, as shown in Fig. 5-23.

The rear axle must be held 3/8 inch from the bottom of the trailer so that the trailer lays level—the front no higher than the rear. To accomplish this, place a 3/8-inch-thick, 1 1/2-inch-wide and 2 3/8-inch-long axle extender between the rear axle and the bottom of the trailer (Fig. 5-24). Glue the axle extender in the center of the rear axle. Then glue this assembly to the bottom of the trailer. Be sure the rear-axle assembly is centered between the sides and 1 1/4 inches away from the rear.

Next, drill a 3/32-inch-diameter hole on the bottom of the trailer near the front end. This hole is where the trailer will be attached to the truck. Insert a peg, the same type

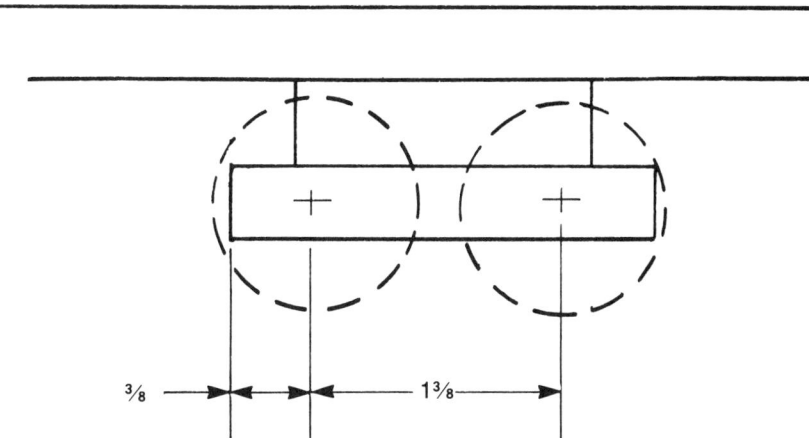

Fig. 5-24. The rear axle support of the Box Trailer must be lowered below the bottom of the trailer. This is done by glueing an axle extender to the bottom of the trailer.

used to hold the wheels in place, through the hole in the trailer bed (from inside the trailer). Then put the end of the peg protruding below the trailer bed into the hole previously drilled in the frame of the semitruck.

As with the flatbed trailer, there are two choices for attaching the box trailer to the semitruck frame. The first alternative is to glue the peg into the trailer bed, to allow the trailer to be removed from the semitruck. The second method is to permanently attach the trailer to the truck by inserting the peg through the trailer bed and glueing it into the truck frame. Either selection works fine. The decision is strictly a personal one.

GAS/MILK HAULER

The Gas/Milk Hauler can be built as a vehicle that travels the countryside collecting milk from dairy farmers and delivering it to a dairy; or it can be a gas truck, one that pumps gas into construction vehicles at the construction site or delivers fuel oil to outlying areas. Whichever you select, it is sure to become a popular truck for resale or a welcomed addition to the fleet.

This truck is also based on the basic truck chassis described in the beginning of this chapter. There are some additional pieces of wood that are required for this project: a ¾-inch length of ¾-inch-diameter dowel, two ⅜-inch-diameter by ¾-inch-long dowels, and a 4½-inch-long by 2½-inch-diameter cylinder. The dowels can usually be purchased at a hardware store or lumberyard.

If a wood-cutting lathe is available, the cylinder can be turned from a 3½-inch-by-3½-inch square. If not, however, do not despair. Many of the toy wholesalers that sell

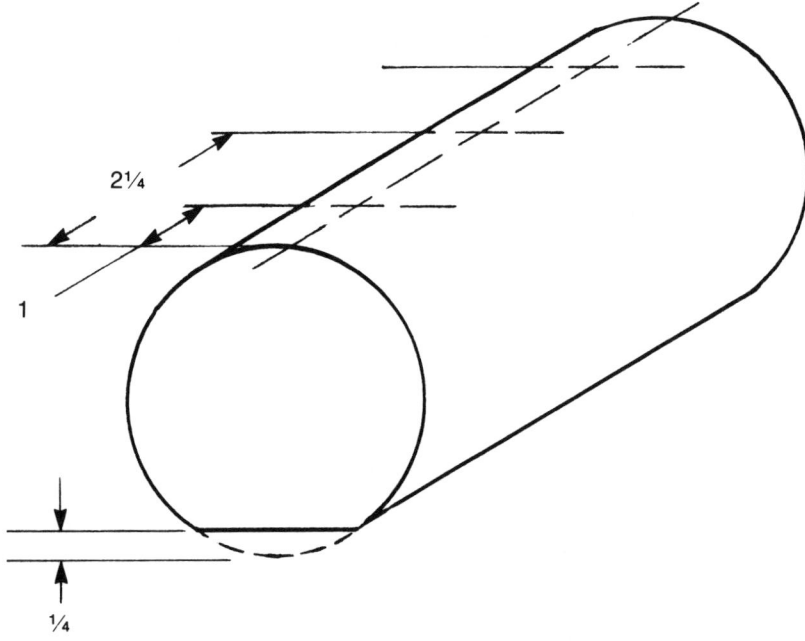

Fig. 5-25. *Drill three holes in the top of the cylinder tank.*

toy supplies sell wood cylinders in a variety of diameters. Find a cylinder approximately 2½ inches in diameter.

Now, flatten the bottom of the cylinder so that it can be permanently glued to the basic truck chassis. This can be done by drawing a line across the end of the cylinder ¼ inch up from the bottom. The material can be removed with a hand plane, wood rasp, Surform tool, or power sander. Whichever method you choose, you should take care not to remove too much material, and to remove it uniformly so that the tank will rest flat on the truck.

Next, drill a ¾-inch-size hole, ½ inch deep, on the top of the tank or cylinder (Fig. 5-25). Then glue the ¾-inch-long dowel into the hole. Also drill two ⅜-inch-diameter holes, ½ inch deep into the top of the tank, 1 inch in from both ends. Glue the two corresponding dowels into the ⅜-inch holes.

The tank is now ready to be glued to the truck chassis. To ensure that the tank adheres permanently, apply a layer of glue to both the frame and the rear of the cab. Also apply a thin layer to the bottom of the tank. Carefully line the tank up in the center of the truck frame. Then put even pressure on the tank. Allow the pressure to remain on the tank until the glue has set.

Now the Gas/Milk Hauler only needs to be finished (painted, varnished, etc.), before it is ready to be put to work in the fleet.

CEMENT MIXER

The next truck seems to hold a particular fascination for youngsters. Children find the Cement Mixer, (Fig. 5-26), with its large, impressive revolving drum, interesting to watch. The Cement Mixer, too, is built on the basic truck frame, detailed earlier in this chapter.

First, cut two vertical drum supports from ⅜-inch-thick material. The first should measure 1⅝ inches wide and 2⅛ inches long. The drawing in Fig. 5-27A shows the top corners have been cut to a 45-degree angle to eliminate sharp corners. Also shown is the center location of a ¼-inch-diameter hole. Glue the front vertical drum support onto the frame and rear of the cab (Fig. 5-27B).

Fig. 5-26. The Cement Mixer is one of the favorites among children because of its large size and revolving drum.

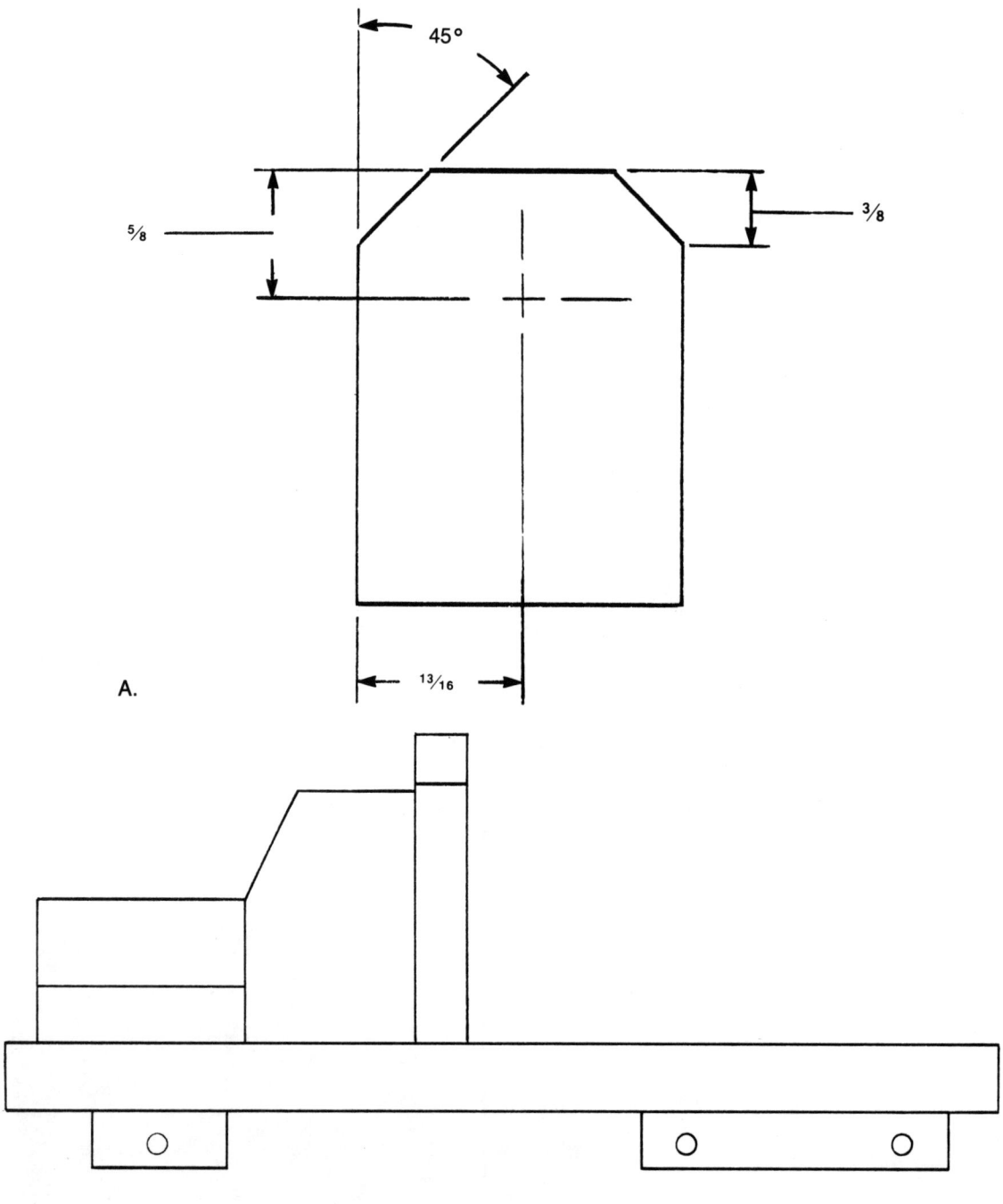

Fig. 5-27. *(A) Drill a ¼-inch hole in the front drum support and make two 45-degree cuts at the upper corners. (B) Glue the front vertical drum support onto the frame and rear of the cab.*

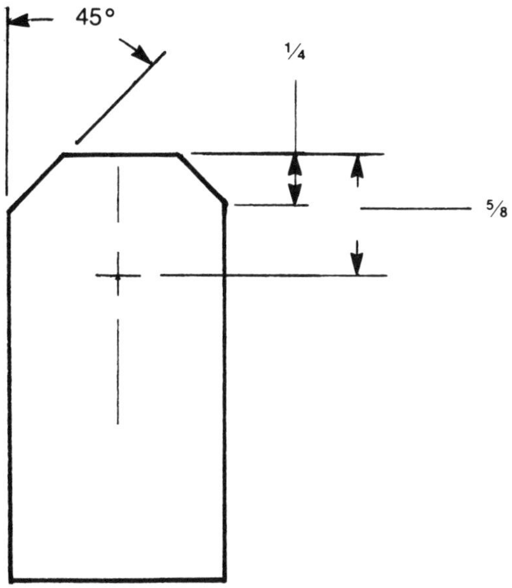

Fig. 5-28. *Drill a hole slightly larger than the axle peg into the rear drum support. Cut the two upper corners at a 45-degree angle.*

Next, cut the rear vertical drum support to ⅜ inch thick, 1⅛ inches wide, and 2⅛ inches long. As you did on the front support, cut the two upper corners slightly to a 45-degree angle and drill a hole into it that is large enough for an axle peg to easily slide through (Fig. 5-28B).

Before glueing the rear drum support onto the frame, glue a ¾-inch length of ¼-

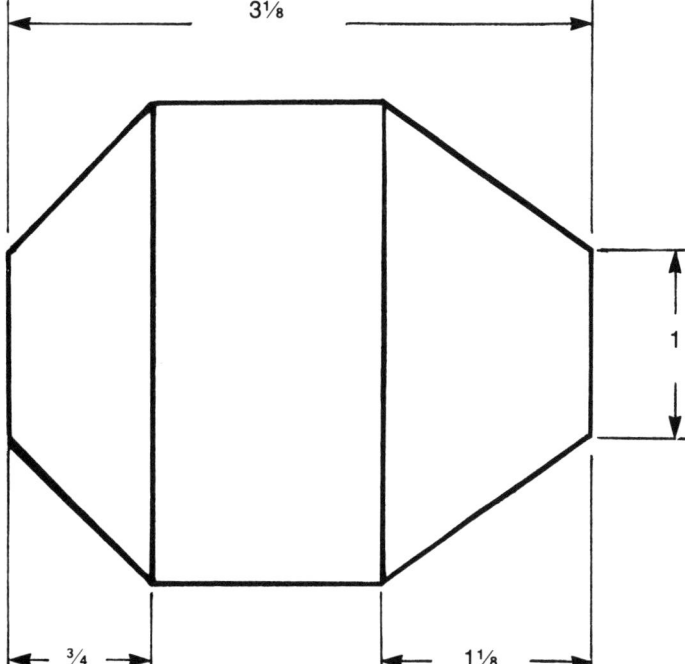

Fig. 5-29. *The mixing drum of the Cement Mixer is turned on a lathe to the proper size.*

57

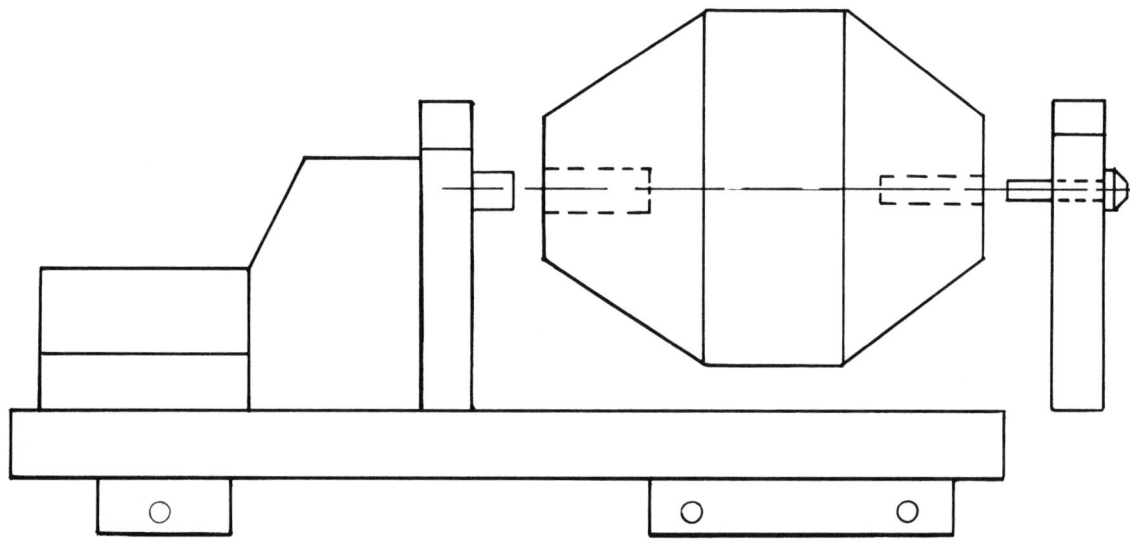

Fig. 5-30. Place the mixing drum between the front and rear drum supports.

inch dowel rod into the ¼-inch hole of the front drum support. Now, it is necessary to make and install the drum.

The drum is made from two 4½-inch lengths of 1½-inch-thick wood, 3½ inches wide. (Two lengths of 2 by 4 will work fine.) Glue the two lengths together surface-to-surface to form a block with a 3-inch thickness. Then turn the block on a wood lathe to the shape shown in Fig. 5-29.

Next, drill a 5/16-inch-diameter hole, ¾-inch deep, into end of the drum that slopes down more severely (1⅛ inch). In the center of the other end of the drum, drill a hole the same diameter as the axle peg.

The next step is to place the mixing drum onto the drum supports. To do this, slide the end of the drum with the 5/16-inch-diameter hole over the ¼-inch dowel on the front drum support. Do *not* glue it in place. The drum must turn freely on the dowel.

The rear drum support can now be glued onto the back end of the truck frame. Insert an axle peg that will easily turn through the hole drilled in the rear drum support. Glue the peg into the drum (Fig. 5-30).

Be sure to allow all of the glued parts ample time to dry. Afterward, give the entire project a quick sanding to ensure that everything is smooth and free from defects. Then finally, a finish, for either protective or decorative purposes, should be applied to the truck. If you use paint or varnish, make sure the drum turns freely while the finish dries.

LIST 5-1. REQUIRED MATERIALS

Basic Truck Component
- 1 – Chassis — ½ × 1⅝ × 7¼
- 1 – Cab — 1½ × 1¼ × 1¾
- 1 – Hood — 1 × 1⅛ × 1⅜
- 1 – Front Axle — ⅜ × 1⅝ × 1
- 1 – Rear Axle — ⅜ 1⅝ × 1
- 6 – Wheels — 1¼-inch diameter
- 6 – Axle Pins — Small Size

Flatbed Truck
- 1 – Basic Truck Component — Standard Size
- 1 – Cab Protector — ⅜ × 2⅜ × 2⅛
- 1 – Enlarged Truck Bed — ⅜ × 2⅜ × 4¼

Variations
- 5 – Logs
- 20 – Pieces of Lumber — From ¼ inch to ½ inch in width. Random lengths - 3½ to 4½ inches.

Dump Box
- 1 – Basic Truck Component
- 2 – Sides — ⅜ × 1¾ × 4⅝
- 2 – Front/Rear — ⅜ × 1¾ × 1⅝
- 1 – Floor — ⅜ × 2⁷⁄₁₆ × 4⅝
- 1 – Dump Pivot Block — ⅜ × ½ × ⅞
- 5 – Pins — ¹³⁄₁₆ × ⁵⁄₃₂

Semitruck
- 1 – Basic Truck Component — Standard Size
- 1 – Sleeping Cab — 1 × 1½ × 2
- 2 – Outboard fuel tanks — ½-inch diameter × 1¼

Flat Trailer
- 1 – Trailer Bed — ⅜ × 2½ × 8½
- 1 – Rear Axle — ⅜ × 1⅝ × 2¼
- 1 – Axle Extender — ⅜ × 1½ × 2⅜
- 4 – Wheels — 1¼-inch diameter
- 5 – Axle Pegs — Small

Box Trailer

1	– Bed	– 3/8 × 1 3/4 × 8 1/2
2	– Sides	– 3/8 × 2 × 8 1/2
2	– Ends	– 3/8 × 1 3/4 × 2
1	– Rear Axle	– 3/8 × 1 5/8 × 2 1/4
1	– Axle Extender	– 3/8 × 1 1/2 × 2 3/8
4	– Wheels	– 1 1/4-inch diameter
5	– Pegs	– Small

Gas and Milk Hauler

1	– Basic Truck Chassis	
1	– Cylinder Tank	– 2 1/2 inch diameter × 4 1/2 inches long
1	– Center Filler	– 3/4-inch-diameter dowel × 3/4 inch long
2	– End Fillers	– 3/8-inch-diameter dowels × 3/8 inch long

Cement Mixer

1	– Basic Frame Assembly	
1	– Front Drum Support	– 3/8 × 1 5/8 × 2 1/8
1	– Rear Drum Support	– 3/8 × 1 1/8 × 2 1/8
1	– Mixing Drum	– 2 1/2 inch diameter × 3 1/8
1	– Dowel	– 1/4 × 3/4 inch long
1	– Axle pegs	

6
CHAPTER

Construction Vehicles

The tracks on which the bulldozer and creeper shovel are built (Fig. 6-1) are the same size and are built in the same manner. In this chapter I will describe the construction procedure for the track, and follow with the directions for the bulldozer and creeper shovel.

THE CREEPER UNIT

Cut the two tracks from a ¾-inch-thick board. The length of each track should be 4¾ inches long and 1⅛ inches wide. On both ends, draw a 9/16-inch radius, as shown in Fig. 6-2. Cut and sand the radius on the ends. Drill two ¼-inch-diameter holes through the tracks where indicated.

Cut the frame from a piece of ⅜-inch-thick wood measuring 1¾ inches wide and 4 inches long. Mark a line on the edges of the board ⅝ inch in from one end and another line 2¾ inches from the first line (Fig. 6-3). Measure 3/16 inch up along the two lines on the edge of the frame. At these two locations, drill a ¼-inch-diameter hole ½ inch deep. Repeat on the opposite edge of the frame.

The parts for the basic creeper track are now ready for sanding and assembly. To assemble the creeper, apply a thin layer of glue on the edge of the frame. Allow a small amount of glue to slip down into the ¼-inch holes drilled in the edges. Also apply a small amount of glue in the holes of the track.

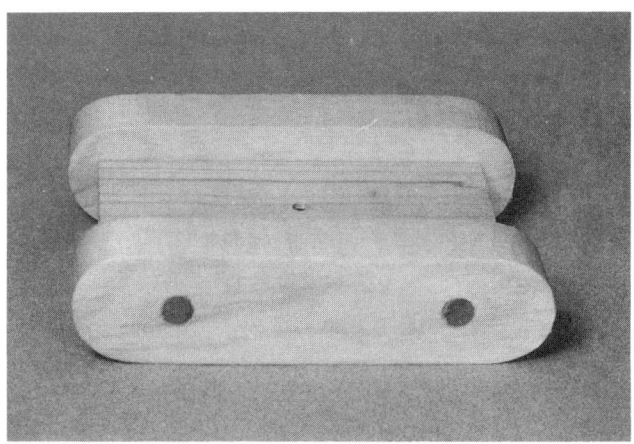

Fig. 6-1. The Bulldozer and Creeper Shovel are both built on the same lower unit, the Creeper Unit.

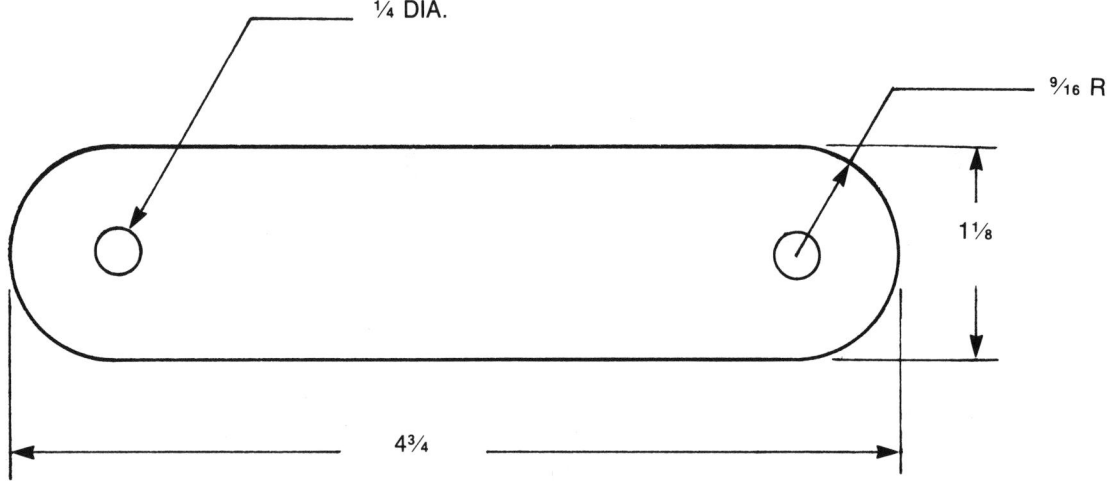

Fig. 6-2. The tracks of the Creeper Unit are shaped as shown.

Carefully line up the holes in the frame with the holes in the track, and insert a 1⅛-inch-long, ¼-inch-diameter dowel into the holes of the track. Push it into the holes in the frame. The dowels should be flush or slightly above the surface of the track. The dowel can be sanded smooth later. Repeat the process for the other side of the creeper track.

We have now assembled the creeper unit, which is the basic component to the bulldozer and the creeper shovel. Next, we must modify the creeper unit and assemble the upper structure for the bulldozer and creeper shovel.

THE BULLDOZER

The Bulldozer is a favorite of most kids. It is a toy that can push imaginary loads or clear a road through the densest forest (Fig. 6-4). The moving dozer blade adds a bit of realism to the child's play.

The engine compartment of the bulldozer is made of a solid block of wood that

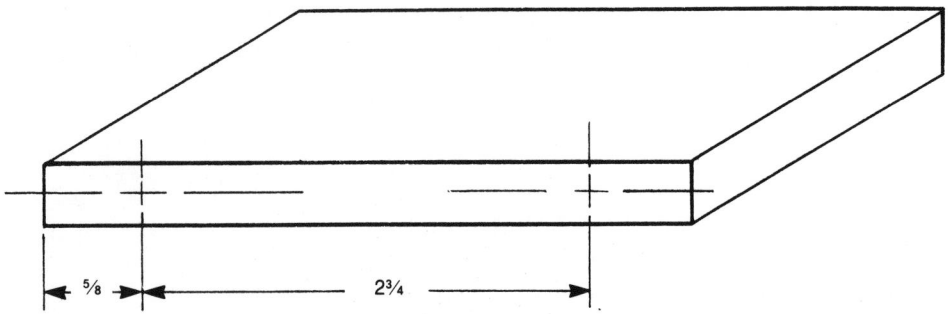

Fig. 6-3. Cut the Creeper Unit frame from a ⅜-inch-thick piece of wood, 1¾ inches wide and 4 inches long. Drill two ¼-inch-diameter holes on both sides.

Fig. 6-4. The Bulldozer, with its tracks and moving blade, is a favorite toy for many children.

measures 1⅛ inches thick, 3½ inches long, and 1½ inches wide. From the block, cut a 1-inch-long by ½-inch-deep area, as illustrated in Fig. 6-5.

Since real bulldozers do not have squared-off lines, this one will not either. The front and edges of the engine compartment should be rounded. Follow the shape shown in Fig. 6-5. After sanding the engine compartment, set it aside. You will later glue it onto the frame.

Drill an axle peg hole 1⅜ inches from the end and centered in the creeper unit. Repeat this on the opposite side. There are two blade arms that are cut from ¼-inch-thick stock. The arms measure 2½ inches long and 1 inch across at the widest point. The shape of the blade arm is shown in Fig. 6-6. Drill an axle peg hole through the blade arm, as indicated on the grid pattern.

Glue the ¼-inch-thick, 1-inch-wide, 3⅛-inch-long blade spreader between the front of the two blades (Fig. 6-7). While the blade arm assembly is drying, build the dozer blade. The blade in the illustration was made from a 4⅜-inch length of cove molding, which can be purchased at any lumberyard. The original shape of the molding must be slightly modified, as shown in Fig. 6-8. This can be done with a saw, or filed and sanded.

All parts of the bulldozer are now ready for a final sanding and assembly. Begin by

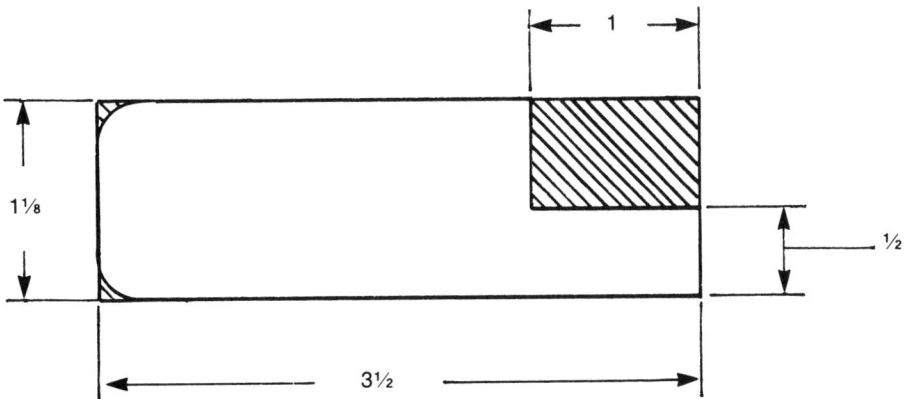

Fig. 6-5. The correct shape of the engine compartment. The shaded areas are to be removed.

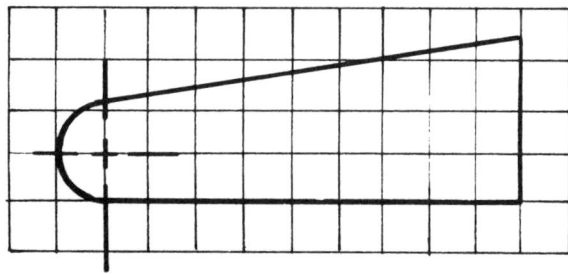

Fig. 6-6. The grid pattern shows the shape of the blade arm.

glueing the engine compartment to the creeper unit frame. The engine compartment should overhang the front of the frame by ½ inch and be centered between the tracks. The front is the end with the axle peg hole drilled in the side of the track. If you want to add a coat of paint or varnish, it is best to do it now, prior to the final assembly.

Slide the blade arm assembly over the creeper unit, lining up the holes drilled through the arm with those drilled in the side of the tracks. The blade arm assembly is held in place with two small axle pegs. Be careful to glue only in the hole drilled in the track. If glue should seep into any other area, it could prevent the blade arm assembly from raising. Test the arm to ensure its movement. The final step in the assembly process is to center the dozer blade on the blade arm assembly and glue it in place.

THE CREEPER SHOVEL

The Creeper Shovel (Fig. 6-9), generally known as the steam shovel, is another all-time favorite. The model discussed here is complete with a swivel cab and operating shovel.

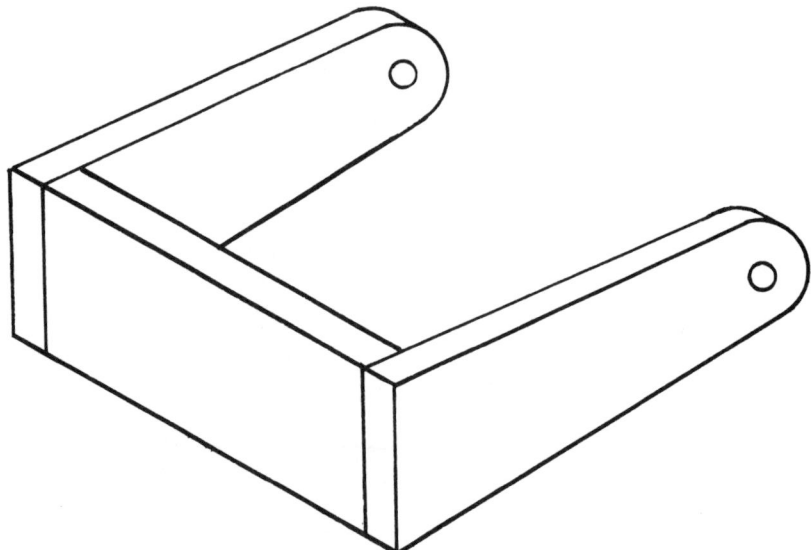

Fig. 6-7. Glue a blade spreader between the blade arms. This will provide a larger glueing surface for the blade.

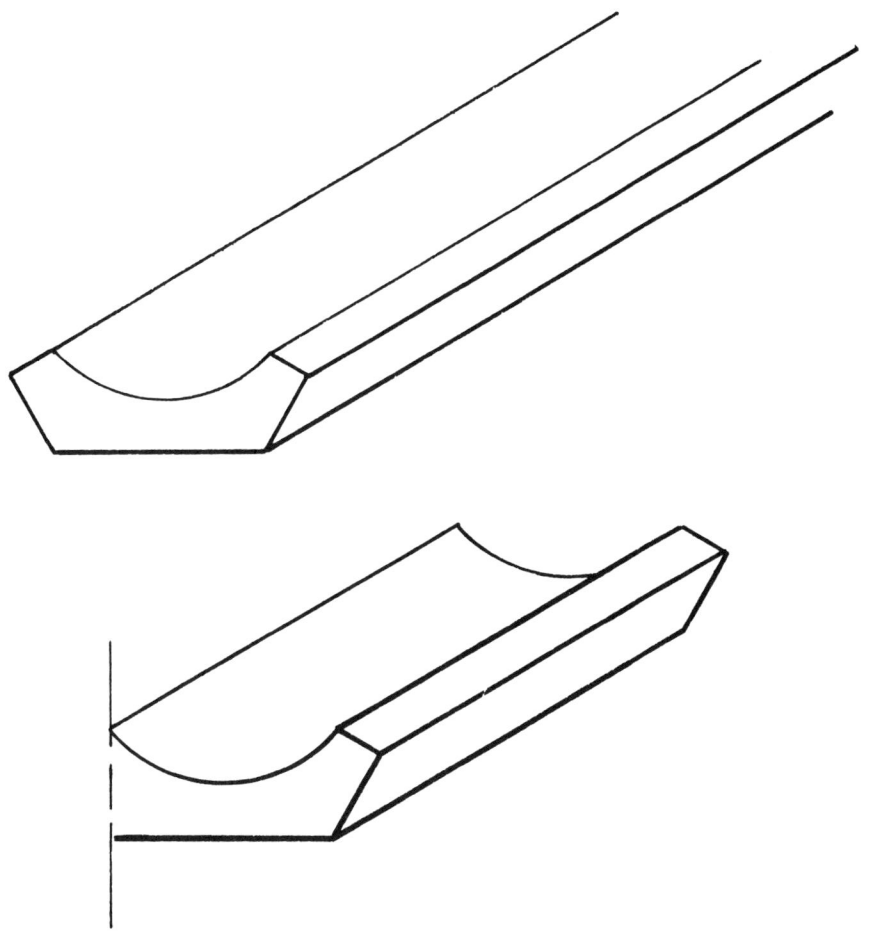

Fig. 6-8. *A short length of cove molding can be used to make the dozer blade, but it must be slightly modified.*

This project starts with the basic creeper unit previously described in this chapter. It requires no alterations in size, just a 3/16-inch hole drilled through the center of the creeper unit frame (Fig. 6-10).

Cut the creeper shovel base from 3/8-inch-thick stock. The length should be 1 3/8 inches, and the width 3 5/8 inches. Next, round the two ends to a radius of 11/16 inch. Drill an axle peg hole at the center of the shovel base, as shown in Fig. 6-11. This is the pivoting point for the base and creeper unit.

The cab and hood are the same as those found on almost all of the vehicles. In this chapter, directions for making both the hood and cab can be found in the basic truck component instructions detailed in Chapters 3 and 5. The only alterations to the basic cab unit are two axle peg holes drilled in the two sides, as shown in Fig. 6-12. The holes are where the crane boom will be attached to the cab.

You are now ready to glue the cab and hood pieces onto the shovel base. Notice

Fig. 6-9. The Creeper Shovel has a swiveling shovel mounted onto the Creeper Unit.

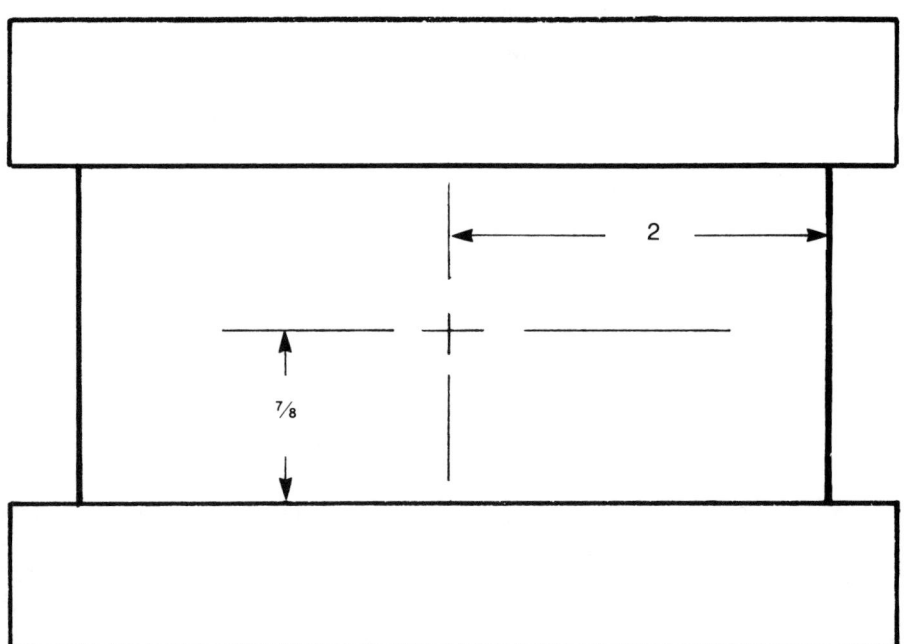

Fig. 6-10. Drill a 3/16-inch-diameter hole through the frame of the Creeper Unit.

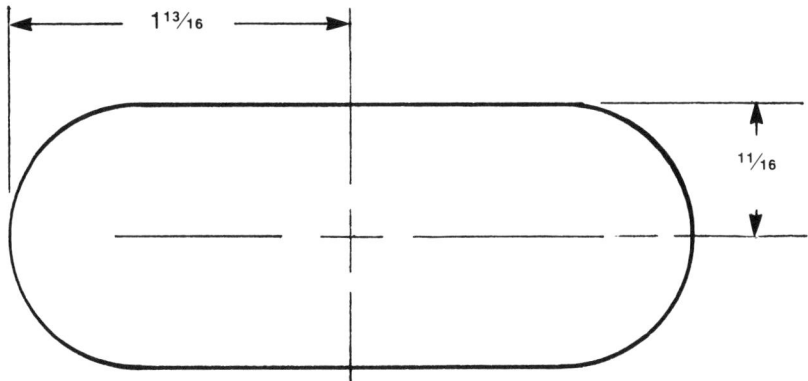

Fig. 6-11. Cut the shovel base and shape as shown.

that, unlike on the trucks, the hood, or motor compartment, on this vehicle is located behind the cab. Set the front of the cab back from the front end of the shovel base ½ inch, centering between the shovel base sides.

The crane boom is made of ⅜-inch-thick wood that measures 1⅞ inches wide by 6⅛ inches long. Draw the boom design, as shown in Fig. 6-13, directly onto the wood. If you are making several cranes, draw the boom on a piece of cardboard or hardboard so that it can be traced.

Next, drill three axle peg holes on the edge of the crane boom, where indicated in Fig. 6-13. The boom extension, which is the piece between the boom and the shovel, is made of one piece of wood ⅜ inch thick, ⅜ inch wide, and 4¼ inches long. Round both ends of the boom extension to permit ease of movement when in operation (Fig. 6-14).

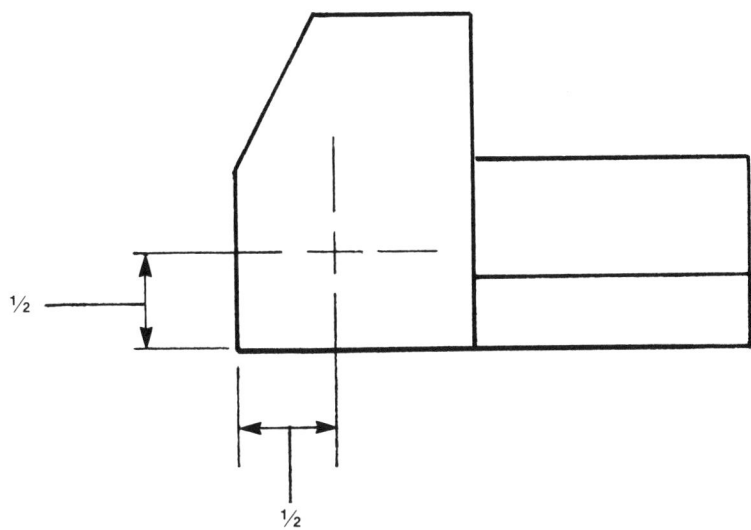

Fig. 6-12. Drill two axle peg holes into both sides of the basic cab.

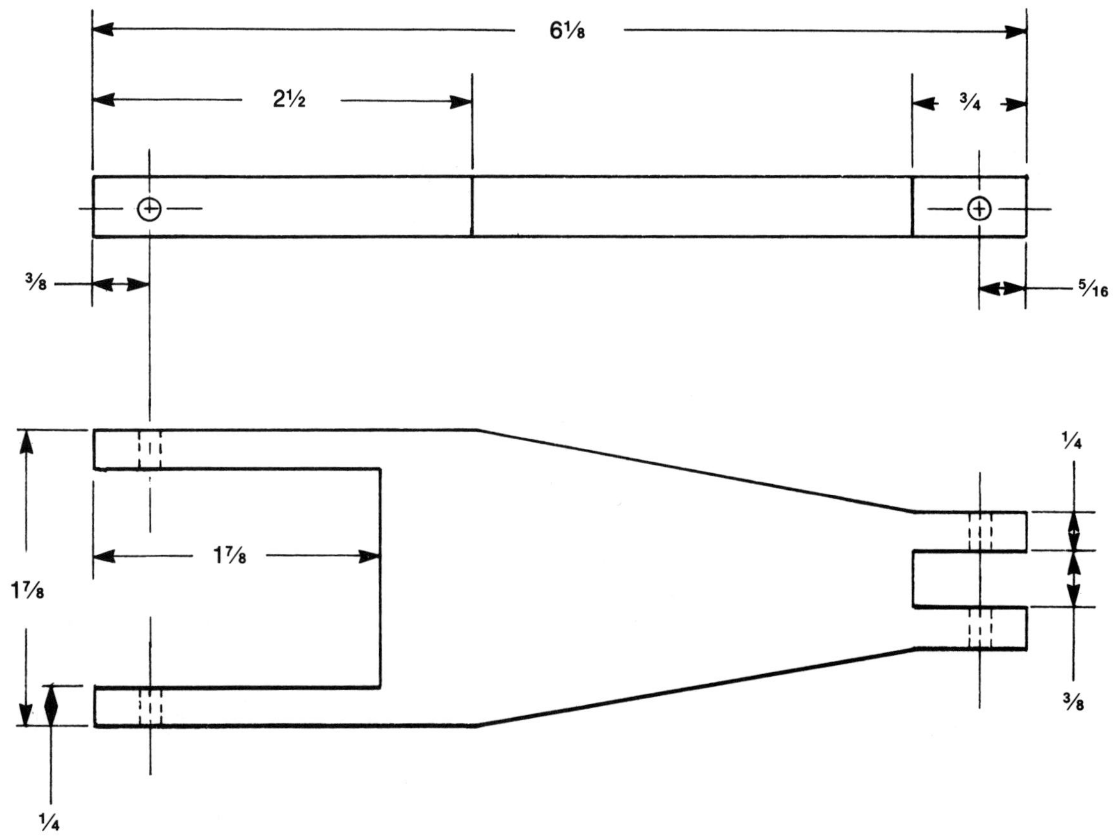

Fig. 6-13. *The crane boom.*

Also, drill two axle peg holes through the ends of the boom extension. This is where the boom extension will be connected to the boom on one end, and the shovel on the other end.

Fit the boom extension loosely into the end of the crane boom and hold in place with two axle pegs. You will have to shorten the pegs somewhat in order to make them

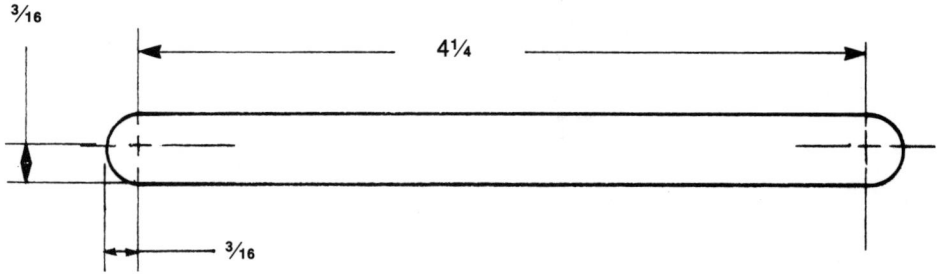

Fig. 6-14. *Round the boom extensions on the ends. Then drill axle peg-size holes through the ends.*

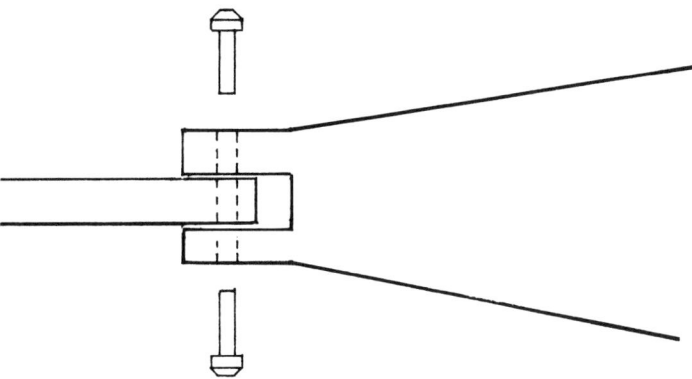

Fig. 6-15. Make sure the boom extension fits smoothly and moves freely in the crane boom.

fit properly. Test fit the two pieces together to make sure they move easily (Fig. 6-15).

The shovel is made from a solid piece of wood, 1¾ by 1⅛ by 1 inch, for maximum strength. Figure 6-16 shows the finished shovel and its dimensions, as viewed from the top (A), and from the side (B).

To construct the shovel, drill a ¾-inch-diameter hole, ⅝ of an inch deep. Then remove

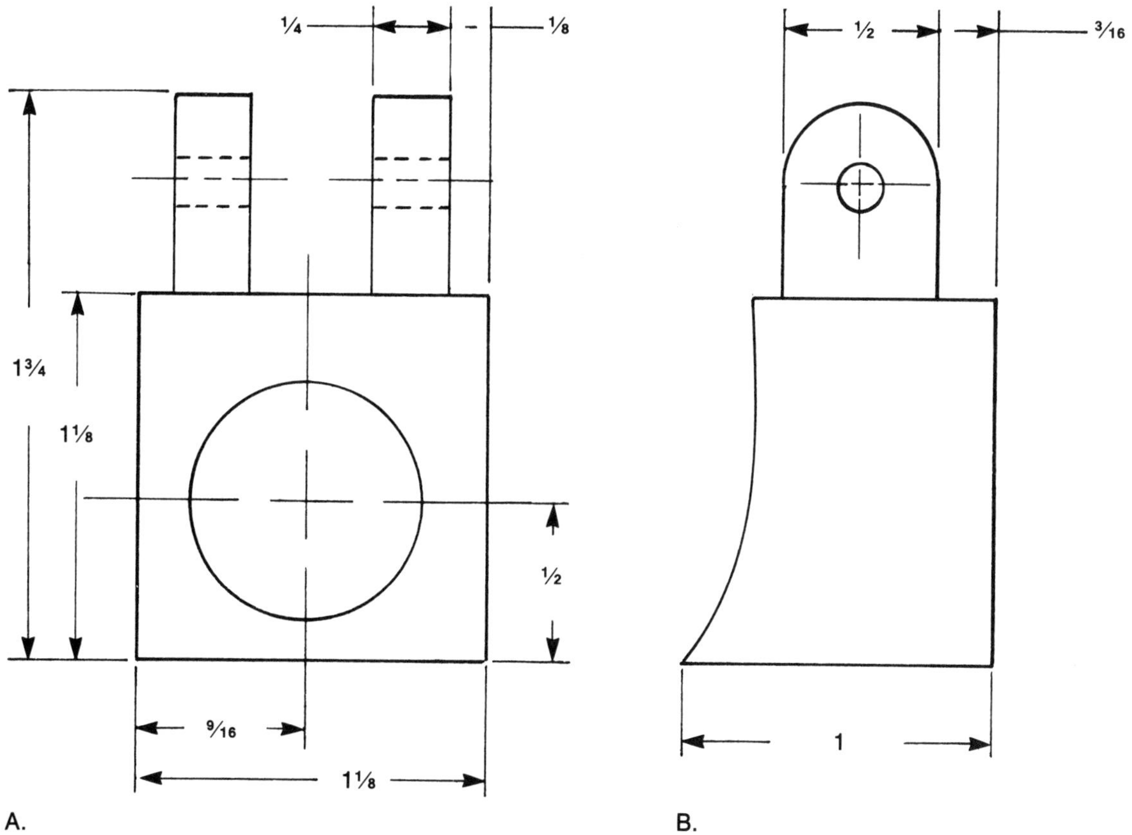

Fig. 6-16. Cutting and shaping the shovel.

an ⅛-inch-thick layer of wood in a slight curve from the top surface of the shovel (see Fig. 6-16B) block. On the side, drill an axle peg hole through the shovel. Refer back to drawing A and cut and shape the shovel as shown. After shaping, the entire shovel will need to be sanded to remove any burrs and sharp edges.

After shaping and sanding, you are ready to begin the final assembly. Insert an axle peg through the Creeper Unit frame from the bottom, through a small, 1-inch-diameter wood wheel, and glue the peg into the hole drilled into the shovel base (Fig. 6-17). Be careful not to get glue on any area of the wood other than in the hole, otherwise, the shovel will not turn freely from side to side.

Next, to assemble is the boom and its related parts. Apply glue in the holes of the cab and then peg the boom into place. The peg should be held in place permanently, while the boom moves freely on the pegs.

Next, attach the boom extender to the boom. At this point, shorten the two pegs,

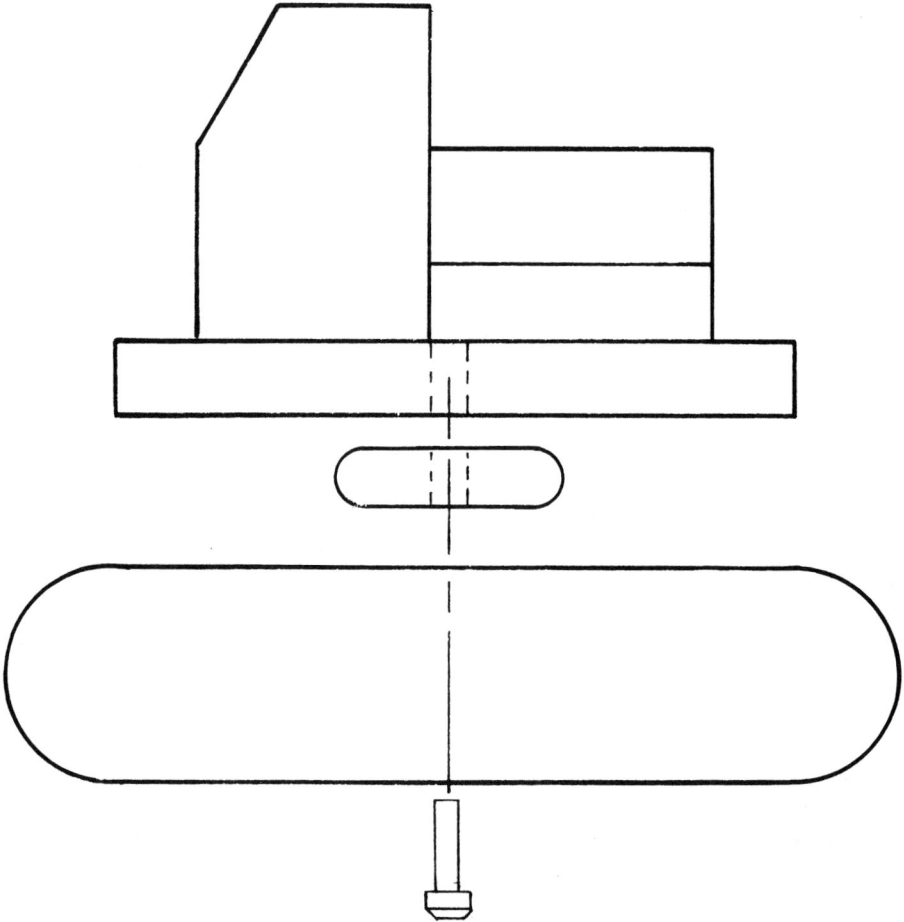

Fig. 6-17. *Assemble the Creeper Shovel by inserting an axle peg through the frame, through a wood wheel, and into the shovel base.*

place through the boom, and glue into the boom extender. While the glued assembly is drying, remember to move each joint occasionally, to make sure they are not being glued together.

PAY LOADER

The Pay Loader vehicle is a masterpiece in design. It is functionality at its best. The machine has been designed to pick up large loads, maneuver in cramped spaces, and operate in deep mud or rough terrain (Fig. 6-18).

Construction begins with the two-piece frame unit. The frame has a swivel joint to allow for movement in cramped places. Select a ⅜-inch-thick piece of wood 1¼ inches wide, and 11 inches long. From this piece of wood, cut two 3¼-inch-long sections and two 1¾-inch-long sections. On one end of the four frame pieces, cut a ⅝-inch radius (Fig. 6-19).

Glue parts a and b together with the squared ends flush, forming half of the frame (Fig. 6-20). Make the second half of the frame by glueing parts c and d together in the same manner.

After allowing time for the glue to set, drill two axle peg holes through parts a and d. (The location of the holes is shown in Fig. 6-21A.) Next, drill four axle peg holes in the edges of the two frame units (Fig. 6-21B).

Using a small axle peg, connect the two frame units together. Be careful to apply the glue only to the hole in the top frame piece (part a) and to insert the peg through the bottom. This will ensure that the frame will swivel properly.

Glue the standard cab and hood components described in Chapters 3 and 5 to the rear of the frame onto part a (Fig. 6-22). Then glue the hood unit flush with the rear of the frame, and glue the cab adjacent to the hood, centering each between the frame edges.

Next to build is the shovel mount. It is made from a piece of wood that measures

Fig. 6-18. *The Pay Loader, with its oversized tires and jointed frame, is able to work in tight areas.*

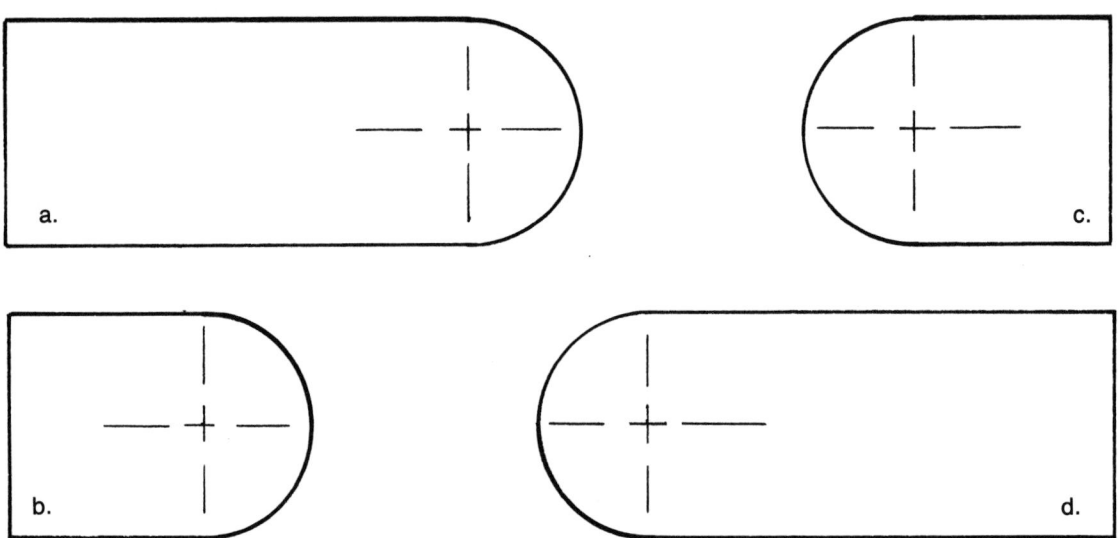

Fig. 6-19. *The four parts of the Pay Loader frame.*

¾ inch thick, 1 inch wide, and 1½ inches long. Along the front top edge of the shovel mount, cut down at an angle, as shown in Fig. 6-23. On both sides of the shovel mount, drill two axle peg holes when indicated. Now glue the shovel mount in place on part c.

Next, glue the 2-inch-diameter wheels into place. Only put glue into the axle holes on the frame, so the axle peg will be held firmly in place, but the wheels can turn freely.

The arms of the Pay Loader are made from four pieces of ⅛-inch-thick wood. Use

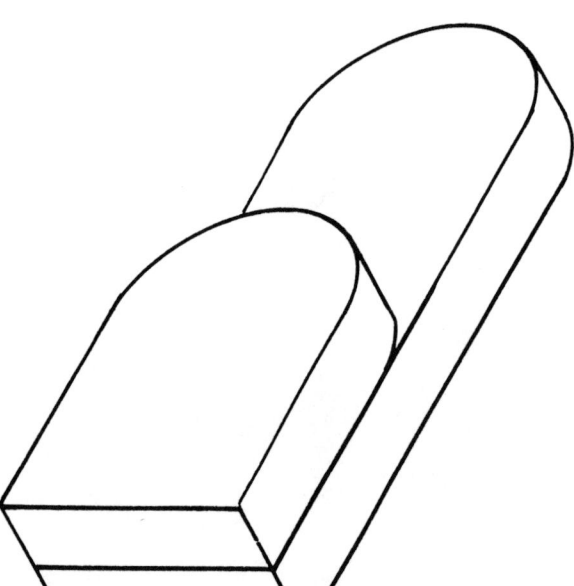

Fig. 6-20. *Glue the Pay Loader frame parts together, as shown.*

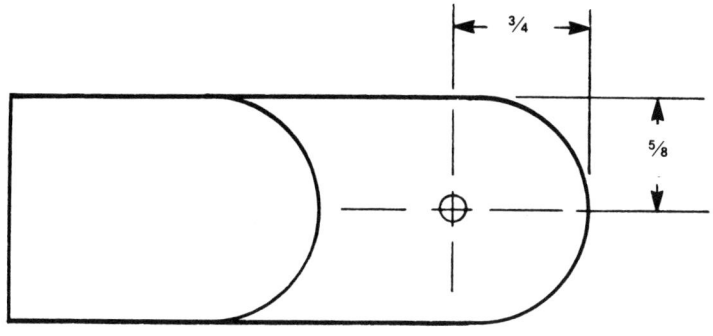

A.

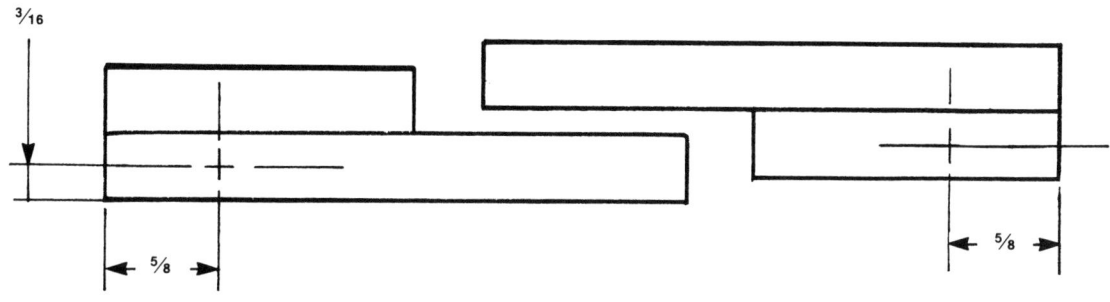

B.

Fig. 6-21. *(A) Drill an axle peg-size hole in parts a and d. (B) Also drill four axle peg holes in the frame edges.*

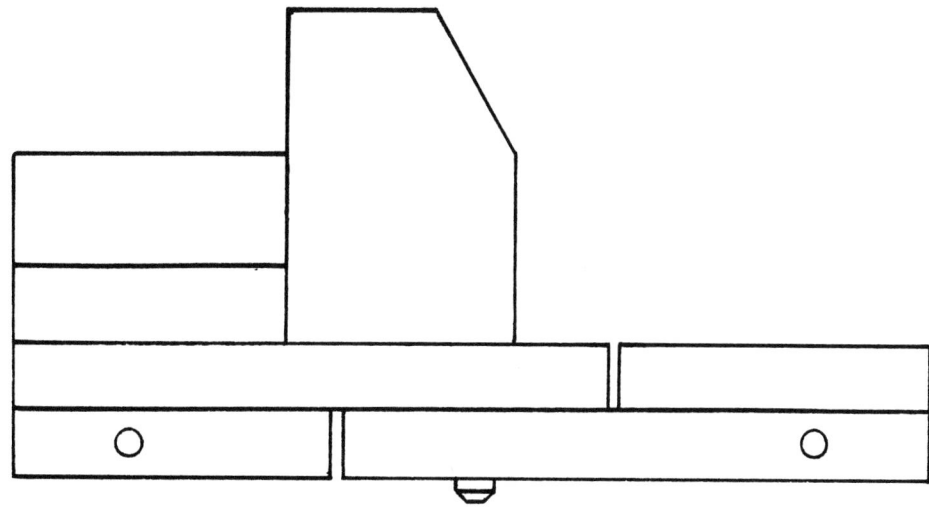

Fig. 6-22. *Glue the standard cab and hood onto the frame as shown.*

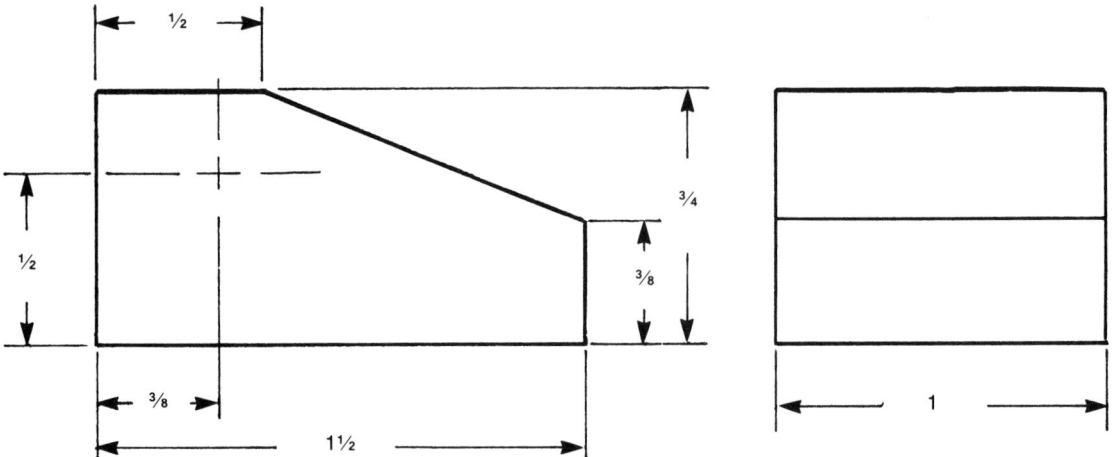

Fig. 6-23. *Shape the shovel mount for the Pay Loader as shown. Also drill an axle peg on each side of the shovel mount at the point indicated.*

either hardwood or some wood that will not easily be broken. The width of the arms is ½ inch, and the length of each is 3⅝ inches. On the ends of each arm, drill a hole large enough for the axle pegs to slide through easily. Also, rout the ends to a ¼-inch radius to remove sharp corners that may cause scratches (Fig. 6-24).

Now make an arm spreader to fit between the arms. The size of the spreader should be ⅜ inch thick, ⅜ inch wide, by 1 inch long. On each end of the spreader, drill a hole for an axle peg (Fig. 6-25). The arms can now be assembled on the Pay Loader shovel mount.

Begin by sliding an axle peg through one end of an arm, and glue the peg into the hole in the shovel mount. Repeat this step on the opposite side of the shovel mount. On another shovel arm, insert an axle peg through one hole, then through the hole on the end of the arm that is attached to the shovel mount. Then glue the peg into the arm spreader. Repeat the process on the other side (Fig. 6-26).

The last part to build is the shovel. This shovel is made from wood that is ¼ inch

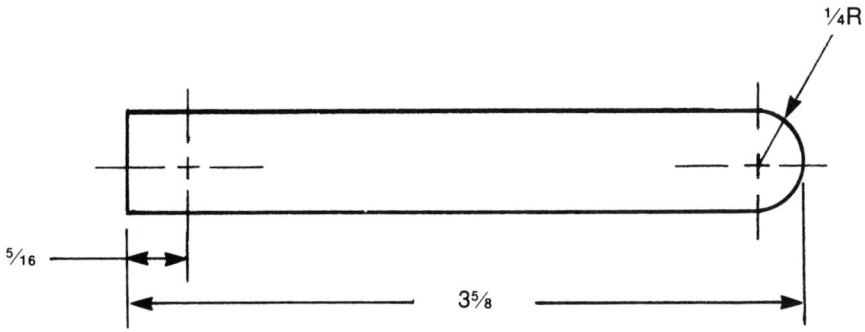

Fig. 6-24. *Round the arms of the Pay Loader to a ¼-inch radius.*

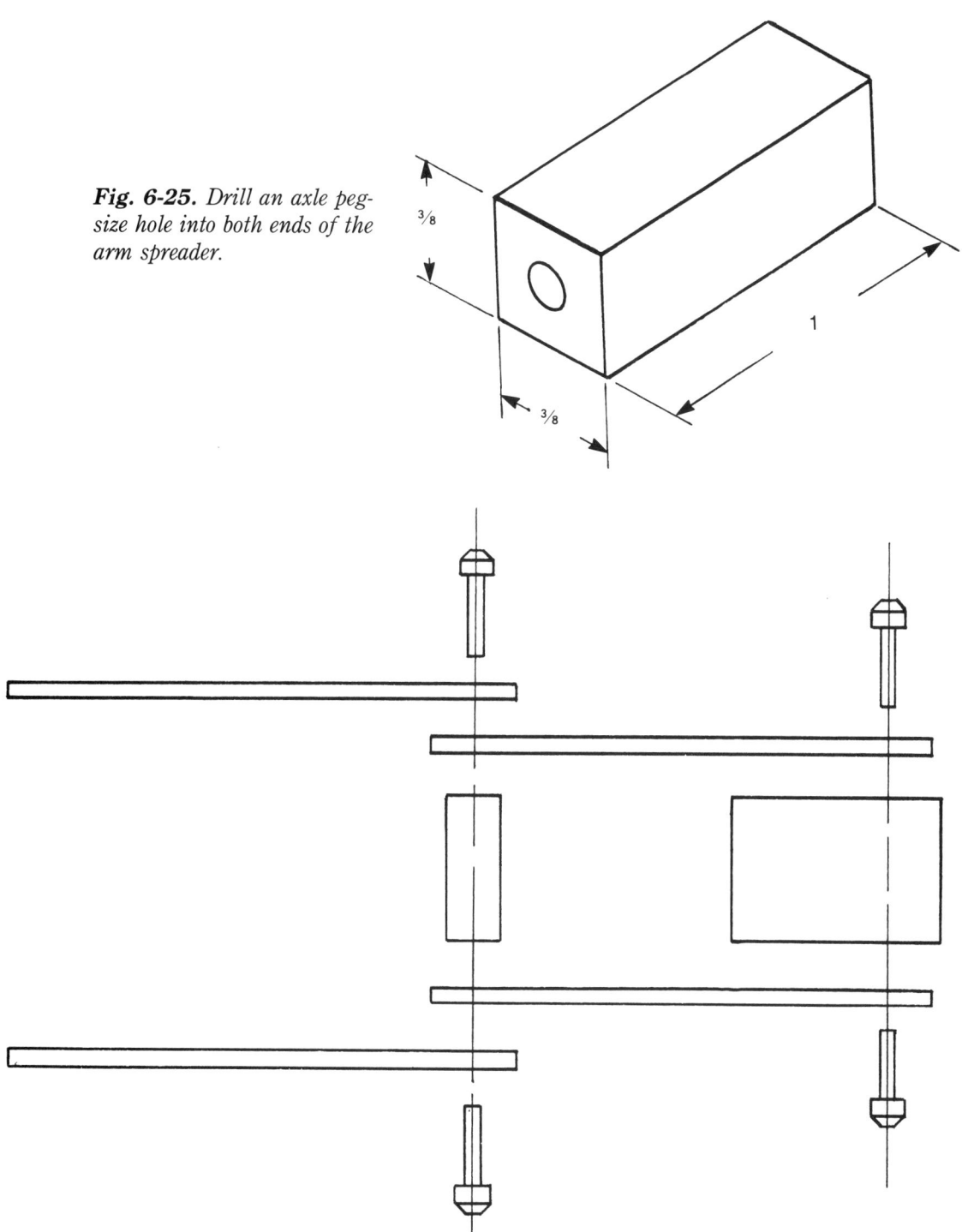

Fig. 6-25. Drill an axle peg-size hole into both ends of the arm spreader.

Fig. 6-26. Assemble the Pay Loader shovel arms to the shovel mount (as viewed from above).

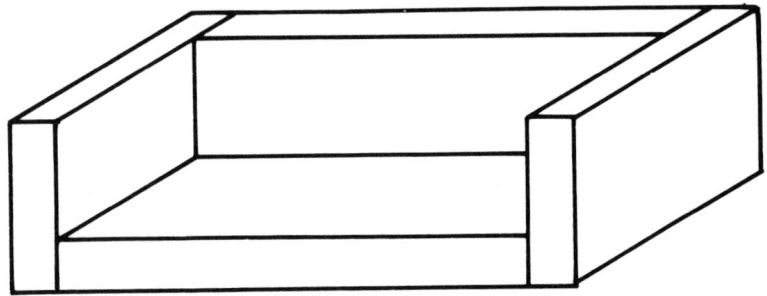

Fig. 6-27. *Glue the Pay Loader shovel together as shown.*

thick. The shovel back and bottom should both be 2½ inches long and ⅞ inch wide, but only 1 inch long.

Glue the parts of the shovel together, as shown in Fig. 6-27. Be sure not to spare the glue, and allow plenty of time for the glue to set.

After sufficient drying time, cut the side pieces of the shovel and sand at an angle (Fig. 6-28A). On the rear of the shovel, glue a ⅜-inch-thick, 1¼-inch-long, ¾-inch-wide block in the center of the shovel back (Fig. 6-28B). Drill two axle peg holes on either end of the block, at the location shown.

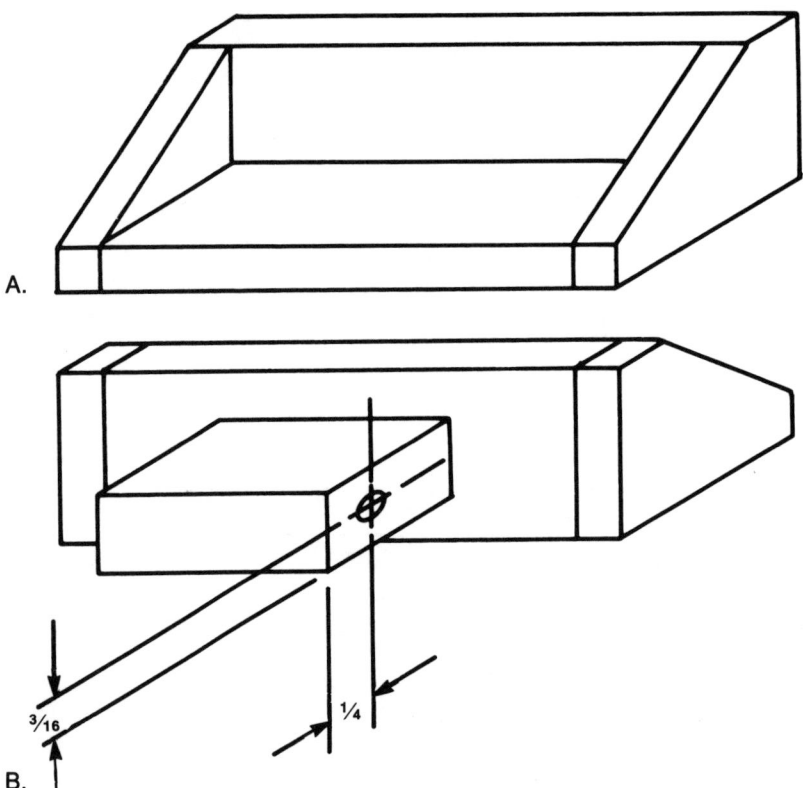

Fig. 6-28. *(A) Cut and sand the shovel sides at an angle. (B) Glue the mounting block on the rear of the shovel.*

Fig. 6-29. Most construction jobs require a Grader to level the roads or to clear snow. The Grader presented here is capable of this and much more.

The final step is to attach the shovel to the Pay Loader. Slip an axle peg through the holes in the end of the shovel arms. Glue the pegs into the holes in the block on the shovel. Take care so that glue only gets in the hole and not between the arm and shovel.

The Pay Loader is one of the more complicated toys in this section, but the result is well worth the effort. This is a project that is a challenge to build, and a welcome gift and fun toy to play with. However, because of its thin wood arms that could break under abuse and cause possible injury, I advise that this toy only be given to children above the age of six.

GRADER

Every road construction job requires at least one grader to level the road bed (Fig. 6-29). The Grader has been built using interchangeable parts, which are used throughout this series of vehicles.

Cut the chassis of the Grader from a single piece of wood that measures 1⅛ by 1¾ by 7⅛ inches. Lay out the design of the grader chassis on the side and top of the board (Fig. 6-30). I recommend you use a band saw for cutting out the chassis, although any saw that is capable of cutting out the design can be used if a band saw is not available. Cut the design that is drawn on the side of the chassis board first.

Tape the upper portion of the board back onto the board. This will allow you to see the lines previously drawn on the top while cutting the design.

Drill six 5/32-inch holes into the chassis: four are for the rear wheels, one for the scraper blade, and the sixth is for the front axle. The location of each of these holes can be found in Fig. 6-31. Sand the edges of the grader chassis, rounding all of the sharp edges.

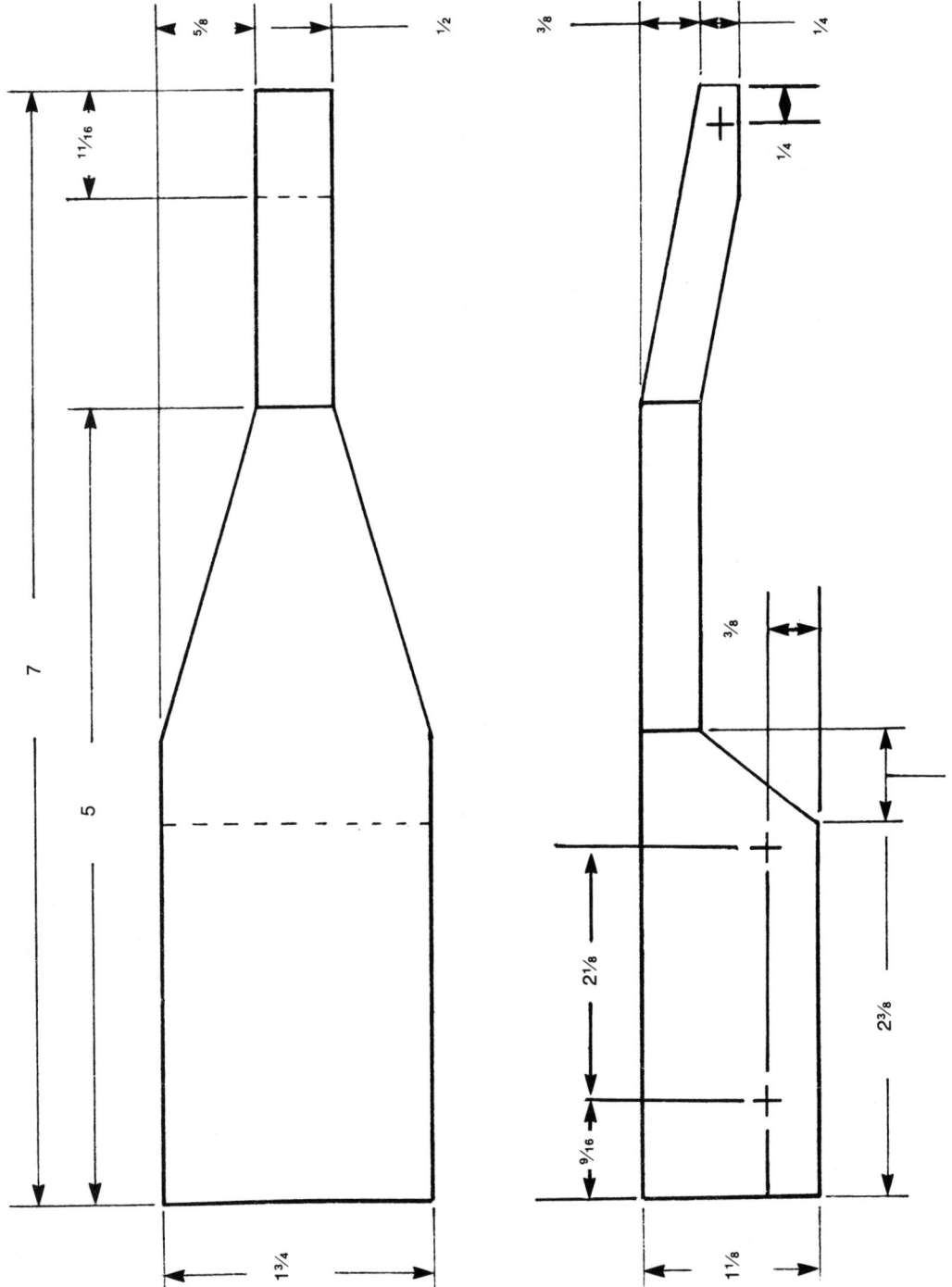

Fig. 6-30. The design of the Grader chassis.

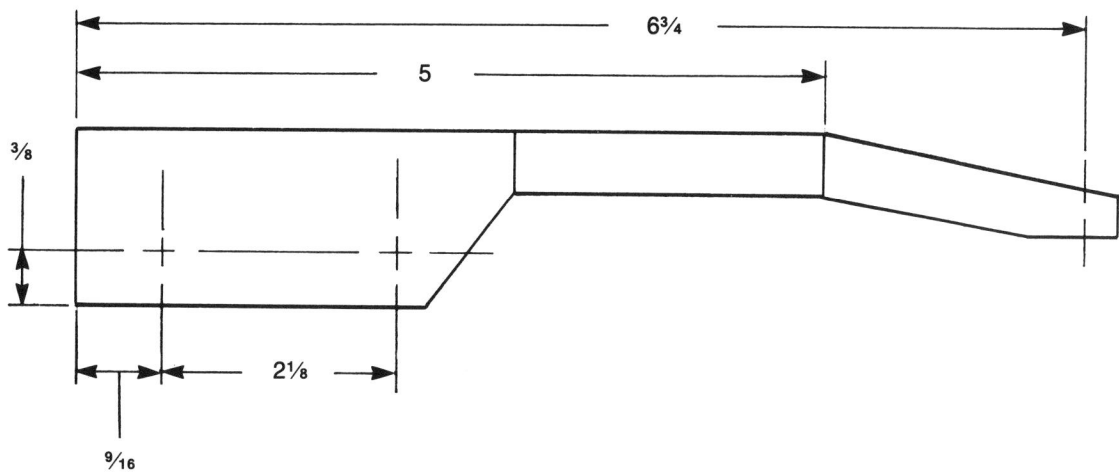

Fig. 6-31. *Drill six 5/32-inch holes into the chassis.*

The front axle of the Grader is made from a piece of wood ½ by ½ by 1½ inches. Drill a 5/32-inch hole in each end and another of the same diameter centered on the top surface.

Next cut the grader scraper blade from a piece of wood that measures ⅜ by ¾ by 3 inches. Along the top edge of the scraper blade, drill a 5/32-inch-diameter hole in the center, as shown in Fig. 6-32. The lower front edge should taper slightly to more closely resemble the real machine.

The cab and engine compartment of the Grader are the same as used on the rest of the vehicles in this series. They are described in Chapter 5.

Now all of the component parts of the Grader are cut and ready for final assembly. The rear wheels should be 1½ inches in diameter and held in place with 13/16-inch-long by 5/32-inch-diameter axle pegs. (If you use another size peg, you will need to adjust the holes throughout this project accordingly.) Also install the 1¼-inch-diameter front wheels with axle pegs into the ends of the front axle. Insert the same pegs through the grader chassis to hold the scraper blade, and the front axle.

When using the pegs, be careful to glue only the end of the peg, not the whole shaft. This will allow the wheels, scraper, and front axle to turn freely, yet remain permanently attached (Fig. 6-33).

The Grader is a fun project that requires little work and little wood; but will result in a toy that is sure to meet the demands of the toughest junior construction boss.

TRUCK MOUNTED SHOVEL

The Truck Mounted Shovel (Fig. 6-34) is the same as the Creeper Shovel, except that it is mounted on the basic truck chassis. This type of shovel is more mobile than the Creeper Shovel, with tires instead of creeper tracks.

Begin with a Basic Truck chassis, the same as described in the beginning of Chapters 3 and 5, a truck bed which is ⅜ inch thick, 2⅜ inches wide, and 4¼ inches long. Next drill an axle peg hole at the point shown in Fig. 6-35.

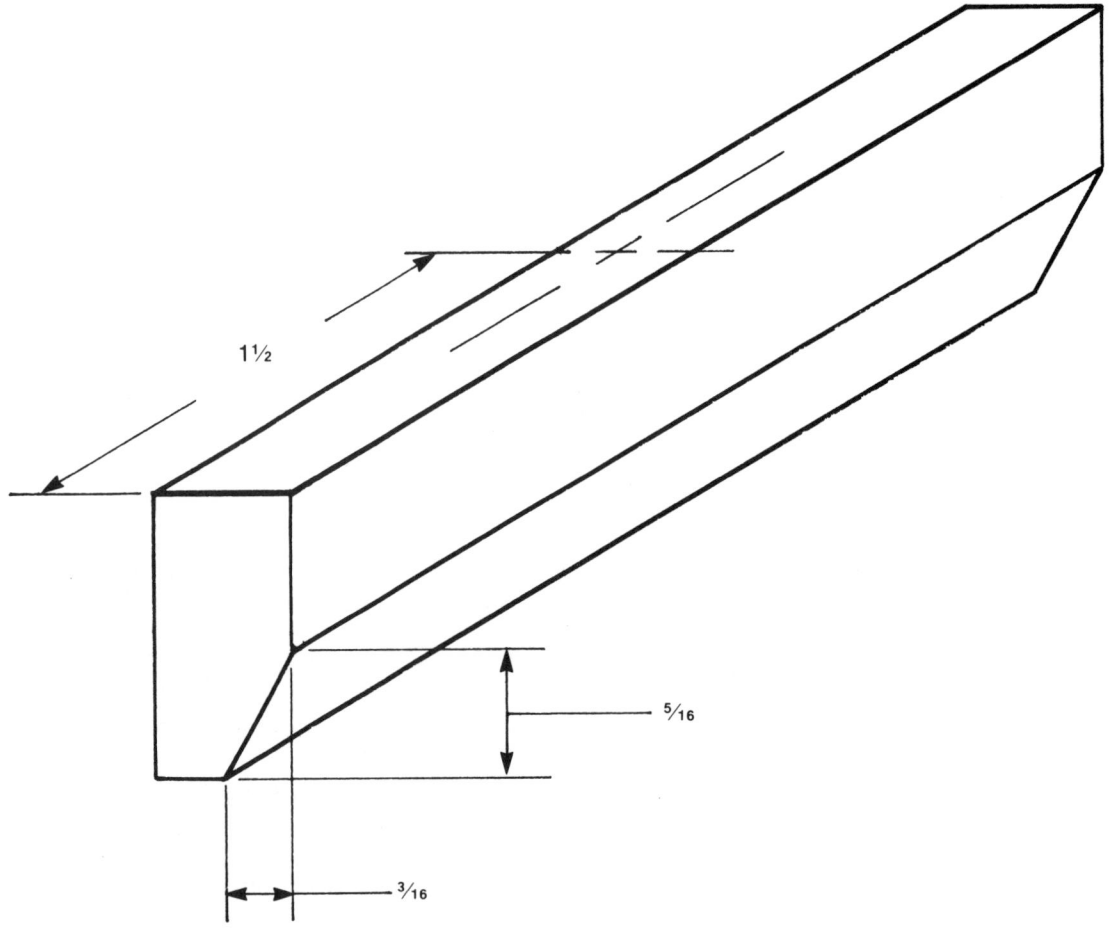

Fig. 6-32. *Drill an axle peg-size hole in the top of the scraper blade. The drawing also shows the method of shaping the scraper blade.*

On the bottom of the truck bed, drill a ⅜-inch-diameter hole, half the thickness of the bed, at the location of the smaller hole just drilled (Fig. 6-36). The large hole provides the head of the axle peg with a recess within the truck bed. When completed, insert an axle peg, and glue the bed onto the basic truck chassis.

Next make the shovel unit by glueing a standard cab and hood, as described in Chapter 5, onto a ⅜-inch-thick, 1¼-inch-wide, 3¾-inch-long frame. Round both ends of the frame. In the center of the frame, drill a hole the size of the axle peg. This will later be used when you attach the shovel to the truck. Also drill two holes into the center of the shovel frame sides, 1 inch back from the front end.

The four shovel arms each should be ⅛ inch thick, ½ inch wide, and 3¾ inches long. On both ends of the shovel arms, drill an axle peg-size hole, centered ⅜ inch from each end.

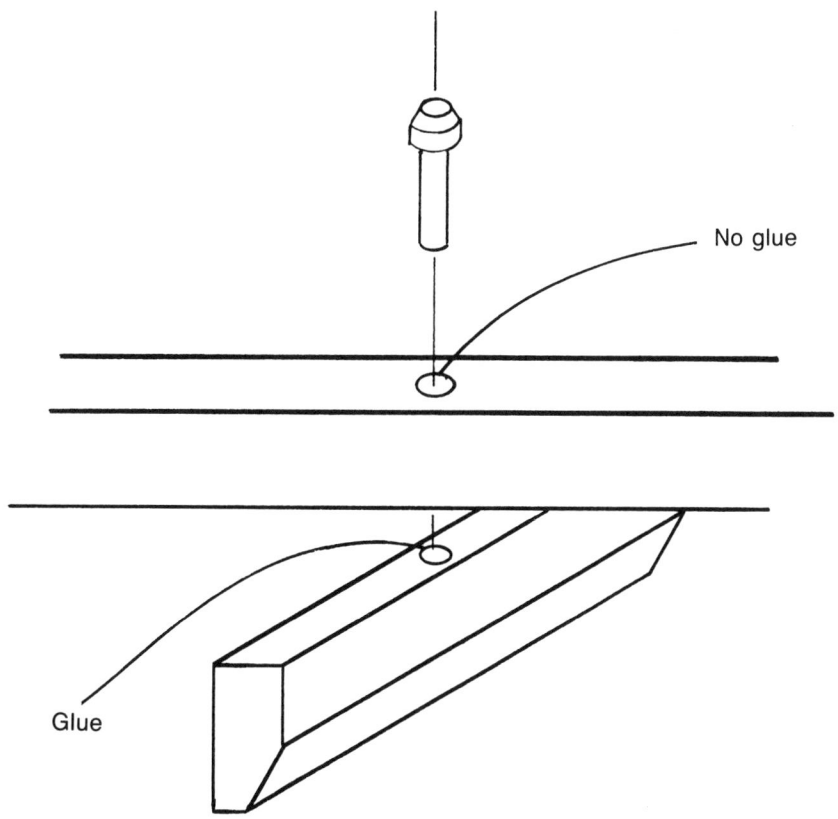

Fig. 6-33. When assembling the scraper blade to the Grader chassis, be careful not to allow glue to get into the chassis hole.

Cut the shovel arm spreader from a 1⅛-inch-long, ⅜-inch-square piece of wood. Through the center of each end of the arm spreader, drill an axle-peg size hole ½ deep.

The shovel arms and arm spreader can now be assembled and attached to the shovel frame (Fig. 6-37). Remember to only put glue in the holes in the shovel frame and arm spreader. By doing this, the axle pegs will be permanently held in place, but the shovel arms will move freely.

The final part to be made for the Truck Mounted Shovel is the shovel. Make the shovel from a block of wood 1⅛ inches thick, 1⅛ inches wide, and 1⅛ inches long. In the center of the top of the cube, drill a ¾-inch-diameter hole, ¾ inch deep. Taper the top of the shovel back into a slight arc from the front edge, to a point that is ¼ inch down (Fig. 6-38).

Finally, on both sides of the shovel, drill an axle-peg size hole for the shovel arms. As with the other parts of the shovel arm assembly, be careful to only allow glue to get into the two holes in the shovel, not in the shovel arms.

All that remains is to mount the shovel onto the truck bed. This is done by placing a narrow wooden wheel over the axle peg sticking out of the truck bed, then glueing the shovel onto the axle peg.

Fig. 6-34. *The Truck Mounted Shovel is built on the standard truck chassis.*

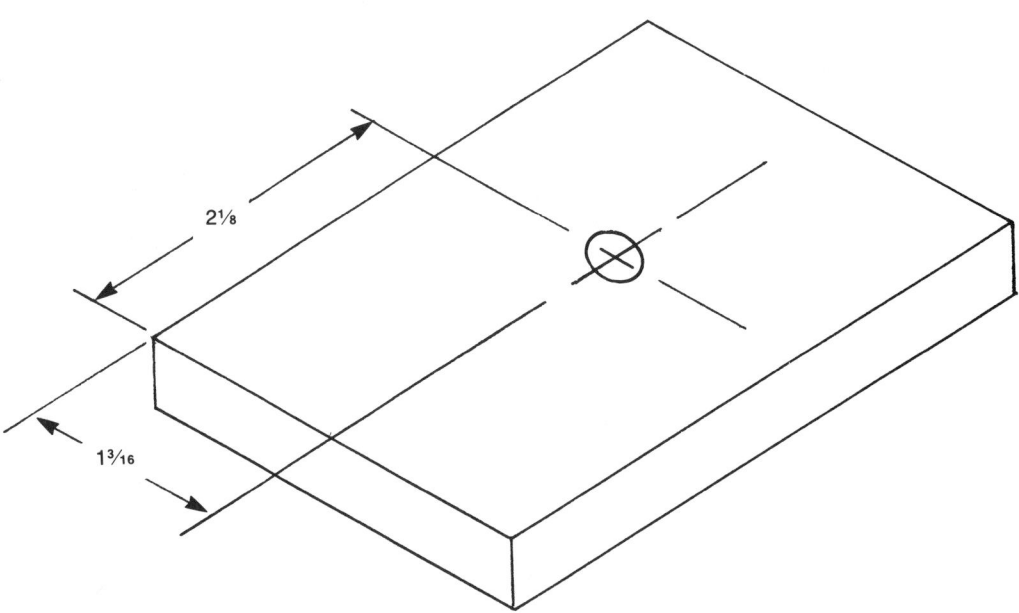

Fig. 6-35. *Drill two holes into the truck bed before glueing it onto the truck chassis.*

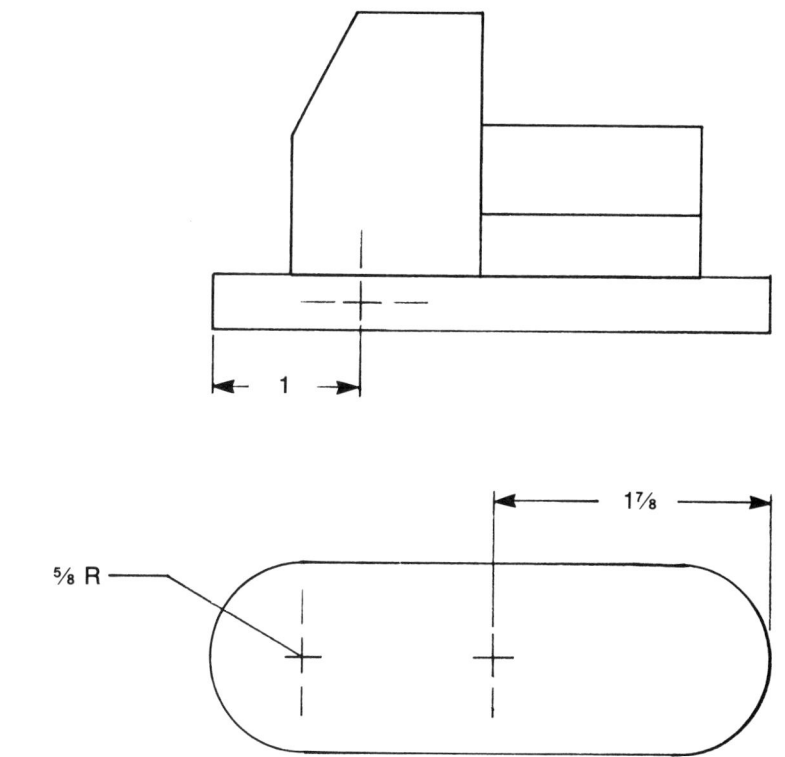

Fig. 6-36. *The shovel frame measures ⅜ inch thick, 1¼ inches wide, and 3¾ inches long. Glue a standard cab and hood to the frame.*

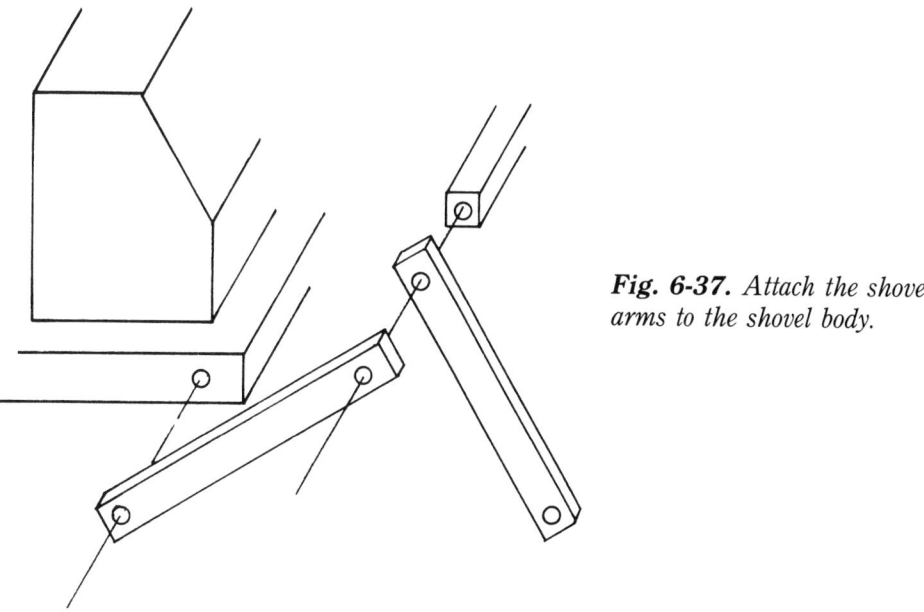

Fig. 6-37. *Attach the shovel arms to the shovel body.*

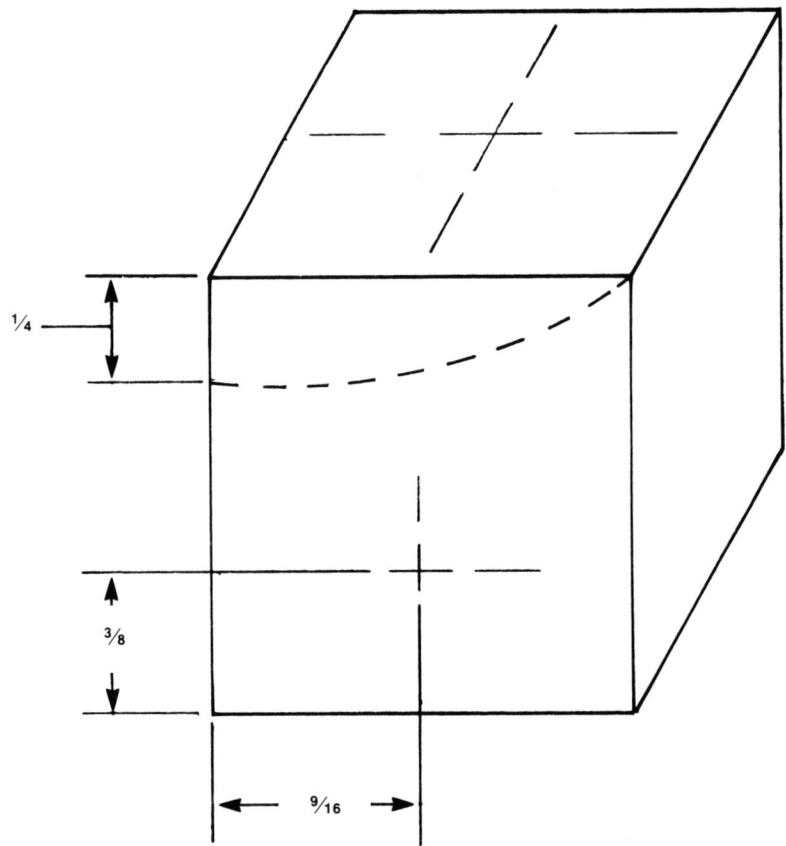

Fig. 6-38. *The shovel is made from a 1⅛-inch cube.*

───────────── **LIST 6-1. REQUIRED MATERIALS** ─────────────

Creeper

2 – Creeper Tracks   – ¾ × 1⅛ × 4¾
1 – Frame   – ⅜ × 1¾ × 4

Bulldozer

1 – Standard Creeper Unit
1 – Engine Compartment   – 1⅛ × 1½ × 3½
2 – Blade Arms   – ¼ × 1 × 2½
1 – Blade Spreader   – ¼ × 1 × 3¼
1 – Blade (cove molding)   – 4⅜-inch length
2 – Axle Pegs   – Small size

Creeper Shovel

1 – Creeper Unit
1 – Shovel Base — 3/8 × 1 3/8 × 3 5/8
1 – Cab Unit — Standard Size
1 – Hood Unit — Standard Size
1 – Crane Boom — 3/8 × 1 1/8 × 6 1/8
1 – Boom extender — 3/8 × 3/8 × 4 1/4
1 – Shovel — 1 × 1 1/8 × 1 3/4
1 – Wheel — 1-inch diameter
7 – Axle Pegs — Size to fit

Pay Loader

2 – Long Frame Halves — 3/8 × 1 1/4 × 3 1/4
2 – Short Frame Halves — 3/8 × 1 1/4 × 1 3/4
1 – Hood Unit — Standard Size
1 – Cab Unit — Standard Size
1 – Shovel Mount — 3/4 × 1 × 1 1/2
4 – Wheels — 2-inch diameter
4 – Shovel Arms — 1/8 × 1/2 × 3 5/8
1 – Spreader — 3/8 × 3/8 × 1
1 – Shovel Back — 1/4 × 7/8 × 2 1/2
1 – Shovel Bottom — 1/4 × 7/8 × 2 1/2
2 – Shovel Sides — 1/4 × 7/8 × 1
1 – Shovel Block — 3/8 × 3/4 × 1 1/4
11 – Axle Pegs — Small Size

Grader

1 – Chassis — 1 1/8 × 1 3/4 × 7 1/8
1 – Front Axle — 1/2 × 1/2 × 1 1/2
1 – Scraper Blade — 3/8 × 3/4 × 3
1 – Cab — Standard Size
1 – Engine Compartment — Standard Size
2 – Front Wheels — 1 1/4-inch diameter
4 – Rear Wheels — 1 1/2-inch diameter
8 – Wood Pins — 13/16 × 5/32

Section III

Toy Box Stuffers

One of the most wonderful things about wooden toy making is the diversity of projects to choose from. This section features the unusual, like the Creature Keeper, and the more conventional, like the Doll Bed. Plus, there are simple projects, the Quick Cutouts, for instance, and more challenging ones, like the unique Clown Doll. So, whatever your tastes or level of ability, something here is sure to please.

7
CHAPTER

Quick Cutouts

The vehicles in this chapter are quick and easy to make, yet sturdy and durable enough to hold up to the tough play of most children (Fig. 7-1). The same basic design can commonly be found at gift shops and craft shows; but the following designs have been expanded to include many new and unique vehicles.

The cars, trucks, and train are all designed to be cut from a piece of inexpensive construction lumber, grade 2-by-4 or 2-by-6 inch. The vehicles are easily cut with a band saw with a fine blade; but a scroll saw, coping saw, or saber saw can also be used with satisfactory results.

The vehicles are purposely void of detail and are meant to be viewed principally in profile. That is the reason the front-rear and top views of them might appear a bit strange. However, the side of each is amazingly full of character.

Because of the ease of production, these vehicles are excellent toys to make for resale. They can be cut, sanded, and assembled in a minimum amount of time. If this is your intention, I strongly suggest that you draw and cut the vehicles out of a piece of hard cardboard or hardboard. You can trace these templets onto the lumber a number of times, saving you much time and effort.

The actual work on the lumber begins with the selection of a portion of the wood that is free of knots or other defects. Defects might detract from the appearance of the

Fig. 7-1. *Car and truck cutouts.*

vehicle or, worse yet, cause scratches or splinters on the hands of their young owners. This is not the object of the toy, so take time to find the wood which is clear and has a straight grain.

Trace the templet or draw the profile of the vehicle on the board. Then carefully cut out the design. If the cutting is done carefully, the amount of sanding required for each car will be greatly reduced.

At the location indicated on the drawings of each vehicle, drill the axle holes and peg the wheels in place. The vehicles described and pictured in this section all use wood axle pegs to hold the wheels in place, though this is not the only method. (Chapter 2, "Tips on Toys," contains instructions for other methods.)

The train in this section is made in the same manner as the other vehicles, but the engine and cars are held together by wood pins. Each car has a hole drilled in the front and rear frame so they may be pinned together, shown in detail in Fig. 7-2. Plans for each vehicle appear in Figs. 7-3 through 7-20. A list of materials is also provided at the end of the chapter for easy reference (Table 7-1).

The Quick Cutouts require very little time to construct, yet make great gifts for all the youngsters in the family. Just think of their faces as they find a fleet of Quick Cutouts under the Christmas tree.

Whatever the reason or occasion, these are projects that are sure to please those who receive the gift, and also the craftsperson who creates them.

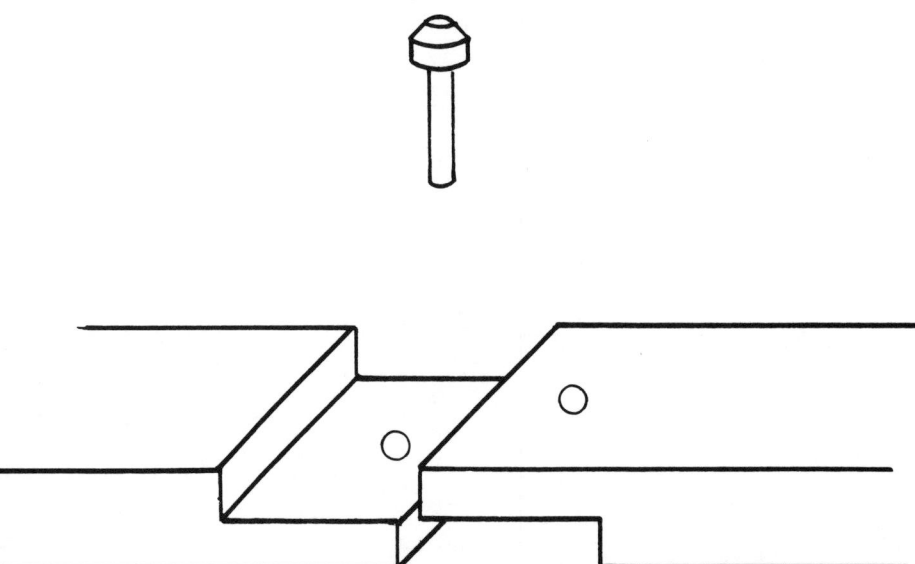

Fig. 7-2. The cars of the train are coupled together by using an axle peg. Drill a hole slightly larger than the diameter of the axle peg, centered through the ends of each car. Then glue the peg into the top hole. Insert the remainder of the peg, protruding from the bottom surface of the train frame, into the hole drilled in the end of the following car.

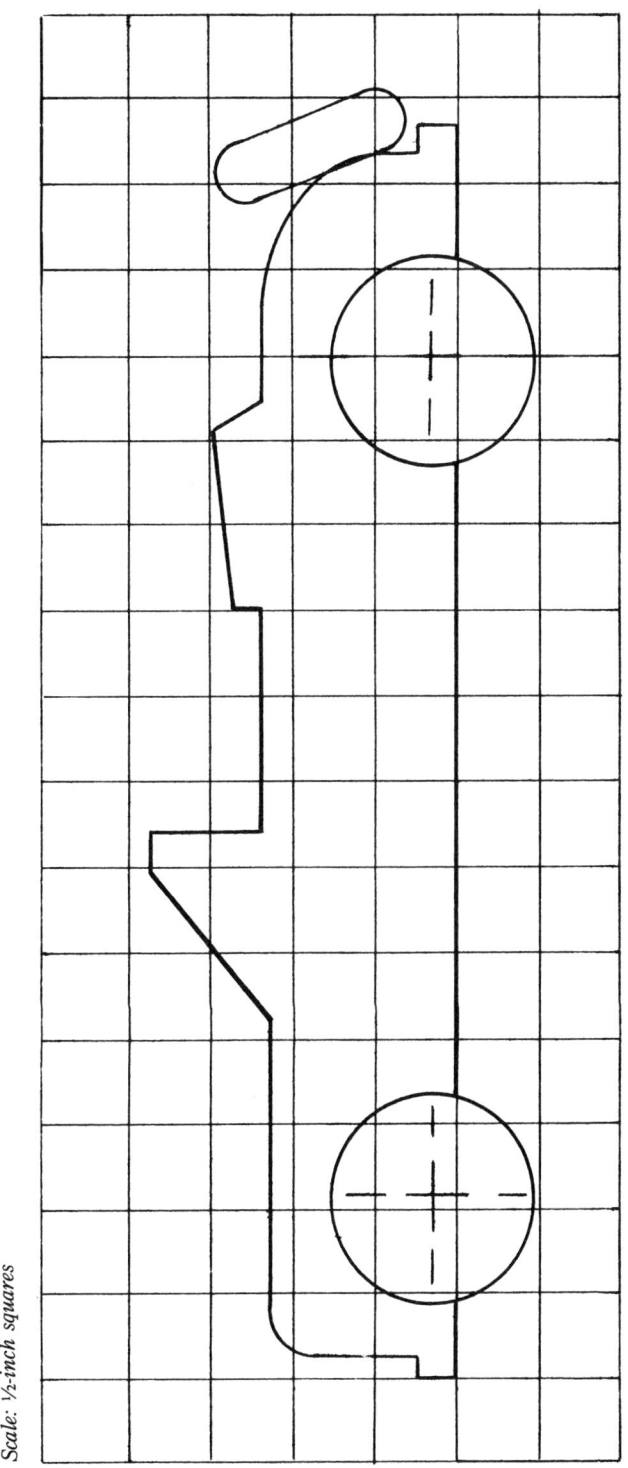

Scale: ½-inch squares

Fig. 7-3. *The Convertible, illustrated here on a grid pattern should be cut from 7½-inch length of 2-by-4-inch lumber.*

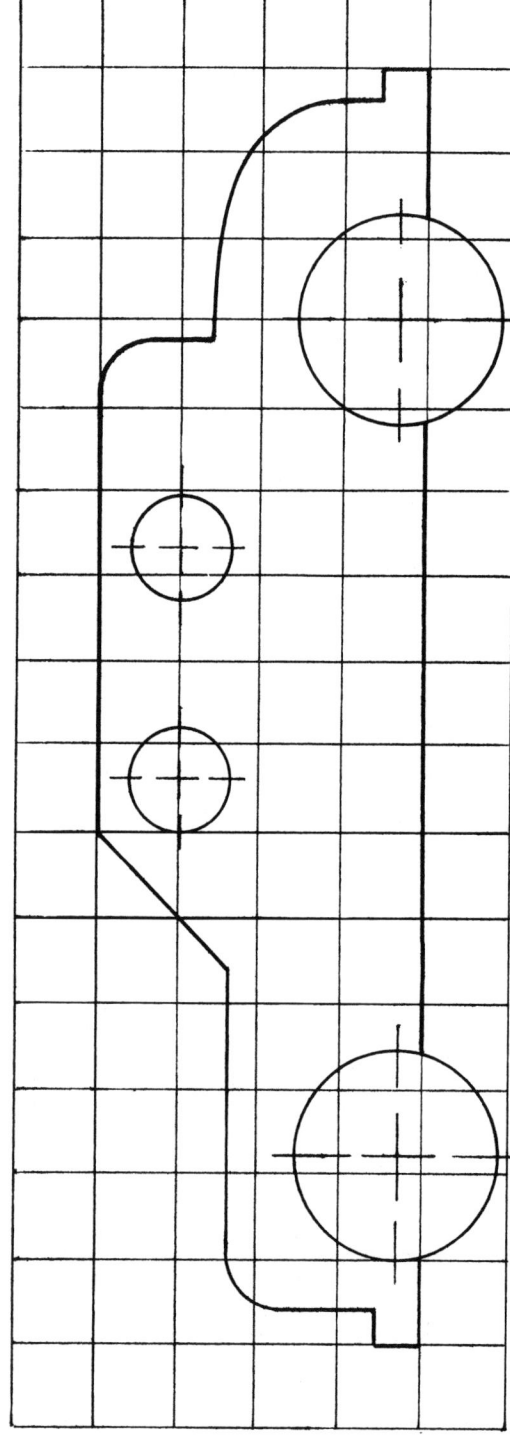

Scale: ½-inch squares

Fig. 7-4. The stately Limousine, with its continental tire mounted on the rear trunk, is a favorite of most. The quick cutout shown here is drawn on a grid pattern. The window holes should be ⅝ inch in diameter.

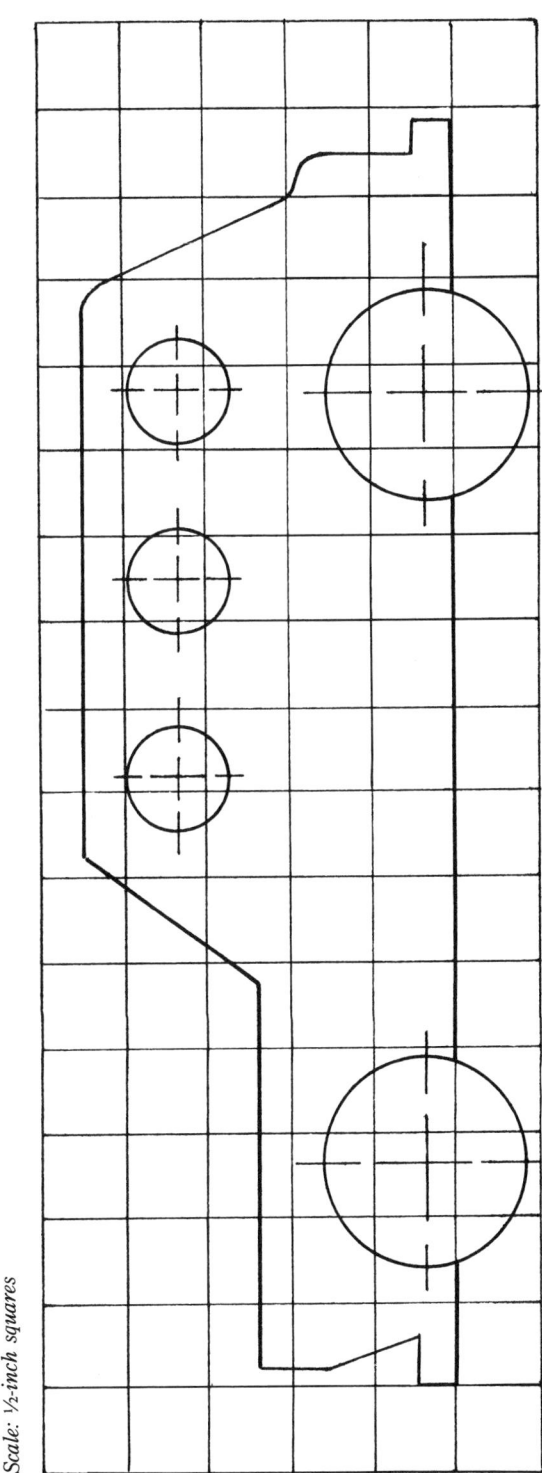

Fig. 7-5. The familiar Station Wagon shown here on a grid pattern, should be cut from a 2-by-4-inch piece of lumber, 7½ inches long.

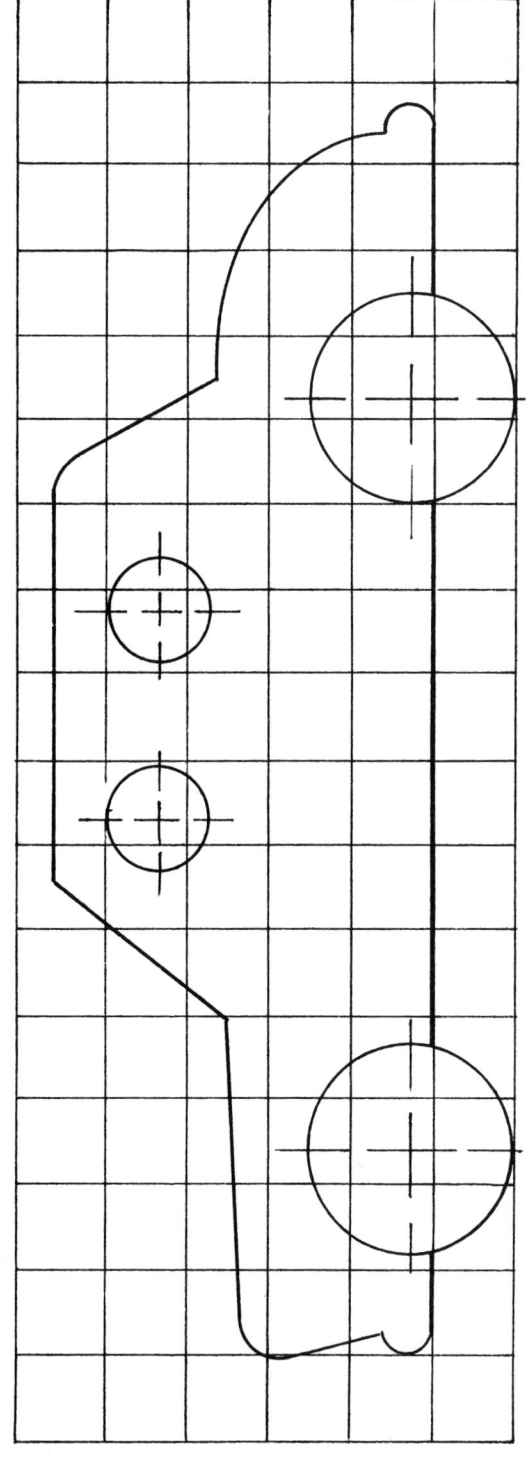

Scale: ½-inch squares

Fig. 7-6. *The most common type of car found on the highways is the sedan. Here is our version, which should be drawn on a ½-inch-square grid.*

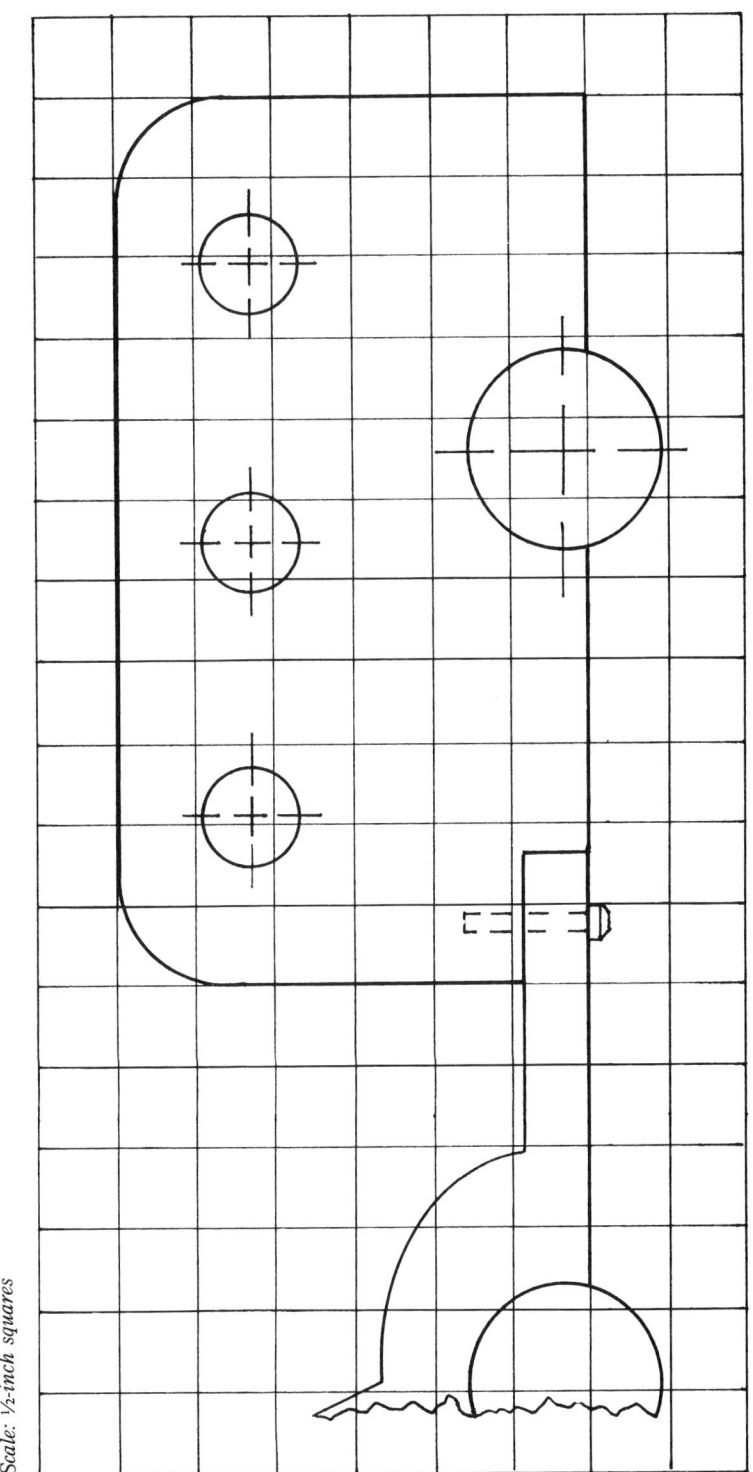

Scale: ½-inch squares

Fig. 7-7. The Camping Trailer shown here on a grid pattern, can be attached to any of the vehicles in this chapter. However, the rear of the car must be extended, as shown, to attach to the trailer. Insert an axle peg through the extended rear of the car and glue into the bottom of the trailer. The window holes should be ⅝ inch in diameter.

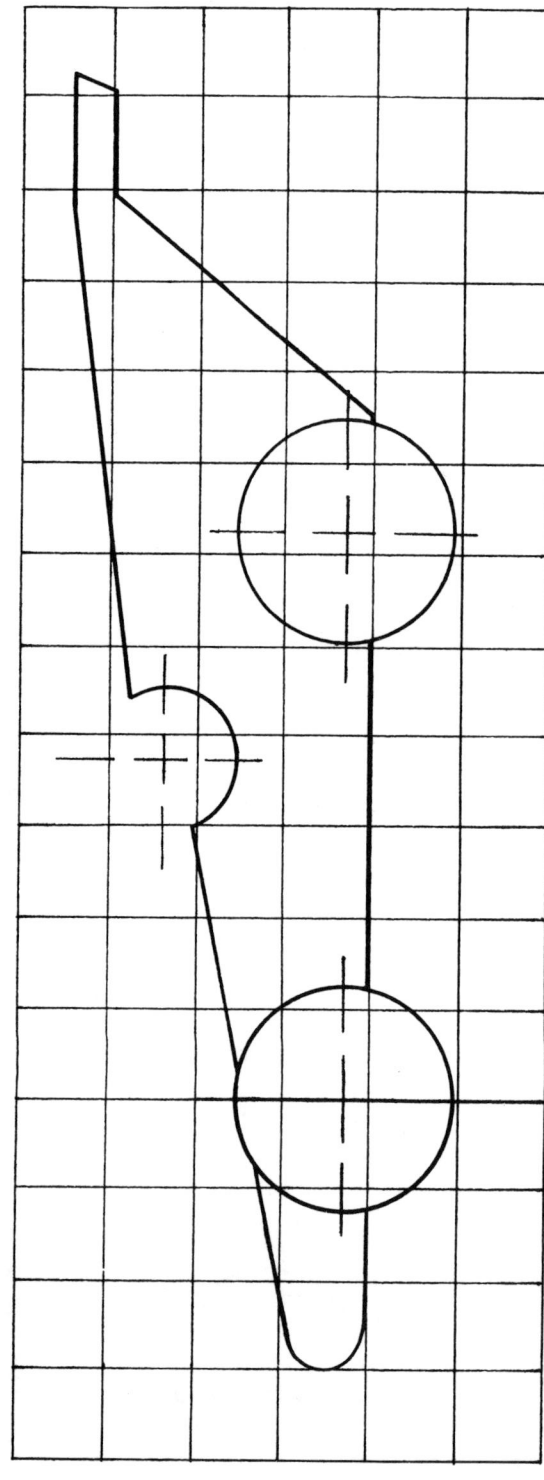

Scale: ½-inch squares

Fig. 7-8. The Racer shown here on a grid pattern, is capable of speeds limited only by the child's imagination.

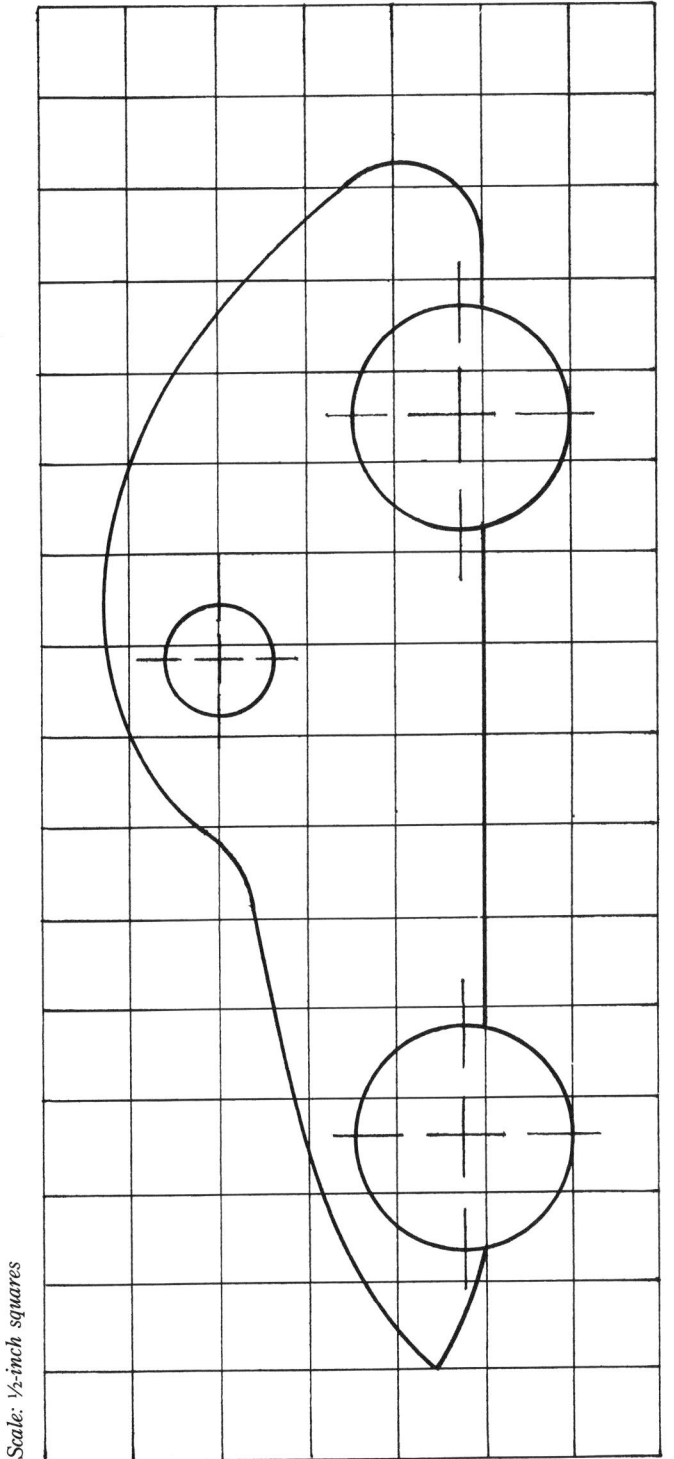

Scale: ½-inch squares

Fig. 7-9. The smooth, flowing lines of the Sports Car allow it to almost effortlessly cut through the wind. Draw the body design on a ½-inch-square grid.

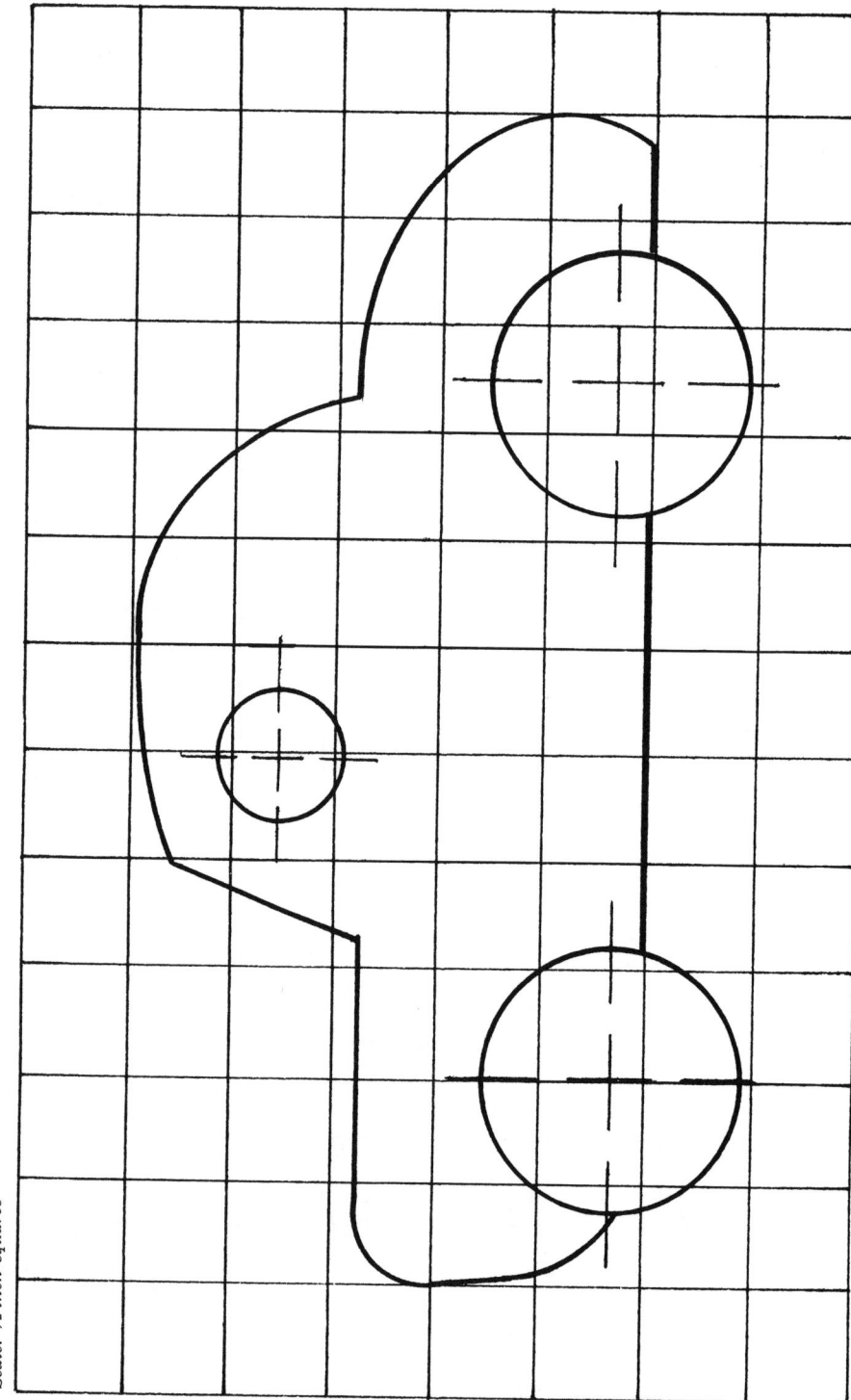

Fig. 7-10. The Old Jalopy, with its classic body lines, should be cut from a 5½-inch length of 2-by-4-inch lumber.

Scale: ½-inch squares

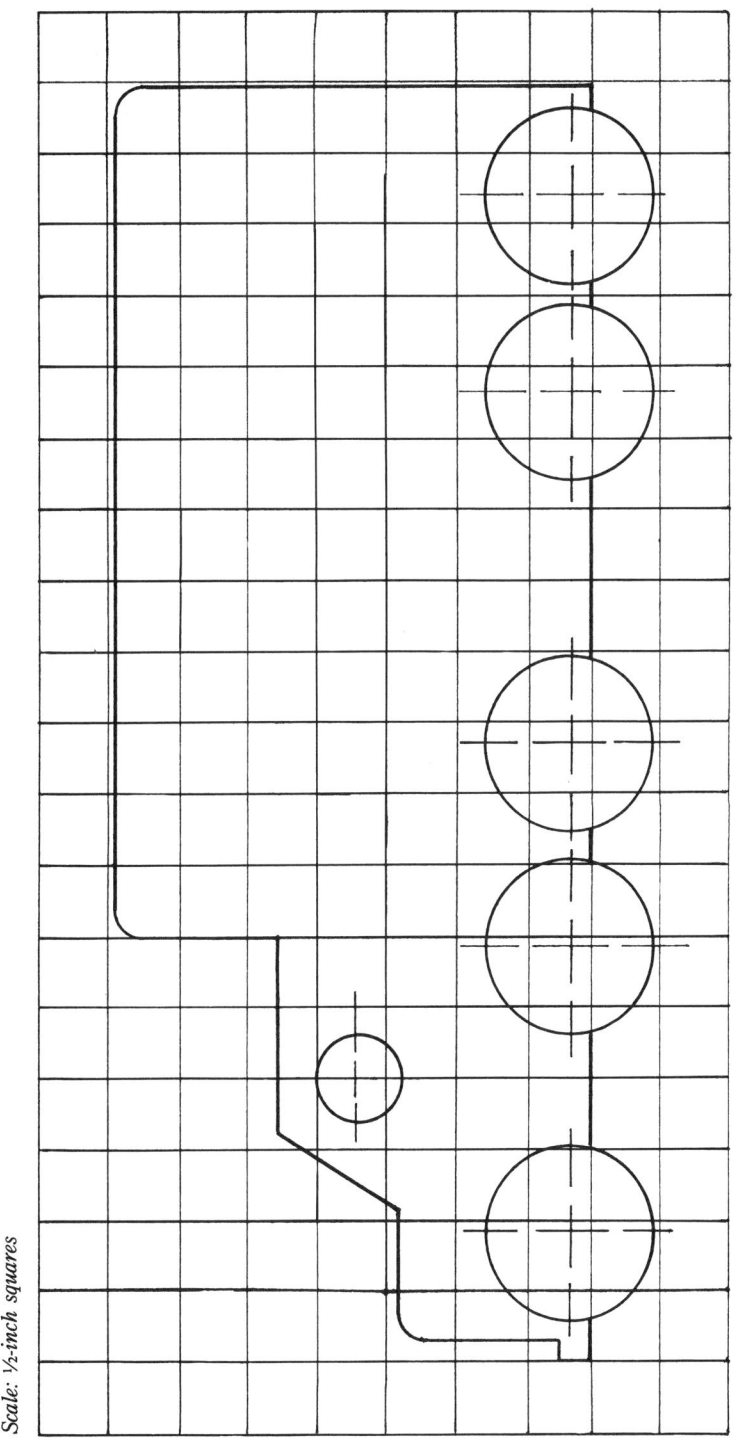

Fig. 7-11. The Local Delivery Truck, should be drawn on a ½-inch-square grid pattern.

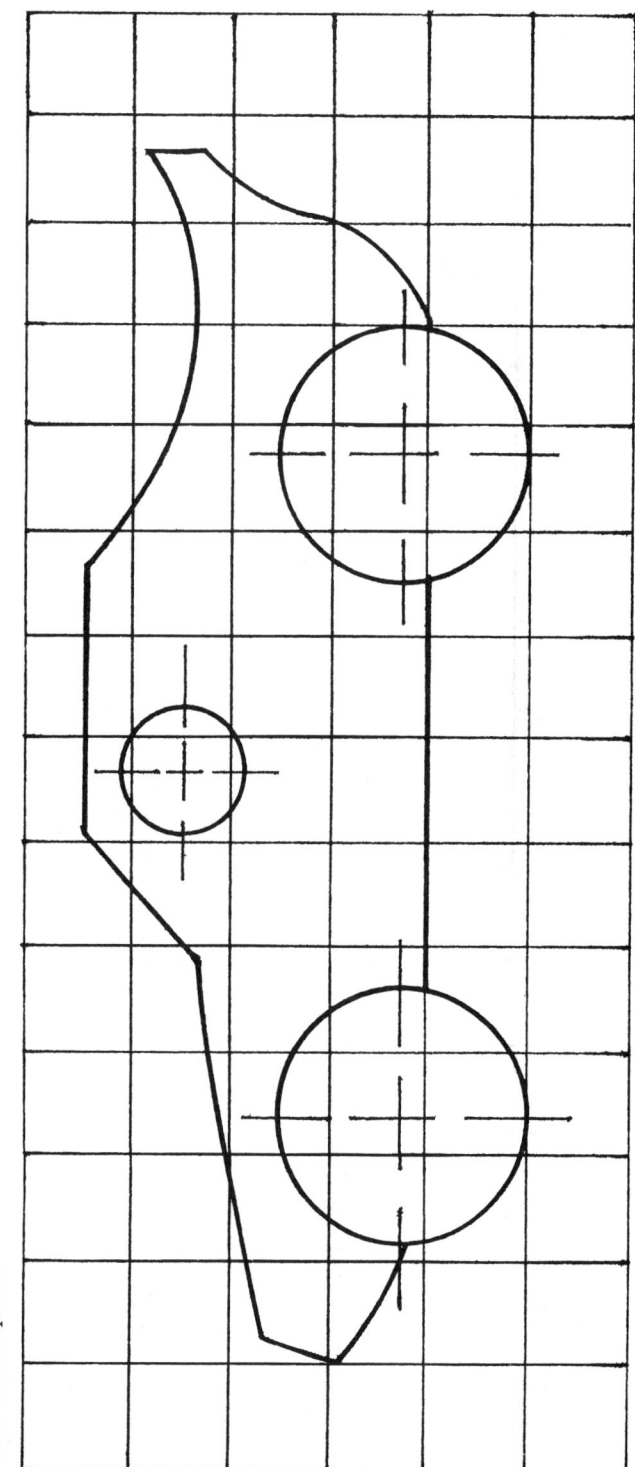

Scale: ½-inch squares

Fig. 7-12. The small car market is being flooded by imported cars. The small Import Car, shown on a grid pattern, is made by drawing its shape onto a 2-by-4-inch piece of lumber, 5¾ inches long.

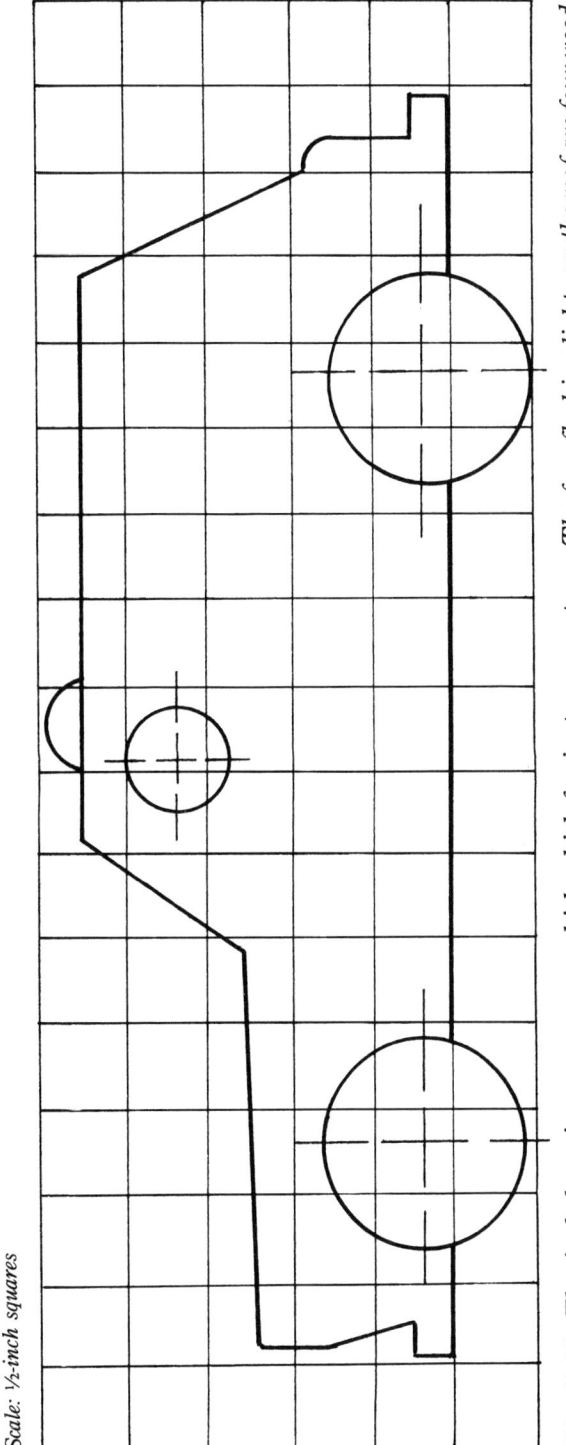

Fig. 7-13. The Ambulance is an emergency vehicle which fascinates youngsters. The four flashing lights on the roof are four wood furniture buttons, which can be purchased from most of the mail order companies listed in the Appendix.

Scale: ½-inch squares

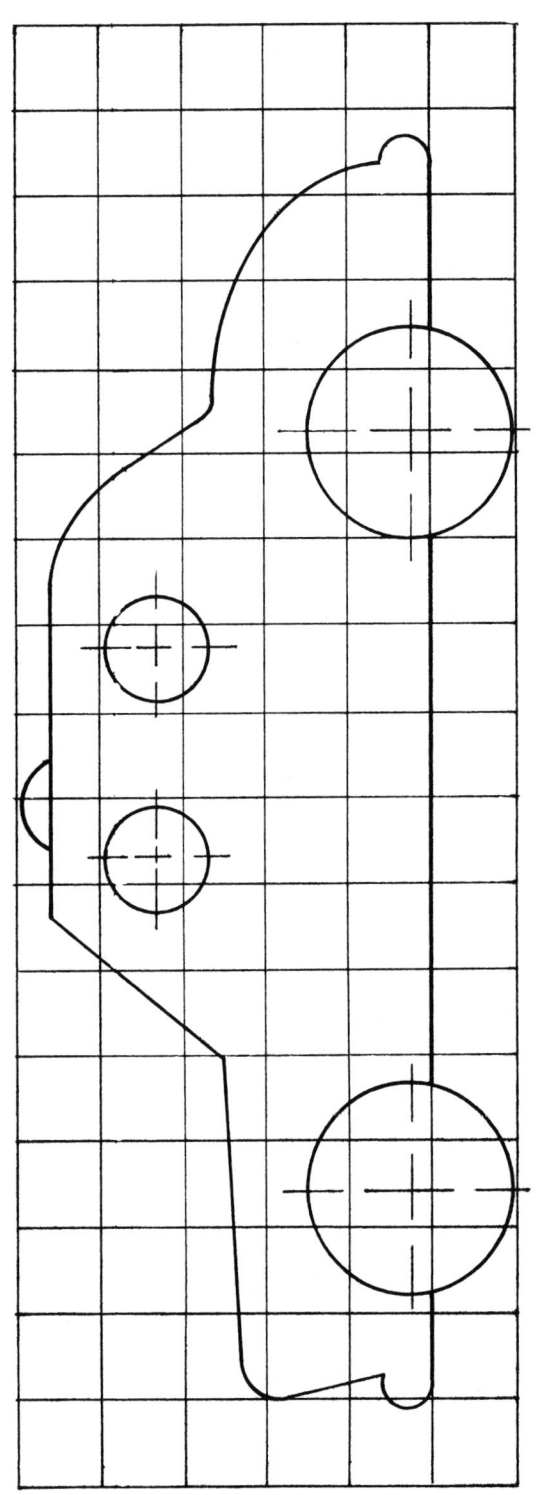

Scale: ½-inch squares

Fig. 7-14. The Police Car is another emergency vehicle that children love to play with. The two flashing lights on the roof are furniture buttons.

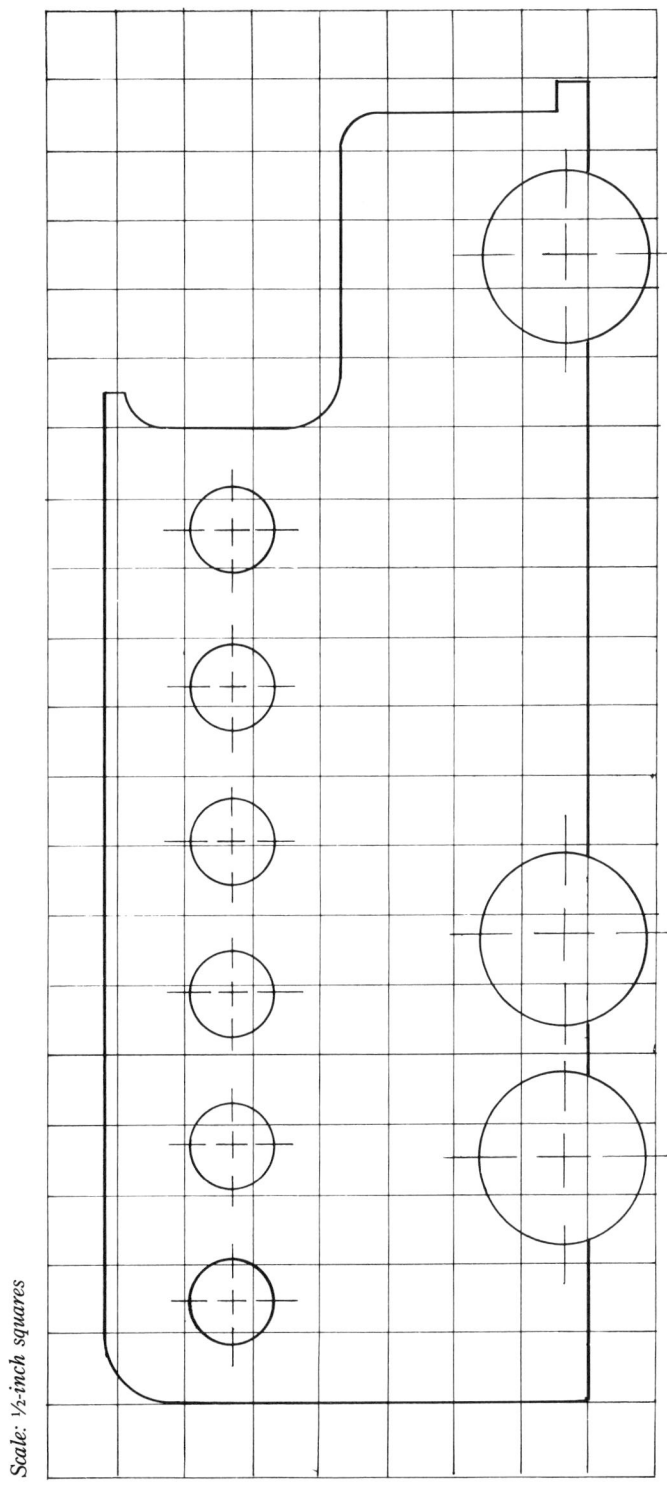

Fig. 7-15. The School Bus should be cut from a 9½-inch length of 2-by-4-inch lumber. The windows are ⅝ inch in diameter.

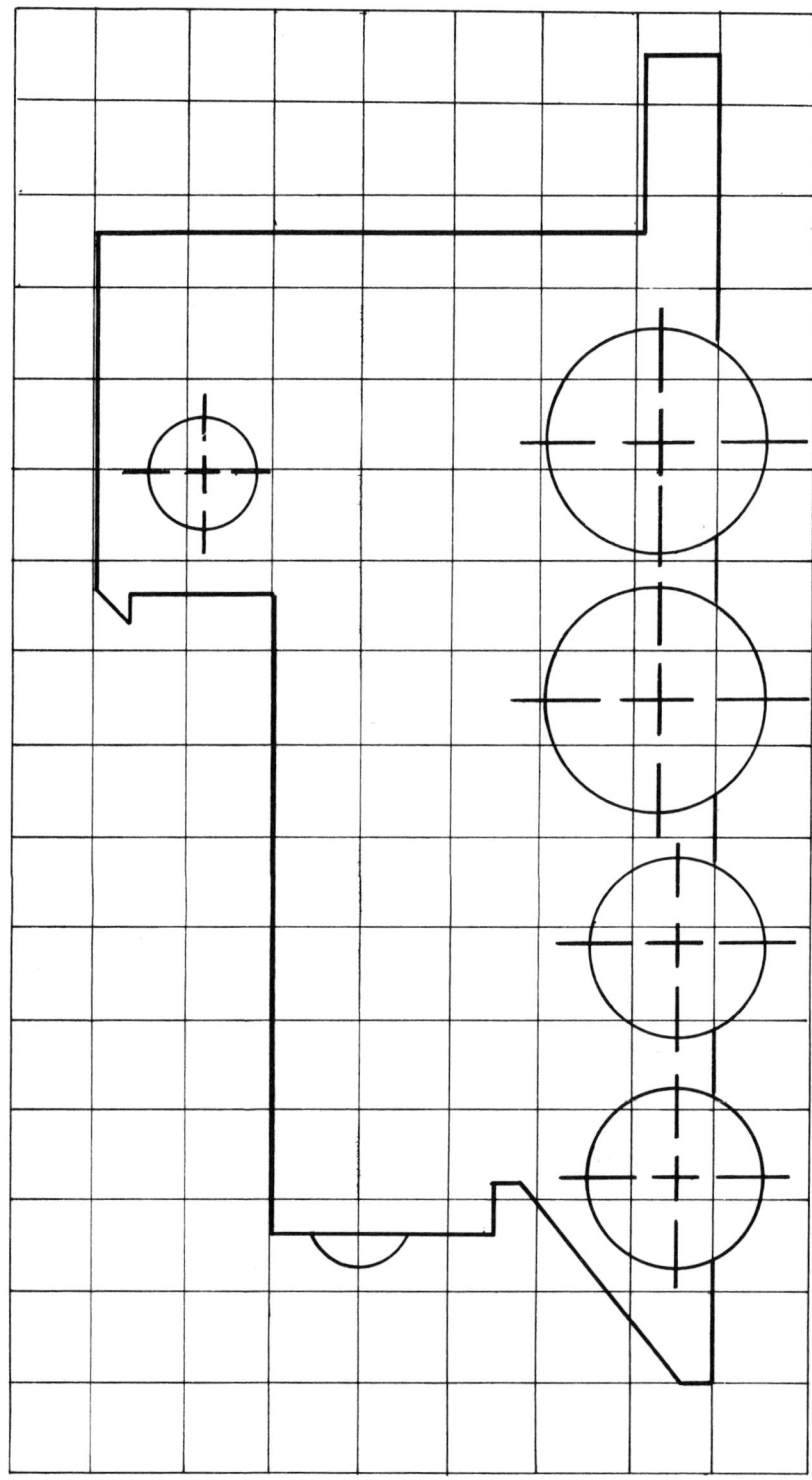

Scale: ½-inch squares

Fig. 7-16. *Each car of the toy train has 1¼-inch wheels, and is coupled to one another with axle pegs. The Engine shown on the ¼-inch-square grid pattern above, uses two 1-inch diameter wheels. Glue a furniture button to the front of the Engine for a head light, and attach the toy train smokestacks, sold by the mail order companies listed in the Appendix, for added realism.*

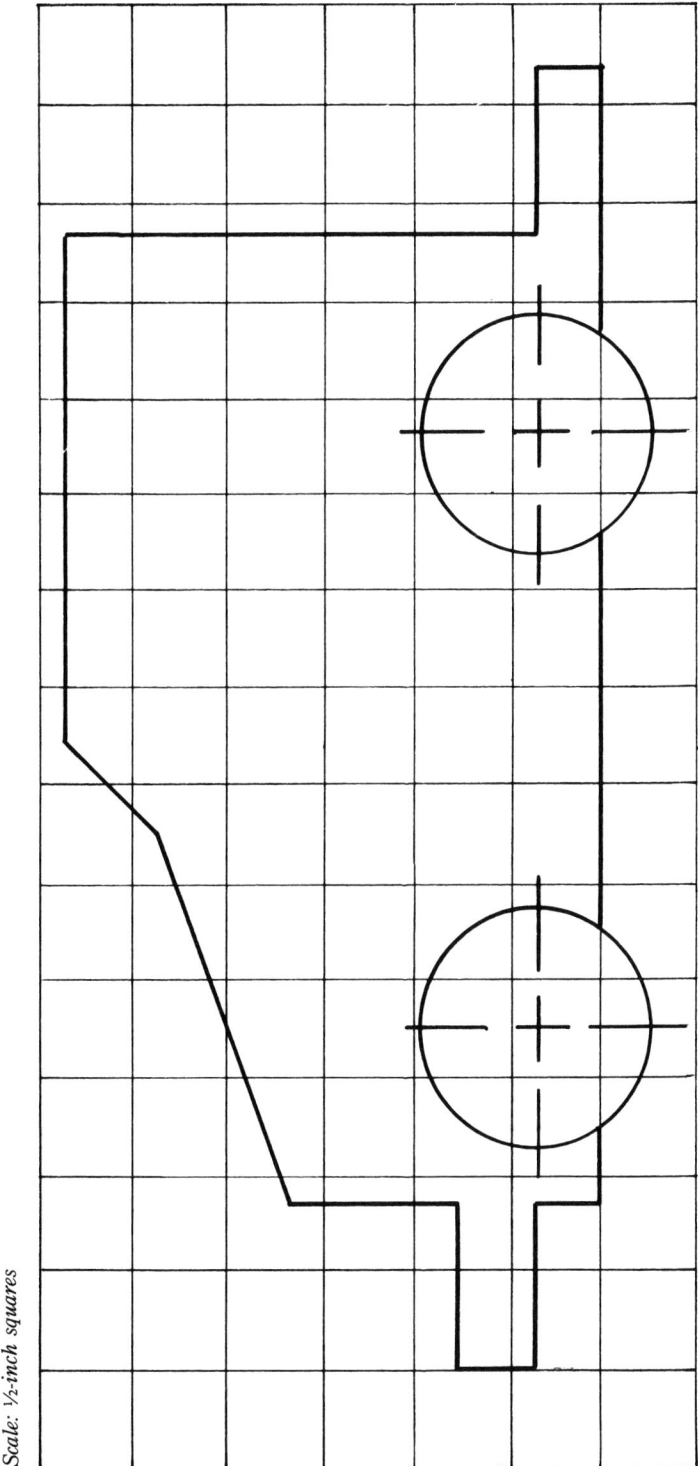

Fig. 7-17. Cut the Coal Car from a 6¾-inch length of 2-by-4-inch lumber.

105

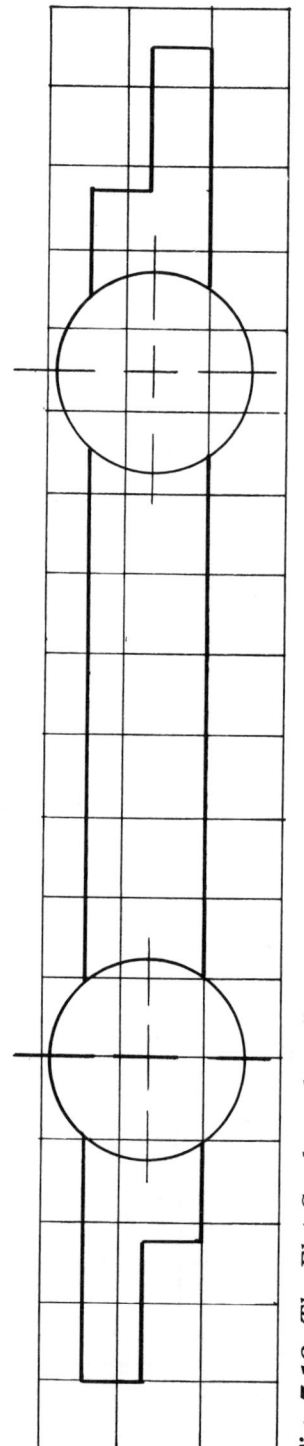

Scale: ½-inch squares

Fig. 7-18. The Flat Car has a low, flat surface that can be used to carry all types of cargo.

Scale: ½-inch squares

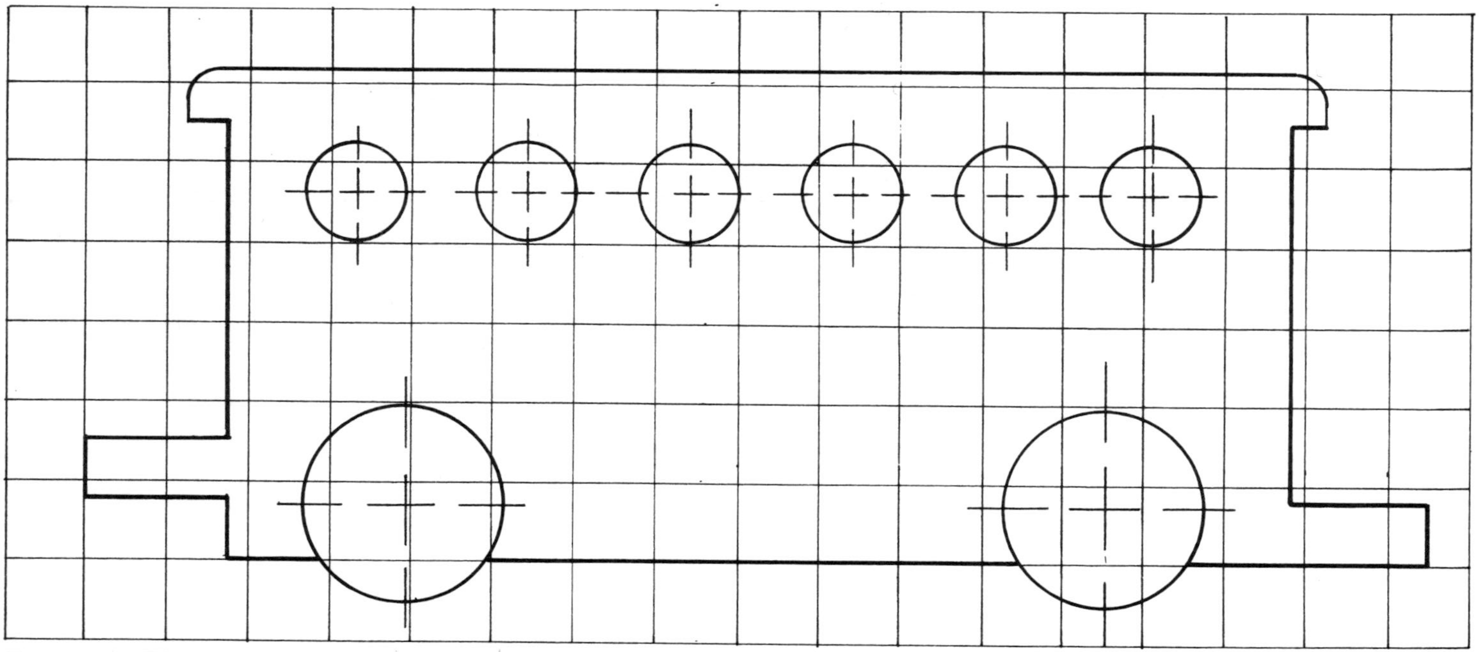

Fig. 7-19. The windows drilled into both sides of the Passenger Car are ⅝ inch in diameter. If no windows are drilled, the Passenger Car quickly becomes a Box Car for carrying cargo.

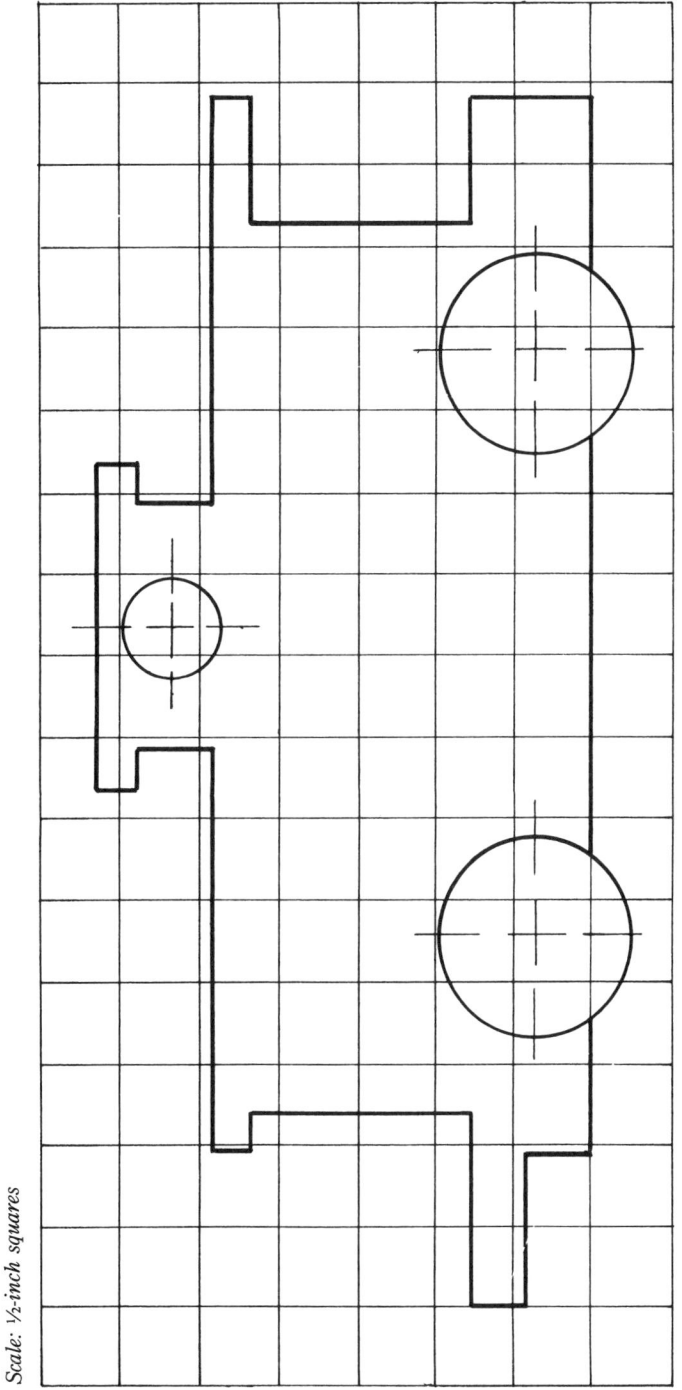

Scale: ½-inch squares

Fig. 7-20. The Caboose is cut from a 2-by-4-inch piece of lumber that is 7½ inches long.

LIST 7-1. REQUIRED MATERIALS

Convertible
1 – 2 × 4 × 7½ Wood Body
4 – 1¼-inch-diameter Wheels
4 – Small Axle Pegs

Limousine
1 – 2 × 4 × 7½ Wood Body
4 – 1¼-inch-diameter Wheels
4 – Small Axle Pegs

Station Wagon
1 – 2 × 4 × 7½ Wood Body
4 – 1¼-inch-diameter Wheels
4 – Small Axle Pegs

Camper/Trailer
1 – 2 × 4 × 5½ Wood Body
2 – 1¼-inch-diameter Wheels
3 – Small Axle Pegs

Racer
1 – 2 × 4 × 7½ Wood Body
4 – 1¼-inch-diameter Wheels
4 – Small Axle Pegs

Sports Car
1 – 2 × 4 × 6¾ Wood Body
4 – 1¼-inch-diameter Wheels
4 – Axle Pegs

Jalopy
1 – 2 × 4 × 5¾ Wood Body
4 – 1¼-inch-diameter Wheels
4 – Small Axle Pegs

Local Delivery Truck
1 – 2 × 4 × 9 Wood Body
10 – 1¼-inch-diameter Wheels
10 – Small Axle Pegs

Import
1 – 2 × 4 × 5¾ Wood Body
4 – 1¼-inch-diameter Wheels
4 – Small Axle Pegs

Ambulance
1 – 2 × 4 × 7½ Wood Body
4 – 1¼-inch-diameter Wheels
4 – Small Axle Pegs
4 – ⅜-inch-diameter furniture buttons

Police Car
1 – 2 × 4 × 7½ Wood Body
4 – 1¼-inch-diameter Wheels
4 – Small Axle Pegs
2 – ⅜-inch-furniture buttons

School Bus
1 – 2 × 4 × 9¼ Bus Body
6 – 1¼-inch-diameter Wheels
6 – Axle Pegs

Engine
1 – 2 × 4 × 7⅜ Engine
4 – 1-inch-diameter Wheels
4 – 1¼-inch-diameter Wheels
1 – Smokestack
8 – Small Axle Pegs
1 – ½-inch-diameter furniture buttons

Coal Car
1 – 2 × 4 × 6¾ Car Body
4 – 1¼-inch-diameter Wheels
5 – Small Axle Pegs

Flat Car
1 – 2 × 4 × 8¼ Car Frame
4 – 1¼-inch-diameter Wheels
5 – Small Axle Pegs

Passenger Car
1 – 2 × 4 × 8¼ Car Body
4 – 1¼-inch-diameter Wheels
5 – Small Axle Pegs

Caboose
1 – 2 × 4 × 7½ Car Body
4 – 1¼-inch-diameter Wheels
5 – Small Axle Pegs

8
CHAPTER

Things That Fly

All too often a toy is designed to look good, but does not function well as a play thing. It breaks too easily. This has given rise to the design of the Piper Cub Airplane (Fig. 8-1). The design is not overly heavy in detail, yet anyone should be able to recognize what it is. It is built to hold up to the hard play with which most toys are greeted. After all, have you ever seen a child just fly a toy airplane? The planes always seem to crash.

PIPER CUB AIRPLANE

The fuselage of the Piper Cub is cut from a 11-inch-long piece of 2-by-4 lumber. The 2-by-4 piece should be ripped to a width of 2 inches and a thickness of 1½ inches.

This project will rely heavily on your ability to lay out the design and shape the wood to the correct shape. The side view of the airplane fuselage is shown in Fig. 8-2A.

Notice that the layout is done with all straight lines. The dimensions given will assist you in drawing them out. Draw the design directly onto the wood using dark pencil lines so that they will show up clearly while being cut.

Fig. 8-1. *The Piper Cub airplane has been designed to be both attractive and sturdy.*

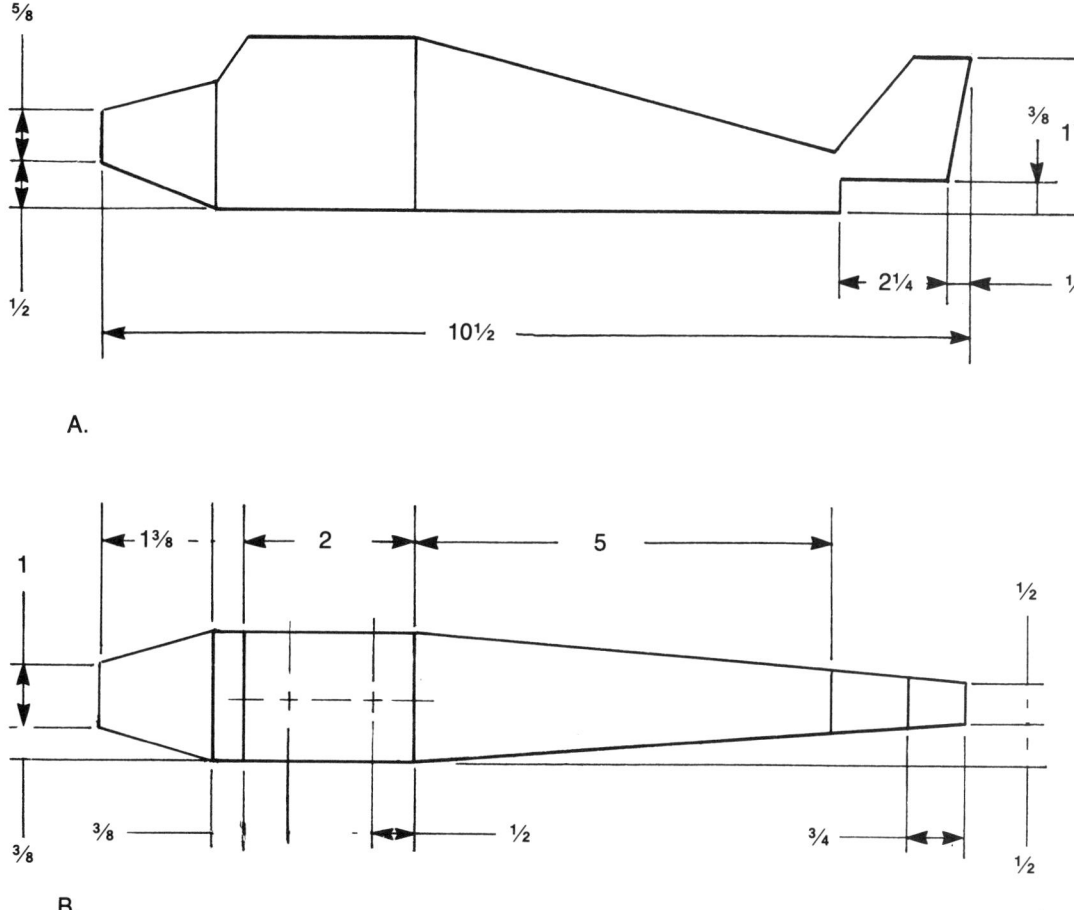

Fig. 8-2. (A) The profile of the Piper Cub fuselage; (B) The top view.

After the layout has been completed, the cutting may begin. A band saw works best, but a jigsaw or coping saw can also do the job.

When the side view, or profile, of the airplane has been cut, the edges should be sanded smooth down to the pencil lines. Now turn your attention to the top edge. Figure 8-2B shows how to lay out the design on the top of the airplane fuselage. First, cut away with a saw, then file and sand down to the line (Fig. 8-3).

The last few parts of the Piper Cub Airplane are all made from ⅜-inch-thick wood. The wing measures 2 inches wide and 12 inches long. The two struts are cut to a width of 1⅜ inches and a length of 2¾ inches.

The stabilizer is the short rear wing on an airplane. It measures 1¼ inches wide and 2¾ inches long. The final ⅜-inch part is the ⅝-inch-wide, 2¼-inch-long propeller. These five parts are drawn on the grid pattern in Fig. 8-4.

Notice that there are ⅜- and ¼-inch-diameter holes marked on some parts. Mark

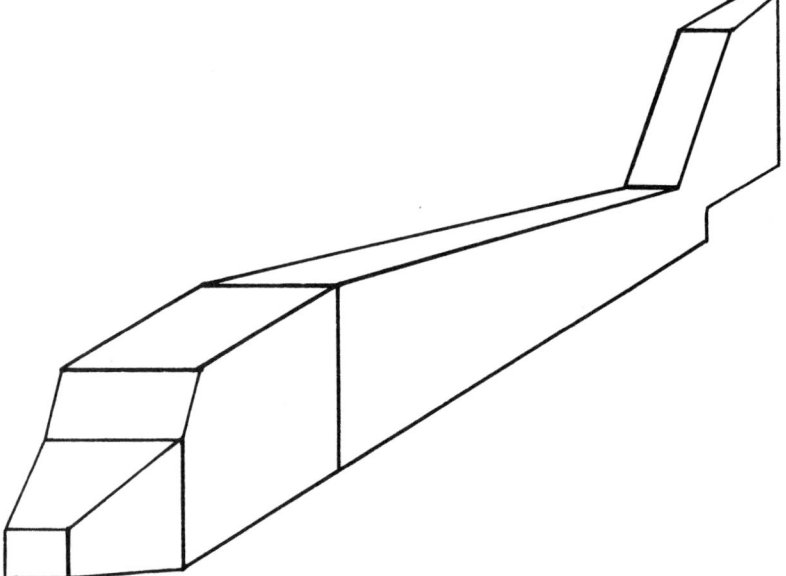

Fig. 8-3. *The fuselage after the profile and top have been cut.*

the center of these holes. They will be used later to dowel the parts to the fuselage or to pin one part to another.

When all of the layout work has been completed, cut out each part, sand down to the line, and drill the required holes. Also, drill axle peg holes in the struts and propeller. The location of these are shown on the grid. The diameter of these holes is determined by the size of the axle pegs that you use to attach the 1-inch-diameter wheels to the struts. The same size drill bit is used to drill a hole in the center of the propeller.

Assembly of the component parts begins with the wing. The wing is centered over the top of the fuselage. The dowel holes are marked, then drilled 1-inch deep. The wing

Scale: ½-inch squares

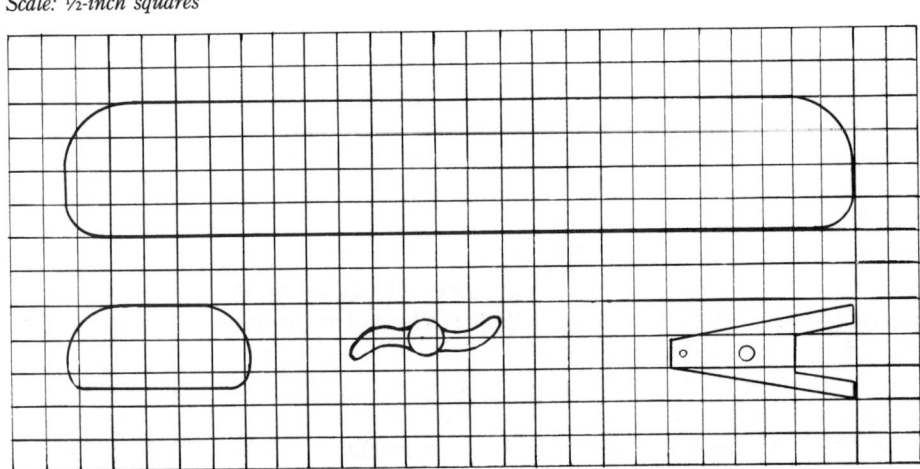

Fig. 8-4. *The grid pattern with the remainder of the Piper Cub parts.*

112

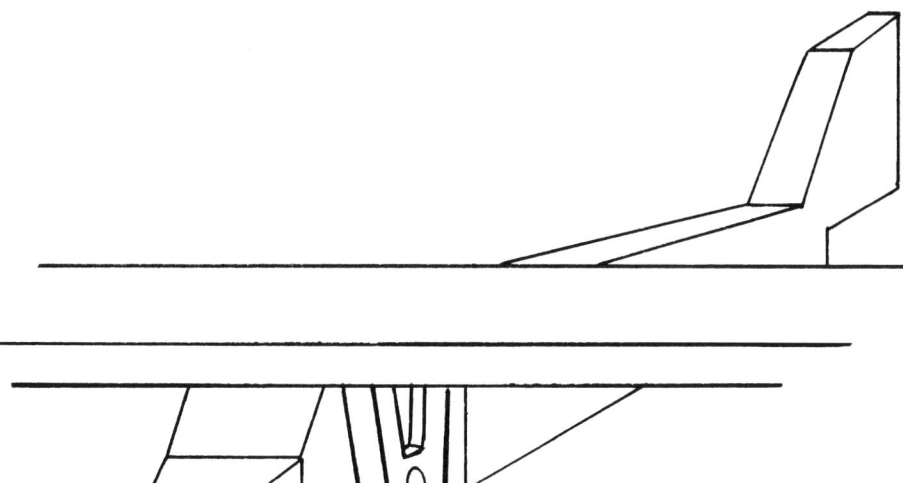

Fig. 8-5. *Glue and dowel the struts to the fuselage under the wing, for maximum durability.*

can now be glued and doweled into position. The dowels should be allowed to extend above the surface of the wing. You can sand them flush with the glue is set.

Next, glue and dowel the stabilizer to the fuselage. Line up the stabilizer on the rear of the fuselage, then mark the location where the dowel hole must be drilled. Be careful not to drill too deep into the tail section, or the hole might come through the top side.

When completed, glue and dowel the stabilizer into position using a ¼-inch-diameter dowel. The dowel may be sanded flush with the surface of the stabilizer or left slightly longer, in order to act as a rear wheel.

The design on this airplane has been slightly altered from the original Piper Cub in that the wing strut on this plane both supports the wing and holds the landing gear. Glue and dowel the struts into the fuselage in the center of the wing (Fig. 8-5). Repeat the procedure on the opposite side of the airplane, making sure to put the glue into the hole in the strut, not the wheel. With the axle peg glued only to the strut, the wheels will be allowed to spin freely.

After the glue has set, sand the dowels flush with the surface of the strut. The wheels (1¼-inch diameter) are now permanently affixed to the struts.

Now, glue the propeller into place in the same manner, by only putting glue into the fuselage hole, not the propeller hole.

The Piper Cub, one of the most stable of designs in the aircraft industry, can be seen at all airports. In fact, most pilots learns to fly with this plane and have a deep admiration for it. The young pilots who "fly" this toy Piper Cub will soon learn to share the pilot's love for the airplane.

HELICOPTER

The Helicopter design provided here is for a helicopter that is capable of landing on both land and water, as it has been provided with pontoons (Fig. 8-6).

The helicopter body is cut from an 8⅜-inch-long section of 2-by-4 lumber. The width of the 2 by 4 must be cut down to 2 inches, making a board that is 1½ inches thick, 2 inches wide, and 8⅜ inches long. On the side of the board, draw out the side view or profile of the helicopter body (Fig. 8-7A). Again, lay out the design in dark pencil lines so that they will be easily seen while cutting. I suggest that the cuts be made close to the line, then filed and sanded down to the line. This will result in a smooth, flat surface at each part cut.

The next step is to lay out the shape of the helicopter body as viewed from the top. The drawing in Fig. 8-7B shows how the top view is laid out. The layout work should be done carefully to ensure that each line is straight and accurately drawn. The shaded areas on the drawing indicate the material that must be removed. As I suggested with the side view, the cuts should be made close to the line, then filed and sanded to smooth the wood down to the line.

The next two pieces to make are the main blade and the tail rotor. Cut both of these from a ⅜-inch-thick piece of wood. The main blade should measure ¾ inch wide and 8 inches long. Round each end of the main blade by drawing a ⅜-inch arc on the ends. In the center of the main blade, drill a hole through the thickness. The location of the hole is shown in Fig. 8-8. The diameter of the hole should be of sufficient size to allow an axle peg to slip through it easily.

Cut the tail rotor from a 2¼-inch-long, ⅝-inch-wide piece of ⅜-inch-thick wood. The shape of the tail rotor is shown in Fig. 8-9. (This is the same propeller that was used on the Piper Cub Plane. If that project has already been completed, you may have saved the templet.) Drill a hole in the center of the propeller. Insert an axle peg through this hole. Be sure the hole is slightly larger than the axle peg so that the tail rotor will spin freely.

Next to build is the pontoon assembly. Begin by cutting two 3¾-inch lengths of ¾-inch-diameter dowel. Drill two ⅜-inch-diameter holes in each pontoon—one 1¼ inches back from the front end, the other 1¼ inches back from the first. Drill the holes ⅜-inch deep. Be sure to round both ends of each pontoon to prevent scratches from sharp edges. Now make four pontoon struts from four lengths of ⅜-inch-diameter dowel, each 1⅜ inches long.

Fig. 8-6. *The wood Helicopter is built to stand up to the use and abuse of children's play.*

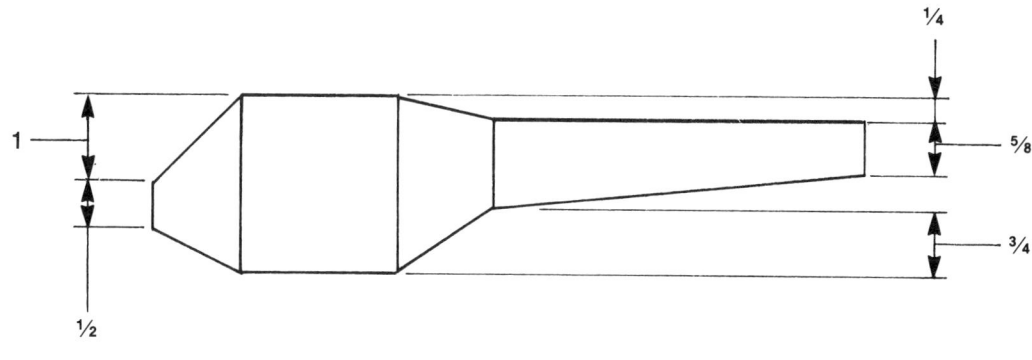

A.

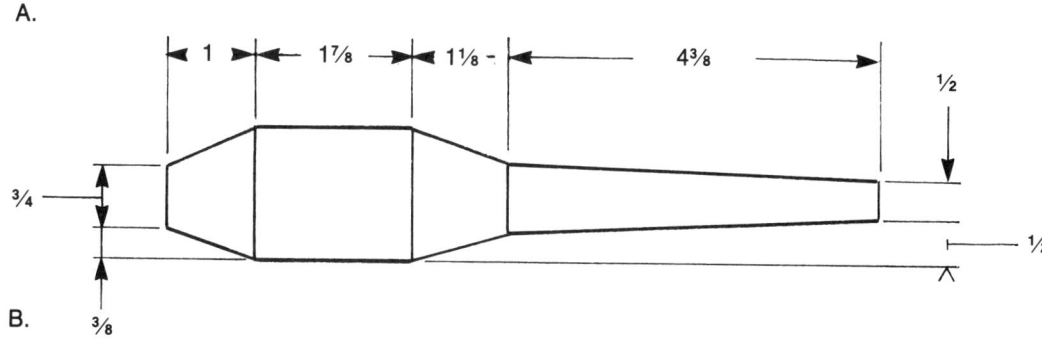

B.

Fig. 8-7. *(A) The profile of the helicopter body; (B) The top of the helicopter.*

To install the pontoons on the underside of the helicopter, drill four ⅜-inch-diameter holes ⅜ inch deep into the belly of the helicopter. The locations of the holes are shown in Fig. 8-11A. The ⅜-inch-diameter holes should be drilled at approximately a 22-degree angle, as shown in Fig. 8-11B.

Sand each piece thoroughly for both appearance and safety reasons. Now you can assemble the component parts.

The main blade and tail rotor are pinned in place with axle pegs. No glue should get into the holes in the blade or rotor, only in the helicopter body. This will allow the parts to turn freely once the glue has set. Now glue the pontoon assemblies into the angled holes drilled in the underside of the helicopter.

This Helicopter toy has been designed to meet two criteria. The first, to be nice enough in appearance to attract and hold the attention of the child, the second to take the use and abuse the child will exert in normal play. The Helicopter has taken this practical aspect into every detail of its design.

INTERSTELLAR FIGHTER

The Interstellar Fighter is a model of the ship that can travel throughout space fighting off the evil spacecraft. To begin construction, cut two 1-by-1½-by-4½-inch pieces of wood. These will form the starboard and port (right and left) sides of the star chaser.

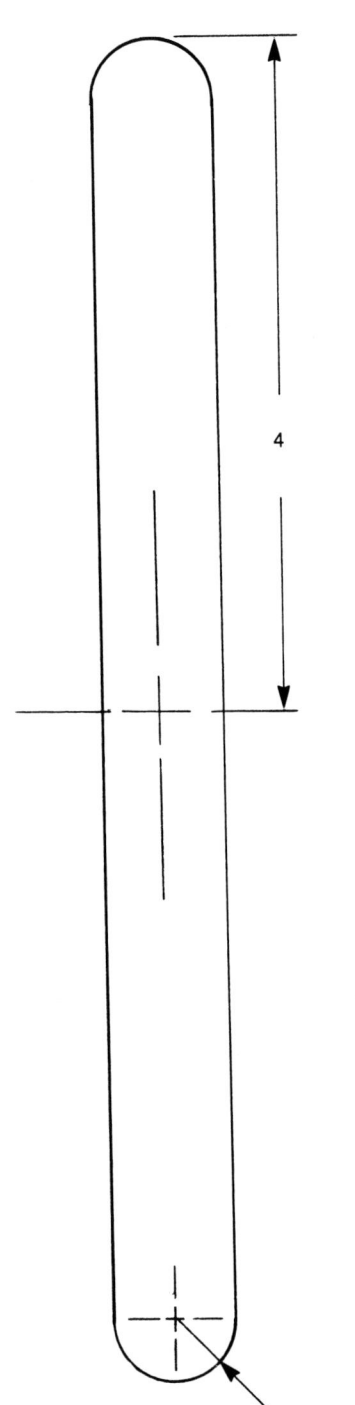

Fig. 8-8. Cut the main Helicopter blade from a piece of wood 8 inches long and ¾ of an inch wide. Drill the center hole where shown.

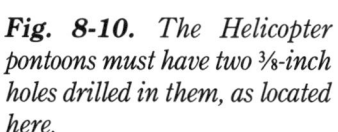

Fig. 8-9. *The outline of the tail rotor.*

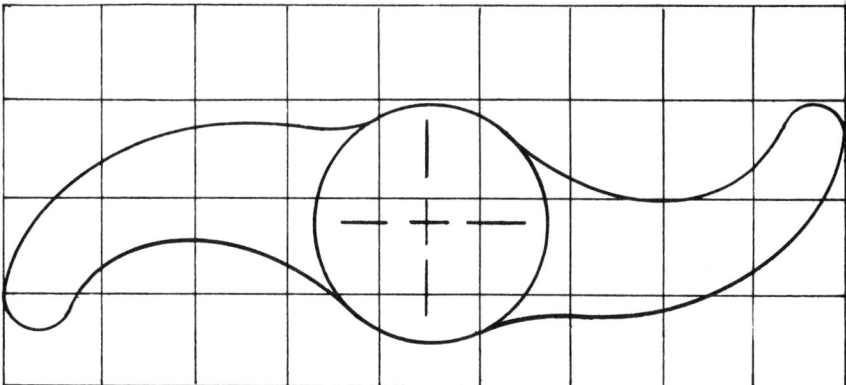

Fig. 8-10. *The Helicopter pontoons must have two ⅜-inch holes drilled in them, as located here.*

The next piece to make is the ⅜-by-2½-by-4¼-inch vertical stabilizer. Glue these three pieces together with the ⅜-inch-thick piece between the other two 1-inch-thick boards (Fig. 8-12). Make sure the bottom edges of all three pieces are flush with one another.

After allowing sufficient time for the glue to set, draw out and cut the horizontal wing cavity. This is a ⅜-inch-deep, 3⅜-inch-long area cut into the bottom edge of the fuselage (Fig. 8-13). This cut can be made using a handsaw or a band saw.

Measure ⅝ inch in from the rear end along the top of the vertical stabilizer, then measure ½ inch up from the ⅜-inch wing recess just cut on the forward-most end of the fuselage assembly (Fig. 8-14). Lay a straight edge on the fuselage connecting the ⅝-inch and ½-inch marks, and draw a line. Using a saw, cut close to the line, removing the upper part. Then sand or file down to the line.

To further shape the fuselage, cut the upper corners of the fuselage off at a 45-degree angle. The drawing of the rear end of the fuselage in Fig. 8-15 indicates where the angle is to be cut. Also shown in the drawing is the location of two ¼-inch-diameter holes. Drill the holes to a depth of 1½ inches. This is where the thruster jets will later be inserted.

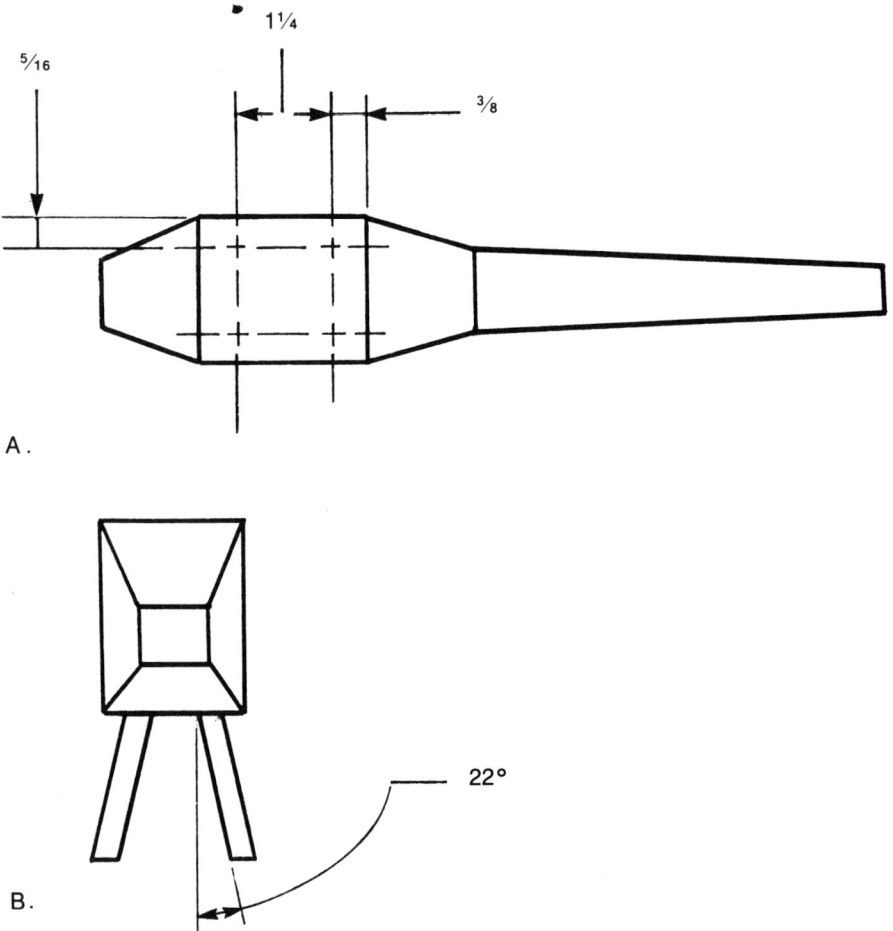

Fig. 8-11. *(A) Drill four ⅜-inch-diameter holes in the exact positions shown, so that the pontoon assembly can be installed. (B) Be sure to drill at an angle.*

Cut the horizontal wing from a ⅜-inch-thick piece of wood, which is 4½ inches wide and 3⅞ inches long. Glue it into the horizontal wing recess cut on the bottom of the fuselage. When the glue has set, refer to Fig. 8-16. For the last of the fuselage shaping steps, measure back along the ends of the wings 2½ inches. Measure 1⅝ inches in from each wing along the forward end of the wing. Draw a line connecting the two points. Cut close to the line, cutting through the wing and fuselage. Then sand the cut smooth.

The pilot control center is cut from a piece of wood measuring 1 inch thick, 1¼ inches wide, and 2½ inches long. Along the top edge, measure back from the front end 1⅛ inches, and draw a line across the top. On the front end, draw a line ⅜ inch up from the bottom. Connect these two lines with a diagonal line on the sides. Cut and sand away the excess material (Fig. 8-17A). Then measure in from one side, along the front end, ¼ inch and draw a line. Measure ⅝ inch over from the ¼-inch line and draw another

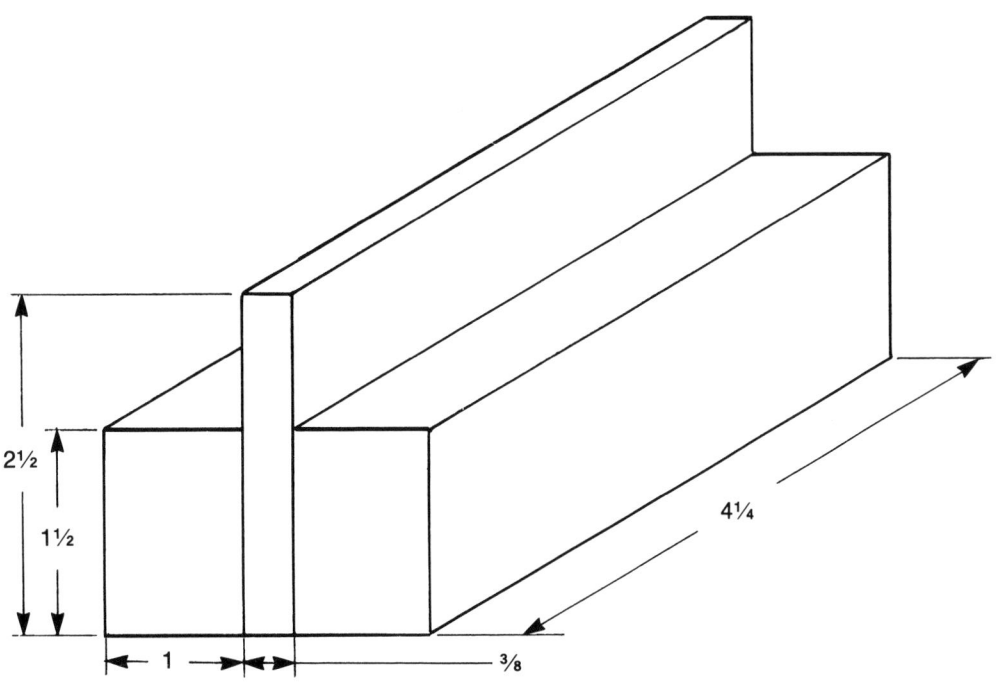

Fig. 8-12. Begin construction of the Interstellar Fighter by glueing two 1-by-1½-by-4¼-inch pieces on both sides of the ⅜-inch-thick vertical stabilizer.

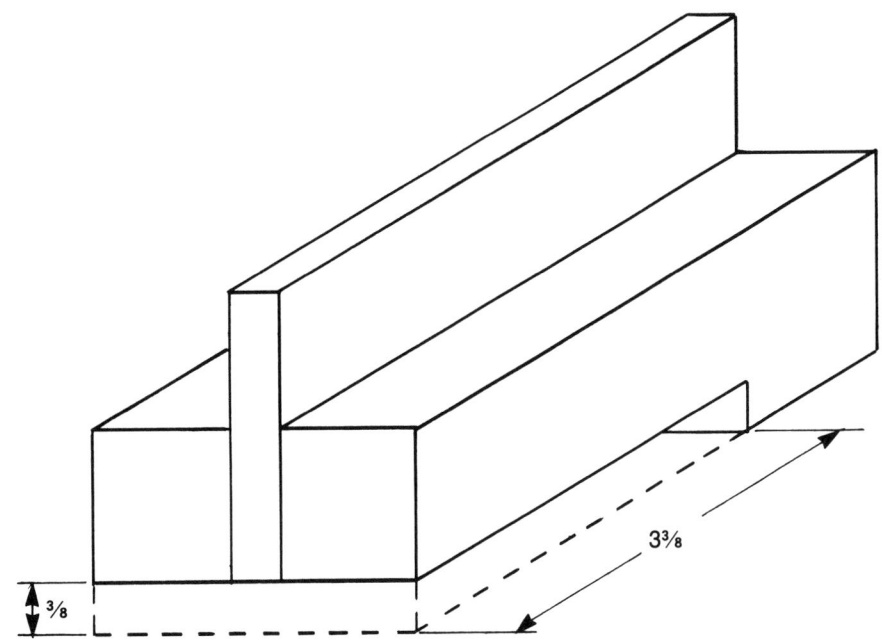

Fig. 8-13. The horizontal wing is recessed in the lower front portion of the fuselage assembly.

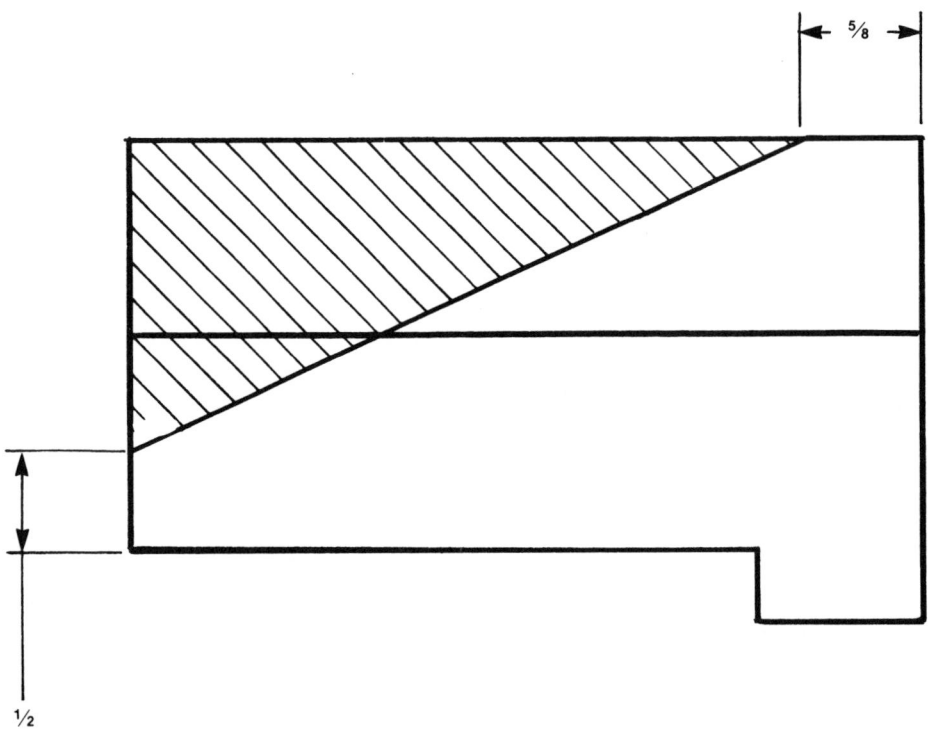

Fig. 8-14. *Shape the fuselage assembly by first drawing a diagonal line from the front edge to the top and removing the shaded area.*

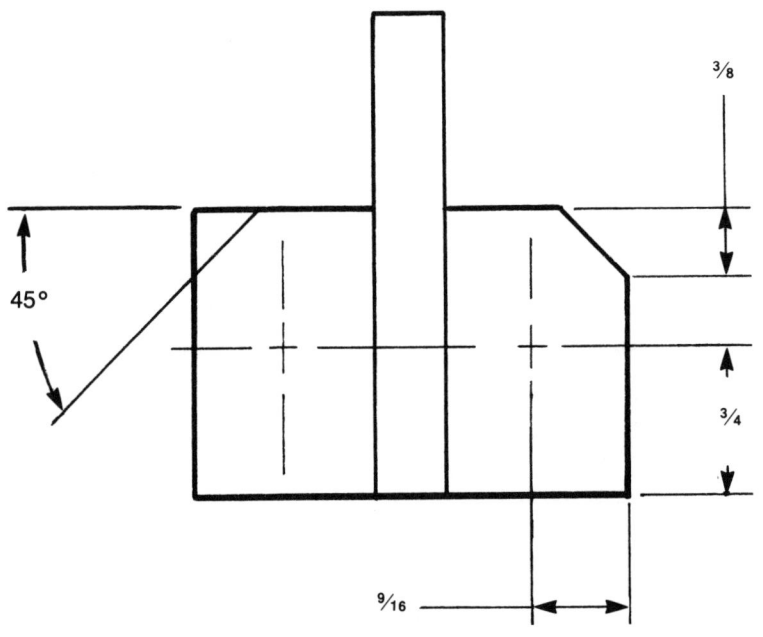

Fig. 8-15. *Cut the port and starboard fuselage halves at a 45-degree angle.*

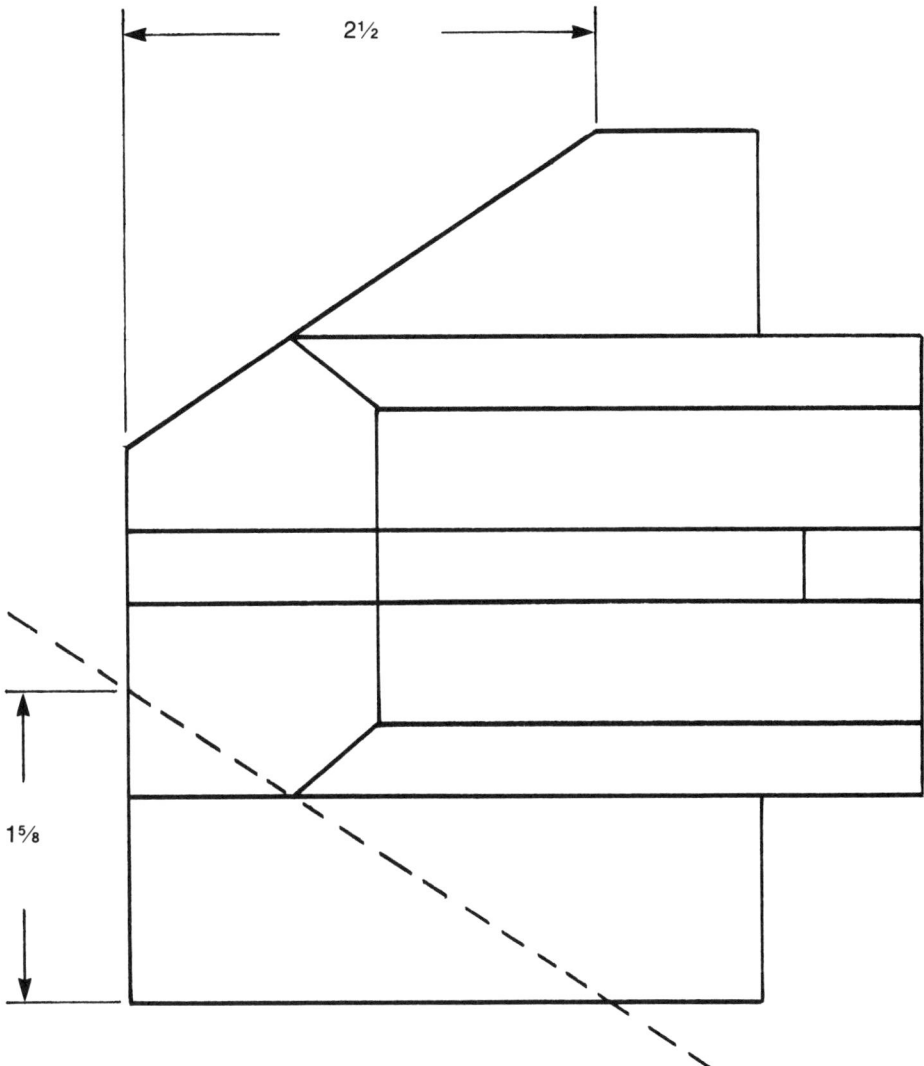

Fig. 8-16. *After glueing the horizontal wing into place, cut the wing and body at an angle.*

line. Draw a diagonal line from the two lines previously drawn along the angled surface to the 1⅛-inch line. Using a saw, cut the excess material from the sides of the pilot control center, then sand (Fig. 8-17B). Figure 8-17C illustrates what the project should now look like.

Next, dowel the pilot control center to the main fuselage assembly. On the front end of the fuselage assembly, draw two diagonal lines, as shown in Fig. 8-18. Repeat on the rear end of the pilot control center. At the point where the two lines cross, on both parts, drill a ¼-inch-diameter hole to the depth of 1½ inches in both sections. Cut a 2½-inch-long section of ¼-inch-diameter dowel. Test fit, then glue the dowel in the

121

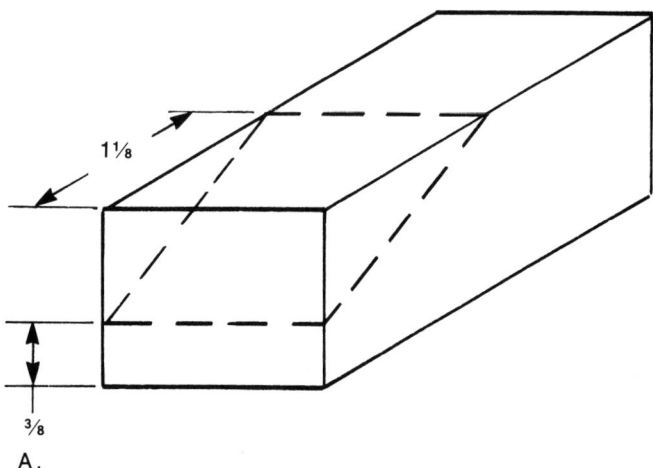

A.

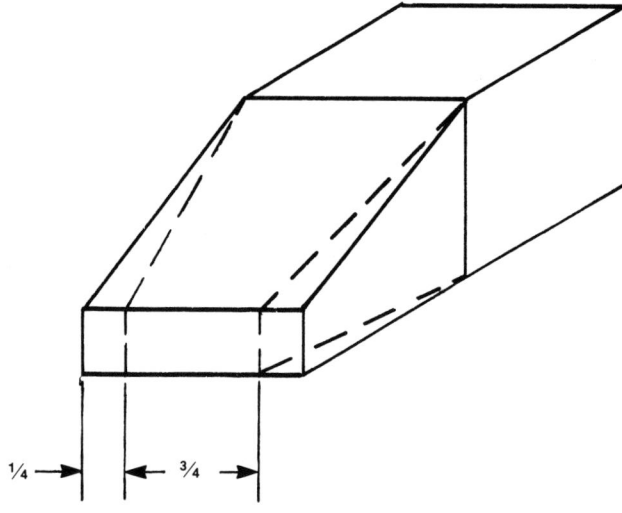

Fig. 8-17. Step-by-step procedure for shaping the control center.

B.

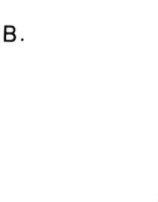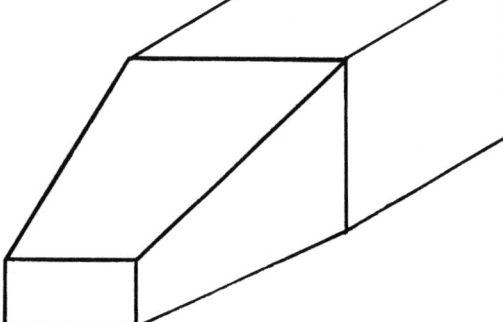

C.

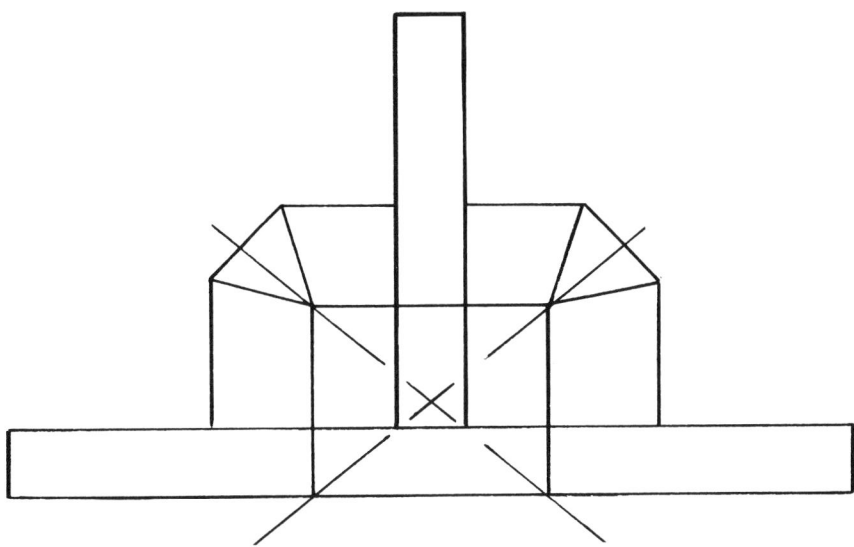

Fig. 8-18. *The two diagonal lines on the front of the fuselage assembly indicated where to drill a ¼-inch-diameter hole.*

pilot control center and the ¼-inch hole in the main fuselage.

The Interstellar Fighter is now ready for its main source of propulsion: the two thruster jets. The jets used on the sample are two small wood train smokestacks inserted into the ¼-inch holes drilled into the rear of the fuselage. If the wood smokestacks are not available, you can drill ½-inch holes instead and insert two 1-inch-long pieces of ½-inch-diameter dowels.

Finally, sand all over and apply some sort of finish to protect the Fighter. Then watch out! There will be interstellar battles taking place in each room of the house, with the Fighter emerging victorious in each instance.

THE ORICAN SHUTTLE

The Orican Shuttle is a small spacecraft used to transport personnel and supplies between larger ships, from ships to space stations, and surface exploratory substations. The project is a quick one that can be built in a short amount of time, costs little for materials, and results in a spacecraft which is a sure fire hit with kids.

The Orican Shuttle is constructed from a single piece of 2-by-4 inch pine lumber 7 inches long, which is free from knots or other defects. On the surface of the 2 by 4, measure back from the left end 2 inches and draw a line across the board. Measure in 1 inch from the 2-inch line and again draw a line. Next, measure in 1 inch from the right end and draw a line across. These measurements are the basis for shaping the Orican Shuttle (Fig. 8-19A).

To continue with the basic layout, draw two horizontal lines on the top surface, parallel to, and 1 inch in from, the sides. On the right side of the board, measure in along the end 1 3/16 inches from both sides, as shown in Fig. 8-19B.

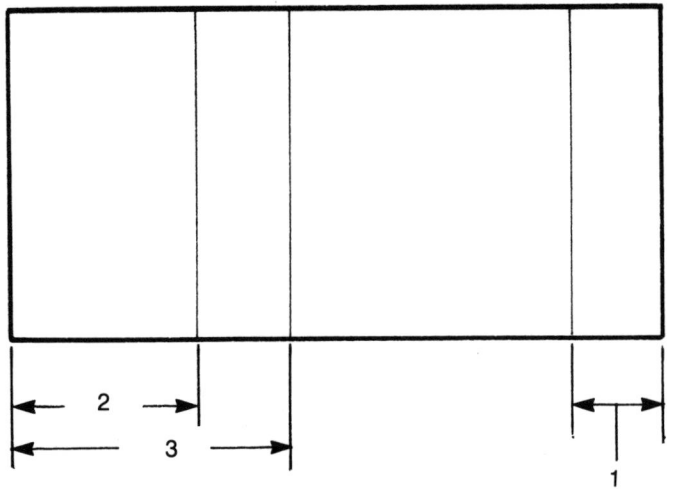

A.

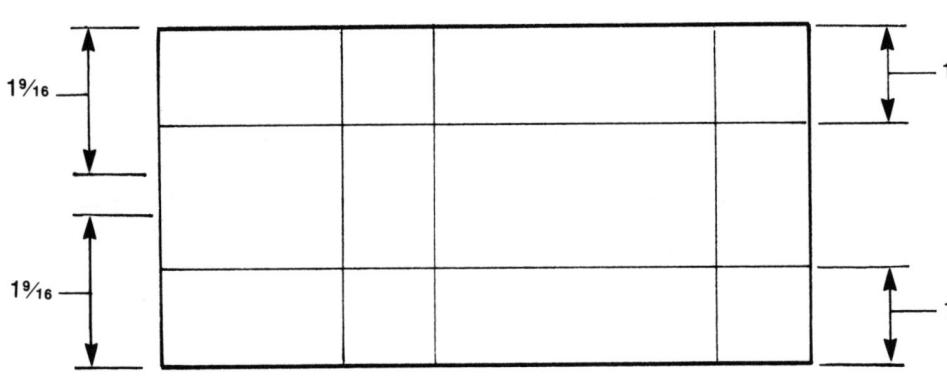

B.

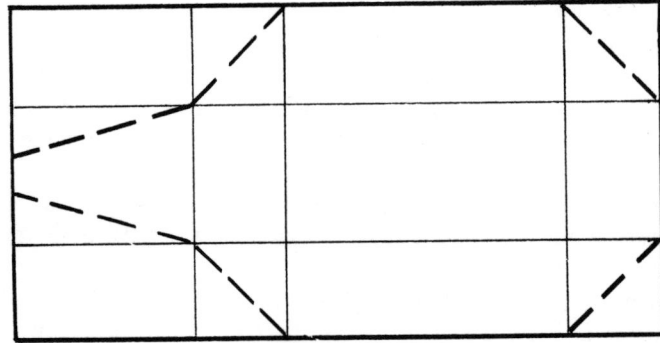

C.

Fig. 8-19. *The three drawings show how to draw the outline of the Orican Shuttle.*

The drawing in Fig. 8-19C shows how the top view of the Orican Shuttle is drawn from the series of lines previously drawn. From the 1 9/16-inch point, draw a diagonal line back until it meets the intersection of the 1-inch horizontal line and the 2-inch lines. From that same point, draw another line diagonal to the line which is 3 inches in from the end. On the right side, draw one more diagonal line from the point where the 1-inch horizontal lines meet the end.

Using a band saw, jigsaw, or handsaw, cut the surface shape of the Orican Shuttle. Remember to cut close to the line, then sand down to the line. This will produce a smoother, cleaner body.

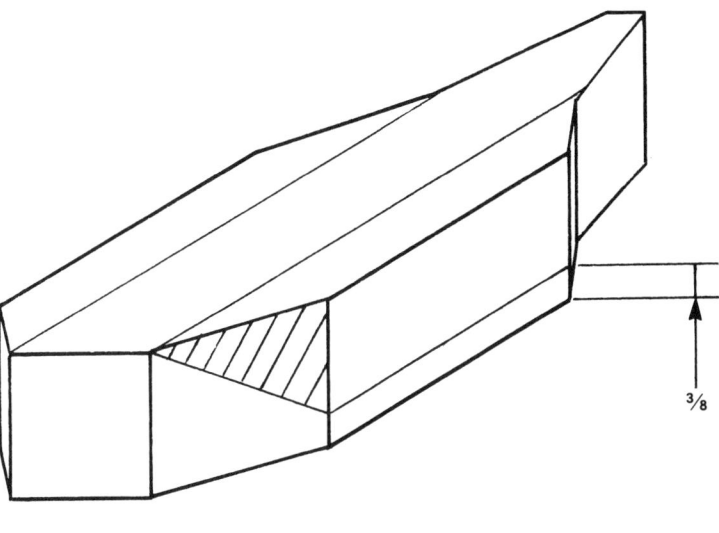

Fig. 8-20. *These drawings shows how the sides of the Orican Shuttle and the pilot house are shaped.*

A.

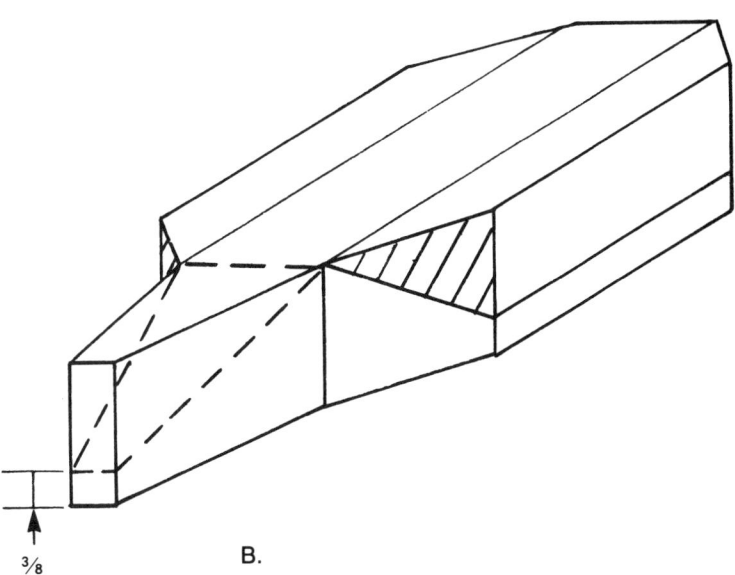

B.

On the rear end of the Orican Shuttle body, measure up from the bottom surface ⅜ inch on both sides. Then draw a diagonal line from the ⅜-inch point, up to the point where the inch horizontal line meets the end board (Fig. 8-20A). On the side of the spacecraft, draw a line the length of the side, ⅜ inch up from the bottom. On the front edge of the shuttle, draw a diagonal line up from the ⅜-inch line, to the top where the 1-inch line has been drawn (Fig. 8-20B). The shaded area shows the material that must be removed.

The final shaping operation for the Orican Shuttle is to cut the front pilot house at a slight downward angle, by measuring up along the front edge ⅜ inch, then filing away the material up to where the pilot house meets the body (Fig. 8-20B).

When the final shaping has been completed, the entire project should be sanded with coarse sandpaper first, then progressively finer paper to produce a smooth surface on the Orican Shuttle. The smooth, scratch-free surface will allow the shuttle to travel almost effortlessly through space, delivering its vital cargo.

PERSONNEL TRANSPORTER

The Personnel Transporter (Fig. 8-21) is the command headquarters, where all navigational decisions are made, and interplanetary battles are planned. The Interstellar Fighters surround the transporter to take on and eliminate any alien ships which dare to attack.

Begin construction by cutting the vertical wing to the correct size of ⅜ inch thick, 5 inches wide, and 6 inches long. Next, cut the two fuselage halves. They measure ¾ inch thick, 1½ inches wide, and 5 inches long. Measure down 2³⁄₁₆ inches on the vertical wing and draw a line all the way across. Next, measure 1½ inches down from the line just drawn, and again draw a line across the wing (Fig. 8-22). Repeat on the other side of the wing. The two fuselage halves are glued onto the wing between the two lines drawn.

Once the glued wing and fuselage assembly has had sufficient time to dry, draw the wing shape on the assembly. Figure 8-23 illustrates the method for cutting the correct wing shape. Draw the shape directly on the assembly, cut away the excess, and sand down to the line.

Fig. 8-21. The Personnel Transporter is the command headquarters for the entire fleet. At first glance, it appears to be a complex project; but by following the step-by-step instructions, the project can be easily built.

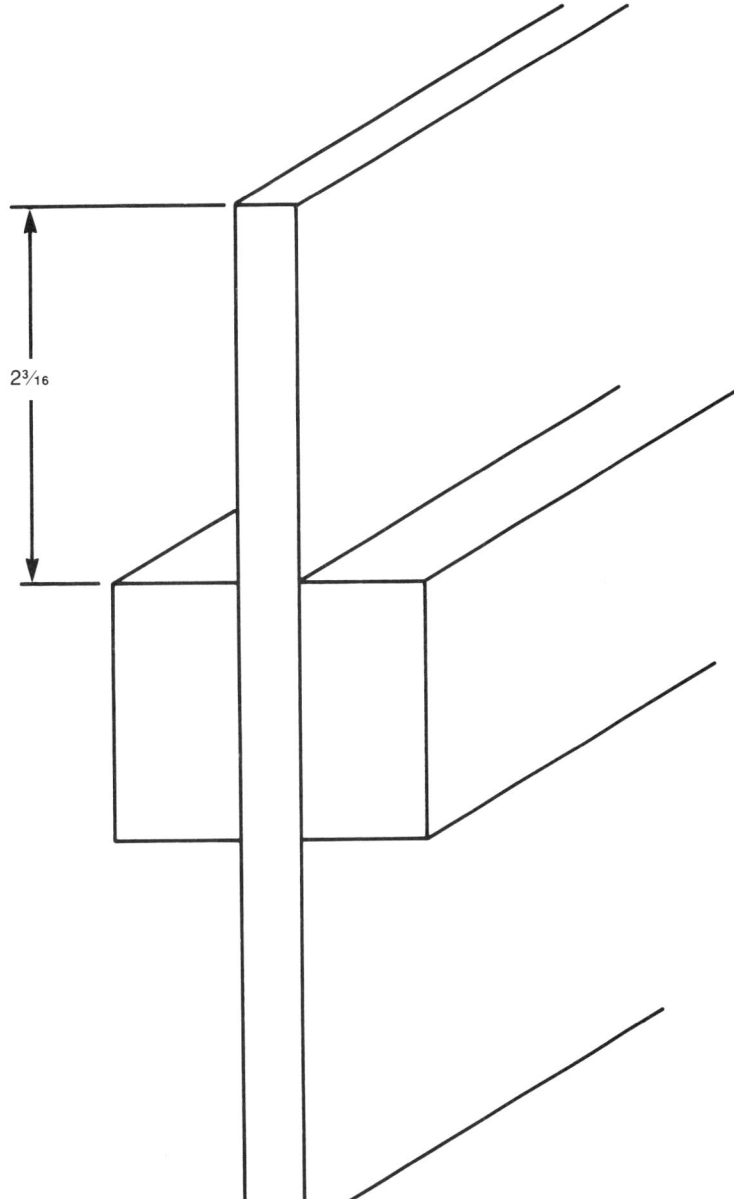

Fig. 8-22. *Glue two fuselage halves 2³⁄₁₆ inches down from the top edge of the vertical wing. I suggest that you draw lines across the wing to assist with lining up the halves.*

On the rear end of the wing/fuselage assembly, drill a hole in which to insert the thruster rocket. In the sample, a ⅝-inch-wide, 1-inch-deep hole was drilled in the exact center of the assembly to accommodate a medium-sized train smokestack (Fig. 8-24).

Next drill a ¼-inch-wide, 1-inch-deep hole in the front of the assembly, as shown in Fig. 8-25. The hole will later be used to dowel the pilot center to the mail fuselage.

On both sides of the fuselage, draw a pencil line ³⁄₁₆ inch up from the bottom edge

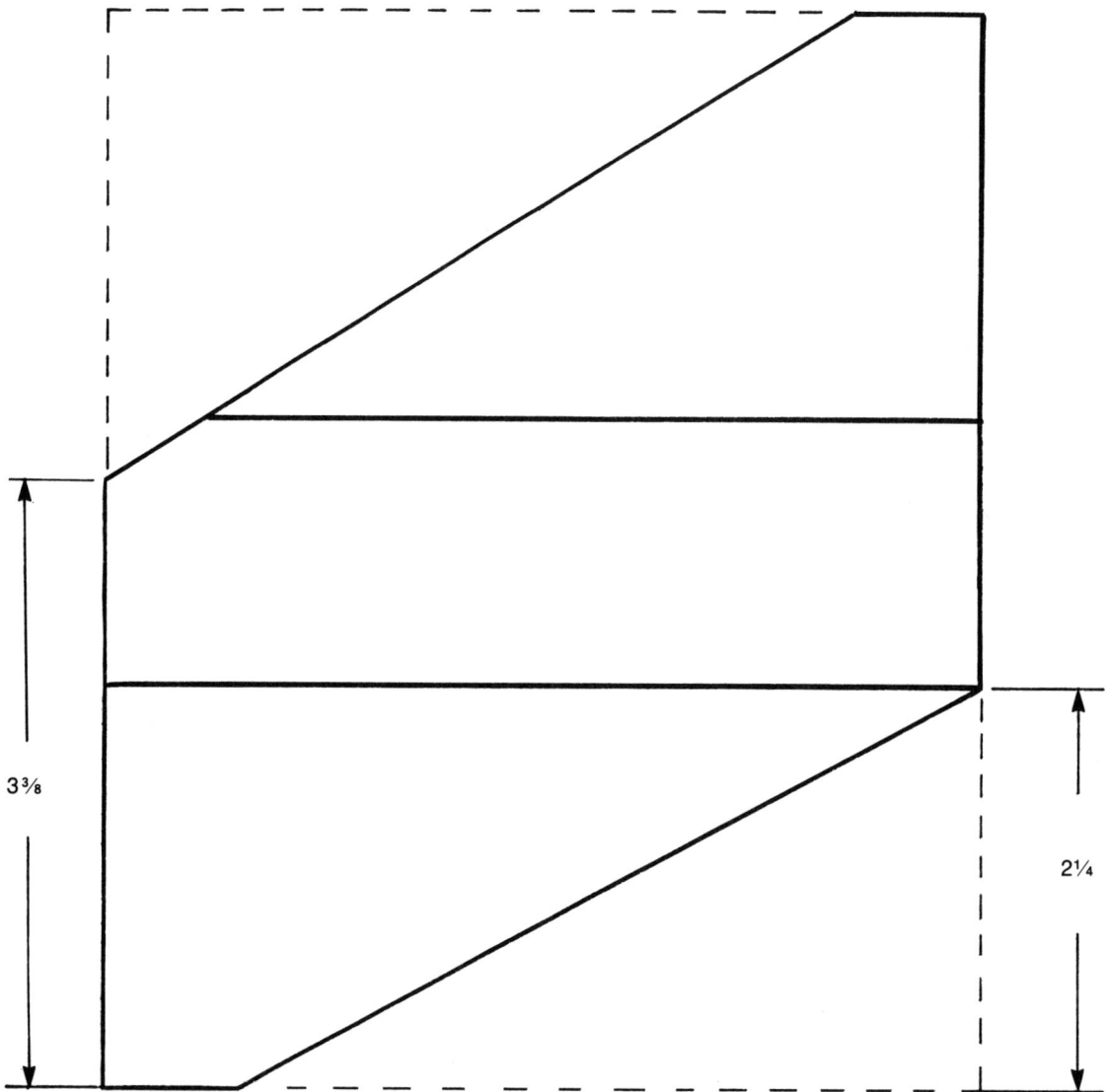

Fig. 8-23. *Draw the shape of the wing on the vertical wing fuselage assembly.*

(Fig. 8-26). From the front end of the fuselage, measure ⅞ inch back along the 3/16-inch line and make a mark. From that mark, measure 1 inch, make a mark, then 1 inch again, mark, then one more inch, and again make a mark. At these four marks, drill 3/16-inch holes ½ inch deep. Drill these holes carefully. They must line up with the other four holes that will later be drilled.

Next cut the two diagonal wings from a ⅜-inch-thick piece of wood that is 3¾ inches wide, and 5 inches long. Measure down along the right side ⅞ inch and make a light pencil mark. On the bottom edge, measure ¾ inch in from the left side, again making a light pencil line. Draw a pencil line diagonally from the two points, as shown in Fig.

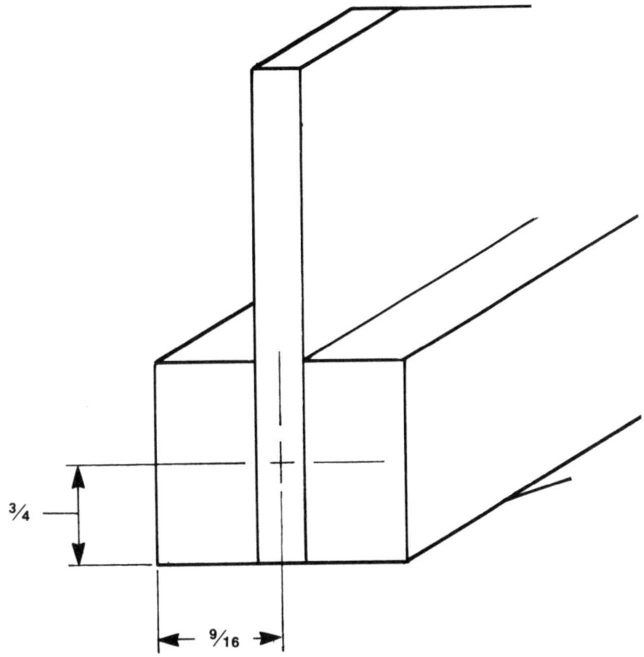

Fig. 8-24. Insert a thruster rocket into the hole in the wing/fuselage assembly.

Fig. 8-25. Drill a ¼-inch hole, 1 inch deep, at the center of the front end of the wing/fuselage assembly.

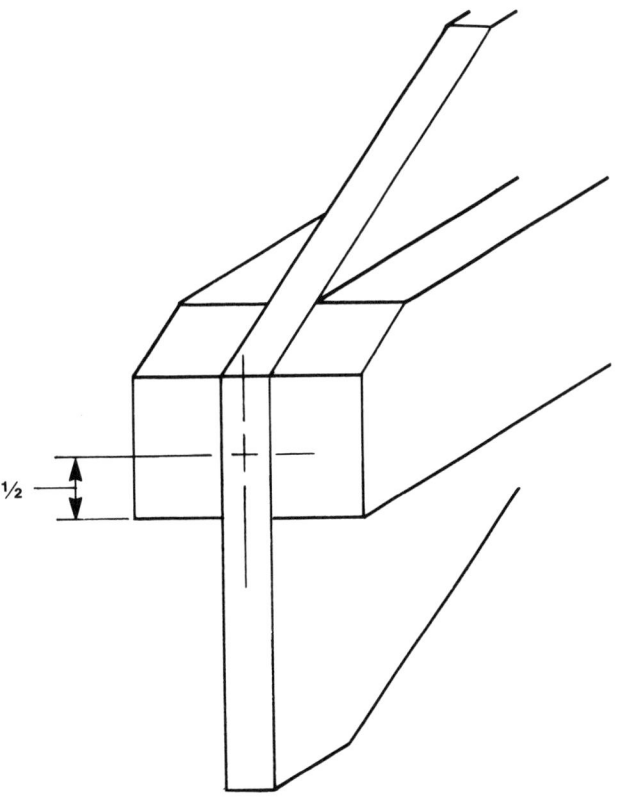

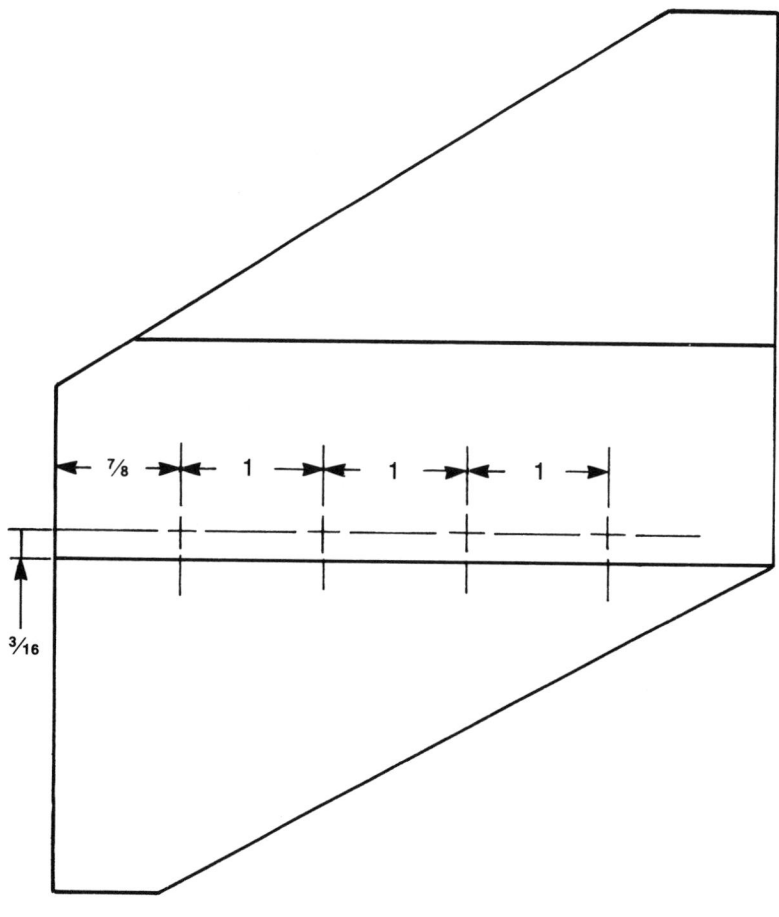

Fig. 8-26. Drill 3/16-inch-diameter holes into the fuselage halves.

8-27. Cut away the waste material and sand down to the line.

Cut the upper edge of the diagonal wings at a 45-degree angle, making sure that the angle is cut in the correct direction on the wings (Fig. 8-28A). Along the top edge of the diagonal wing, measure down 9/16 inch and draw a line across. From the front of the wing, measure back along the 9/16-inch line 7/8 inch, then 1 inch, then 1 more inch, then 1 inch again (Fig. 8-28B). At each point, drill a 3/16-inch-diameter hole. To do this, set the wing on a piece of scrap wood resting on the angled upper edge (Fig. 8-29). Then drill the holes, keeping the drill bit at a 90-degree angle to the scrap wood. Repeat this process with the other wing.

After applying a small amount of glue, insert four of the 3/16-inch-diameter, 1 1/4-inch-long dowel rods through the holes in the diagonal wings. The dowels should line up with the holes drilled in the fuselage assembly.

Using a toothpick, apply some glue in the fuselage holes, and also a thin layer along the angled edge of the wing. Lightly tap the dowels into the fuselage until they will not sink any deeper; The dowels cannot be made flush with the wing. Repeat on the other side.

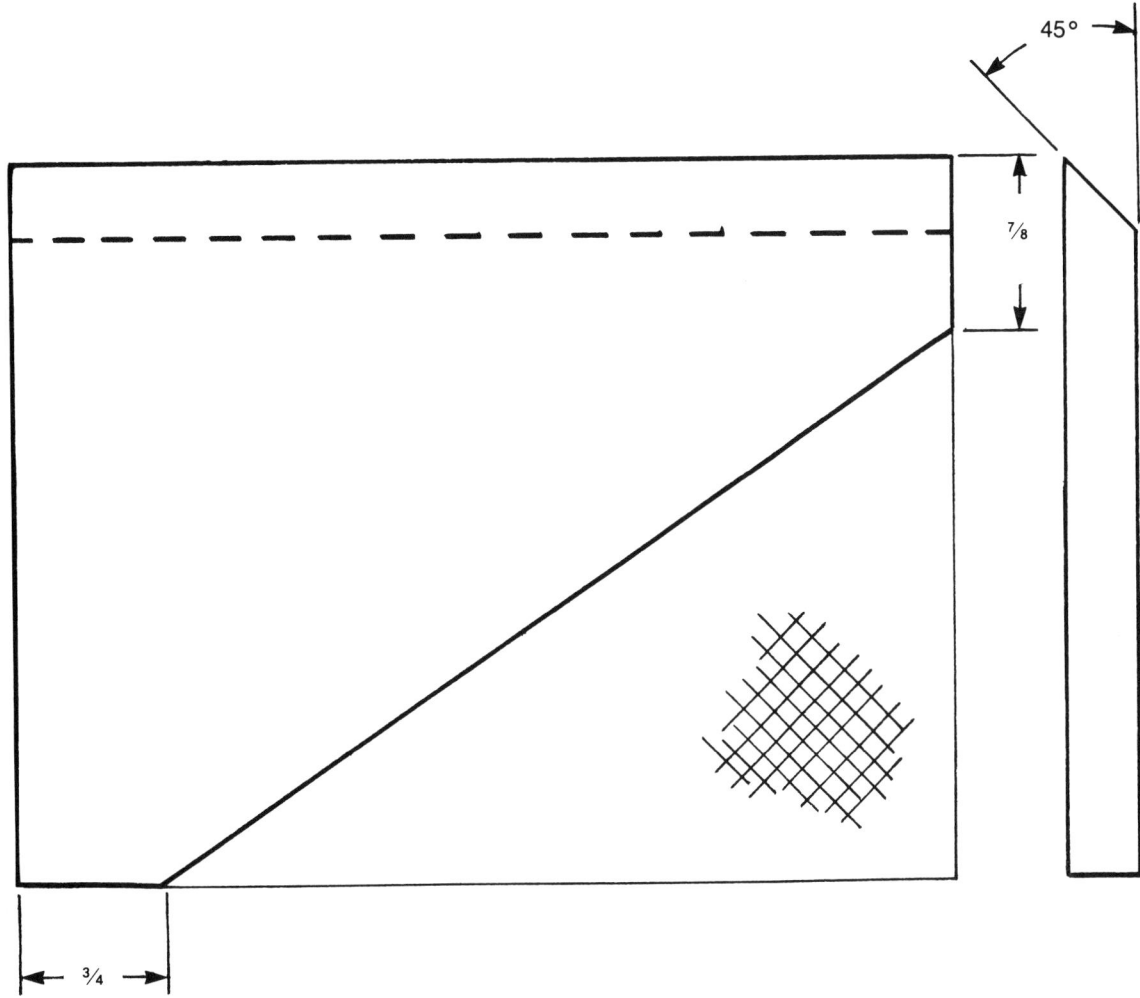

Fig. 8-27. *Cut the diagonal wings from a piece of ⅜-by-3¾-by-5-inch piece of wood.*

After the glue has had sufficient time to set, cut off the dowel ends that are protruding out of the wing and sand flush with the wing surface.

The command center is constructed from a piece of 1-inch-thick wood, 1¼ inches wide and 2⅝ inches long. Along the top surface, measure back from the front end 1⅛ inches, and draw a line across the top. On the front end, draw a line ⅜ inch up from the bottom. Connect these two lines with a diagonal line on the sides. Cut and sand away the excess material (Fig. 8-30A).

Measure in from one side, along the front end, ¼ inch, and draw a line. Measure ⅝ inch over from the ¼-inch line, and draw another line. Draw a diagonal line from the two lines previously drawn along the angled surface, to the 1⅛-inch line on the top surface. Using a saw, cut then sand the excess material from the side of the command center (Fig. 8-30C).

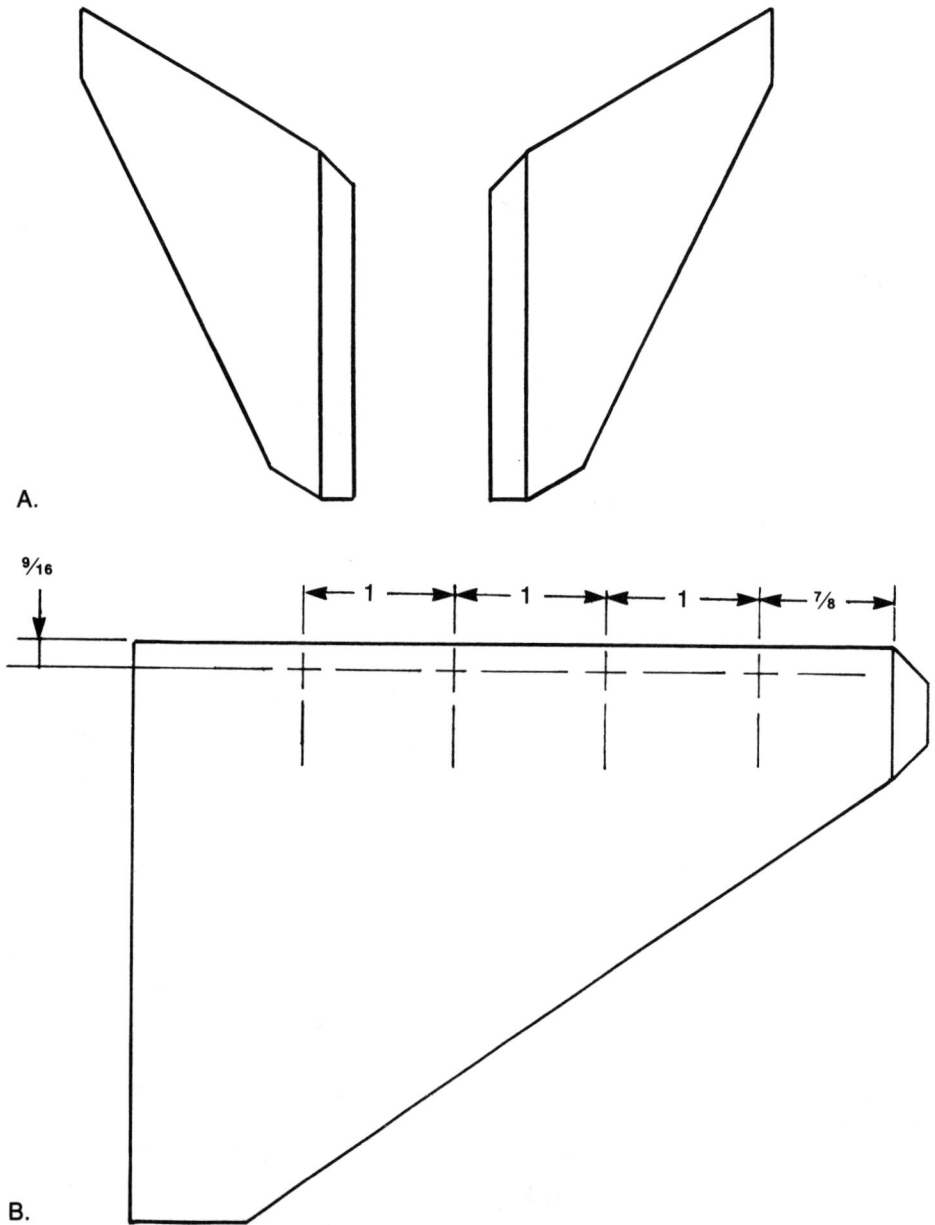

Fig. 8-28. *(A) Along the top edge of the wing, make a 45-degree angle cut. (B) The location of the 3/16-inch holes along the wing.*

On the rear end of the command center, draw two diagonal lines from corner to corner (Fig. 8-30D). Drill a ¼-inch-wide, ¾-inch-deep hole where the two lines cross, and apply a small amount of glue into the hole with a toothpick. Also apply some glue into the ¼-inch hole already drilled into the front portion of the fuselage. Into this hole,

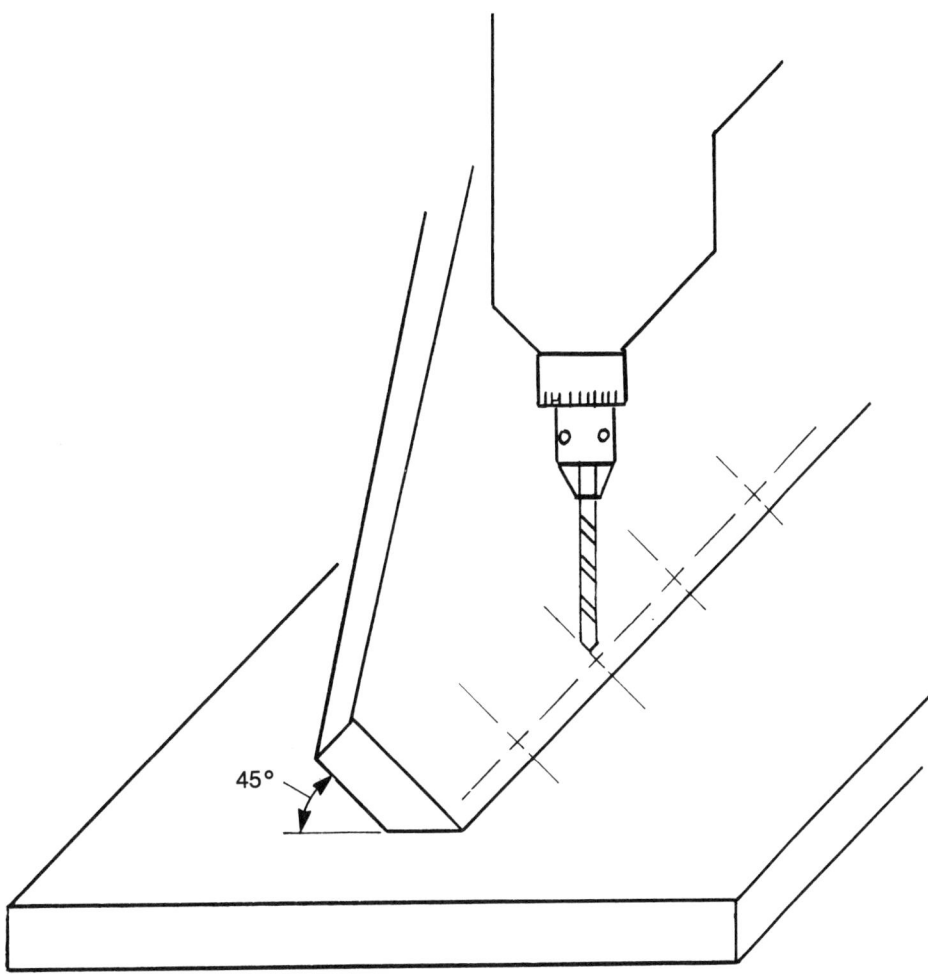

Fig. 8-29. Keep the drill bit at a 90-degree angle to the scrap wood.

insert a 1¼-inch length of ¼-inch dowel rod. Then apply a layer of glue on the rear portion of the command center and slide it onto the ¼-inch dowel.

PLANETARY LANDING VESSEL

A ship capable of traversing the vast unknown of space must be a very large craft. Landing this ship at each planet would be a monumental task. To eliminate this problem, the Planetary Landing Vessel has been developed (Fig. 8-31). It is a small pod-type vessel that can be sent down to the surface of a planet to perform vital scientific experiments, then return to the mother ship via its thruster rocket, mounted in the bottom center of the main body.

The main body of the Planetary Landing Vessel is made from two pieces of common

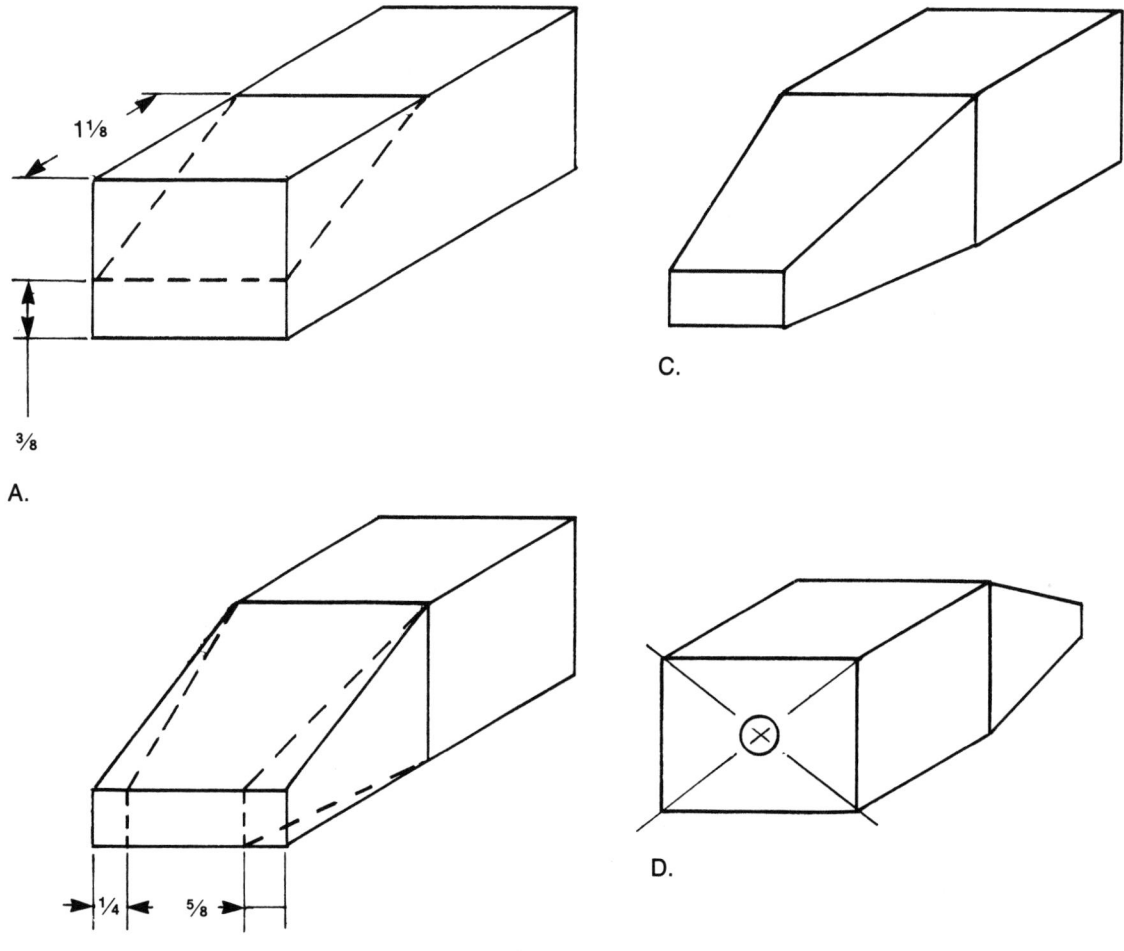

Fig. 8-30. *These four drawings detail the steps involved in creating the command center from a single block of wood.*

2-inch-by-4-inch lumber (actual size: 1½ by 3½ inches), cut to a length of 3¼ inches that are free of knots and other defects. Each piece must be cut down to a width of 3 inches. Then glue the two pieces together, surface to surface to form a block that measures 3 inches thick, 3 inches wide, and 3¼ inches long (Fig. 8-32A).

Once dry, draw two lines on the top end of the main body block. The first line is ⅞ inch in from the right edge, and the next is 1¼ inches in from the ⅞-inch line (Fig. 8-32B). Repeat this again on the front end. The result will be a 1¼-inch square drawn in the center of the wood block. Also draw a line 1¼ inches down along the four sides.

The next step is to file and sand away the wood material between the ⅞-inch lines on the top and the 1¼-inch line drawn on the sides. Repeat this process on the other three sides. When finished, the top of the landing vessel should look as shown in Fig. 8-33.

Fig. 8-31. The Planetary Landing Vessel has been developed to transport explorers and/or warriors from the mother ship to the planet surface.

Turn the main body upside down. Measure in from each side along the bottom 1⅛ inches. This will result in a ¾-by-¾-inch square drawn in the center. Next, on each side, measure ½ inch down from the end the ¾-inch square is drawn on. Draw a line around the main body at the ½ inch marks, as illustrated in Fig. 8-34A. File and sand from the 1⅛ inch line on the bottom end to the ½ inch line on the sides (Fig. 8-34, B and C).

While the main body is still in the inverted position, drill a ⅝-inch hole in the center of the ¾-inch square. The hole is for the rocket, which is actually a train smokestack sold by many of the toy parts mail order companies listed in the Appendix. The rocket/smokestack used on the Planetary Lander is the medium size (⅝ inch diameter

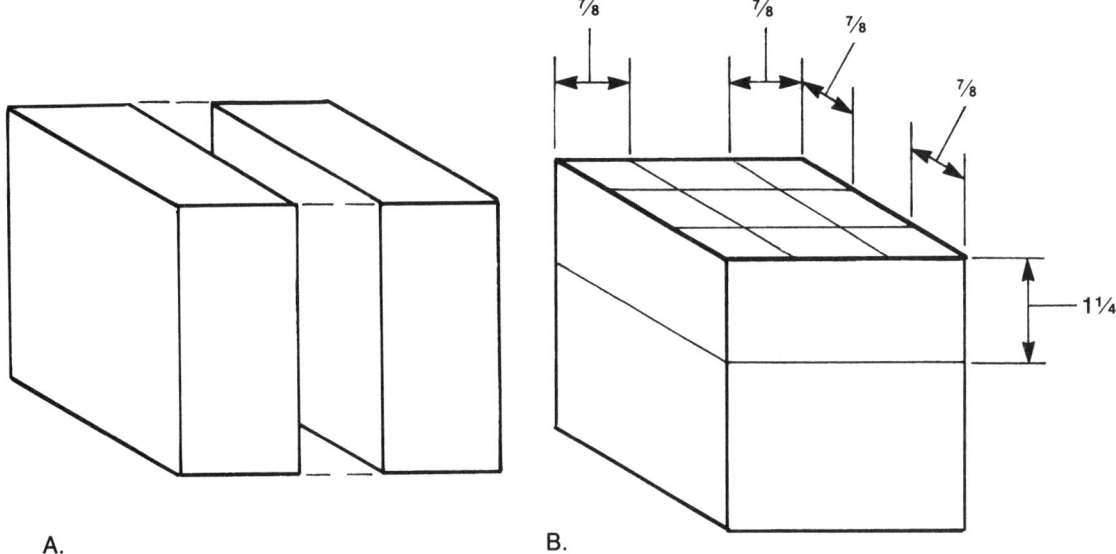

Fig. 8-32. (A) Glue the two pieces of lander body together. (B) Lay out the shaping lines on the lander body.

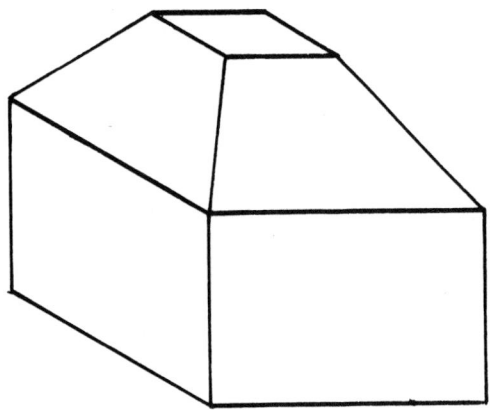

Fig. 8-33. The top of the lander body.

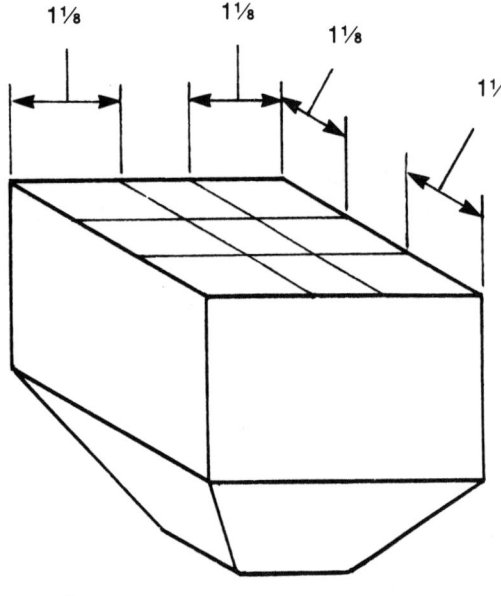

A.

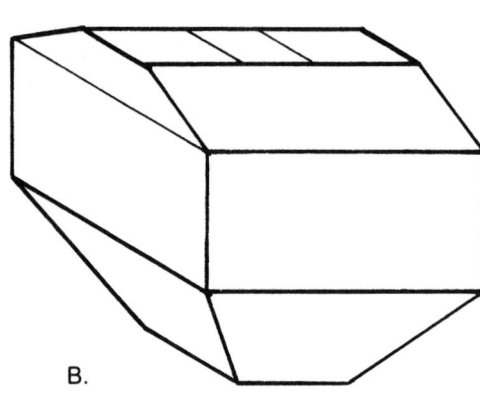

B.

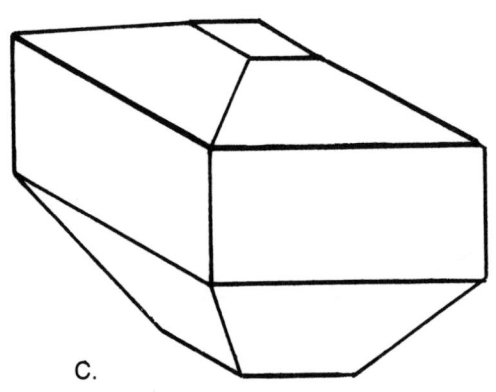

C.

Fig. 8-34. The three drawings in this illustration show (A) the measurements used in the layout of the bottom of the lander, (B) the first step in the shaping process, and (C) the finished shape.

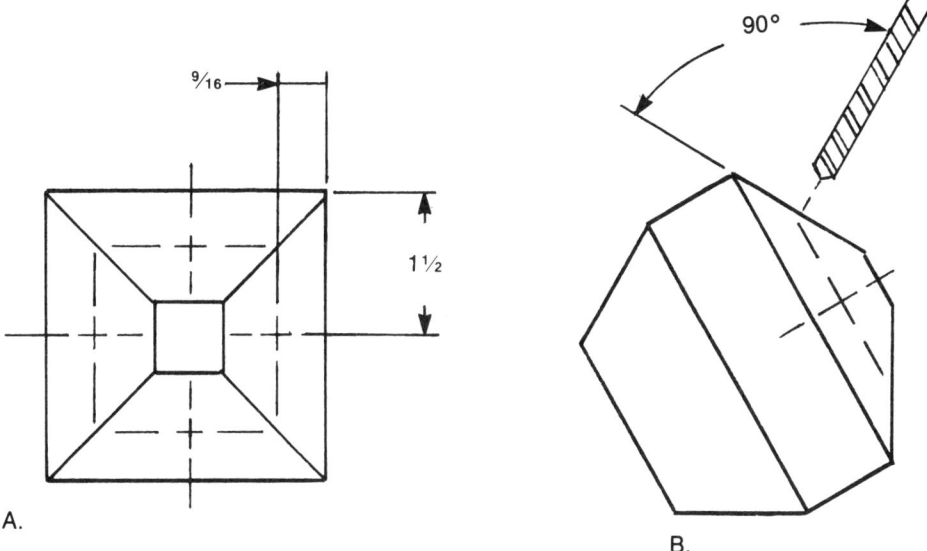

Fig. 8-35. *(A) The location of the four ⅜-inch-diameter holes in the bottom of the lander body's slanted sides. (B) Drill the holes at a 90-degree angle.*

shaft, 2⅝ inches long) sold by Toymaker Supply Company of Tahoe City, California.

The landing appendages, actually four lengths of ⅜-inch dowel, require that four ⅜-inch-diameter holes be drilled into the center of the slanted surfaces on the bottom of the main body. The center of the ⅜-inch-diameter holes is located along the slant ⁹⁄₁₆ inch in from the outside edges, and centered (Fig. 8-35A). These holes *must* be drilled at a *90-degree angle* to the slanted surface (Fig. 8-35B). If this is not done, the Planetary Landing Vessel will not be capable of standing properly.

Next, draw a line ⅝ inch in from each corner on the sides of the main body. The corners between the lines are removed with a file and sanded smooth (Fig. 8-36).

The final operation, prior to the assembly of the Landing Vessel, is to drill four ½-inch-diameter holes in the center of the flat portions of each side. Glue a ½-inch birch furniture button into these holes. These are the Lander's portholes.

For the assembly of the vessel, cut four pieces of ⅜-inch-diameter dowel rod to a length of 2¾ inches. Then glue dowels into the holes on the bottom of the Lander. Also glue the rocket into place. The rocket might be too long to fit into the hole, so the shaft must be cut to fit accordingly.

After allowing sufficient time to dry, sand the bottom of the Lander's appendages so that they sit flat. This is most easily done by moving the entire landing vessel across a full sheet of sandpaper laid on a bench. The vessel should be moved across the paper until the four legs are all flattened and set even.

The Planetary Landing Vessel is now assembled. Prior to the application of some form of protective material (oil, varnish, or paint), thoroughly sand the Lander. First use a medium/coarse sandpaper (80 to 100 grit) to remove any defects, then proceed with a sandpaper of a finer grit (150 grit) to smooth the surface.

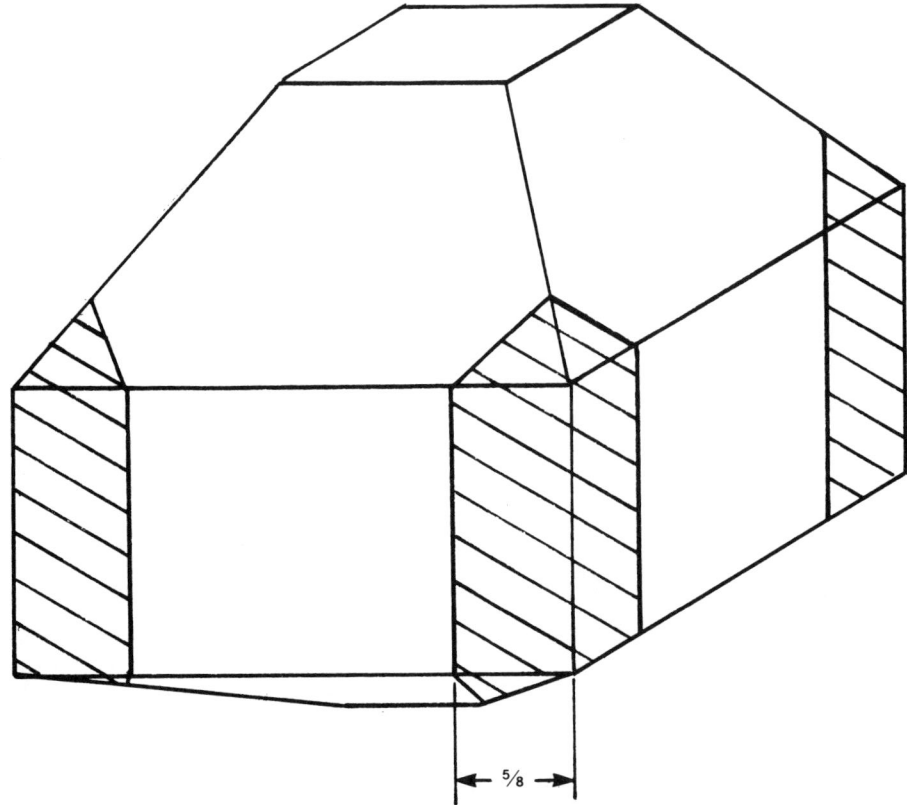

Fig. 8-36. *The final step involved in the shaping of the lander body is to remove the areas shaded here.*

The Planetary Landing Vessel is a necessary piece of equipment to be carried aboard the mother ship of a fleet and is a project that is sure to provide hours of healthy, safe, imaginative playtime for junior astronauts.

PLANETARY MOBILE UNIT (P.M.U.)

Astronauts who have been sent light years away to other planets and maneuvered multimillion dollar landing crafts to a soft landing, cannot be expected to simply walk around collecting soil and rock samples. The astronauts need a "car" to get around. That is why the Planetary Mobile Unit, P.M.U. has been designed (Fig. 8-37).

The P.M.U. has been designed to be built of materials commonly found in the shop. The forward section should be cut from a short piece of 2-by-4-inch lumber, while the rear unit should be cut from a short (3⅞ inch), narrow (2¼ inch) piece of ¾-inch-thick wood.

First, cut the 2-by-4 piece of lumber used for the forward compartment to a size of 1½ inches thick, 2¼ inches wide, and 4¾ inches long. On this piece of stock, measure back along one surface 2 inches and ⅜ inch up from the bottom on the front end (Fig.

Fig. 8-37. *The Planetary Mobile Unit (P.M.U.) is the astronaut's main source of transportation once on the planet surface.*

8-38A). Now draw a diagonal line on the side, from the line drawn on the front end, to the line drawn 2 inches back on the top surface (the broken line shown on the illustration).

Cut the excess material from the front of the forward compartment with a hand or power saw. Sand or file down to the line, as shown in Fig. 8-38B.

The next step in the forward compartment shaping is to measure ¾ inch in from each side (Fig. 8-38C) along the front end. Then draw a diagonal line from the front, along the incline surface previously cut, to a distance of 1¼ inches back from the front end. The forward compartment and the rear unit are attached to one another at a recess cut into the back of the front compartment and another on the rear unit. The recess in the forward compartment is cut 1 inch deep, and 1¼ inches in from the rear edge (Fig. 8-38D).

There are only two steps left in the shaping process. First, round the lower frame portion of the front compartment. Second, drill a 3/16-inch-diameter hole in the recessed area (Fig. 8-38E).

The rear unit of the P.M.U. is built from a small piece of ¾-inch-thick wood that is 2¼ inches wide, and 3⅞ inches long (Fig. 8-39A). Along the top surface, measure back ⅞ inch from the end and draw a light line. Also measure in from the edge 1⅛ inches, along the line just drawn. Where these two lines intersect, drill a ¾-inch-diameter hole, ½ inch deep. This hole will later be for the rotating antenna.

Next drill a 3/16-inch-diameter hole through the center of the ¾-inch hole, completely through the rear unit. Measure back from the rear end along the top surface 2 inches, and draw a line across the top surface. Along the rear end, draw a line ⅜ inch up from the bottom surface (Fig. 8-39B).

Like the front compartment, the rear unit must have a recess cut into the front end

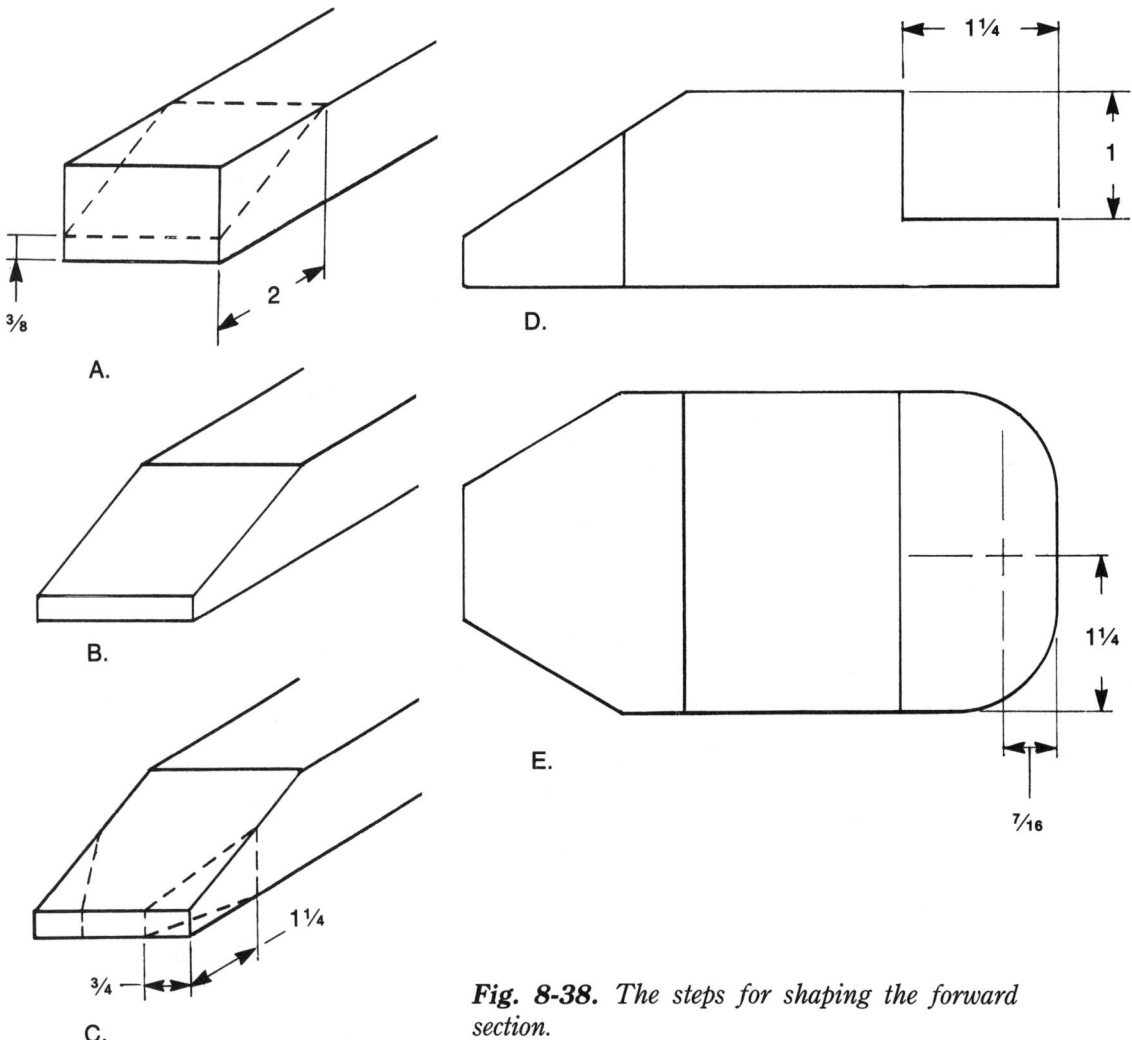

Fig. 8-38. The steps for shaping the forward section.

of the bottom surface. Figure 8-39C shows the exact size of the recess, which is ⅜ inch deep and ⅞ inch long. On the top surface of the rear unit, cut the back end at a light angle (Fig. 8-39D). Measure in from one side ½ inch and make a mark. Do the same from the other side. Now draw a diagonal line from the ½-inch marks to the 2-inch line previously drawn.

The last step is to round the front end of the rear unit. To do this, measure back from the front end 1⅛ inches. Set a compass for a radius of 1⅛ inches, strike the arc, then cut and sand the curve (Fig. 8-39E). Next, measure back from the end ⁷⁄₁₆ inch, and 1⅛ inches in from the side. Drill a ³⁄₁₆-inch-diameter hole.

The three axle supports that are glued to the bottom of the front and rear units each measure ¼ inch thick, ½ inch wide, and 2¼ inches long. Two of the three axle

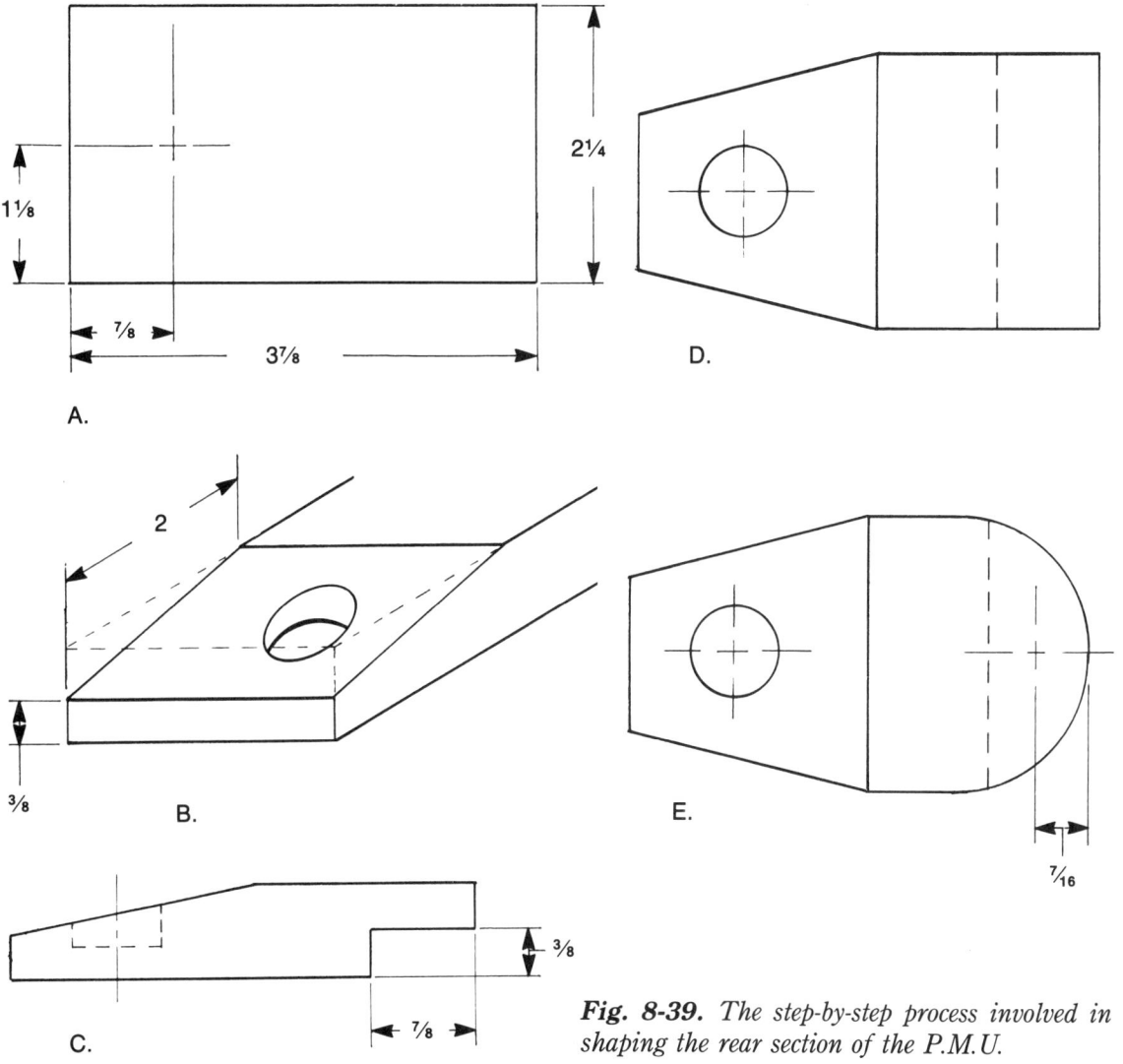

Fig. 8-39. The step-by-step process involved in shaping the rear section of the P.M.U.

supports are glued to the bottom of the front compartment, while the third is glued into place on the rear unit. The positions of each axle support are shown in Fig. 8-40. Notice that the rear axle support, once glued in place, is sanded at an angle equal to the angle already cut on the rear unit.

Drill 5/32-inch-diameter axle holes, 1 inch deep into the axle supports. Drill the holes on the forward-most axle support and the one located on the rear unit along the glue joint between the main body and the axle support. Drill the hole on the middle axle support slightly (⅛ inch) below the glue joint (Fig. 8-41), since the middle wheels are smaller than the forward and rear wheels.

After sanding the front compartment and rear unit, the main parts of the P.M.U.

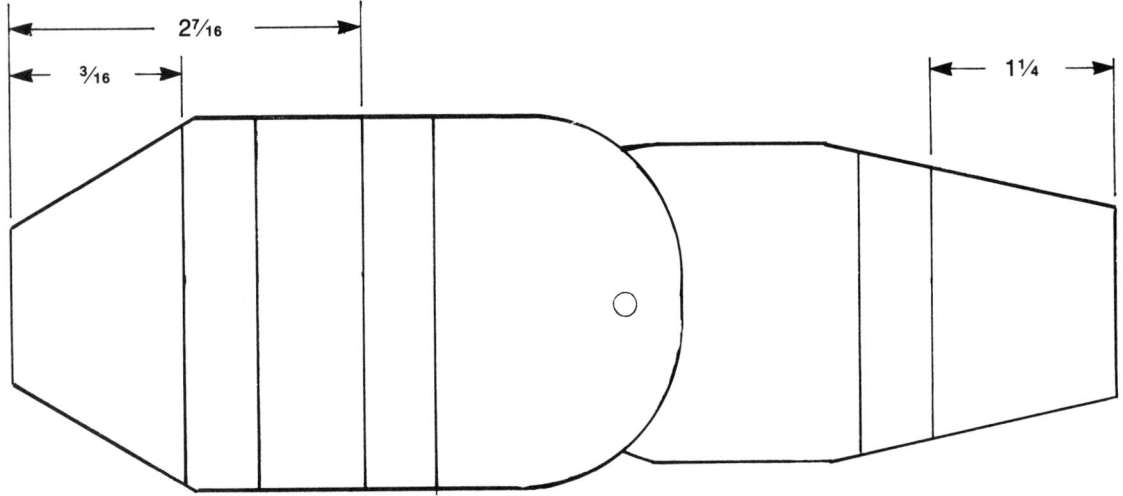

Fig. 8-40. *Glue axle supports onto the bottom of the Planetary Mobile Unit.*

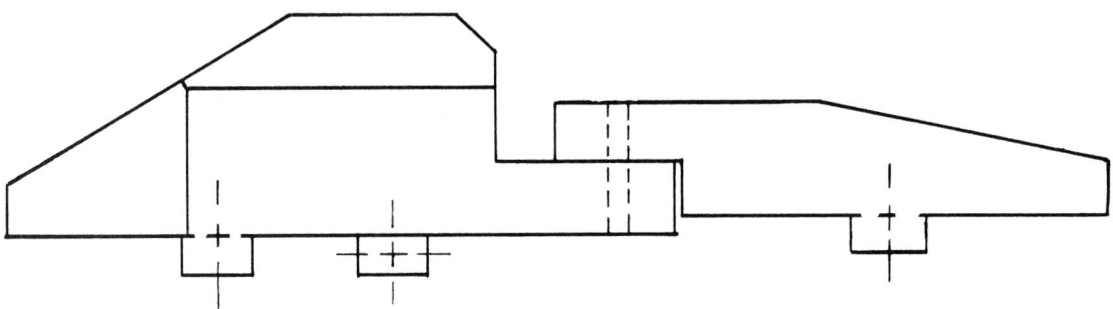

Fig. 8-41. *Drill the axle holes at two different heights. The forward and rear axle holes are drilled at the glue line between the body and the axle support, while the middle hole is drilled ⅛ inch below the glue line.*

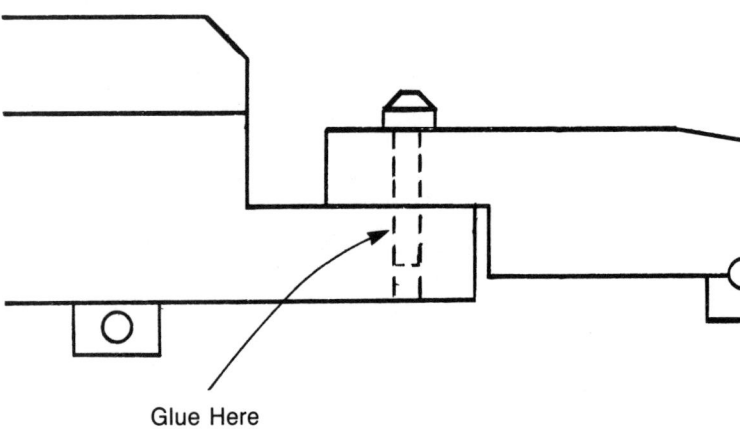

Glue Here

Fig. 8-42. *The forward and rear sections of the P.M.U. are permanently attached to one another by the use of an axle peg.*

can be assembled. Insert a 5/32-inch-by-7/8-inch axle peg into the two 3/16-inch holes drilled through the ends of the front and rear units (Fig. 8-42). Place a small amount of glue into the lower hole so the peg will go through the rear unit and be permanently secured to the front compartment.

Be careful not to allow glue to get into the upper hole, or the two units will be glued together and not swivel. The same is true with the axle pegs that are used to hold on the wheels. Only apply glue to the holes, not the wheels and holes. Otherwise, the wheels will not spin freely on the axle peg. The wheels on the sample are the wood wheels available from most toy parts suppliers, but they are put on backwards, to give them a more space-age appearance.

All that remains is to install the space-type gear to the P.M.U. The first to be assembled and installed is the rotating antenna. Cut a 1¼-inch length of ¾-inch dowel rod. On one end of the dowel, drill a 3/16-inch hole through the center to a depth of 5/8 inch. Cut the other end and sand to an angle. Figure 8-43 shows how the dowel should be cut. Also shown is the location of a hole drilled into the angled end of the dowel. The size of the hole is the same diameter as the axle pegs used, 3/16 inch, and is drilled to a depth of ¼ inch. Insert the axle peg through a 1¼-inch wood wheel and glue it into the hole just drilled.

The next three parts that are attached to the rear unit of the Planetary Mobile Unit are all cut from short pieces of dowel rod. The energy pods are cut from a piece of 3/8-inch-diameter and ½-inch-diameter dowel rod. Cut the ½ inch energy pod to a length of 1½ inches, and the 3/8-inch-diameter pod to 1⅜ inches. Round both ends of the dowels, then flatten one side slightly so it will lay flat. Glue the two energy pods into place on the flat surface of the rear unit.

The resource recovery compartment is cut from a 5/8-inch-diameter dowel. Cut it to a length of 1 inch, with one end rounded. Next drill a 5/8-inch-diameter hole 1¼ inches

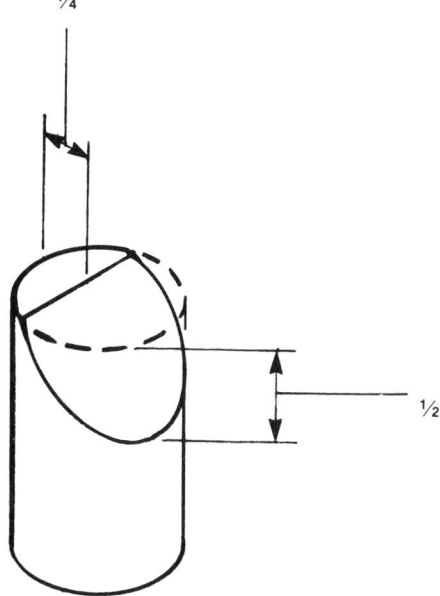

Fig. 8-43. The rotating antenna support is made from a length of ¾-inch diameter dowel rod, with an angle cut on top.

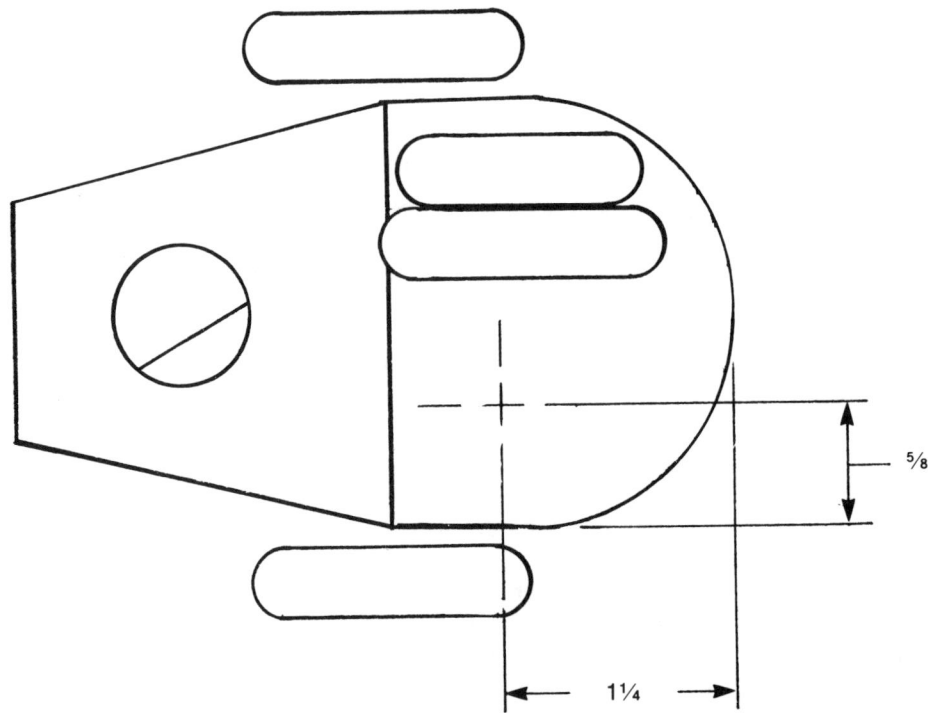

Fig. 8-44. *Glue the resource recovery compartment into the ⅝-inch hole in the rear section.*

from the front end and ⅝ inch in from the left side. The hole should be drilled to a depth of ½ inch (Fig. 8-44). Glue the resource recovery compartment into the ⅝-inch hole previously drilled.

The Planetary Mobile Unit is now ready for finish, oil, varnish, or paint. The choice is up to you. Then prepare to watch the junior astronauts explore even the roughest terrain and most bizarre planets.

VENUSIAN STAR CRUISER

Any junior astronaut will delight in receiving this space toy. The Venusian Star Cruiser (Fig. 8-45) consists of a main fuselage with two outboard propulsion pods. The project, from the toymaker's point of view, is a fun and easy-to-build spacecraft that requires very little material and only a few hours of time.

Construction begins with the main fuselage made up of three parts: the port (left) and starboard (right) halves, and the vertical stabilizer wing. The fuselage halves should both measure ¾ inch thick, 1⅞ inches wide, and 7 inches long. Cut the vertical stabilizer wing from a ⅜-inch-thick piece of wood, 3½ inches wide by 7 inches long.

Glue the three parts together to form the main fuselage. Then glue the ¾-inch-thick pieces on either side of the stabilizer wing (Fig. 8-46). Take care to align the bottom edges of the three parts flush with one another. Allow the parts to dry before any other work is done.

Fig. 8-45. The Venusian Star Cruiser is a spacecraft equipped for long-range flight.

The next step is to shape the main fuselage. First, draw the design directly on the wood (Fig. 47A). Next, cut excess material close to the line just drawn and sand down to the line (Fig. 8-47B).

To shape the main fuselage, draw out the design, place a ruler or straightedge along the bevel just cut (Fig. 8-48A); then draw a straight line from the front edge of the ⅜-inch-thick board in the center of the fuselage to the outside top of the bevel. Cut and sand down to the line on both sides (Fig. 8-48B).

On both sides of the fuselage, drill two 1-inch-diameter holes as shown in Fig. 8-49.

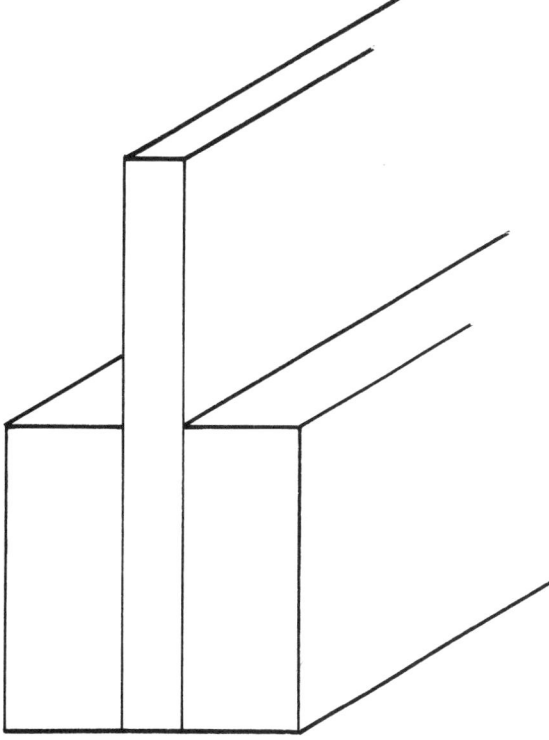

Fig. 8-46. Glue the two fuselage halves, port and starboard, onto the lower end of the vertical stabilizer wing.

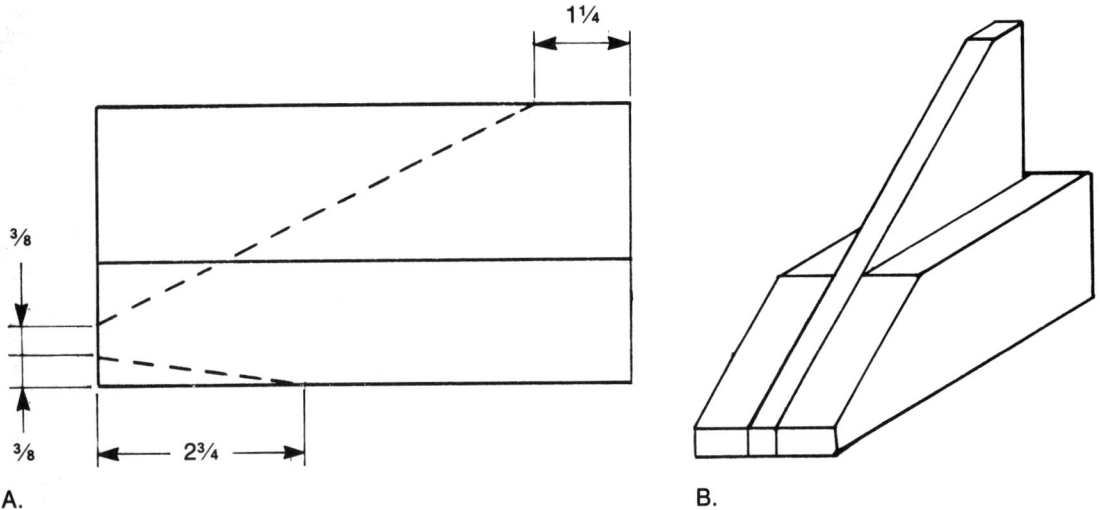

Fig. 8-47. *The fuselage/stabilizer unit needs to be shaped. Drawing (A) provides the design to be cut, while drawing (B) illustrates the fuselage unit once cut.*

These holes are where the traversing tubes connect to the outboard propulsion pods.

The outboard propulsion pods are each made from a piece of wood that measures 1¼ inches thick, 1½ inches wide, and 7 inches long. These may be cut from a piece of wood that is 1½ inches thick, then reduced to 1¼ inches.

To shape the front edge of the propulsion pods, follow the lines in Fig. 8-50A. On

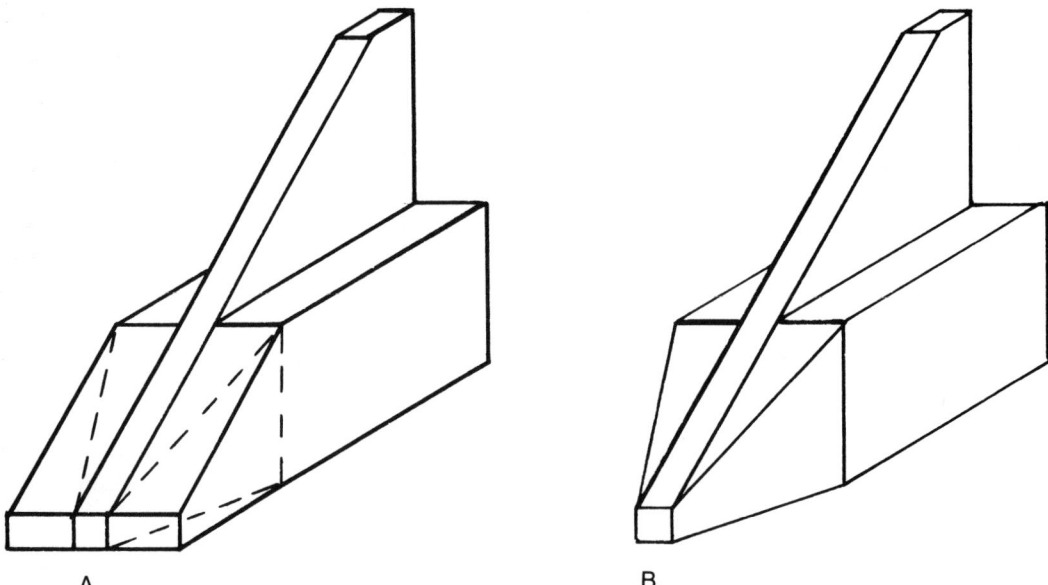

Fig. 8-48. *The next shaping operation for the fuselage unit is to (A) draw a diagonal line on each side of the front end, then (B) remove the material.*

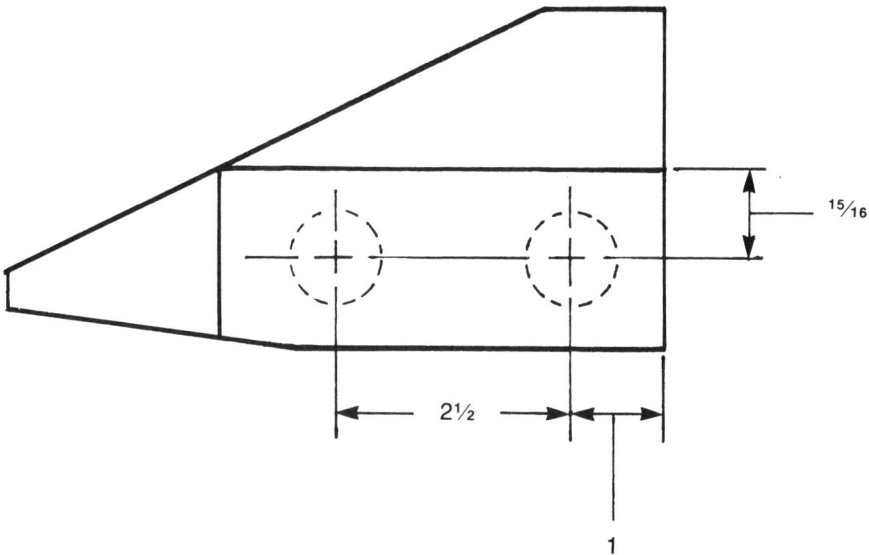

Fig. 8-49. *Drill two 1-inch-diameter holes on the port and starboard sides of the fuselage unit, at the points shown.*

the side, draw a straight diagonal line. As was done on the main fuselage, cut away the excess material and sand down to the line (Fig. 8-50B).

Next, measure along the front edge of the propulsion pods ½ inch in from the side and ¼ inch in from the point just marked. Draw a diagonal line with a straightedge. Drill two 1-inch-diameter holes in one side of the propulsion pods. These holes are located so that they will line up with those previously drilled in the main fuselage (Fig. 8-51). The holes need only be drilled in one side of the propulsion pods, to a depth of ¾ inch.

On the rear end of the propulsion pods, drill a ⅝-inch-diameter hole. This is the point where the thruster jets will be inserted. The thruster jets can be a short length of ⅝-inch dowel rod, cut to extend ¼ inch past the rear end of the propulsion pods, or a medium- to large-size smokestack (as shown in this example) sold by toy parts suppliers of toy trains.

Now, drill the jet thruster hole in the center of the end of the propulsion pod. To determine the exact location, draw two straight lines from corner to corner, then drill where the lines intersect. Another option is to insert another wood smokestack into the end of the main fuselage. The example built here has a large smokestack in the main fuselage and two smaller ones in the propulsion pods.

Next, cut four 1-inch-diameter dowel rods to a length of 2¼ inches. The dowel rods, when glued in place between the main fuselage and the propulsion pods, become the traversing tubes that allow for easy movement of the crew in the ship.

Sand all parts of the Venusian Star Cruiser, the main fuselage and the outboard propulsion pods. All rough surfaces and sharp corners *must* be rounded to prevent accidents. Once sanded, glue the star cruiser together, taking care not to allow glue to squeeze out and mar the surface. If clamps are not available to securely hold the ship

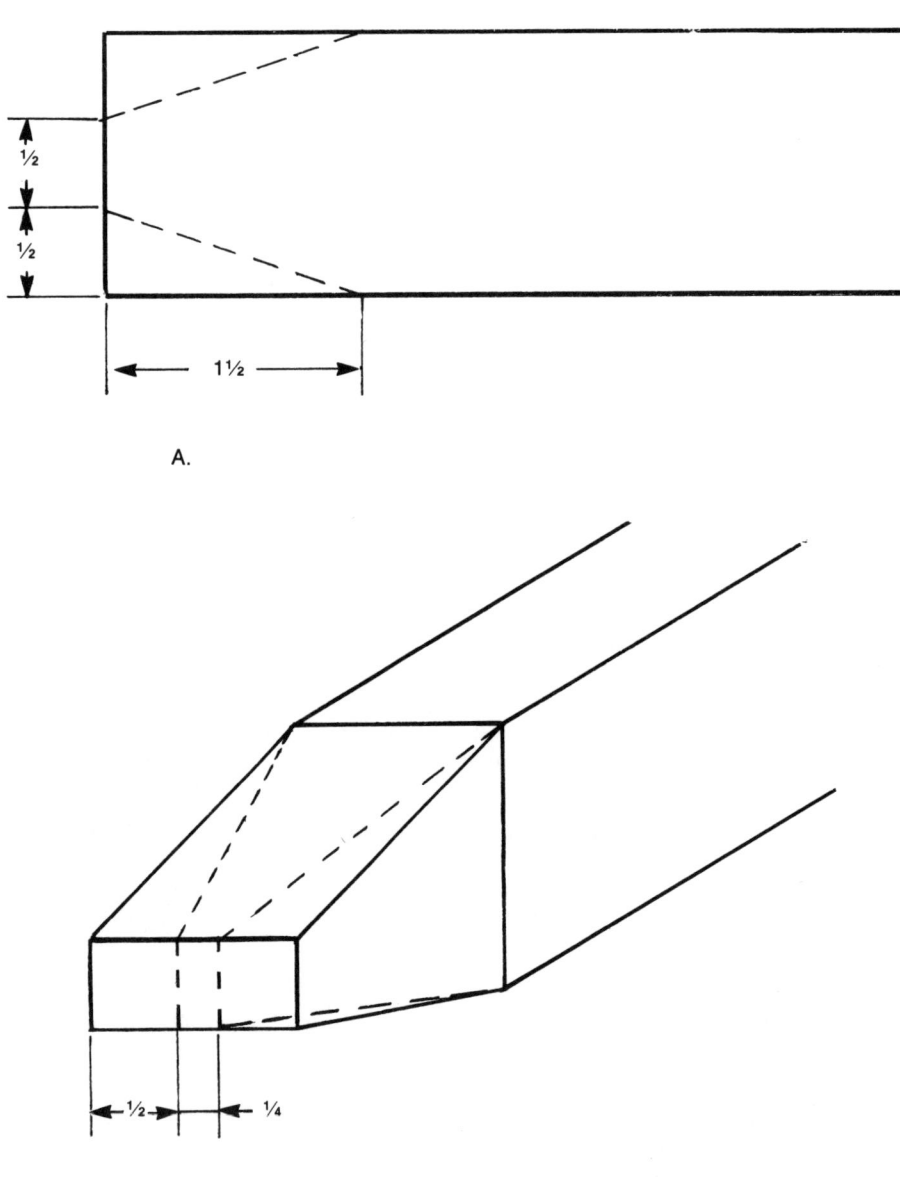

Fig. 8-50. Shape the front end of the propulsion pods in the same manner as the main fuselage. Drawing (A) illustrates the outline work necessary for shaping the side. Drawing (B) shows the shape for the top and bottom.

while the glue sets, two or three strong rubber bands can be used.

The Venusian Star Cruiser, like most of the projects in this book, does not require much of an investment in materials. In fact, the majority of the pieces required for the star cruiser can be found in the shop scrap box.

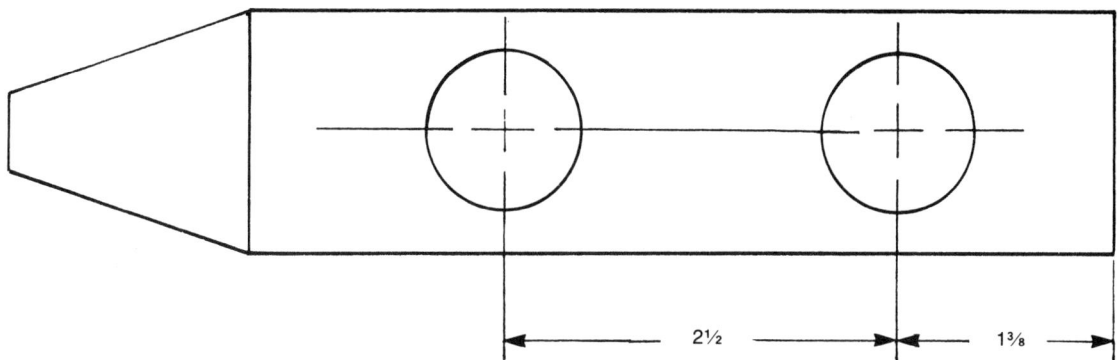

Fig. 8-51. *Drill two 1-inch-diameter holes in the outboard propulsion pods. These must be drilled in their exact location, in order to match the holes drilled in the main fuselage.*

TABLE 8-1. REQUIRED MATERIALS

Piper Cub

1	– Fuselage	– 2 × 4 × 11
1	– Wing	– ⅜ × 2 × 12
2	– Struts	– ⅜ × 1⅜ × 2¾
1	– Stabilizer	– ⅜ × 1¼ × 2¾
1	– Propeller	– ⅜ × ⅝ × 2¼
3	– Axle Pegs	– Small Size
2	– Wheels	– 1¼-inch diameter
3	– Dowel Pins	– ⅜-inch diameter × 1⅜
3	– Dowel Pins	– ¼-inch diameter × 1¼

Helicopter

1	– Helicopter Body	– 2 × 4 × 8⅜
1	– Main Blade	– ⅜ × ¾ × 8
1	– Tail Rotor	– ⅜ × ⅝ × 2¼
2	– Axle Pegs	– Small
2	– Pontoons	– ¾-inch diameter × 3¾
4	– Pontoon and Struts	– ⅜-inch diameter × 1⅜

Interstellar Fighter

2	– Port and Starboard Sides	– 1 × 1½ × 4¼
1	– Vertical Stabilizer	– ⅜ × 2⅛ × 4¼
1	– Horizontal Wing	– ⅜ × 4½ × 3⅞
1	– Pilot Control Center	– 1 × 1¼ × 2½
1	– Dowel Pin	– ¼-inch diameter × 2½
2	– Thruster Jets	– Small Train Smokestacks

Personnel Transporter

1 –	Vertical Wing	– ⅜ × 5 × 6
2 –	Fuselage Halves	– ¾ × 1½ × 5
1 –	Thruster Rockets	– Medium Toy Train Smokestacks
2 –	Diagonal Wings	– ⅜ × 3¾ × 5
8 –	Dowel Pins	– 3⁄16-inch diameter × 1¼
1 –	Command Center	– 1 × 1¼ × 2⅝
1 –	Dowel Pins	– ¼-inch diameter × 1¼

Planetary Landing Vessel

1 –	Main Body	– 3 × 3 × 3¼
4 –	Landing Appendages	– ⅜ inch diameter × 2¾
1 –	Rocket	– Medium Size Toy Train Smokestack
4 –	Furniture Buttons	– ½-inch diameter

Planetary Mobile Unit

1 –	Forward Compartment	– 1½ × 2¼ × 4¾
1 –	Rear Unit	– ¾ × 2¼ × 3⅞
3 –	Axle Supports	– ¼ × ½ × 2¼
9 –	Axle Pegs	– Size to Fit
1 –	Rotating Antennae Shaft	– ¾-inch diameter × 1¼
1 –	Energy Pod	– ½-inch diameter × 1½
1 –	Energy Pod	– ⅜-inch diameter × 1⅜
1 –	Resource Recovery Compartment	– ⅝-inch diameter × 1¼
4 –	Wheels	– 1¼-inch diameter
2 –	Wheels	– 1½-inch diameter
1 –	Antennae	– 1¼-inch diameter

Venusian Star Cruiser

1 –	Port Fuselage	– ¾ × 1⅞ × 7
1 –	Starboard Fuselage	– ¾ × 1⅜ × 7
1 –	Vertical Stabilizer Wing	– ⅜ × 3½ × 7
2 –	Propulsion Pods	– 1¼ × 3½ × 7
4 –	Traversing Tubes	– 1-inch diameter × 2¼

- Optional -

2 –	Thruster Jets	– Small Smokestacks
1 –	Main Pocket	– Medium or Large Smokestack

Orican Shuttle

1 –	Body	– 2 × 4 × 7

9
CHAPTER

Project Potpourri

The love and tenderness that is lavished on dolls by their young "mothers" is of amazing proportions. Dolls are taken everywhere, changed when they are wet, dressed, hugged, and loved. Why not build a cradle for the doll to sleep in? This cradle has been designed to resemble those which are used by "real" babies, but is down-sized for dolls. Although this cradle is of the proper size for "Cabbage Patch" dolls, the dimensions can be increased or reduced to fit any size doll.

DOLL CRADLE

Construction begins by cutting two pieces of wood that measure ¾ inch thick, 11 inches wide, and 11⅛ inches long. These will be the cradle ends. On the ends of the cradle, draw the shape in Fig. 9-1. First, reproduce the grid onto a sheet of paper or cardboard, drawing the shape onto the grid, and cutting out the shape. Then trace the pattern onto the end boards. Be sure to mark the center location that is shown on the grid pattern. At this center point, drill a ¼-inch hole, then cut the cradle ends to shape using a jig, band, scroll, or coping saw.

The cradle sides are made from two pieces of wood that measure ¾ inch thick, 4⅝ inches wide, and 20 inches long. You will then have to cut off a 1-inch-wide strip from each side (Fig. 9-2). The 1-inch-wide pieces will be used as the top rails of the cradle sides, while the remainder will become the cradle side bottoms. Place the two 1-inch-wide top rails and the cradle side bottom pieces next to one another, as shown in Fig. 9-3A. Clamped in this position, the boards will be easier to mark for the spindle holes which are to be drilled in each of the parts. Figure 9-3B shows the location where a line should be drawn across the boards.

At each line which crosses the edges of the side pieces, draw another line perpendicular to the first line, ⅜ inch in from the edge (Fig. 9-4). At each of these cross marks, drill a hole to attach the spindles. The exact diameter and depth of the hole is determined by the spindles that will be used.

The next step involves the lower inside surface of the sides. Cut a ¼-inch-wide, ⅜-inch-deep groove (Fig. 9-5). The ¼-inch-thick, 10-inch-wide, 20-inch-long bottom will fit between the grooves. The bottom can be made of ¼-inch-thick plywood or hardboard. The hardboard is suggested because it is smooth and free from splinters. Set the bottom aside for now, until the rest of the cradle is ready for assembly.

Scale: ½-inch squares

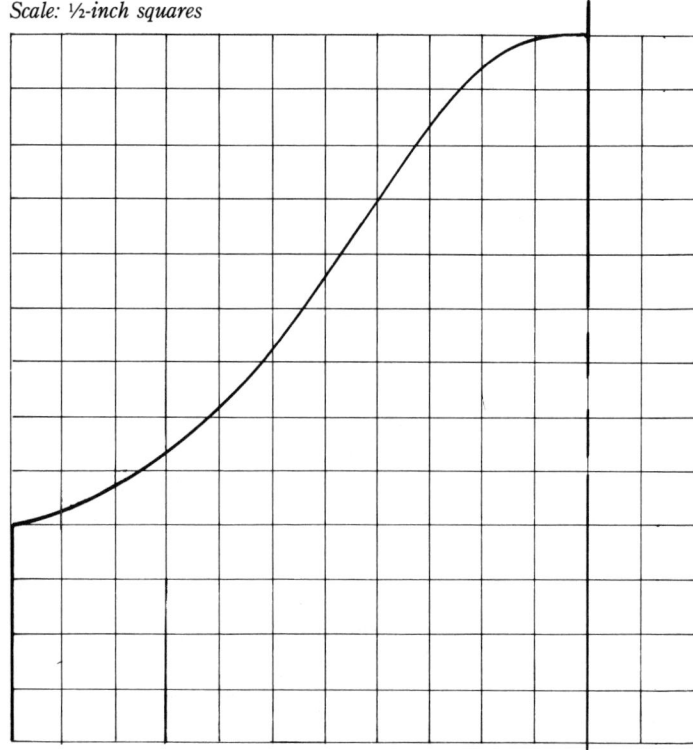

Fig. 9-1. The grid pattern shows the design of the top of the cradle ends.

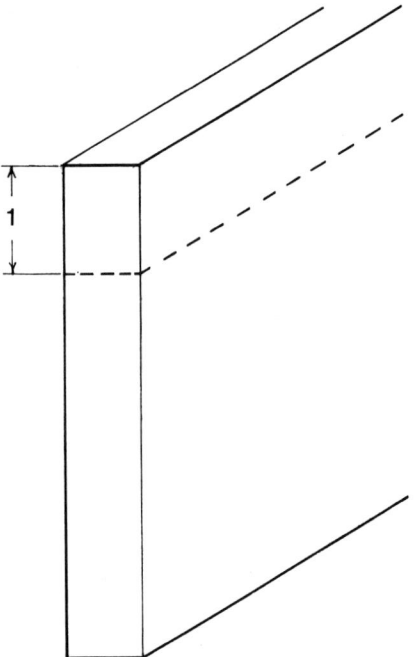

Fig. 9-2. Cut a 1-inch-wide strip off the side pieces, which will form the top rail.

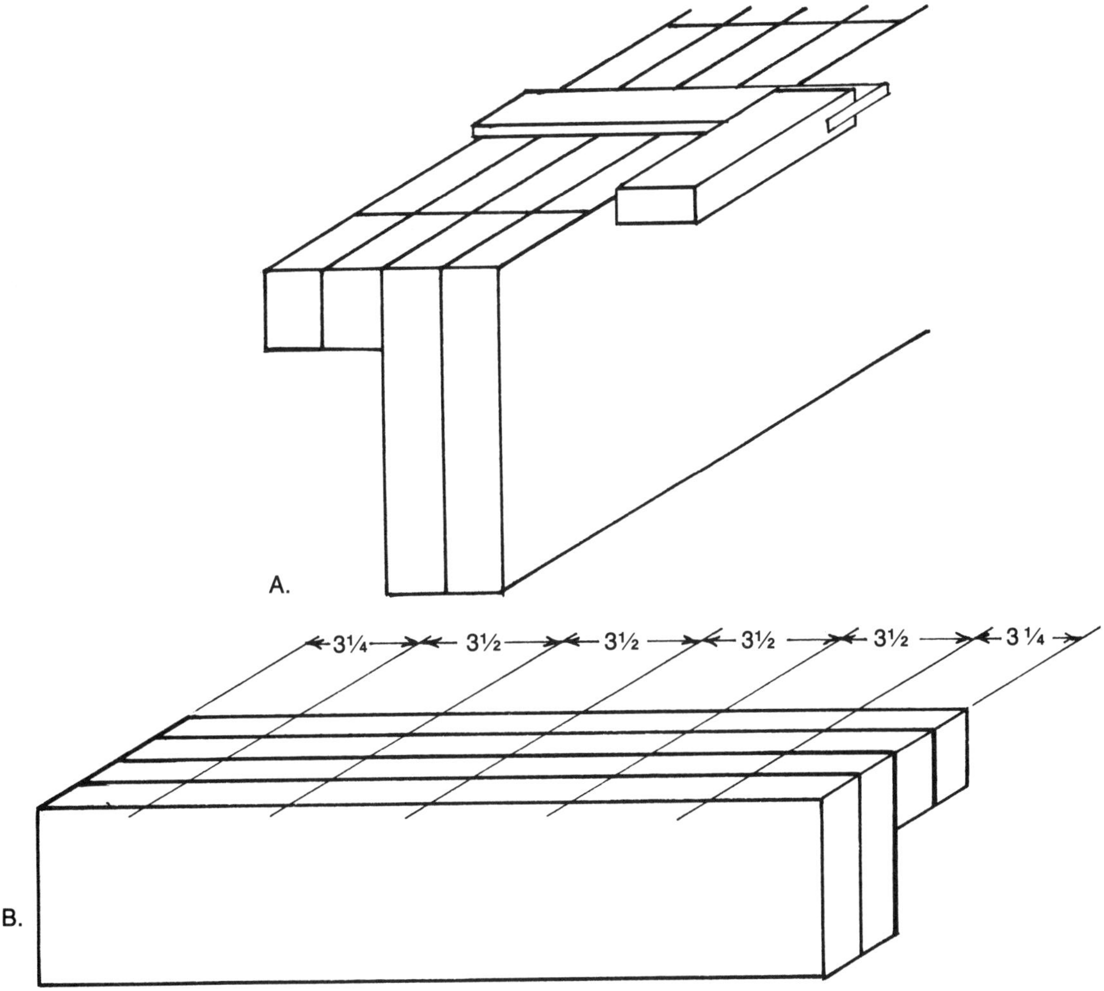

Fig. 9-3. The two drawings show an easy way to lay out the locations of the spindle holes.

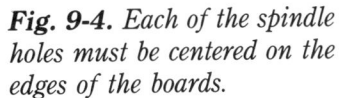
Fig. 9-4. Each of the spindle holes must be centered on the edges of the boards.
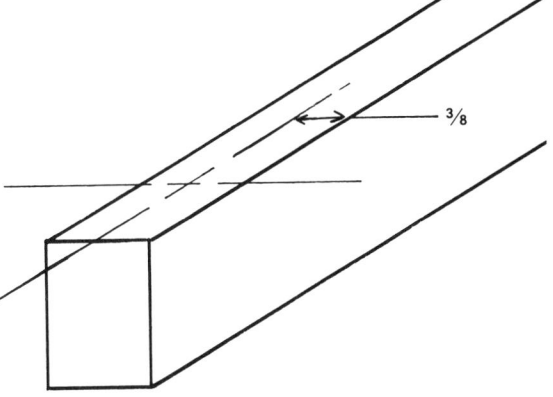

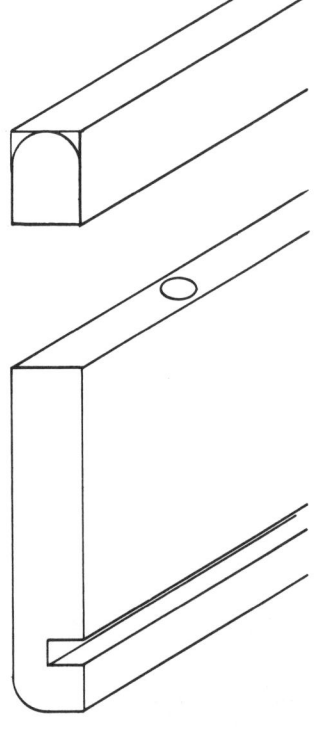

Fig. 9-5. On the inside bottom surface of the cradle sides, cut a ¼-inch-wide by ⅜-inch-deep groove.

The side pieces must have the sharp edges rounded to eliminate the possibility of scratches. This can be done with a router or with a file and sandpaper. Round the top edges of the 1-inch-wide strips and the lower outside edge of the side bottom. Once the rounding of the edges is completed, the side assemblies and ends should be sanded.

The doll cradle shown in the photographs has been assembled completely with wood dowels, although this is not necessary. Screws covered by furniture buttons may also be used for the assembly. In either case, when assembling the cradle, it is important

Fig. 9-6. The uprights, two bases, and horizontal support are the five pieces that make up the cradle support.

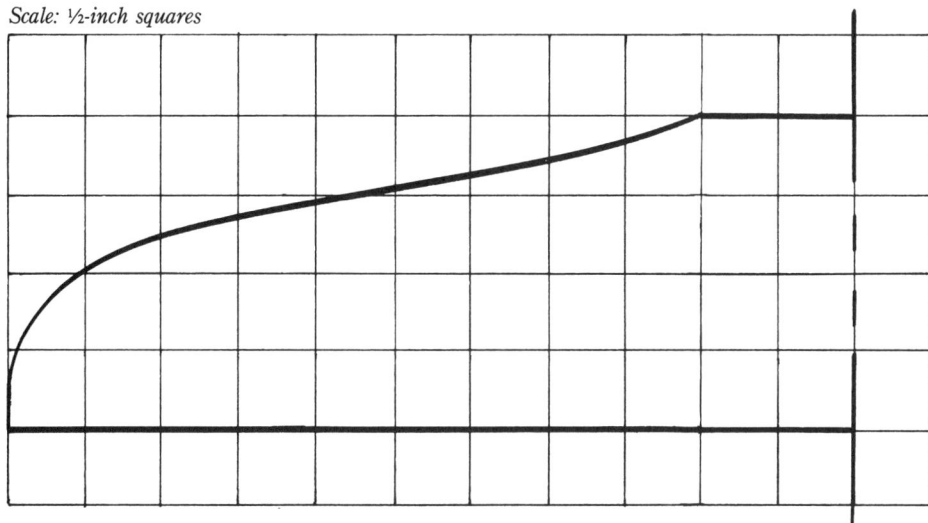

Fig. 9-7. *The design of the base pieces shown on a grid pattern.*

to remember to first insert and glue the ¼-inch-thick bottom between the two sides. Then attach the cradle ends to the sides. Set this assembly aside and allow it to dry.

Next to build is the cradle support. It is constructed of two 2-inch-wide-by-11-inch-long-by-¾-inch-thick bases, two 2-inch-wide-by-15¼-inch-long uprights, and one 1¾-inch-wide, 22-inch-long horizontal support (Fig. 9-6). Rip these pieces to their correct width, then crosscut to their appropriate lengths. Round the top ends of the two uprights by drawing a 1-inch radius with a compass, then cutting and sanding down to the line. Drill a 5/16-inch-diameter hole through both uprights where the compass point is set.

The two bases should also be cut to a decorative shape (see Fig. 9-7). Draw the design on a grid pattern, cut it out, then trace it onto the two ¾-inch-thick bases. The design should be cut out with a saw capable of cutting curves, then sanded. Then glue the two bases and screw (or dowel) onto the uprights (Fig. 9-8).

The horizontal supports can now be glued and screwed (or doweled) between the two uprights. The horizontal support is meant to hold the two uprights apart at the appropriate distance, so that the cradle will easily fit between and swing freely. When the parts are glued together, before the glue has had time to set, place the assembly on a flat surface, checking to be sure the two bases sit evenly.

Now the cradle and support should be either stained and varnished or painted. When dried, attach the two assemblies by inserting two ¼-inch dowels through the support upright and glueing them into the holes previously drilled into the cradle ends. If you wish, the dowels can be replaced with two 1½-inch-long axle pegs, shown in the photograph.

This is a sturdy, well-built cradle design that should easily last for many years, passing down from generation to generation. Build for today; but remember it could be tomorrow's heirloom.

Fig. 9-8. *The Creature Keeper is a great way to hold all types of creepy, crawling insects for youngsters to view and study.*

THE CREATURE KEEPER

Kids love to catch and keep all types of creepy crawling creatures that roam around the deepest jungles of our backyards. The Creature Keeper (Fig. 9-8) is an inexpensive project that results in a great place for bugs of all types to temporarily reside.

Begin with two pieces of wood that measure ¾ inch thick, 3½ inches wide, and 4¼ inches long. These two pieces will be the front and rear of the Creature Keeper. On the front piece measure down from the top 1¾ inches, and in from the edge 1¾

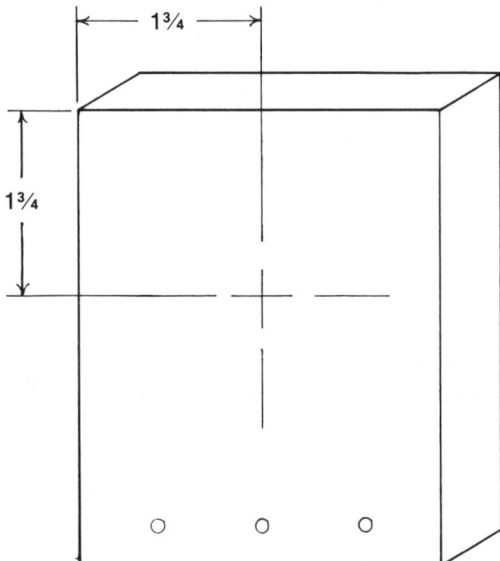

Fig. 9-9. *Drill a 1½-inch hole at the point indicated for the creature hole.*

inches (Fig. 9-9). Where these two points meet, drill a 1½-inch-diameter hole.

Another piece of wood ¾ inch thick, 3½ inches wide, and 4½ inches long will be needed for the Creature Keeper base. Nail the base between the front and rear ends. Three nails in each end should hold the ends securely to the base.

A piece of nylon screen is needed for the sides and top of the Creature Keeper. Conventional metal window screen should not be used, for this will result in sharp pointed ends that pick and scratch. The nylon, fabric type, will provide safe cage walls. A piece of screen that measures 6 inches by 12 inches should be large enough to cover the sides and top, and still allow the ends to be turned under to keep the ragged screen ends out of harm's way. The screen is readily held in place by small tacks with a head large enough not to pull through the screen holes. Space the nails about 1¼ inches apart.

Cut a cage door from a section of ¼-inch plywood. The door measurements are 2½ inches wide by 3 inches long. The top end of the door can be rounded for appearance's sake. Drill a ⅛-inch-diameter hole ½ inch down from the top of the door and center between the edges. Through the hole, insert a 1-inch long, number 6 roundhead screw, and screw it into the front of the cage. The exact location of the screw is 1¾ inches in from the sides and ⅝ of an inch down from the top edge. The door should now swing freely from side to side to provide access to the cage.

The Creature Keeper can be left natural—paint or varnish is not necessary on this project. All that remains to complete the Creature Keeper is to place a few leaves and a bit of grass on the floor of the cage. Then it's off to search for the "wild creature" in the backyard!

35MM CAMERA

Thirty-five-millimeter cameras can be seen everywhere. Everybody seems to have one. Why not make one for the kids? Our camera is made entirely out of wood (Fig. 9-10). Although the camera in the photograph has been built using two different colors of wood, this is not necessary. Each piece is made from readily accessible ¾-inch-thick wood.

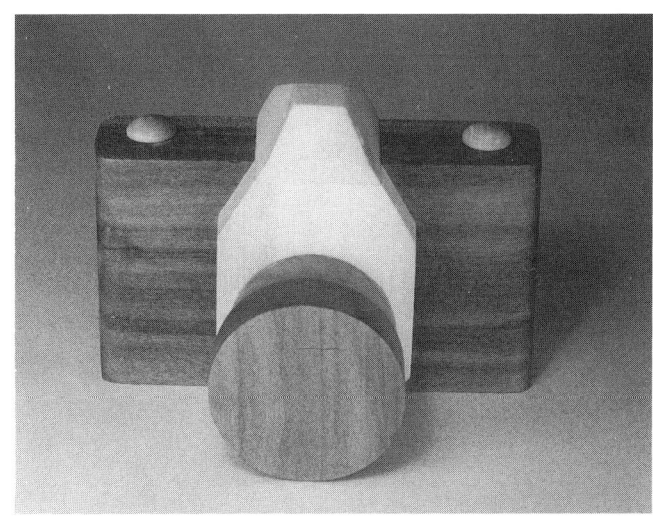

Fig. 9-10. Children enjoy doing as they see parents and other adults do. This includes taking photographs with a 35MM camera. The camera shown here will provide hours of fun for youngsters.

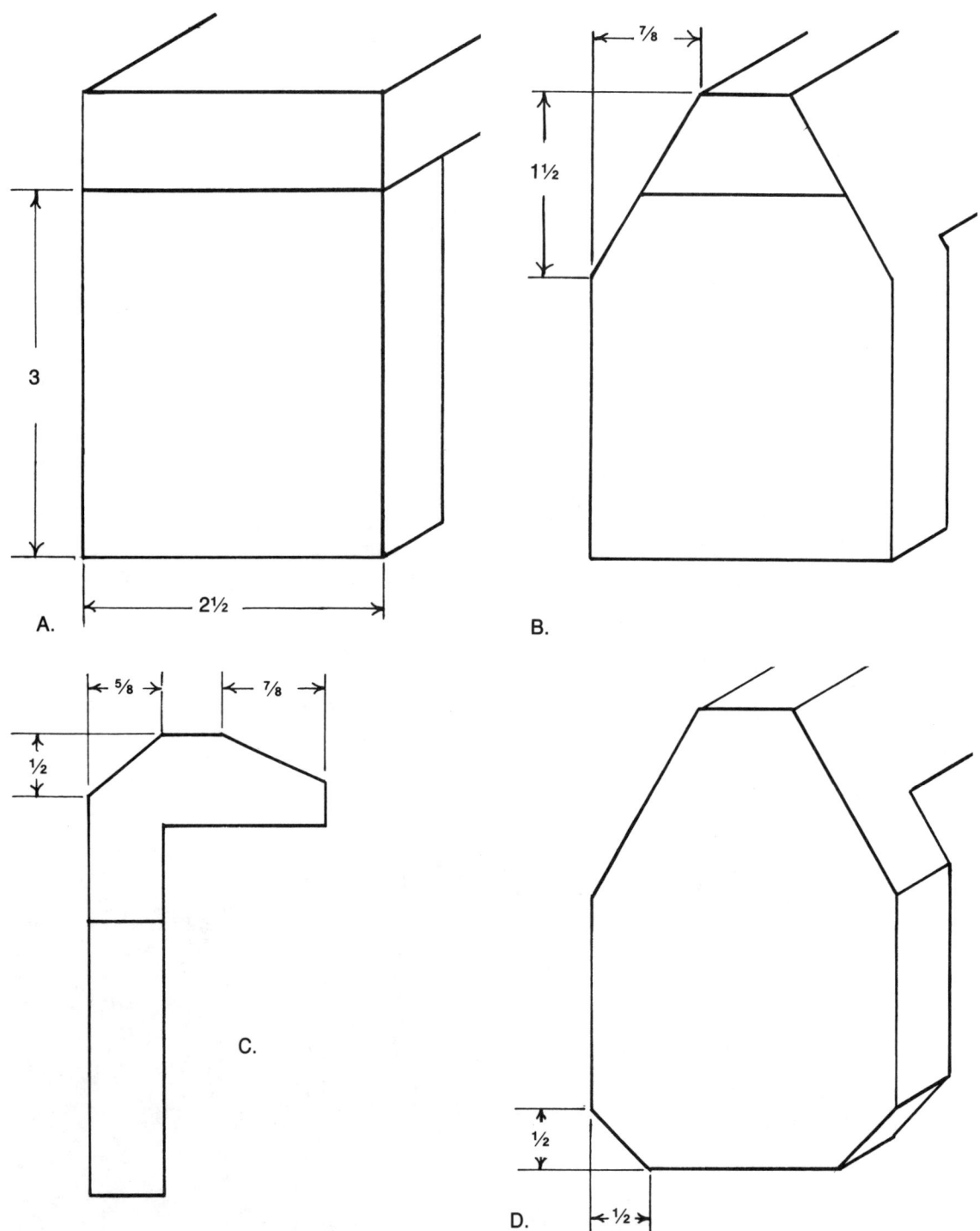

Fig. 9-11. *This series of drawings shows the steps involved in shaping the 35MM camera viewfinder.*

Begin by building the camera body, which is 1½ inches thick. First glue two ¾-inch-thick, 3-inch-wide, and 5½-inch-long boards together. Join them surface to surface, creating a solid block 1½ inches thick, 3 inches wide, and 5½ inches long.

The lens area is made from a piece of ⅝-inch-thick wood that is 2½ inches wide and 3 inches long. Glue to the top edge of this the ¾-inch-thick, 2½-inch-wide, and 2-inch-long viewfinder (Fig. 9-11A).

When the glue between the viewfinder and the lens area has set, measure down 1½ inches on both sides of the front edge and ⅞ inch in from both sides along the top (Fig. 9-11B). Draw a line from the lower mark, up diagonally, to the upper mark. Then cut away the excess material and sand down to the line.

The next step involves the side of the assembly (Fig. 9-11C). Measure down ½ inch from the leading edge, and ⅝ inch in from the leading edge back. Draw a diagonal line between these two points. Along the top edge, measure back from the rear edge ⅞ inch. Also on the rear edge, measure up ⅜ inch and again draw a diagonal line between these two points. Cut and remove the material down to the two diagonal lines (Fig. 9-11D). Notice that there are two ½-inch-by ½-inch cuts on the bottom of the lens area. These are made for appearance's sake only. All that needs to be done with the lens/viewfinder assembly is to glue it in place, centered on the camera body.

The lens is made up of two wood disks. The first disk is ¾-inch thick and 2 inches in diameter, while the outside disk is the same thickness, but 2¼ inches in diameter. Carefully glue the two disks together, centering the smaller disk in the larger. There should be ⅛-inch difference around the disk. Clamp this and allow it to dry. While it is drying, turn your attention to the lens area that has been glued onto the camera body.

Measure up from the bottom, as shown in Fig. 9-12, 1⅛ inches and make a light

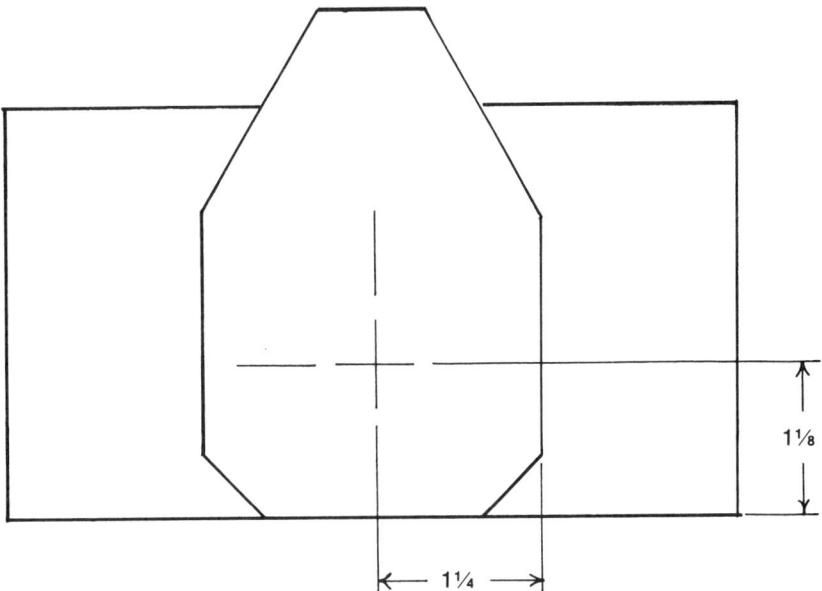

Fig. 9-12. Glue the camera lens to the camera viewfinder at the exact location shown in this drawing.

pencil mark. Next, measure in from the side of the lens area 1¼ inches, and form a cross where the two marks meet. This shows where the center of the small disk must be glued. To ease the job of aligning the lens, draw a 2-inch-diameter circle with a compass, using the point where the lines cross as the center mark. Then glue the lens assembly (the two glued disks) to the lens area, centering within the 2-inch-diameter circle just drawn. Clamp this, allowing plenty of time for it to dry.

For a finishing touch, the camera shown in the photograph has two large furniture buttons glued into the top of the camera body. The centerpoints of the buttons are located ¾ inch in from both ends and ¾ inch in from the rear of the camera.

The camera should then be examined carefully for any rough edges or sharp corners that might cause injury to young photographers. Once all sanding is completed, the camera can be finished in a number of ways. It can be painted to resemble your favorite "35," stained, varnished, or oiled.

Whatever the finish, this is one project that will be a big hit with the kids. They can imitate adults and take it on trips. The 35MM Camera is also a nice project for the craftsperson. After all, it is a "snap" to make.

KRAYON KEEPER

Most parents with young children are sure to find at least one of the kids' coloring crayons under the couch or bed, fallen behind the desk, or the whole box scattered on the floor. This is a problem, for the crayons are easily broken if stepped on, and might even permanently stain the carpeting. Sure, they may be kept nice in the cardboard box they are sold in, but though they appear to be sturdy enough to hold up to abuse, they often fall apart. Anyway, it's more fun for youngsters to use a Krayon Keeper (Fig. 9-13).

Fig. 9-13. *Krayon Keepers are a great way for a child to organize his or her coloring crayons.*

Krayon Keepers can be built from common 2-by-4 pine material, in a variety of familiar shapes. The construction of the Krayon Keeper only requires you to transfer the pattern onto wood, cut out the pattern, sand, and drill a series of holes in the upper edge. These general instructions apply to each of the designs presented in this section; but they may also be used to build any other shapes you can dream up.

The four grid patterns shown in Fig. 9-14 illustrate the design for a pig, a whale, a truck, and a snowmobile. Each design has been drawn on a ½-inch-square grid pattern

Scale: ½-inch squares

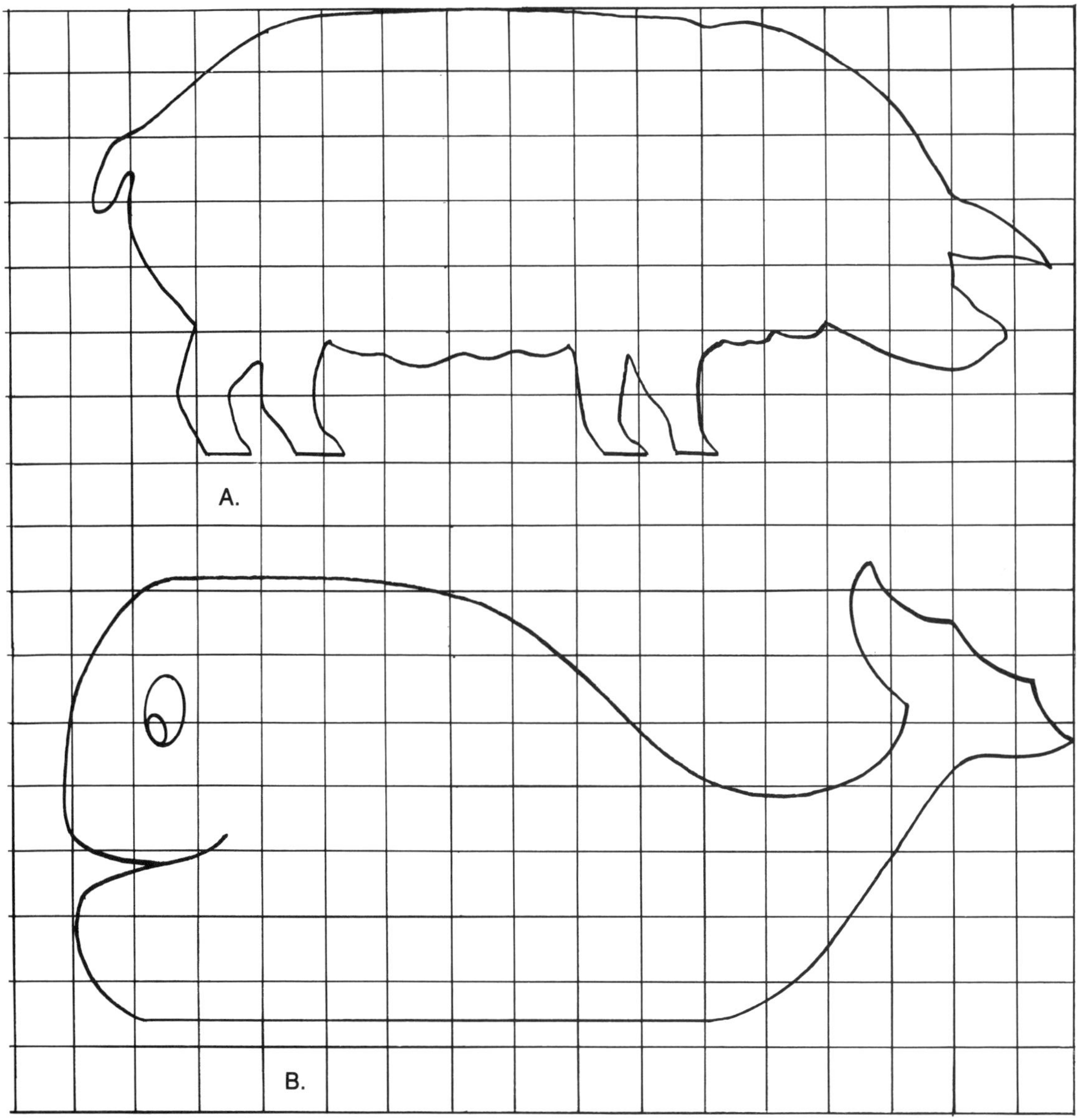

Fig. 9-14. *This illustration shows the four Krayon Keepers drawn on a grid pattern.*

161

to assist you in transferring the designs onto wood. If you plan to make several of these, perhaps for resale at craft shows or for gifts, I advise you to draw the designs onto a heavy piece of cardboard or hardboard to create a templet that can be used several times.

After cutting and sanding the shapes, drill the holes into the top edge at ½-inch intervals, with the center of each hole ⅜ inch in from the edges (Fig. 9-15). The best diameter for the crayon holes is 7/16 inch. This size will allow plenty of space for a crayon to be easily put into and removed from the Krayon Keeper. If a 7/16-inch drill bit is not available, a ⅜-inch-diameter hole will work for most crayons. The crayon holes should be drilled to a minimum depth of ½ inch. If the project design permits the holes to be drilled deeper, the depth should be increased to ¾ inch or 1 inch.

The four designs shown in the text are by no means the only designs that can be made. These are only examples. With this project, you can let your imagination run wild and create a wide variety of Krayon Keepers. The more designs presented to the buying public at craft stores, the better the sales. Whichever design you select, this project will sell well, and will also be a gift welcomed by parents and children alike.

CLIPBOARDS AND LAP BOARDS

Clipboards are handy items for the child who enjoys sitting on the floor while writing, drawing, or coloring. The small clipboard is the size and shape of those commonly found in office supply stores. They are also great to keep in the car for entertaining the children on long trips (Fig. 9-16).

The second project is a larger board, shaped and sized to be used as a lap board. It is large enough to be supported by the knees of a child sitting cross-legged on the floor, or for a child (or adult) who is confined to a bed. The clip holds the drawing paper, crossword puzzle, or coloring book securely in place while the crayon holders on the left side (or right side for left-handed users) holds twenty crayons within easy reach of the user. Both boards have rounded corners; but the larger lap board also has a curved bottom to fit against the user's waist.

Only the size and shape are different between the two boards. Construction is similar. Both boards can be made with either ⅛-inch or ¼-inch-thick hardboard. The small board measures 9¼ inches wide by 13 inches long (Fig. 9-17). Be sure to round the four corners to a radius of ¾ inch. Center the clip on the top of the board and pop rivet in place. Since not all clipboards have the same size clip, you must determine the location of the rivet holes by measuring the clip to be used.

The large lap board is also cut from either ⅛-inch or ¼-inch-thick hardboard. However, the ¼-inch-thick hardboard offers more support for a longer piece of wood. The width and length of the lap board are 16½ inches wide by 24 inches long. You can alter these dimensions, if necessary, to meet the needs of the user. Refer to Fig. 9-18 to determine the exact size and shape.

Determine the location of the rivet holes by measuring the clip that will be used. The clip itself is located 7 inches in from the right side, measured from the edge to the center of the clip. (For left-handers, the clip is on the left side.)

The lap board can be equipped with crayon holders made from pieces of wood 1½ inches thick, 2 inches wide, and 4⅛ inches long. To make the wood crayon holder shown, drill ten ⅜-inch-diameter holes, 1¾ inches deep. Figure 9-19 illustrates where to drill the holes.

Scale: ½-inch squares

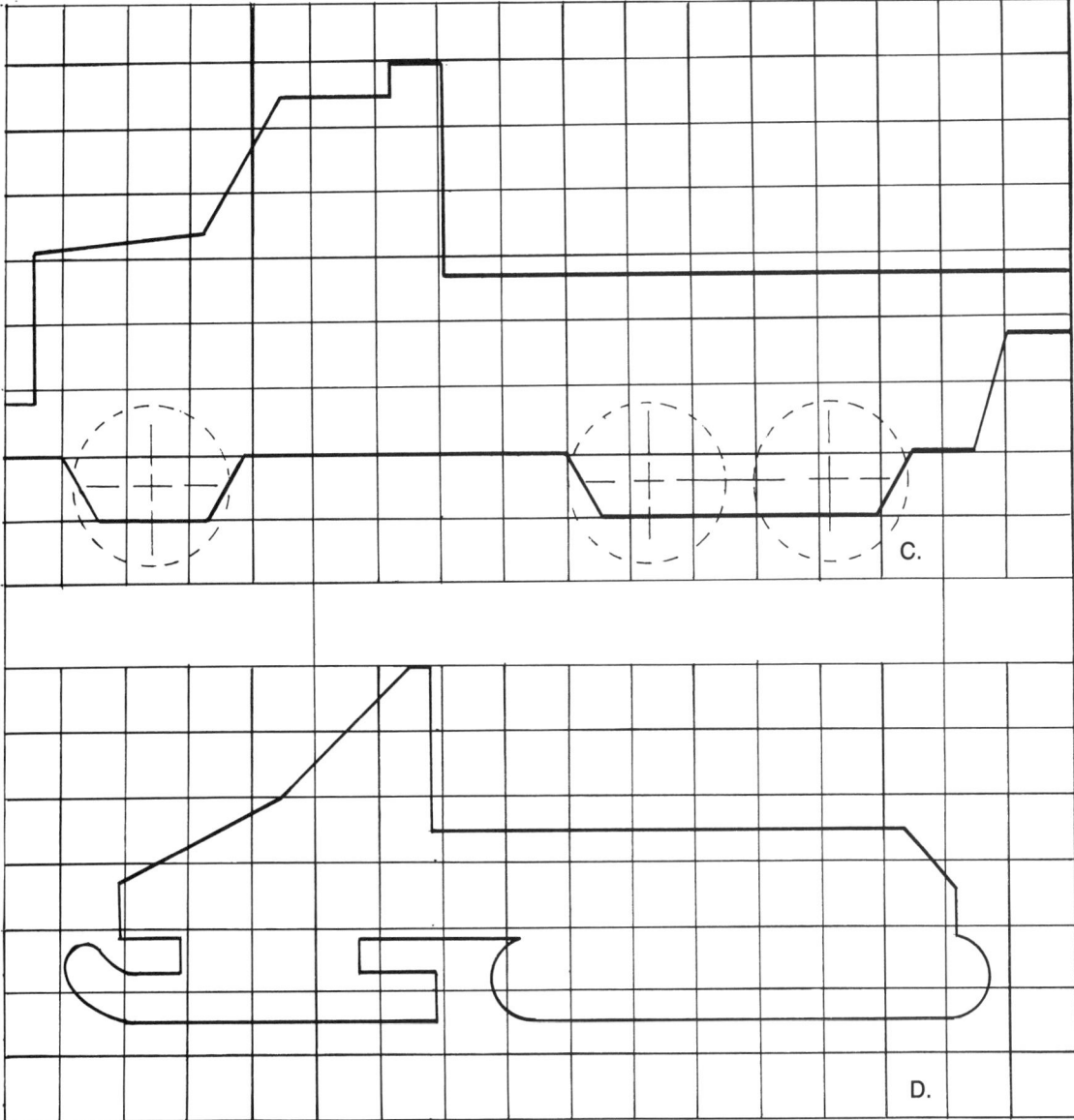

Fig. 9-14. *Continued.*

Round the front edges of the crayon holders to eliminate scratches or bruises from sharp corners. Next, glue the top crayon holder onto the lap board, 6 inches down from the top edge and the bottom holder 6 inches down from that. Then using two number 6, ¾-inch-long flathead wood screws, screw from the back, through the board, and into the crayon holder. Be sure the heads of the screws are recessed below the surface of the hardboard so they will not snag clothing.

The large lap board can be modified for adults by simply eliminating the crayon holders

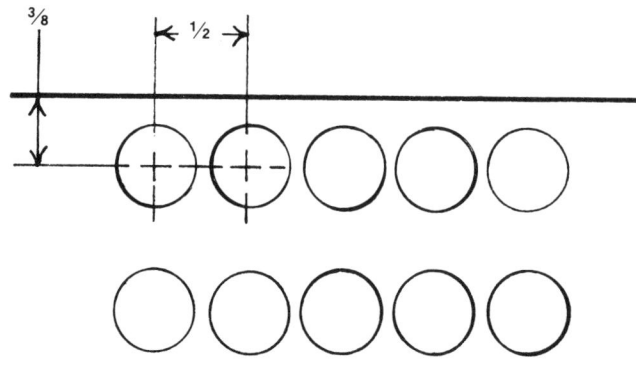

Fig. 9-15. *Drill the Krayon Keeper crayon holes as shown.*

and centering the clip, to become a newspaper crossword puzzle board. The clipboards are easy-to-make projects that are not only fun, but also functional.

DOLL BED

The Doll Bed project (Fig. 9-20) can be built from a 39-inch length of 1-by-10 pine. (The actual size of a 1 by 10 is ¾ inch thick and 9¼ inches wide.) Begin construction by cutting the board into three pieces. The headboard is 14 inches long; the footboard is 10 inches long; and the mattress board is 14 inches long.

There are two methods to build the doll bed. The first is for those who have access to power machines that are capable of cutting dado joints. These dado joints will be used to attach the head, foot, and mattress supports (Fig. 9-21A). The second method is to glue and nail two glue blocks to the head and footboards. These blocks are then used to support the mattress board (Fig. 9-21B).

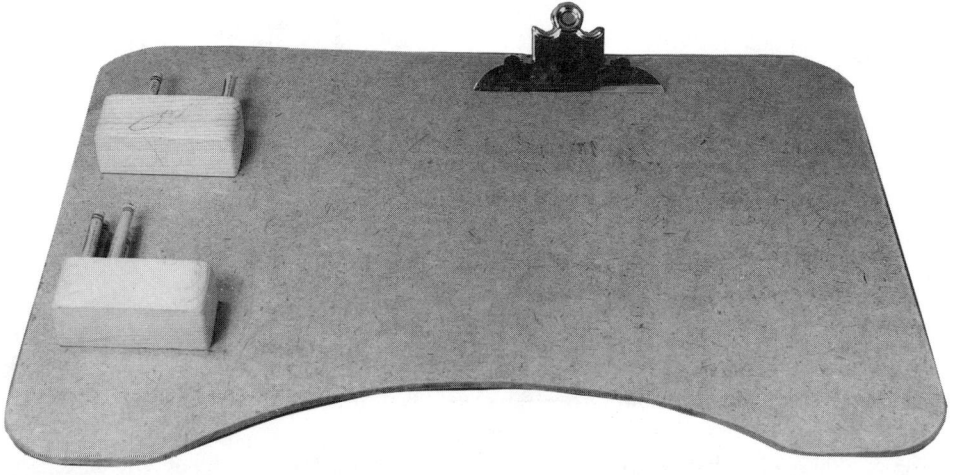

Fig. 9-16. *The clipboard and lap board are great projects that enable kids to color or write while sitting comfortably.*

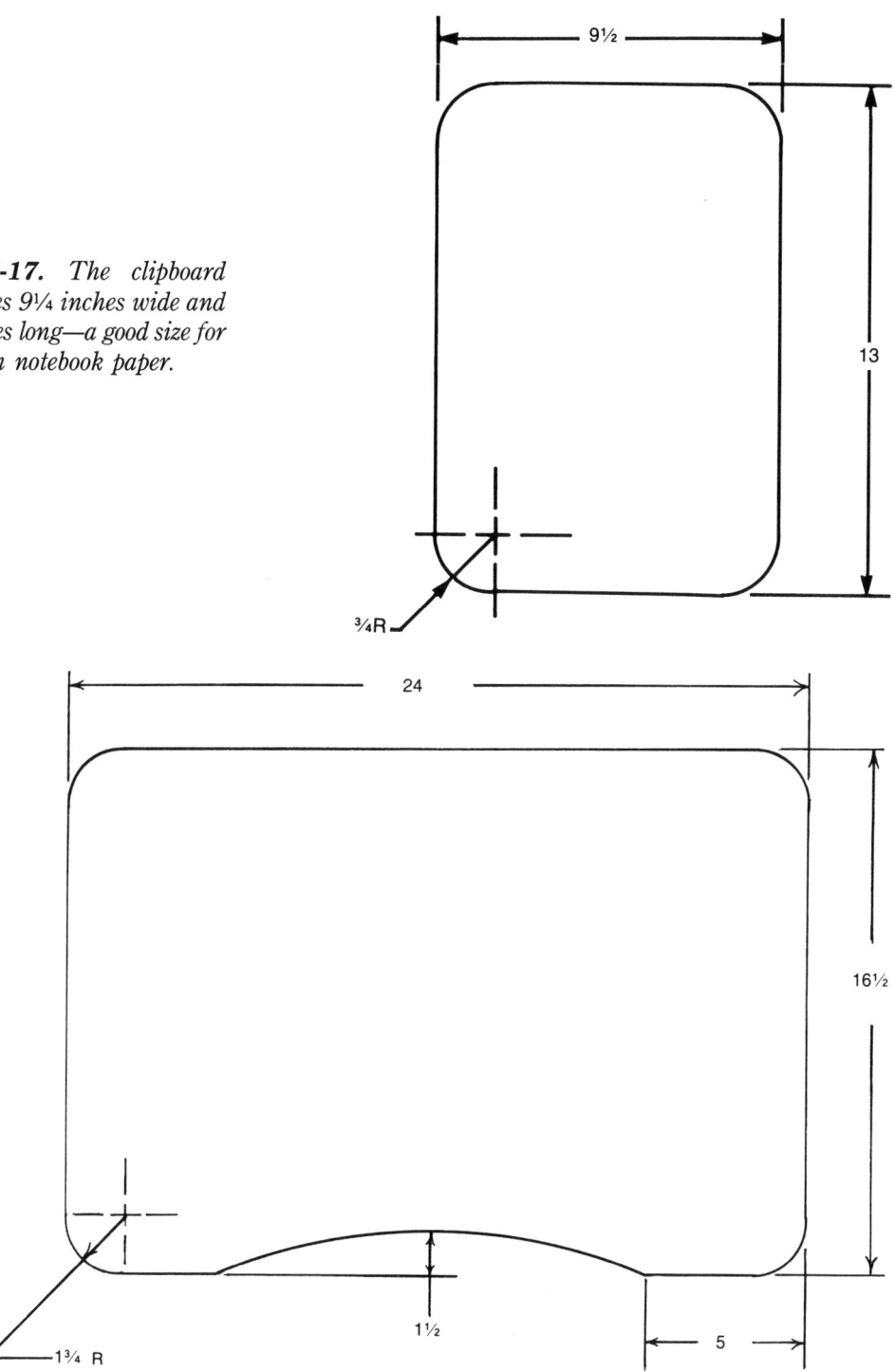

Fig. 9-17. The clipboard measures 9¼ inches wide and 13 inches long—a good size for use with notebook paper.

Fig. 9-18. The large clipboard.

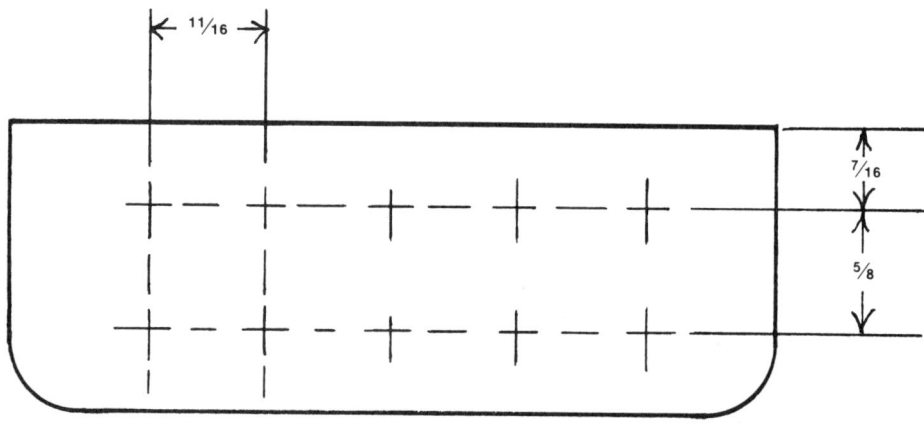

Fig. 9-19. The location of the holes of the crayon holder are shown here.

Either method will do the job. The dado joint is stronger; but the glue block method is quicker. Both methods require you to draw a line across the head and footboards, 2⅝ inches up from the bottom. This line marks the bottom of the dado or glue block.

For the dado method, set the table or radial-arm saw for a ¾-inch-wide, ⅜-inch-deep dado. Cut the dado across both the headboard and footboard with the bottom of the dado on the line previously drawn.

For the glue block method, cut two pieces of wood, measuring ¾ inch thick, ¾ inch wide, and 8¼ inches long. Then glue and nail these glue blocks to the headboard and footboard, again with the bottom of the glue block along the line drawn 2⅝ inches from the bottom ends. The glue blocks should be held ½ inch in from either side.

The next step is to draw out the head and footboard design. Since the design is

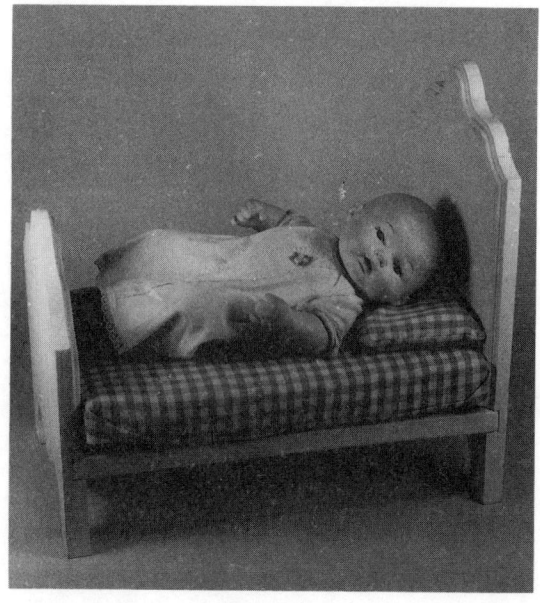

Fig. 9-20. The Doll Bed is a simple project made from a single piece of pine. It will be a welcome accessory for most any doll.

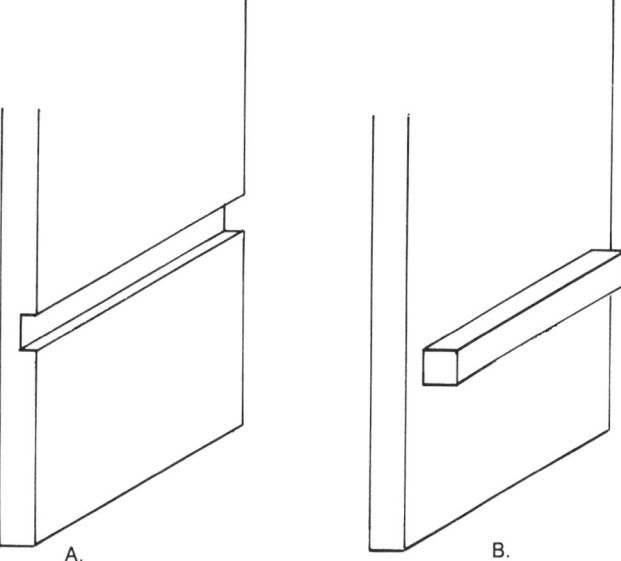

Fig. 9-21. *The two methods for connecting the head- and footboard to the mattress board: (A) the dado method; and (B) the glue blocks method.*

the same on both, I suggest that you draw it on a piece of cardboard first, cut it out, then trace it onto the boards. Figure 9-22 provides a ½-inch grid pattern that illustrates the top and bottom design.

Be sure to line up the top of the pattern with the top edge of the headboard and footboard. Next, lower the pattern down until it rests along the bottom edge of the boards, then trace the pattern. Now cut the designs on the two boards, using a coping, band, jig, scroll, or any other saw capable of cutting curves.

The curved edges just cut should be filed down to the line, then sanded smooth. As an option, the headboard and footboard can be edge-routed to produce a more professional appearance. Again, this is an option, not a requirement.

Now, sand each piece before assembly. Also, if you wish to stain or varnish the doll bed, it is easier to do so prior to assembly.

Depending on which method you selected earlier, the dado method or the glue block method, assembly will differ. To assemble the dado, simply glue the mattress support board into the two dado joints cut in the headboard and footboard.

If you used the glue block method of construction, glue and nail the mattress support board into place. Use finish nails that are 1¼ inches long. Be sure to glue and nail the parts together. Nails or glue alone do not offer the strength necessary for the project.

This bed will be a welcome gift to the child, a gift that is sure to become a cherished possession. You might want to include a foam mattress, sheets, a blanket or quilt, or a pillow and pillow case. These will add a touch of realism that is sure to enchant the young ones.

"OLD 99" TOY TRAIN

No book about toys would be complete without a wood toy train. This book is no exception. The "Old 99" Toy Train has been designed to be safe and easily handled

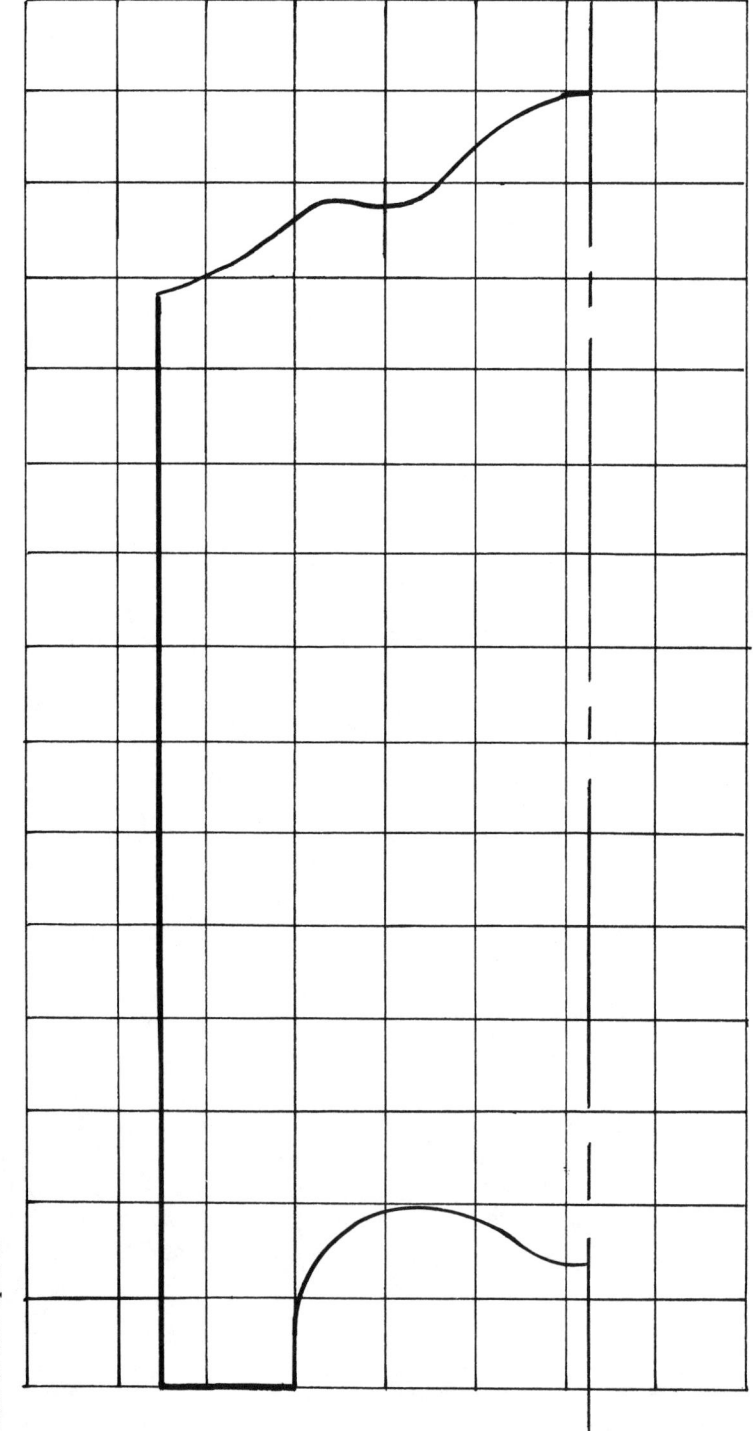

Scale: ½-inch squares

Fig. 9-22. *The grid pattern shows the shape of the top of both headboard and footboard.*

Fig. 9-23. The "Old 99" Steam Train is a great toy for children of all ages. It can carry imaginary loads of cargo in its box cars or real loads on the flat cars.

a child's small hands (Fig. 9-23). The cars are coupled to one another by the use of axle pegs, rather than potentially dangerous hooks and eyes. The frames for all of the cars, including the engine, are made from the same size wood.

Cut to size a piece of wood ¾ inch thick, 2 inches wide, and 40 inches long, then crosscut into individual lengths. The 40-inch length will supply enough frame material for one engine (6 inches long), a coal car (5 inches long), a passenger car (6 inches long), a boxcar (6 inches long), a flat car (5 inches long), a tanker car (5 inches long), and a caboose (5 inches long). If you want to add more cars to the train, increase the length for the additional car frames.

For each of the railroad car frames, you must cut a *coupler*. The coupler is a ⅜-inch-deep, 1⅛-inch-long recess cut into the ends of the frame. Figure 9-23 shows how the cars are coupled together, while Figs. 9-24A through 9-24D provide the dimensions for the frames of each railroad car.

Figure 9-24E shows a top view of a car frame. Notice that both ends are rounded with a 1-inch radius. This will allow the cars to turn freely when they are coupled together. The caboose and engine only have one end rounded. All the other cars are rounded on both ends.

Once you have cut the coupling recess and completed the rounding, drill the axle peg holes in the edge of the frames. These holes are spaced for use with 1-inch-diameter wheels on the cars and front of the engine, and 1¼-inch wheels on the rear of the engine.

The Engine. The train engine (Fig. 9-23) is made from materials that can easily be found at the local lumberyard. The cylinder shaped boiler is a 2½-inch-long length of 1¼-inch-diameter wood rod. The rod is sold as closet clothes rods.

In the center of the front of the boiler, drill a ⅜-inch-diameter hole approximately ½ inch deep. Into this hole, glue a ¾-inch length of ⅜-inch-diameter dowel. This will be the headlight.

Next, flatten the boiler cylinder on the bottom to provide it with more surface for glueing. This can be done by holding the cylinder and rubbing it against coarse sandpaper placed on a flat surface. After flattening, the boiler can be glued onto the frame. The boiler should be glued in the center of the 2-inch-wide frame, about 3/16 inch back from the top, front of the frame.

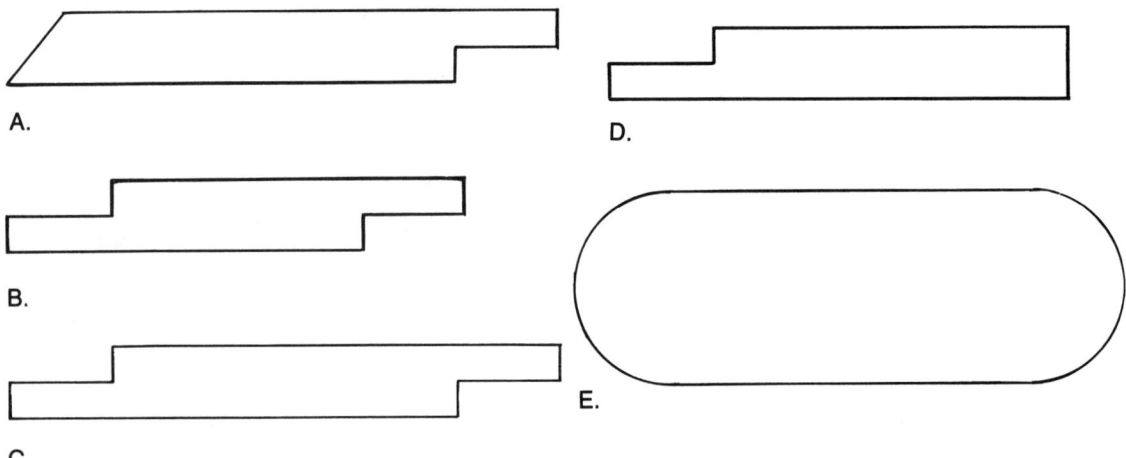

Fig. 9-24. This illustration provides the correct size, and coupling recess for the train frames.

The train in the photographs has a commercially produced smokestack glued into a hole drilled in the boiler. These may be purchased from most of the toy part suppliers listed in the Appendix. If you do not wish to use a commercially produced smokestack, you can use a length of ⅜-inch dowel instead.

The cab of the engine is cut from a short piece of 2-by-4 lumber. Begin by cutting a length of 2 by 4 to 1¾ inches long. Next, cut the height to 2 inches (Fig. 9-25A). Then make a diagonal cut from the front surface to the top (Fig. 9-25B). Glue the cab into place behind the boiler. Again, make sure it is centered on the frame.

Now the engine is ready for the finish. It may be painted (with nontoxic paint), stained and varnished, varnished, or simply oiled.

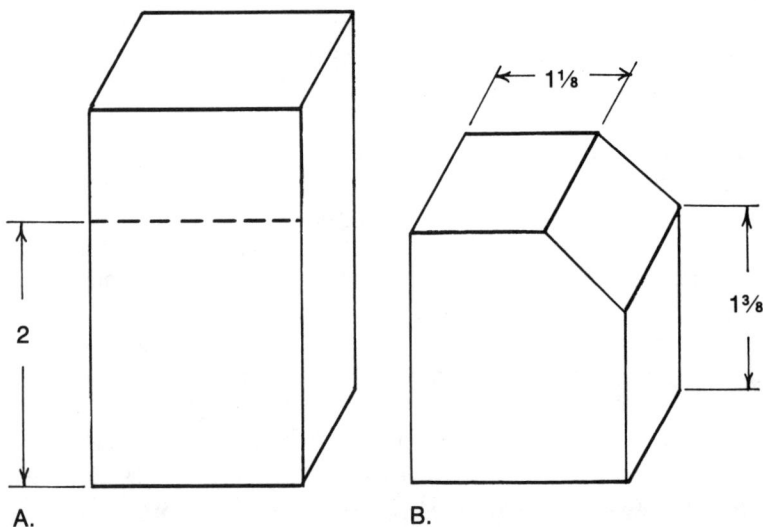

Fig. 9-25. The two steps involved in shaping the train engine cab.

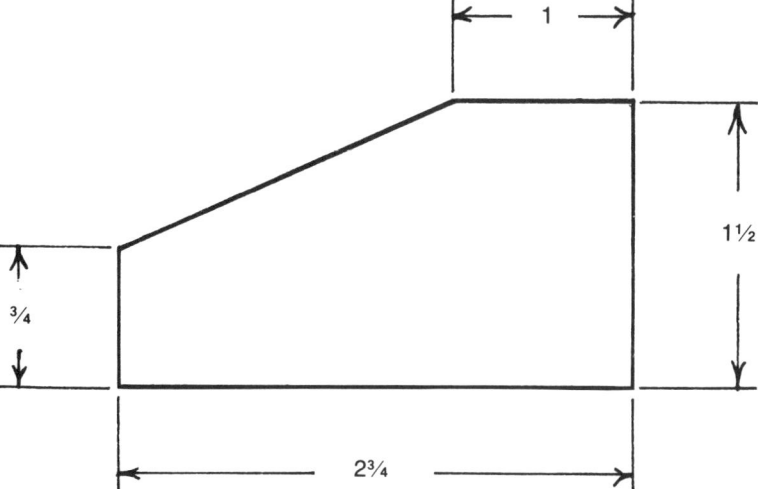

Fig. 9-26. *The Coal Car body.*

Coal Car. The car that follows the engine is the Coal Car (Fig. 9-23). The Coal Car is built on one of the 5-inch-long frames previously cut.

Cut the coal compartment from a small piece of scrap 2-by-4 material. Since the car is 1½ inches wide, the 2-by-4 material is ideal for this use. Figure 9-26 shows the layout of the coal car. This layout can be cut with any saw capable of making straight, precise cuts. After cutting the coal car, sand thoroughly.

Box Car. The most common car found on a train is the Box Car (Fig. 9-27). The Box Car is built on the 6-inch frame previously cut. Cut the freight compartment from a 3¾-inch length of 2 by 4. Then rip the 2 by 4 to a width of 2 inches. This forms the freight compartment, which can now be glued in the center of the frame.

Fig. 9-27. *The Box Car is an enclosed freight handling car made of a singular 2-by-4 block and a ¼-inch-thick top mounted to a frame.*

Fig. 9-28. The Passenger Car is a variation of the box car. It is built the same way; but it has three ½-inch-diameter holes drilled in it for windows.

Passenger Car. The Passenger Car (Fig. 9-28) is a very simple car to make. Using the 6-inch-long frame previously made, drill three ½-inch-diameter holes through it where shown. Then, glue a ¼-inch-thick, 1¾-inch-wide, by 4½-inch-long top to the top surface of the passenger car. Be sure to leave a ¼-inch overhang on the front end.

Tanker Car. In today's highly industrialized society, it is common to see chemicals carried in railroad tanker cars (Fig. 9-23). The Tanker Car on this train is built on a 5-inch-long frame. The tank itself is a 2¾-inch length of 1¼-inch-diameter closet rod. (The same rod was used for the boiler on the engine.) Flatten the rod on the bottom, so that it will better adhere to the frame when glued. On top, centered on the tank, drill a ⅜-inch hole approximately ½ inch deep. Glue a ¾-inch length of ⅜ dowel into the hole.

Flat Car. The Box Car carries freight which must be kept from the elements. However, there are many pieces that are too large to be confined to a Box Car. They must be carried on a Flat Car (Fig. 9-23). The Flat Car is very simple to construct. All you need to do is attach the wheels to the frame.

Caboose. The final car in the train is the Caboose (Fig. 9-23). It is built on a 5-inch-long frame, with only one end cut with a coupling recess. The caboose has two levels. The first is a 1-inch-thick piece of wood, which is 1½ inches wide and 2½ inches long, cut from a piece of 2-by-4 material. Be sure to drill two ⅜-inch-diameter holes through it (Fig. 9-29).

When glueing the lower level of the caboose to the frame, make sure the front end

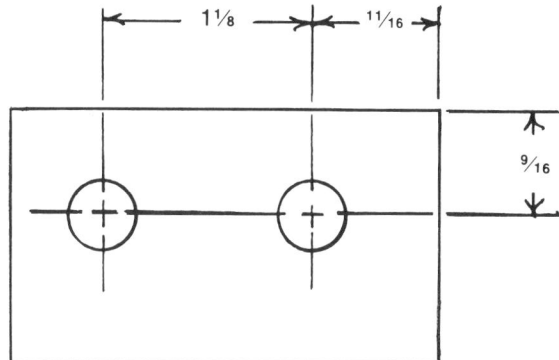

Fig. 9-29. Drill the window holes into the Caboose body at the locations shown.

sits back ⅜ inch from the front edge. Next, glue a piece of wood that is 1¾ inches wide, 3⁹⁄₁₆ inches long, and ¼ inch thick, onto the lower level. Then glue the ¼-inch top in place, leaving a ¼-inch overhang at the front.

The second level is ¾ inch thick, 1 inch wide, and 1 inch long. Through the center of this, drill a ⅜-inch-diameter hole, as was done on the lower level. After glueing the second level onto the ¼-inch roof of the lower level, cap the second level with a ¼-inch-thick, 1-inch-wide, by 1¼-inch-long top.

NAME TRAIN

The Name Train (Fig. 9-30) is built using the same instructions for the "Old 99" train, but it only consists of the engine, a caboose, and as many flat cars as there are letters in the name. Because it's personalized, this train makes an attractive, thoughtful gift that will enhance any child's bedroom.

The only additional instructions for the Name Train require you to cut out the letters

Fig. 9-30. The Name Train is a variation of the "Old 99" train previously described.

of the name from ¾-inch-thick material. The letters should be 2½ inches wide by 3 inches tall. (Simple block letters work best.) For letters that require the centers be cut out, such as a "P" or "D," first drill a hole then use a coping saw to remove the area. Another option is to simply paint the area black instead of removing it.

Next, glue letters onto the flat cars. Since this particular train is designed to be a decorative item and not necessarily for play, the letters are merely glued in place. No additional strengthening is required.

This is a project children will love. Most children have a natural affection for a train; but one that is hauling their name as its cargo is all the more exciting.

TICTACTOE

Tictactoe has been a longtime favorite game for children. It is not only entertaining; it is also an enjoyable way to pass time on long trips. The Tictactoe game described in this section (Fig. 9-31) has a new twist to the old pencil and paper game. It is made to be played as a table or lap game, and animal shapes are the X's and O's.

The board is made from a piece of wood that measures 1½ inches thick, 9¼ inches wide, and 9¼ inches long. A 9¼-inch-long piece of 2-by-10 lumber will do just fine. The ends, edges, and top surface of the board should be sanded smooth. After sanding, cut the grooves on the top of the board with a table saw, set to a ⅛-inch depth. The table saw fence should be set 3 inches away from the blade. Run the board across the blade

Fig. 9-31. Tictactoe is a long-time favorite with children. The toy shown here is a new twist to an old game.

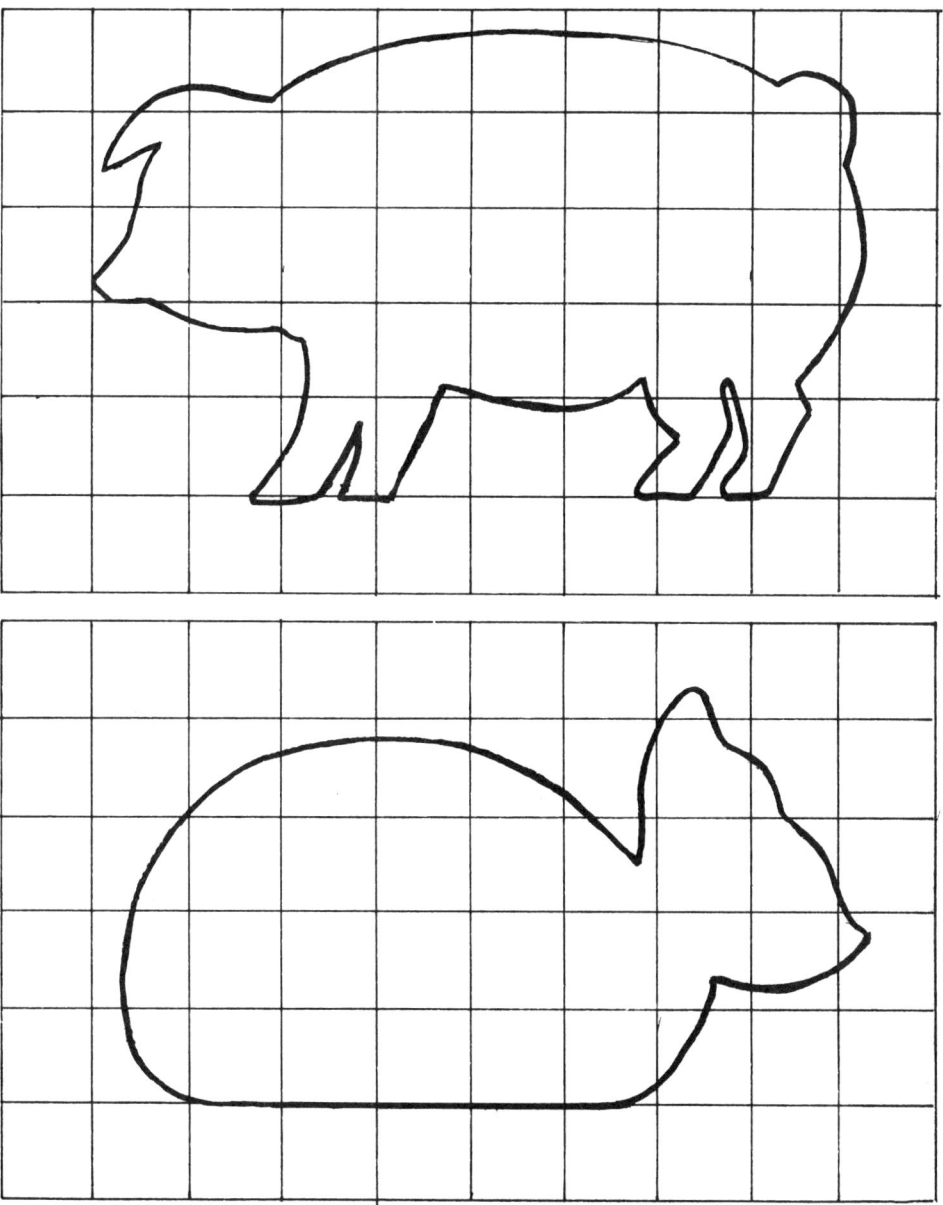

Fig. 9-32. *The grid pattern for the pig and whale.*

four times, once with each edge held against the fence, and two more times for the two ends.

In the center of the nine squares, drill a ⅜-inch hole to an approximate depth of 1 inch. The dowels I used are 5/16 inch in diameter. They will easily slide into the ⅜-inch holes drilled in the board. If another size dowel is used, alter the size of the holes accordingly.

The top edges and ends of the board can be routed with almost any router bit to produce a decorative appearance. As an alternate to the router, the top ends and edges can be rounded with a file, or even left at a square edge. The decision is up to you. You can also sand it smooth, sand and varnish, or simply varnish it.

The instructions provided here show a whale and a pig as the two animals used in the game. The type of animal used is of no importance, but the size of the animals provided is the maximum that should be used.

Cut the animals from ¾-inch-thick material, with an approximate width and length of 2½ inches and 4 inches, respectively. I suggest that the outline of each animal be transferred from the grid patterns in Fig. 9-32 onto a piece of cardboard. The cardboard, once cut out, is then traced onto the ¾-inch-thick material. While cutting out wood animals, remember that careful cutting will result in less sanding.

Next, drill a 5/16-inch hole in the center bottom of the animals. The depth of the hole should be about ¾ inch. Then paint, stain, or varnish the animals to your liking. After the finish dries, glue 3-inch lengths of 5/16-inch dowels into the hole.

The Tictactoe project is now ready. It can be kept in the camper to pass long trips, stored in the child's bedroom ready at a moment's notice, or kept in a family room. It also makes a great conversation piece.

STILTS

Children of all ages seem to enjoy heights. Babies love to stand. Toddlers climb on everything, and youngsters and trees always go together. For this reason, I have

Fig. 9-33. Children love to climb on almost anything. These stilts will enable the children to walk tall.

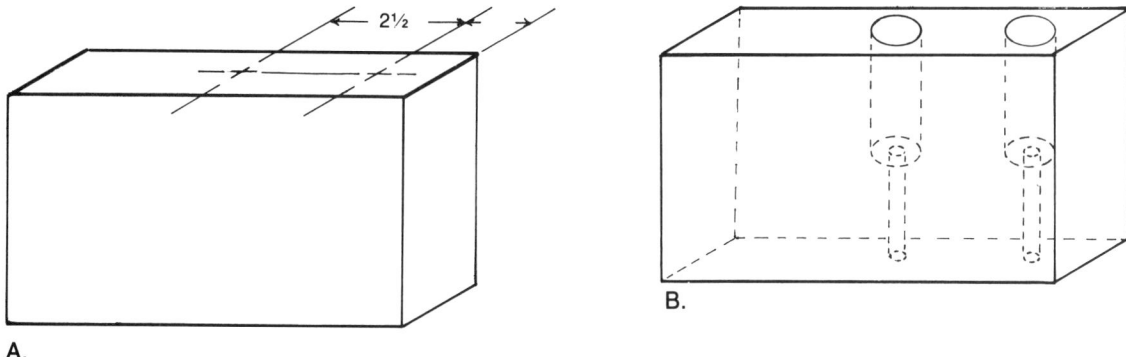

Fig. 9-34. *The drawings in this illustration show (A) the locations of the 5/16-inch holes, and (B) the location of the 3/4-inch-diameter holes.*

included stilts in this chapter. They are relatively simple to build out of easily obtained materials that can be found at any lumberyard.

The entire project can be built from a straight 2 by 4, 8 feet long. First, crosscut the 2 by 4 into a 6-foot length. The remaining two feet will be used for the foot holders. Then rip the 6-foot piece down the center, into two 1½-by-1½-by-6-feet lengths. These two pieces will be for the stilt posts. Be sure to round all the corners of the stilt posts with either a router or a file. Then sand the entire length of both stilt posts to eliminate the possibility of scratches or splinters.

Cut the foot holders, each 6 inches long, from the 2-foot length of 2-by-4 material. On each of the foot holders, drill two 5/16-inch-diameter holes through the block (Fig. 9-34A). Next, drill down through the 5/16-inch-diameter hole with a 3/4-inch-diameter drill bit. The larger-size hole is only drilled to a depth of 1½ inches (Fig. 9-34B).

Cut the foot holders at a slight diagonal, as shown in Fig. 9-35. Next, sand, being careful to remove any sharp edges.

The final woodworking operation is to drill several 5/16-inch-diameter holes in the

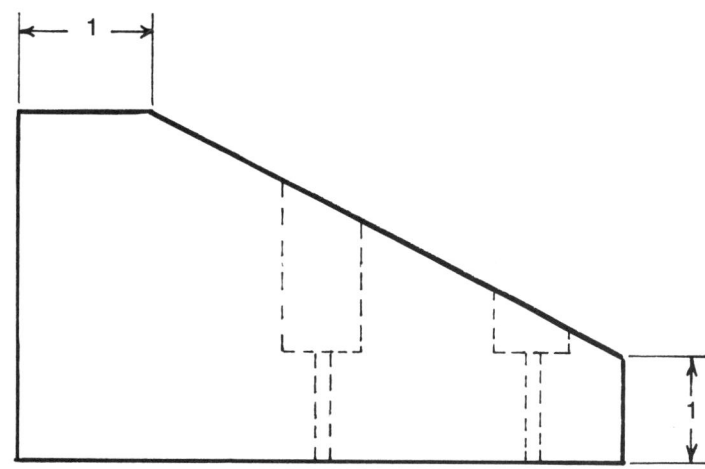

Fig. 9-35. *The correct shape of the foot holders is shown here. Cut the diagonal from a point 1 inch in from the upper end to a point 1 inch up on the lower end.*

177

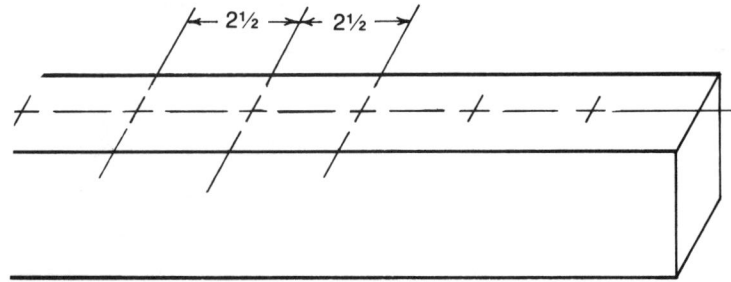

Fig. 9-36. Drill several 5/16-inch-diameter holes, 2½ inches apart, along the lower end of the posts. These holes are used to connect the foot holders to the posts.

stilt posts (Fig. 9-36). These holes should be centered 2½ inches apart. It is important to drill the holes accurately, because they must line up with the holes drilled in the foot holders. The series of holes allow for the youngster to learn to walk on the stilts while the foot holders are set in a low position. The foot holders can be gradually moved higher as the child's skill increases.

Lastly, the stilt project needs a protective coating of either paint or varnish. Regardless of your choice, the stilts project is a relatively inexpensive project that is easy to make. Yet, it is a project that will encourage many hours of outdoor play.

DOLL HIGH CHAIR

The Doll High Chair (Fig. 9-37) has been designed to accommodate the Cabbage Patch dolls. However, many other dolls will also fit quite nicely in the chair. If the size is too small or large, the seat, back, and tray can be altered to fit the doll in question.

This project has been designed to produce an attractive and functional high chair, but is fairly simple to build. Nearly all of the cutting that needs to be done are straight cuts, and even the curves are slight and should not present a problem.

A good place to start this project is with the legs. All four of them can be cut from a board that is ¾ inch thick, 5½ inches wide, and 60 inches long. Figure 9-38A shows one method of how they can be laid out. Figure 9-38B provides the dimensions and shape of the pieces. (Only one back leg and one front leg is shown, but two of each are needed.) When you are finished cutting, sand the legs smooth and round the sharp corners of the edges slightly.

Next to cut is the seat piece. Cut the seat to its size of ¾ inch thick, 9 inches wide, and 9 inches long. Then cut four slots where indicated in Fig. 9-39. These slots allow the legs to fit through the seat. As you've done with all parts of the project, sand the seat and remove all sharp edges.

Cut the chair back to a size of ¾ inch thick, 6 inches wide, and 7½ inches long. The top of the chair back is cut with a decorative curved top (Fig. 9-40). Again, sand the chair back and round all edges.

You are now ready to begin temporary assembly of the basic high chair components. Use four 1½-inch-long, number 8 wood screws to hold the legs to the chair seat at the points indicated in Fig. 9-39B. Figure 9-37 illustrates the assembly of these parts.

The chair back can also be temporarily screwed in place. The same-size screws are used, and the location of the screw holes are shown in Fig. 9-38B.

As you might have noticed, the high chair, in its present condition, is a bit wobbly.

Fig. 9-37. This doll high chair is built so the child's doll can take its proper place at the family dinner table.

This can be corrected by adding leg supports. First screw a ¾-inch-thick, 1¼-inch-wide, 7½-inch-long support between the two front legs (Fig. 9-41). Next, screw in an identical support between the two rear legs, at the same height as the front support.

You should also add two supports that act as spreaders between the front and rear legs. These both should be ¾ inch thick, 1¼ inches wide, and 9½ inches long. Figure 9-38B shows where to screw these spreaders into place, using 1¼-inch-long, number 8 screws. Note that the ends of the spreaders protrude beyond the legs. This must be cut off flush with the legs, so as not to scratch the youngsters.

Allow the high chair to sit on a hard, flat surface—not carpeting. Look to see that all four legs touch the surface. Check to see that the seat is level, and that the general appearance of the chair, as it sits, does not look twisted or awkward. In the event that any of these conditions exist, it is important that they be corrected now, prior to permanent assembly.

If all four legs do not touch the surface, each of the longer legs will need to be cut to the length of the shortest. If the seat is not level with the surface the chair is sitting on, one or more of the legs might be of an incorrect length. The seat may also have been screwed to the leg at the wrong place. To check this, refer back to the drawing in Fig. 9-38B.

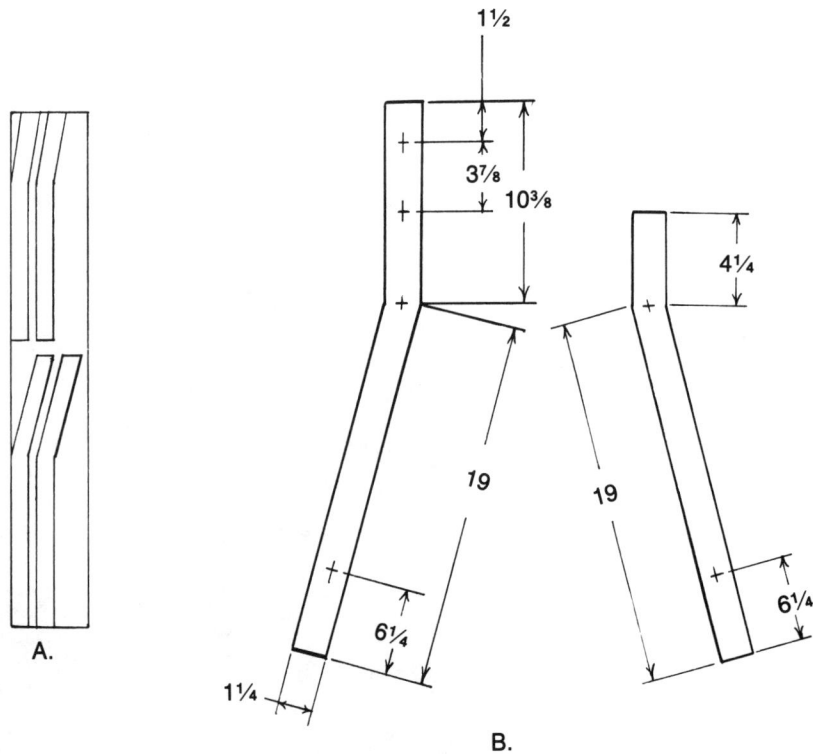

Fig. 9-38. *Drawing (A) illustrates how the high chair legs can be cut from a single piece of wood. Drawing (B) indicates the exact size and shape of the legs.*

If all of the conditions listed above check out all right, but the high chair still appears to be awkward or twisted, a few other techniques might be necessary. The first is to simply twist the legs in the direction which they need to be turned. The legs might have been screwed onto the seat crookedly, or the leg supports might have been shifted during construction. If the high chair still does not sit well, I advise you to review the instructions up to this point and check that the size of each part and the location of each screw hole is correct. When everything checks out, the high chair assembly should be permanently glued and screwed together.

The next parts to be made are the two tray supports. Cut these from ¾-inch-thick material, with a minimum width of 3 inches. The length of each should be 11½ inches. Figure 9-42 illustrates the shape and size of the tray supports, as well as the location of the screw holes where the tray supports are attached to the rear of the chair.

After these pieces have been made and sanded, screw the tray supports into place with two 1¼-inch-long, number 8 screws. This is most easily done by laying the tray support parallel to the seat, so that it is resting on the top of both the front and rear legs.

Measure the distance between the top of the tray support and the seat top at several locations to make sure the tray support and seat are parallel. When everything is set, the tray support can be screwed in place. Turn the high chair over and repeat the process on the other side.

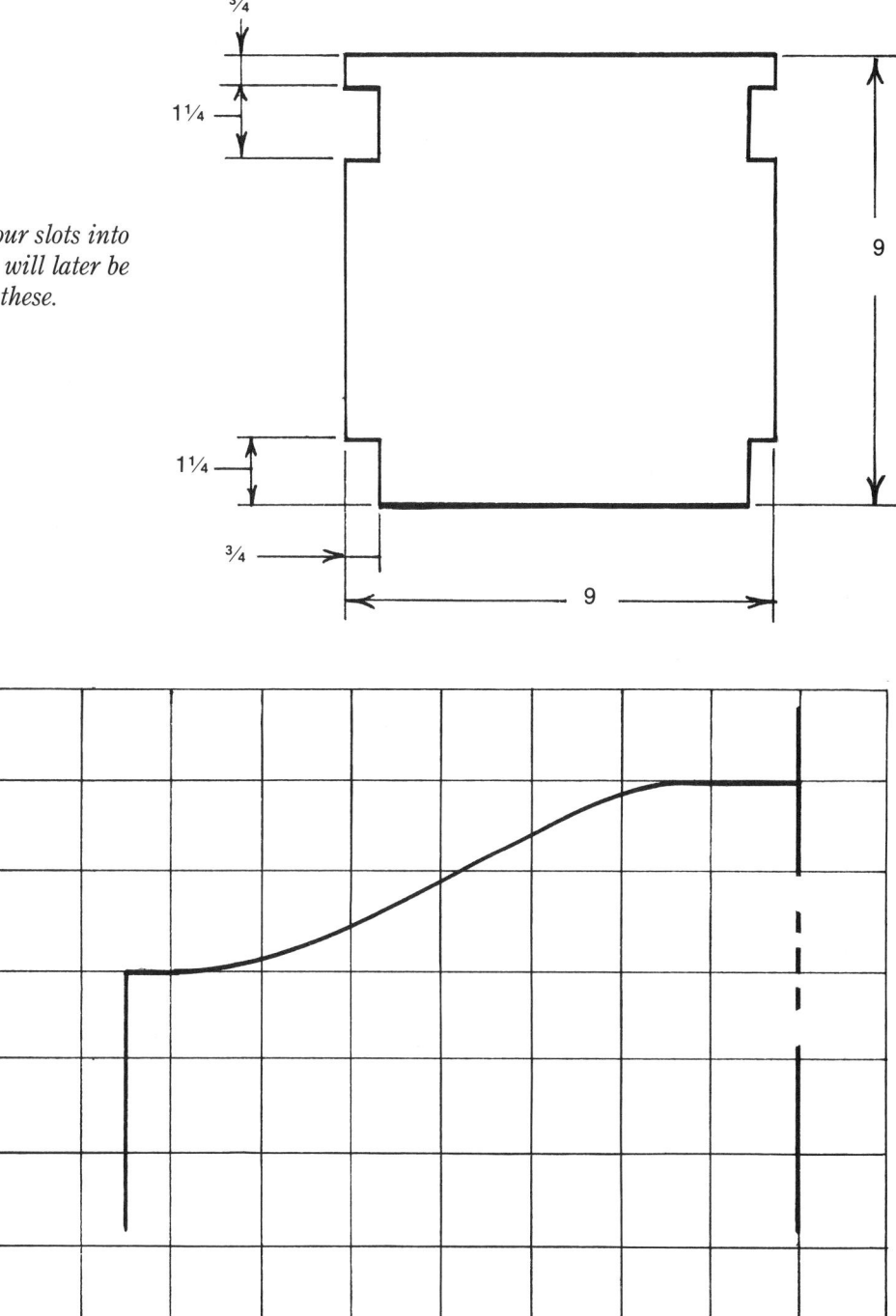

Fig. 9-39. *Cut four slots into the seat. The legs will later be inserted through these.*

Fig. 9-40. *This grid pattern illustrates the decorative curve along the top of the chair back.*

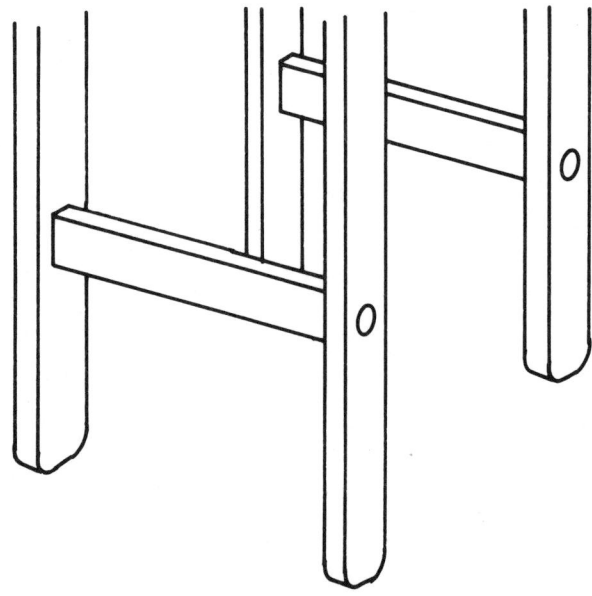

Fig. 9-41. *Screw the leg supports between the front and rear legs as shown.*

The final part to be made for the Doll High Chair is the tray. Cut the tray from a piece of wood that is ¾ inch thick, 7 inches wide and 12 inches long. The grid pattern in Fig. 9-43 provides the shape for the high chair tray. Draw and cut this out of the wood. The grid pattern also marks the locations of four points where 1½-inch-long, number 8 wood screws are used to hold the tray securely to the tray supports. Once the tray is sanded, and the edges rounded to remove the possibility of scratches or splinters, you can mount the tray onto the tray supports.

The Doll High Chair, at first glance, might look like a complicated project better left to the professional. Yet, after carefully making this project and following the step-by-step instructions, you will learn that it is relatively easy to build. Each piece is fairly simple to cut out and, when assembled, they create a project that will impress everyone who sees it.

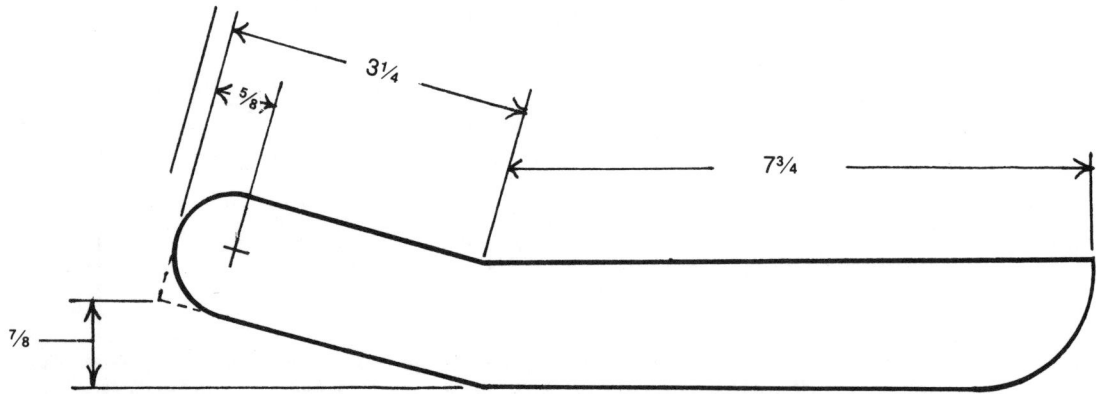

Fig. 9-42. *The dimensions required to cut the tray supports to the correct size and shape.*

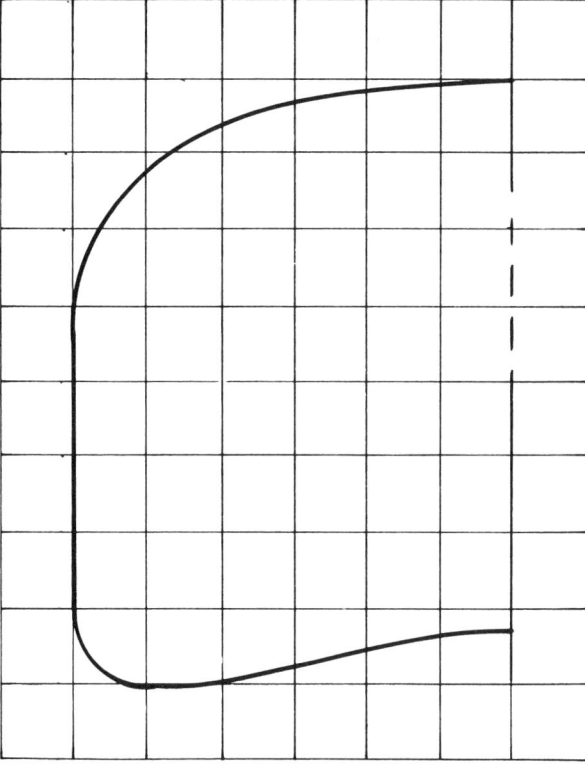

Fig. 9-43. The high chair tray has a curved shape, as illustrated in the grid pattern.

HYDROPLANE

The thrill and excitement of hydroplane racing provides a lasting memory for all who have seen the sleek, trim boats skimming inches off the water. Depending on the size and class of the hydroplane, they can reach speeds in excess of 100 miles per hour. Yet, the hydroplane described in this section is capable of any speed a child can create in his or her imagination (Fig. 9-44).

Hydroplane construction begins with the rounded front of the boat, which is cut from

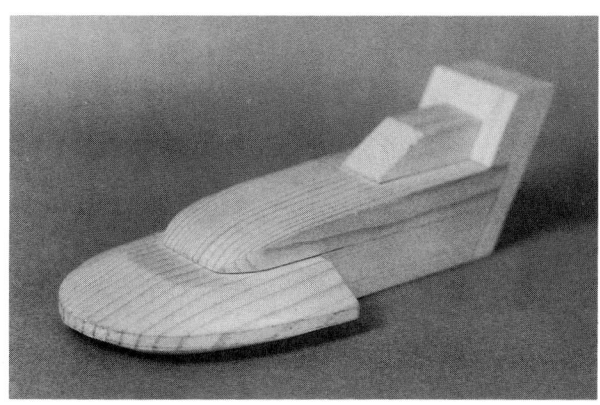

Fig. 9-44. The Hydroplane is a fast, exciting boat capable of speeds in excess of 100 miles per hour.

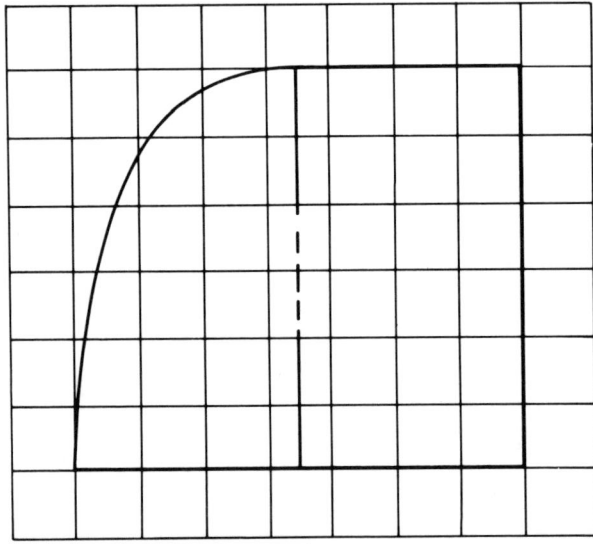

Fig. 9-45. The grid pattern shows the shape of the front hull.

a 3½-inch-wide, 3-inch-long piece of ¾-inch-thick wood. Round the front of the boat to the shape shown in Fig. 9-45.

On both the top and bottom surface of this piece, draw a pencil line 1 inch in from the curve edge just cut (Fig. 9-46A). On the front and side edges of the curved piece, draw a line ¼ inch down from the top surface and up from the bottom surface (Fig. 9-46B). Remove the material between the lines with a file and sandpaper. The final result is shown

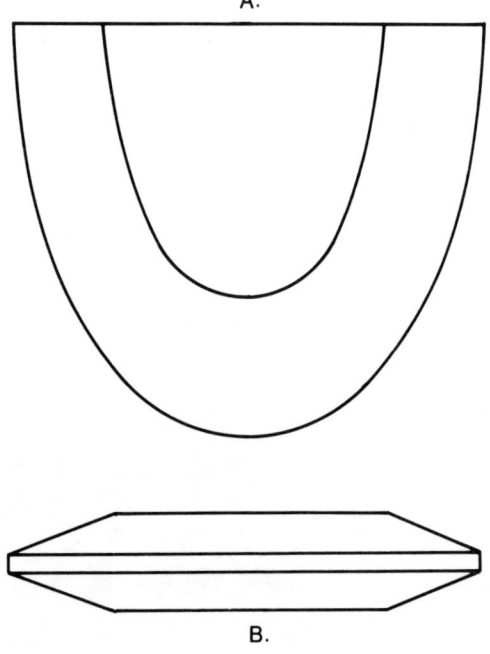

Fig. 9-46. The series of drawings shows the steps in shaping the front of the hull.

Fig. 9-47. *Cut the lower hull half from a piece of ¾-inch-thick wood that is 1¾ inches wide and 3⅛ inches long.*

in the photograph of the finished hydroplane at the beginning of this section.

The next step is to make the lower hull half from a length of ¾-inch-thick wood, cut to a width of 1¾ inches, and a length of 3⅛ inches. Toward the rear (stern) of this piece, cut the angle as shown in Fig. 9-47.

The top half of the hull is also cut from a ¾-inch-thick piece of wood, which is 1¾ inches wide, but is 4¾ inches long. Cut the stern end of the top hull half to the same angle as the lower stern. On the edge of the top half of the hull, draw out the design shown in Fig. 9-48A. The material that is shaded should be removed. The next step

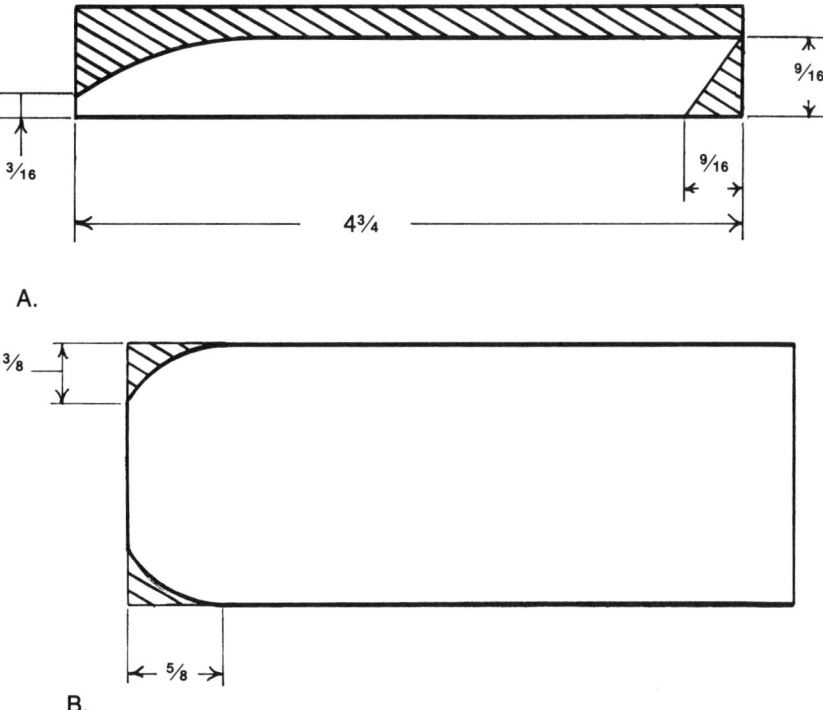

Fig. 9-48. *Shape the upper hull half as shown. The shaded areas are to be removed.*

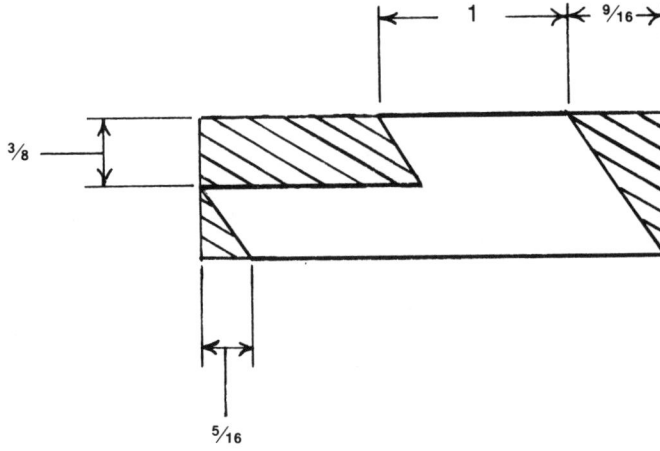

Fig. 9-49. Cut the stern riser of the Hydroplane to the size and shape shown here.

on the upper hull half is to slightly curve in the front, as shown in Fig. 9-48B. Glue together the two hull halves, being careful that the angles cut at the rear of each piece are lined up, and the edges of both are kept flush. When the glue has set on the stern hull halves, they can be glued onto the front hull.

On the extreme rear of the hydroplane, there is a diagonal stern riser that is ¾ inch thick, 1¾ inches wide, and 2½ inches long. There is a recess cut out of the stern riser, the size and shape of which is shown in Fig. 9-49. Now, glue the stern riser on the stern end of the rest of the boat, as shown on the model in Fig. 9-44.

The final part to be cut to size and shape is the pilot compartment. Cut the compartment from a ½-inch-thick piece of wood, ¾ inches wide and 1¾ inches long (Fig. 9-50). Then glue the pilot compartment into place, centered, toward the rear of the hydroplane.

The hydroplane will require some sort of finish. The bare wood will quickly deteriorate if put in the water and, worse yet, the water will cause the glue to dissolve. One or two coats of varnish or paint will protect the wood, eliminating possible problems.

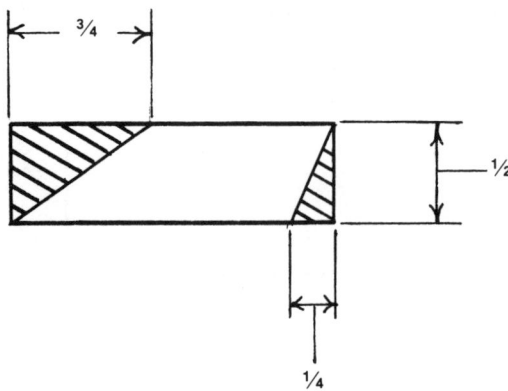

Fig. 9-50. Cut to shape the pilot compartment as shown.

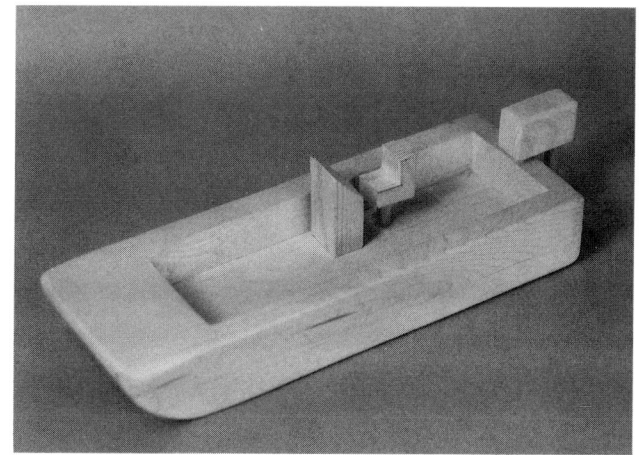

Fig. 9-51. The Bass Boat has been designed to get the fishermen quickly from the boat launch to the shallows, where all the bass are.

BASS BOAT

Specialty boats, such as the deep sea trollers, ski boats, and the bass boats, have all been designed to perform a specific function. The Bass Boat (Fig. 9-51) has been designed to get the fisherman into the shallow water where fish, like bass, feed.

The hull of the Bass Boat is made from one piece of ¾-inch-thick wood, which is 3 inches wide and 8¼ inches long, and another piece with the same width and length, but only ½ inch thick. The ¾-inch-thick piece will require a rectangular hole, which measures 6¼ inches long and 2¹⁄₁₆ inches wide, to be cut out of the board (Fig. 9-52). Next, glue the ¾-inch-thick piece to the ½-inch-thick board. Be careful not to get glue inside the rectangular cutout (Fig. 9-53).

Round the front end of the boat, so that the bow will push the water and waves

Fig. 9-52. Cut a rectangular hole out of the center of the ¾-inch-thick hull half.

Fig. 9-53. Glue the hull halves together.

out of the way. This can be done by cutting away some material with a saw and filing and sanding it smooth. Figure 9-54 illustrates the curve for the bow. While the sandpaper is out, the entire hull should be sanded to eliminate the possibility of scratches to young sailors.

This boat is equipped with a large outboard engine, to get it quickly to the fishing spots. The engine is made from a block of wood that measures ½ inch thick, ¾ inch wide, and 1¼ inches long. On the bottom of the engine block, drill two ¼-inch-diameter holes, ⅜ inch deep. The location of the holes is shown in Fig. 9-55.

Next, glue a ¾-inch length of ¼-inch dowel into one of the two holes. Then glue a 1¼-inch length of ¼-inch dowel into the second ¼-inch hole. The first short dowel is used to secure the motor to the rear of the boat, or *transom*. The larger dowel represents the propeller shaft.

The Bass Boat is characterized by a center command console. The console is made from a single block of wood that measures ½ inch thick, ¾ inch wide, and 1¼ inches long. The top end of the console has a slight angle cut (Fig. 9-56). The shaded area

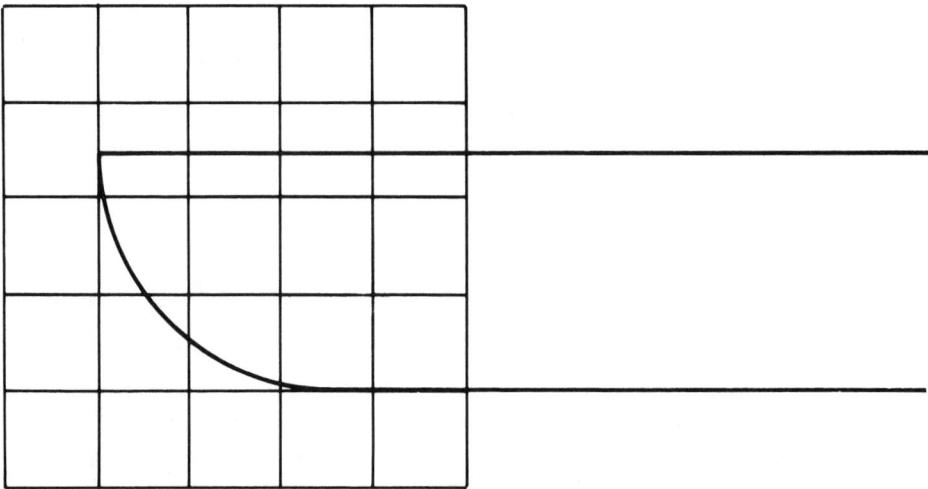

Fig. 9-54. The grid pattern shows the shape of the front of the Bass Boat.

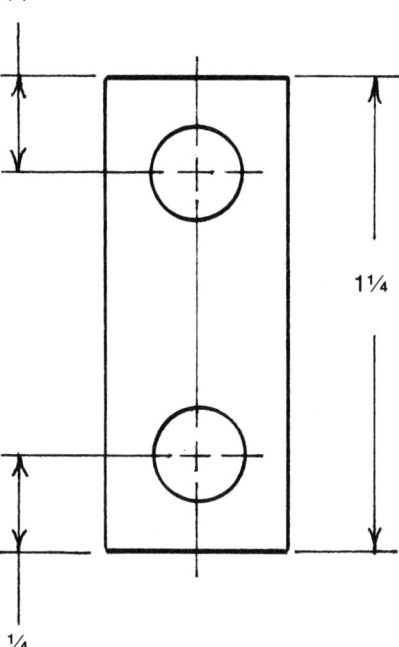

Fig. 9-55. Drill two ¼-inch holes in the bottom of the engine block.

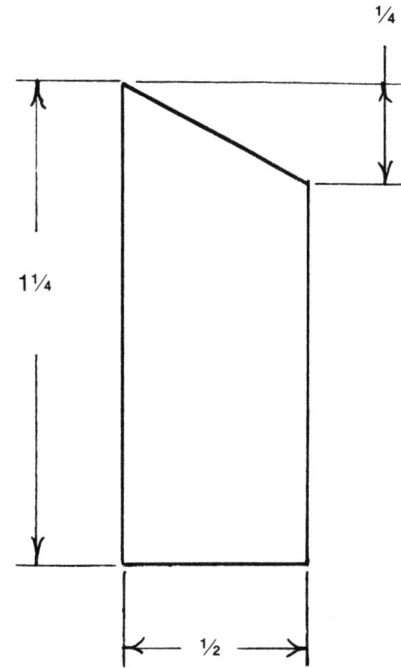

Fig. 9-56. Cut to shape the center command council from a ½-inch-thick, ¾-inch-wide, 1¼-inch-long piece of wood.

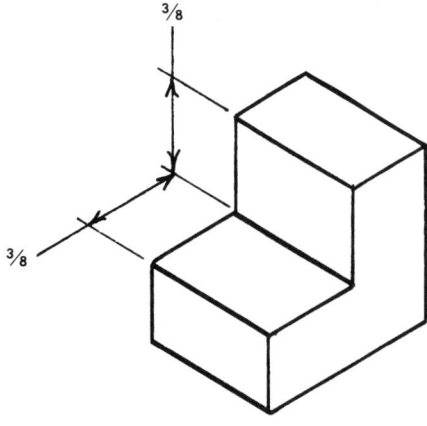

Fig. 9-57. The seat is made from a small block of wood that has a 3/8-by-3/8-inch block cut from it.

is the material that must be removed. Drill a ¼-inch-diameter hole one inch deep in the bottom of the console. Then glue a 1¼-inch length of ¼-inch dowel into this hole. This will later be used to secure the console to the boat bottom.

There is a swivel bucket seat that is raised above the deck for easy casting into shallows. The seat is made from a piece of wood that measures ½ inch thick, ¾ inch wide, and ¾ inch long (Fig. 9-57). On the bottom of the seat bottoms, drill a ¼-inch-diameter hole, 3/16 inch deep. Glue a ¼-inch-diameter dowel rod that has been cut to a length of ⅝ inch into the hole.

Now that all of the parts that make up the Bass Boat have been cut, it is time for assembly. Begin by drilling a series of ¼-inch holes. These holes indicate where the parts are affixed to the hull. Figure 9-58 shows where to drill the ¼-inch-diameter holes. Be careful not to drill the holes deeper than ⅜ inch. (The bottom of the hull is only ½ inch thick.)

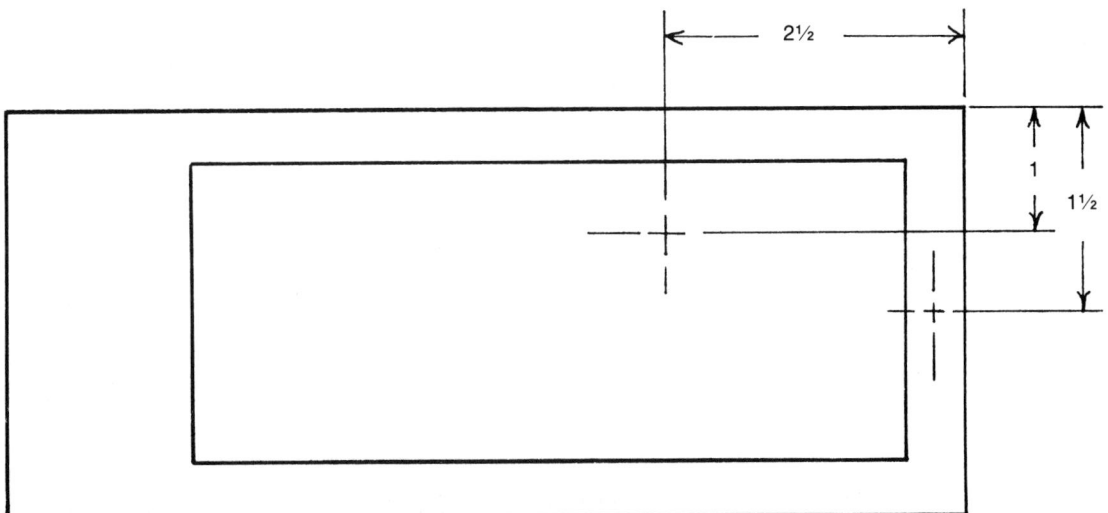

Fig. 9-58. Drill two ¼-inch-diameter holes in the hull at the points shown.

Next, glue one of the pedestal seats into the foreward-most hole, facing the seat forward. The next hole back is for the ¼-inch-diameter dowel, extending out the bottom of the console. Glue the console in place with the chamfer (beveled edge) facing the rear. Immediately behind the console, glue the second seat into the ¼-inch hole. Finally glue the short ¼-inch-diameter dowel, protruding from the outboard motor, into the hole in the transom.

After allowing the glue sufficient time to set, sand the *entire* boat (including the motor and seats) to remove any sharp edges. The sanding should be completed prior to applying any finish.

The finish is important because most glue used in woodworking is water soluble, meaning that it will dissolve in water; therefore the boat must be somehow protected. Paint or varnish will accomplish this very well.

The Bass Boat will run just as smoothly on the water in the tub as it will on the living room carpet. The younger fisherman will have fun speeding along the imaginary lake, in search of the "big one that got away."

GREAT LAKES FREIGHTER

The Great Lakes Freighter is the workhorse of the modern marine industry. It can be found carrying loads of coal, iron ore, lime, quarry stone, and assorted agricultural products around mid America on the world's greatest inland waterway, the Great Lakes (Fig. 9-59).

Construction of the Great Lakes Freighter begins by selecting a 13-inch piece of 2-by-4 lumber that is free from knots and other defects, to use as the hull. Glue a ¾-inch-thick, 3½-inch-wide, 2¼-inch-long raised-forward deckhouse to the front of the hull. To the rear of the hull, glue a ¾-inch-thick, 3½-inch-wide, 3-inch-long rear deck house (Fig. 9-60).

While the glue is setting, draw out a ½-inch-square grid pattern on two pieces of cardboard that is at least 4 inches wide and 4 inches long. Figure 9-61 illustrates the proper layout for the bow and stern. Transfer the design onto the cardboard grid pattern, then cut the outline of the ship ends. The next step is to trace the cardboard templet onto the wood hull.

Next to make is a templet for the side of the hull. Figure 9-62 provides a ½-inch-square grid pattern that displays the proper design for the profile of the hull. As was done before, cut the templet and trace it onto the hull.

Now the shaping of the hull begins. Start by filing and sanding the bottom edges of the front and rear hull. File and sand down to the lines traced from the profile templet.

Fig. 9-59. *The Great Lakes Freighter is the workhorse of the modern marine industry.*

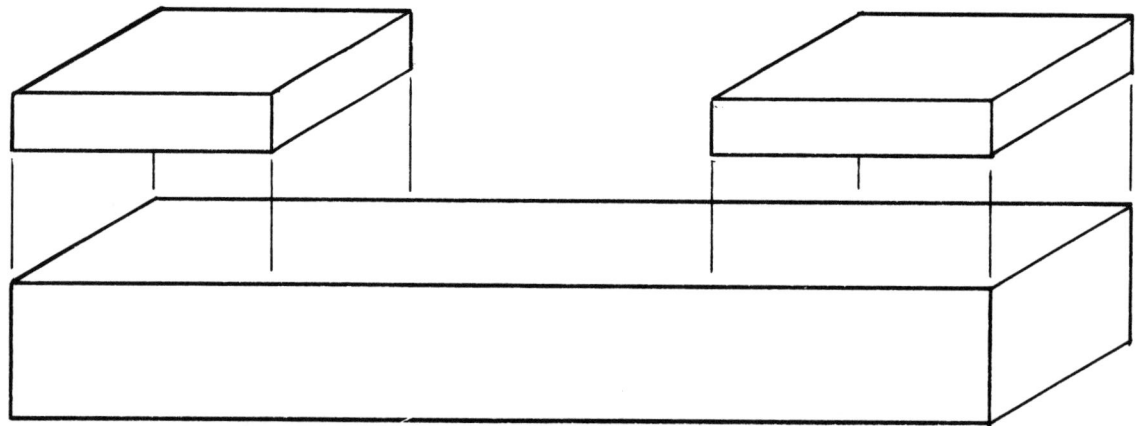

Fig. 9-60. *Glue the raised parts of the freighter to the front and rear of the freight hull.*

Shape the top of the hull by first cutting away excess material, then filing and sanding down to the templet lines on the bow and stern.

The basic boat is now completed. The hull and forward and stern deckhouses are in place and shaped. Next, cut out and glue in place the wheel house and upper rear deck, according to the plans in Fig. 9-63. The first drawing, (A), is the forward wheel house. This is where the ship is piloted. It is composed of a single block of wood that measures ¾ inch thick, 2 inches wide, and 1¾ inches long. This may be cut from a small scrap piece of wood. The second drawing, (B), illustrates the size and shape of the stern deck house. It is cut from a ¾-inch board with a width and length of 2½ inches and 2¼ inches, respectively. This piece should be slightly rounded in the rear, yet the front should be kept square. Also, drill a 1-inch-diameter hole through the center of this piece, at the point indicated. Then glue a 1¾-inch length of 1-inch dowel into this hole. The dowel is the smokestack.

To add a bit of realism to the Great Lakes Freighter, there are five cargo hatch covers glued onto the deck. The cargo hatch covers are each ⅛ inch thick, by 1 inch wide, and 2½ inches long. Glue the covers to the deck between the front and rear raised hull sections, spacing approximately 7⁄16 inch apart. They should also be centered between the sides of the ship.

All of the parts for the Great Lakes Freighter have been cut and assembled. Now you must sand and remove any sharp edges or corners that might exist, then apply some sort of finish.

The finish can be almost anything. The ship can be painted in realistic colors, stained and varnished, or just varnished. That decision is up to you.

If you use white glue (the type normally used for woodworking), you should remember that it is water soluble—not a desirable condition in toy boat construction. Therefore, to help prevent the freighter from slowly falling apart, the entire surface should be painted or varnished.

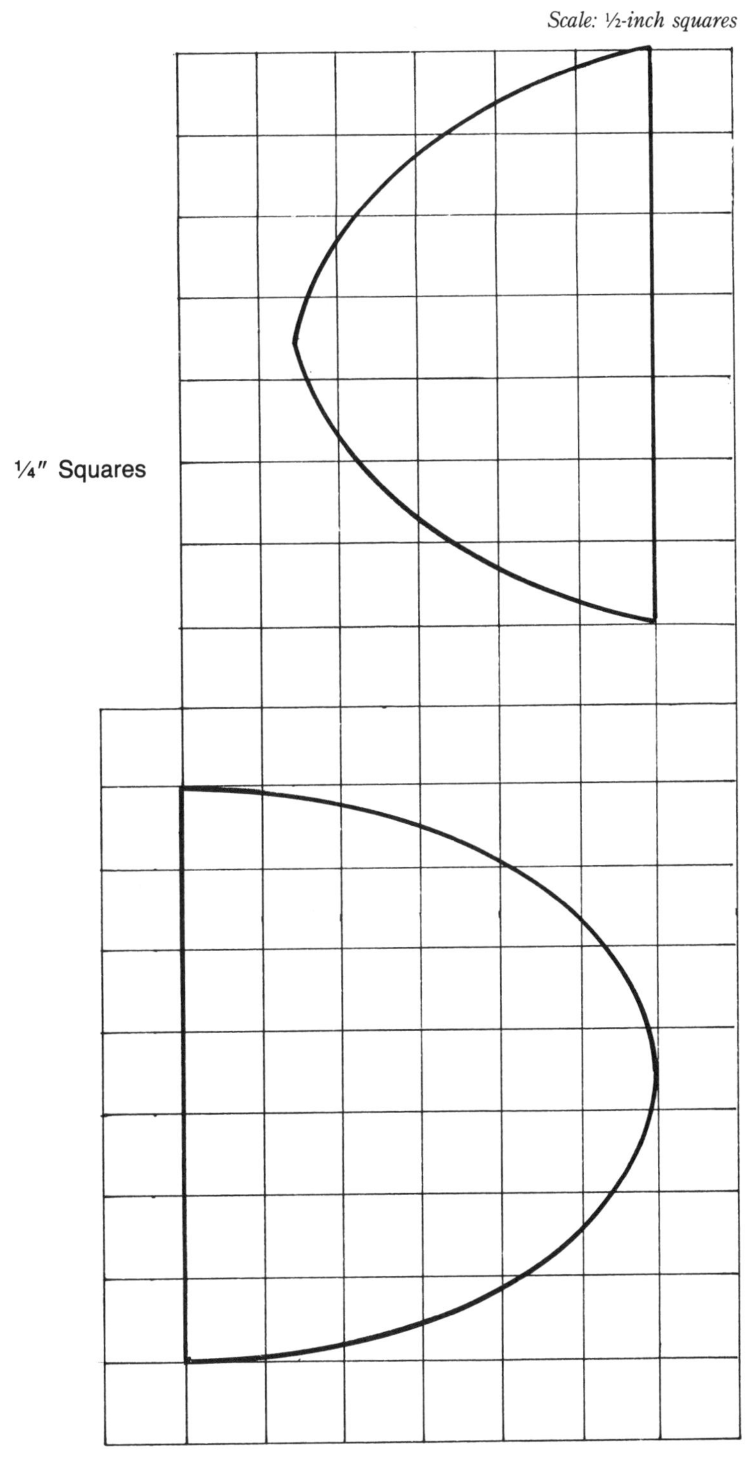

Scale: ½-inch squares

¼" Squares

Fig. 9-61. *The grid patterns show the shape of the bow and stern of the freighter (as seen from the top).*

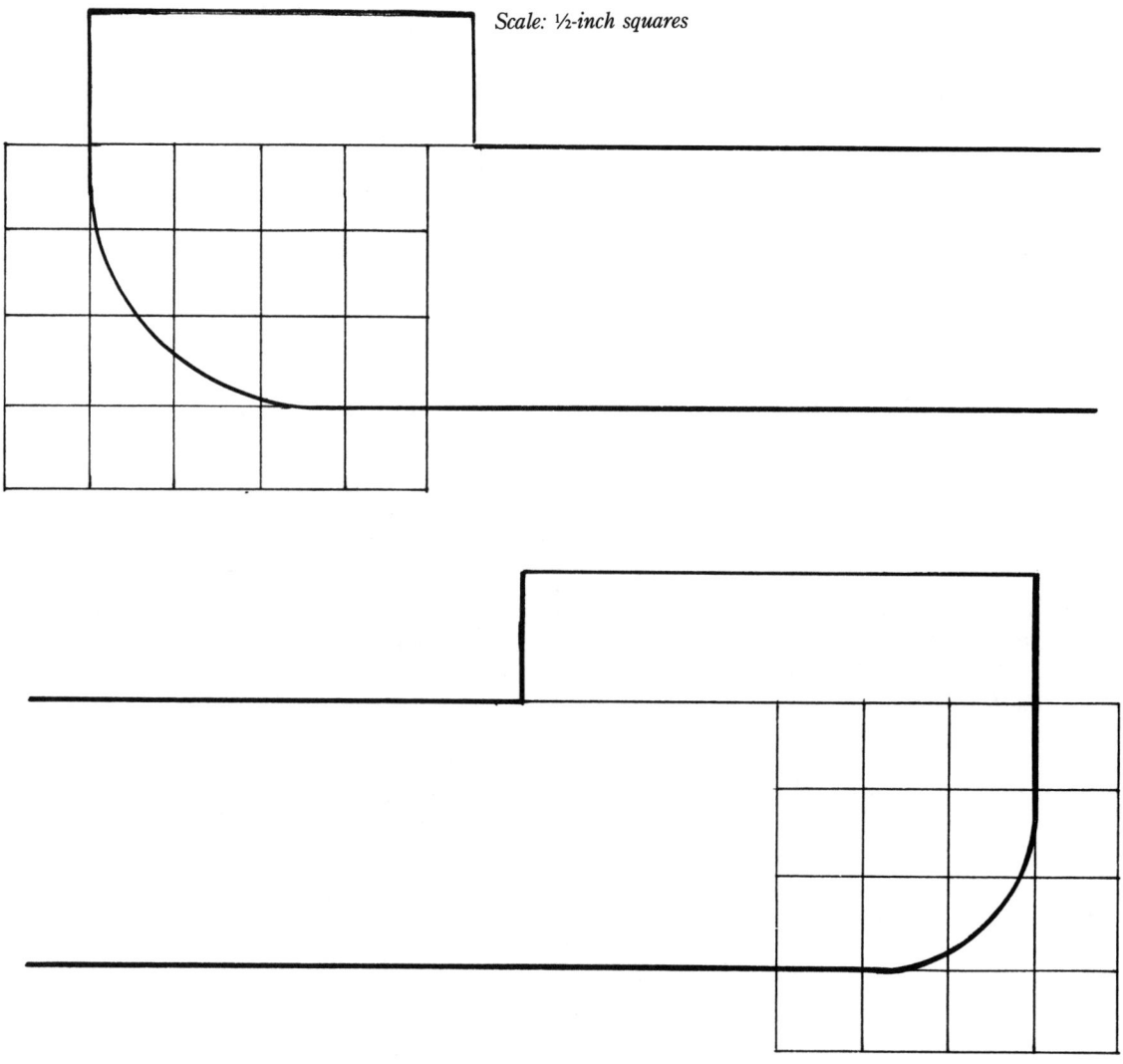

Fig. 9-62. *The shape of the front and rear of the Great Lakes Freighter (as viewed from the side) is shown in this grid pattern.*

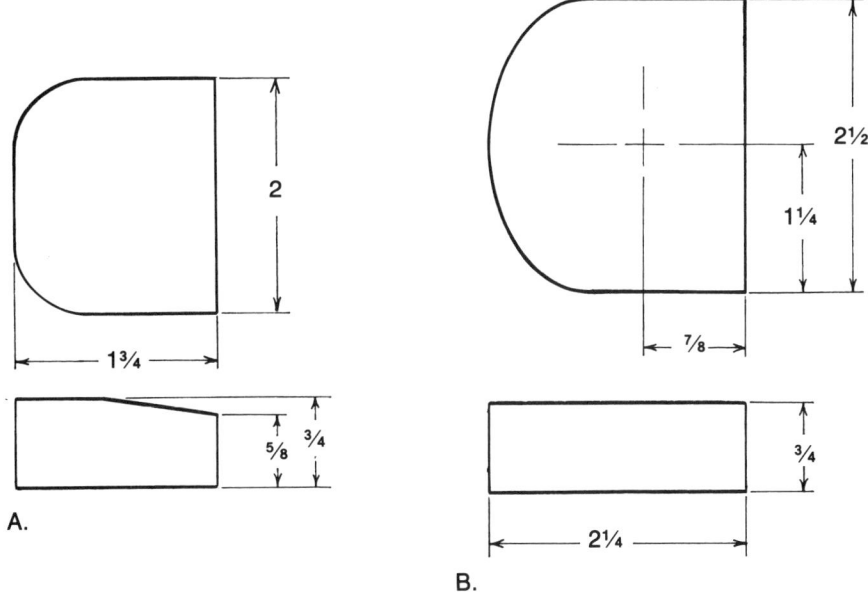

Fig. 9-63. The drawing shows the correct size and shape of the forward deck house and the raised rear deck.

LIST 9.1. REQUIRED MATERIALS

Doll Cradle

2	− Cradle Sides	− ¾ × 11 × 11⅛
2	− Cradle Sides	− ¾ × 4⅜ × 20
1	− Bottom	− ¼ × 10 × 20
2	− Cradle Support Bases	− ¾ × 2 × 11
2	− Cradle Support Uprights	− ¾ × 2 × 15¼
1	− Horizontal Support	− ¾ × 22
	Spindles	− 1¾ inches long

Creature Keeper

2	− Ends	− ¾ × 3½ × 4¼
1	− Base	− ¾ × 3½ × 4¼
1	− Piece of Screen	− 6 × 12
1	− Plywood Door	− ¼ × 2½ × 3
1	− Round Head Screw	− 1 inch, no. 6
6	− Finish Nails	− 1¾ inches long
22	− Tacks	− ¾ inch long

35MM Camera

2	– Camera Body	– ¾ × 3 × 5½
2	– Lens Area	– ¾ × 2½ × 3
1	– Viewfinder	– ¾ × 2½ × 2
1	– Lens Disk	– ¾-×-2-inches diameter
1	– Lens Disk	– ¾-×-2¼-inches diameter
2	– Buttons	– 1-inch diameter

Krayon Keepers

1	– Pig	– 2 × 4 × 7⅝
1	– Snowmobile	– 2 × 4 × 7¼
1	– Whale	– 2 × 4 × 8¼
1	– Truck	– 2 × 4 × 8½
6	– Wheels	– 1¼-inch diameter
6	– Axle Pegs	– Small Size

Clipboard

1	– Board	– ¼ × 9½ × 13
1	– Clip	– Large
2	– Pop Rivets	

Lap Board

1	– Board	– ¼ × 16½ × 24
1	– Clip	– Large
2	– Pop Rivets	
2	– Crayon Holders	– 1½ × 2 × 4⅛
4	– Screws	– ¾, no. 6

Doll Bed

1	– Headboard	– ¾ × 9¼ × 14
1	– Footboard	– ¾ × 9¼ × 10
1	– Mattress Support	– ¾ × 9¼ × 14
2	– Glue Blocks	– ¾ × ¾ × 8¼ (Optional)

Old 99 Toy Train

Engine

1	– Frame	– ¾ × 2 × 6
1	– Boiler	– 1¼-inch diameter × 2½ Rod
1	– Front Light	– ⅜-inch diameter dowel ¾ inch long
1	– Smokestack	– Medium Size
1	– Cab	– 1½ × 2 × 1¾
2	– Wheels	– 1¼-inch diameter
4	– Wheels	– 1-inch diameter
6	– Axle Pegs	– Small Size

Coal Car
- 1 – Frame — ¾ × 2 × 5
- 1 – Coal Compartment — 1½ × 1½ × 2⅜
- 4 – Wheels — 1¼-inch diameter
- 5 – Axle Pegs — Small Size

Box Car
- 1 – Frame — ¾ × 2 × 6
- 1 – Box Compartment — 1½ × 2 × 3¾
- 4 – Wheels — 1¼-inch diameter
- 5 – Axle Pegs — Small Size

Passenger Car
- 1 – Frame — ¾ × 2 × 6
- 1 – Compartment — 1½ × 2 × 3¾
- 4 – Wheels — 1¼-inch diameter
- 5 – Axle Pegs — Small Size

Tanker Car
- 1 – Frame — ¾ × 2 × 5
- 1 – Tank — 1¼-inch dowel × 2¾ inches long
- 1 – Fill Spout — ⅜-inch dowel × ¾ inches long
- 4 – Wheels — 1¼-inch diameter
- 5 – Axle Pegs — Small Size

Flat Car
- 1 – Frame — ¾ × 2 × 5
- 4 – Wheels — 1¼-inch diameter
- 5 – Axle Pegs — Small Size

Caboose
- 1 – Frame — ¾ × 2 × 5
- 1 – First Level — 1 × 1½ × 2½
- 1 – First Level Roof — ¼ × 1¾ × 3⁹⁄₁₆
- 1 – Second Level — ¾ × 1 × 1
- 4 – Wheels — 1¼-inch diameter
- 5 – Axle Pegs — Small Size

Name Train

- 1 – Engine Assembly
- 1 – Caboose Assembly
- 1 – Flat Car Assembly for each letter in the name
- 1 – Letter Block for each letter in the name — ¾ × 2½ × 3

Tictactoe Board

- 1 – Board — 1½ × 9¼ × 9¼
- 4 – Animal Shapes — ¾ × 2½ × 4
- 4 – Animal Shapes — ¾ × 2½ × 4
- 8 – Dowels — ⁵⁄₁₆-inch diameter × 3 inches long

Stilts

2 –	Posts	– 1½ × 1½ × 72
2 –	Foot Holders	– 1½ × 3½ × 6
4 –	Bolts	– ¼ × 4 inches long
4 –	Wing Nuts	– ¼ inch

Doll High Chair

2 –	Front Legs	– ¾ × 1¼ × 25
2 –	Rear Legs	– ¾ × 1¼ × 31
1 –	Seat	– ¾ × 9 × 9
1 –	Chair Back	– ¾ × 6 × 7½
2 –	Leg Supports	– ¾ × 1¼ × 7½
2 –	Spreaders	– ¾ × 1¼ × 9½
2 –	Tray Supports	– ¾ × 3 × 12
1 –	Tray	– ¾ × 7 × 12
8 –	Screws	– 1½, no. 8
8 –	Screws	– 1¼, no. 8

Hydroplane

1 –	Hull Front	– ¾ × 3½ × 3
1 –	Hull Bottom	– ¾ × 1¾ × 3⅛
1 –	Hull Top	– ¾ × 1¾ × 4¾
1 –	Stern Riser	– ¾ × 1¾ × 2½
1 –	Pilot Compartment	– ½ × ¾ × 1¾

Bass Boat

1 –	Hull Top	– ¾ × 3 × 5¼
1 –	Hull Bottom	– ½ × 3 × 8¼
1 –	Motor	– ½ × ¾ × 1¼
1 –	Dowel	– ¼ × 1¼
1 –	Dowel	– ¼ × ¾
1 –	Command Center	– ½ × ¾ × 1¼
1 –	Seat	– ½ × ¾ × ¾
1 –	Dowel	– ¼ × ⅝

Freighter

1 –	Hull	– 2 × 4 × 13
1 –	Forward Hull	– ¾ × 3½ × 2¼
1 –	Rear Hull	– ¾ × 3½ × 3
1 –	Wheel House	– ¾ × 2 × 1¾
1 –	Upper Rear Deck	– ¾ × 2½ × 2¼
1 –	Smokestack	– 1-inch-diameter dowel × 1¾ inches long
5 –	Cargo Hatch Covers	– ⅛ × 2½

10
CHAPTER

For The Little Ones

Almost any toy will occupy a child's attention for a while. It might entertain them for a short time, or be so engrossing that it becomes the child's favorite toy.

SHAPE BOX

The Shape Box (Fig. 10-1) is a fun toy for a child, one that looks like dad's, grandpa's, or mom's toolbox, and one that helps the child develop his or her hand-eye coordination.

The Shape Box is built of ¾-inch thick material and dowel rod, which is easily found at any local lumberyard. Begin by cutting out the two sides, two ends, and bottom. The sides should measure ¾ inch thick, 3 inches wide, and 9 inches long. Cut the ends to ¾ inch thick, 3½ inches wide, and 5½ inches long. Cut off the upper corners at an angle,

Fig. 10-1. *The Shape Box is a toy that the younger child can play with and carry around.*

as shown in Fig. 10-2. Next, drill a ¾-inch-diameter handle hole at the central point as shown in the illustration. Cut the bottom with care, making sure the ends are square (at a 90-degree angle to the sides).

After the five parts have been cut, draw and cut out the shape cavities. On one side piece, draw out the designs shown in Fig. 10-3. Drill a round hole with a wood bit

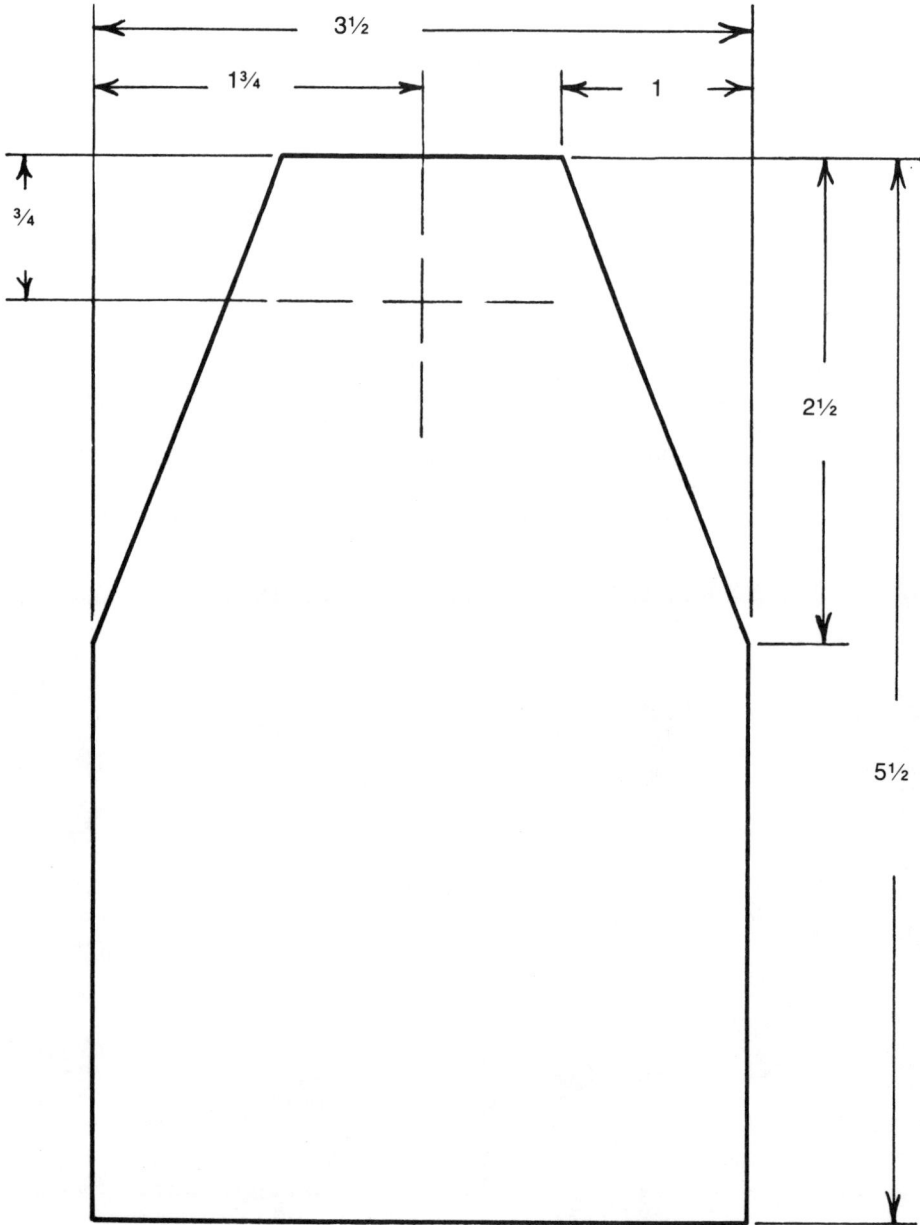

Fig. 10-2. *Cut the ends of the shape box to the shape shown.*

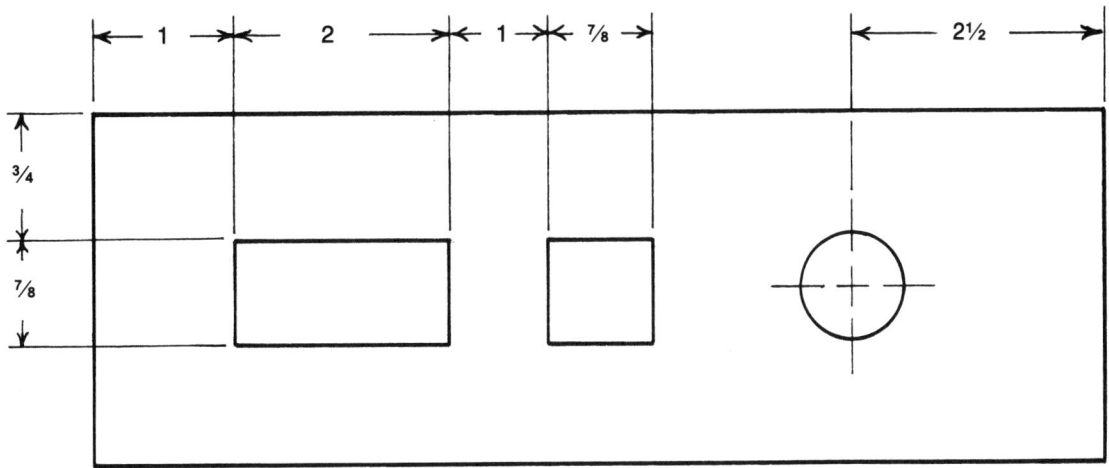

Fig. 10-3. *One side of the child's shape box and the size, shape, and location of the shape holes.*

that measures ⅞ inch in diameter. This will allow a 3-inch-long, ¾-inch-diameter dowel rod to easily fit through. Cut the square hole ⅞-inch square, allowing a ¾-by-¾-by 3-inch-long block to fit into the hole. Cut the rectangle on the side to a size of ⅞ inch tall by 2 inches wide. This will permit a ¾-inch-by-1⅞-inch-wide and 3-inch-long block to fit through.

On the other side piece, cut out a diamond-shape hole, with each side measuring ⅞ inch (Fig. 10-4). Next, cut a 3-inch-long by ¾-inch-wide square block, which will fit through the diamond-shape hole.

The next shape to cut out is a triangle. Cut the triangle hole so that it has a ⅞-inch-

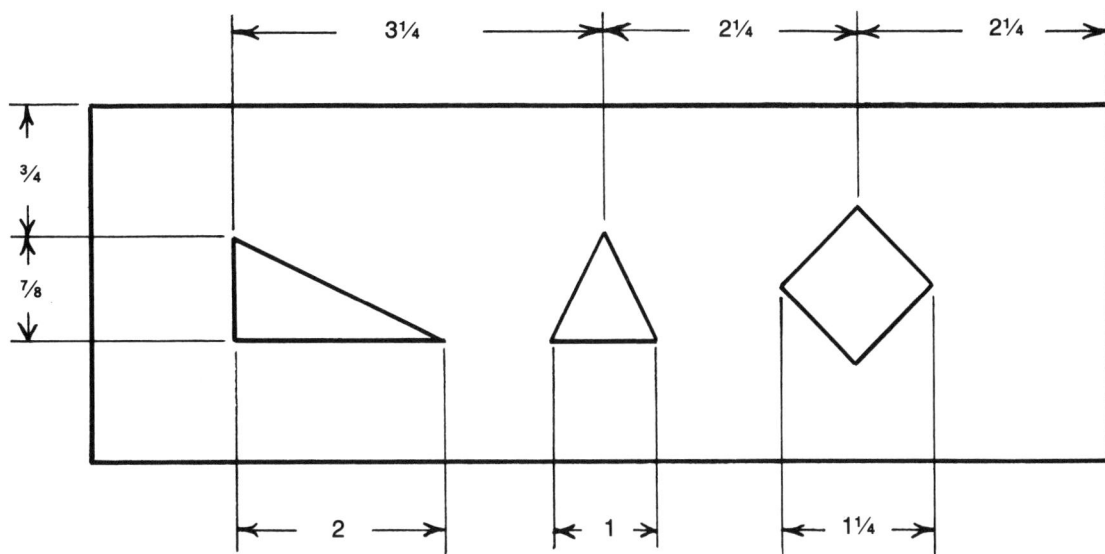

Fig. 10-4. *The second side of the child's shape box.*

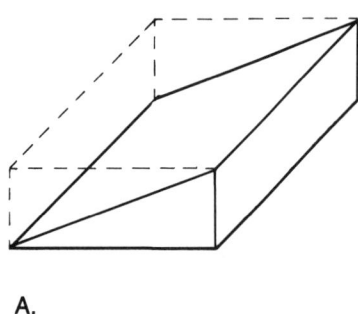

A.

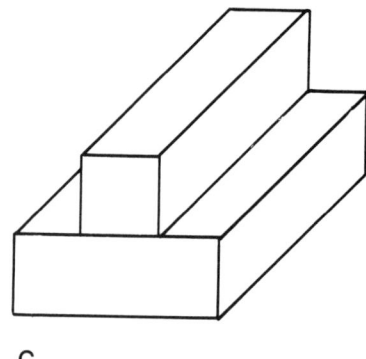

C.

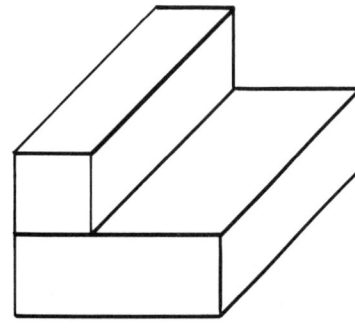

B.

Fig. 10-5. *The correct size and shape of the wedge-shaped piece.*

wide base and 1-inch-long sides. This hole will accept a shape cut from a ¾-inch-by-¾-inch-by-3-inch square block. You will have to cut or file the block into a triangular shape.

The final hole and block to cut in the side is similar to a ¾-inch-thick, 1⅞-inch-wide rectangular cut; but it has a diagonal cut from the upper corner to the opposite lower corner. The block that fits into this hole is a wedge that measures ¾ inch thick by 1⅞ inches wide, by 3 inches long (Fig. 10-5A). The diagonal can be cut or shaped with a file.

One end of the Shape Box should have an "L" shape cutout (Fig. 10-6A). The shape of the block that fits into the hole is shown in Fig. 10-5B. The block is made from one ¾-inch-by-¾-inch-by-3-inch long part glued onto a second piece which is also ¾ inch thick and 3 inches long, but 1¾ inches wide.

On the other end of the Shape Box, cut out an upside-down "T". The size and location of this cutout is shown in Fig. 10-7. The dimensions of the block to fit into the hole is shown in Fig. 10-5C. To make the block, begin by cutting a ¾-by ¾-by 3-inch piece of wood. Then glue it in the center of a piece that measures ¾-inch-by-1¾-inch-by 3 inches.

Figure 10-2A shows the central point for the ¾-inch-diameter hole that must be drilled for the handle. Care must be taken to ensure that the hole is drilled in the identical place on both end pieces, or the ¾-inch dowel handle will not properly fit.

Now that all of the parts have been cut out and their shape holes made, it is time to assemble the parts. Since this project will be used by young children, it is important that it is sturdy. A simple, glued butt joint will not be sufficient. Instead, you should use sixteen dowels, each ⅜ inch in diameter by 1½ inches long, to strengthen the joints.

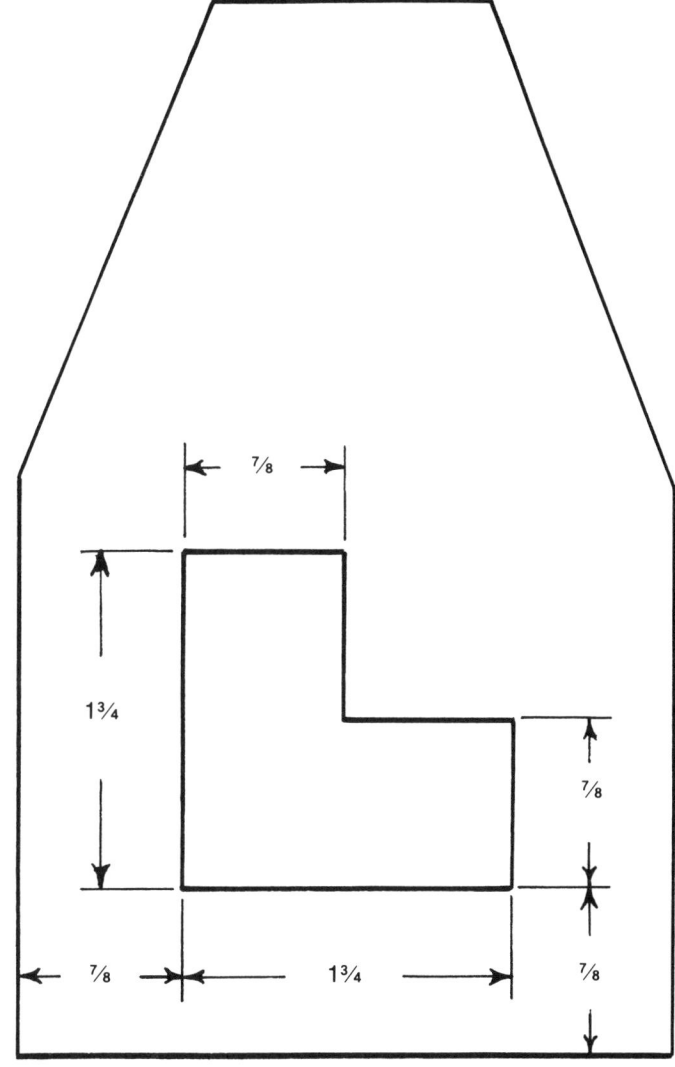

Fig. 10-6. *On one end of the shape box, cut an L-shaped hole as shown.*

Begin by temporarily clamping the box together so that the dowel holes can be drilled. Figure 10-8 shows where to drill the holes. The remainder of the 16 holes are drilled in the opposite corners in the same manner as shown.

Remove the clamps, apply glue to all surfaces that will be glued together, then put the clamps back on. Before the glue has had time to set, apply some glue into each of the dowel holes with a small paintbrush or toothpick, and insert the dowels. It might be necessary to tap the dowels lightly with a hammer to make sure they are firmly in place.

After allowing ample time for the glue to dry, the clamps can be removed. The portion of the dowels that extends out from the surface of the box can be cut off. A handsaw, such as a backsaw, is ideal for cutting the dowels. Take care, however, not to cut the dowels off so low that the saw teeth damage the surface of the project. Cut the dowels,

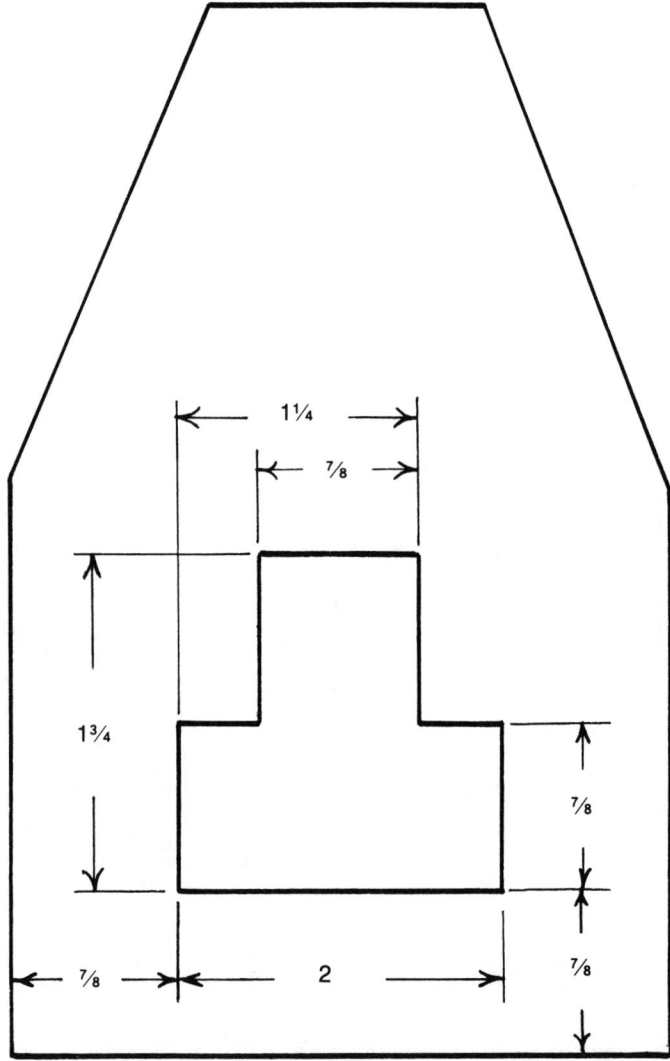

Fig. 10-7. On the other end, cut a T-shaped hole, as shown.

leaving about ⅛ inch above the surface. The remainder can then be filed off and sanded smooth.

Before sanding the entire project, glue a 9-inch length of ¾-inch dowel in the handle hole previously drilled. If the dowel sticks out beyond the end pieces, file and sand the ends flush.

After the entire project has thoroughly dried, sand each piece, taking time to eliminate splinters or sharp edges. The project can be stained, varnished, or brightly painted. Whichever finish you select, the project is sure to quickly become a favorite of the child.

TOOLBOX AND TOOLS

Child psychologists tell us that one of the largest sources of children's play is the

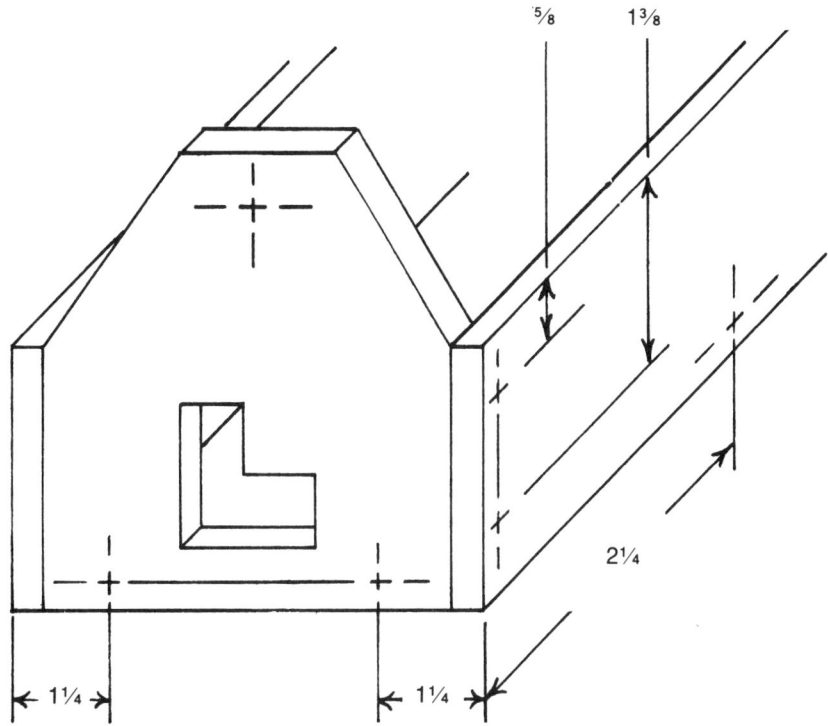

Fig. 10-8. The ends of the shape box can be doweled to the sides.

emulation of adult activities. In simple terms, kids love to play at what they see adults do. The child watches his or her parents drive the car for example, and, as soon as possible, the child grabs the steering wheel and pretends to drive.

The child's toolbox and tools (Fig. 10-9), are toys that the children can use to pretend to build, repair, or dismantle anything their imagination can dress up. But although the tools look real, they are completely nonfunctional, and are designed to be sturdy and safe. The key is for the children to use their imagination and exercise their creativity.

The toolbox is made of six pieces of wood, each measuring ¾ inch thick. The ends are each cut from a board measuring ¾ inch thick by 5½ inches wide by 6 inches long. Figure 12-10 shows how the two ends should be cut. Also shown is the location for a ¾-inch-diameter hole to be drilled through both ends of the end pieces. The handle will fit through the ¾-inch-diameter holes.

Glue the side boards, which measure 3½ inches wide by 17¾ inches long, to the two ends (Fig. 12-11). Make sure that the ends of the side boards and the end pieces of the box are flush.

After allowing sufficient time for the glue to set, drill ⅜-inch-diameter holes through the side boards and 1 inch into the box ends (Fig. 10-12). These ⅜-inch holes are made to accept ⅜-inch-diameter, 2-inch-long dowels. Glue them into place. They will greatly improve the strength of the assembly.

The bottom of the toolbox measures ¾ inch thick, 5½ inches wide, and 16 inches

Fig. 10-9. Children love to imitate others. The wood toolbox and tools will allow young carpenters to build all types of imaginary projects.

long. The bottom is designed to fit between the sides and ends and should also be doweled into place. Figure 10-13 illustrates where to drill the 3/8-inch-diameter holes. Drill them through the sides and one inch into the bottom. Glue the 2-inch-long dowel rods into the holes. Then allow the glue to set before sanding all of the dowel ends flush with the board's surface.

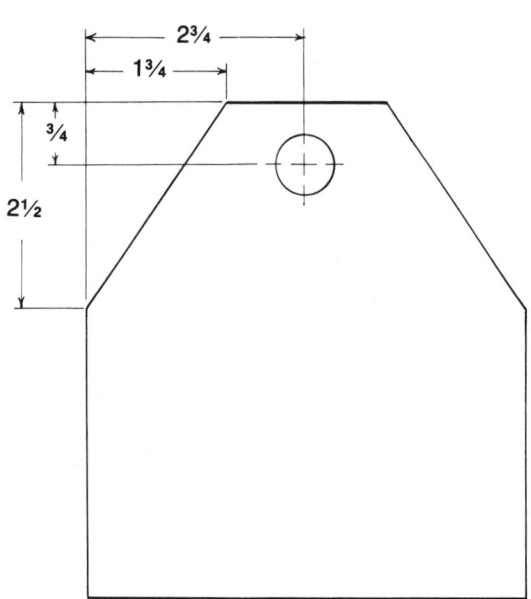

Fig. 10-10. The ends of the toolbox are cut from a board that is 3/4 inch thick, 5½-inches wide and 6 inches long.

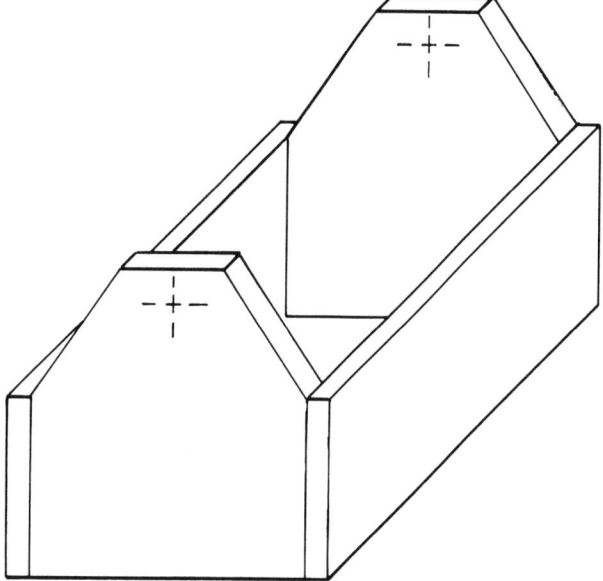

Fig. 10-11. *Glue the sides of the toolbox onto the ends as shown.*

There are only three steps that remain in the construction of the toolbox. The first step is to cut a 17½-inch length of ¾-inch dowel rod. Glue the rod into the two ¾-inch-diameter holes drilled in both ends. The last two steps are to sand the box to remove sharp edges or corners, and to apply some type of finish (varnish, paint, oil).

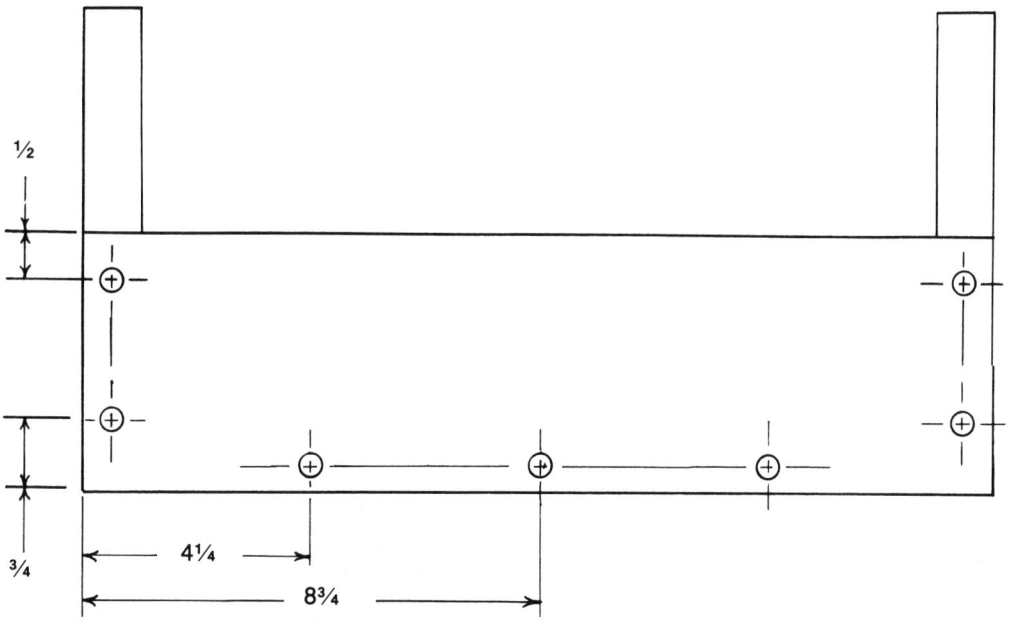

Fig. 10-12. *The location of the dowel holes. Glue and dowel the toolbox bottom between the sides and ends of the box.*

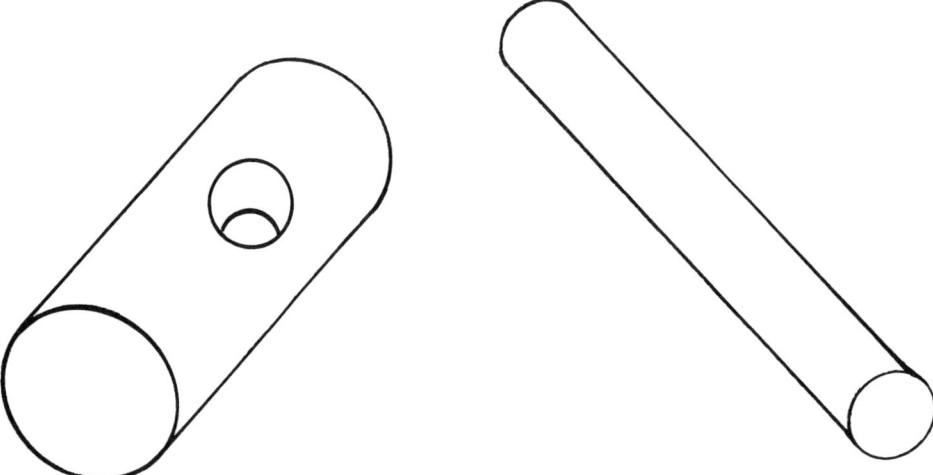

Fig. 10-13. *Drill the ¾-inch-diameter hole into the center of the 1⅛-inch-diameter dowel.*

Mallet

Begin building the collection of tools by making a wooden mallet. The wood mallet is made of two pieces of dowel rod. The head of the mallet is a 3-inch length of 1¼-inch-diameter dowel (clothes closet pole), and the mallet handle is a 6½-inch length of ¾-inch dowel.

Once you have cut the dowels to the correct length, drill a ¾-inch-diameter hole, ¾ inch deep in the middle of the mallet head (Fig. 10-14). Then glue the ¾-inch dowel into the hole. Sand all even and the assembly is completed.

Clawhammer

Like the mallet, the Clawhammer is made of two parts, a hammerhead and a ¾-inch-diameter dowel handle. Shape the hammerhead from a piece of 1½-inch-thick, 1¼-inch-wide, and 3½-inch-long piece of wood. The grid pattern shown in Fig. 10-14A shows the shape of the hammerhead. Draw the shape out of the board, then cut it out with a saw capable of cutting curves.

On the bottom of the hammerhead, locate the center by drawing two diagonal lines, as shown in Fig. 10-14B. Where the two lines intersect, drill a ¾-inch-diameter hole, ¾ inch deep. Also shown are the dimensions of the V-shaped claw.

After sanding the entire hammerhead to remove any sharp edges, cut a 6½-inch length of ¾-inch-diameter dowel rod. Glue the dowel rod into the hole in the bottom of the hammerhead.

Open-End Wrench

The Open-End Wrench is cut from a ⅜ inch thick piece of wood that is 1½ inches wide and 7 inches long. Figure 10-15 shows the shape of the wrench drawn on a grid

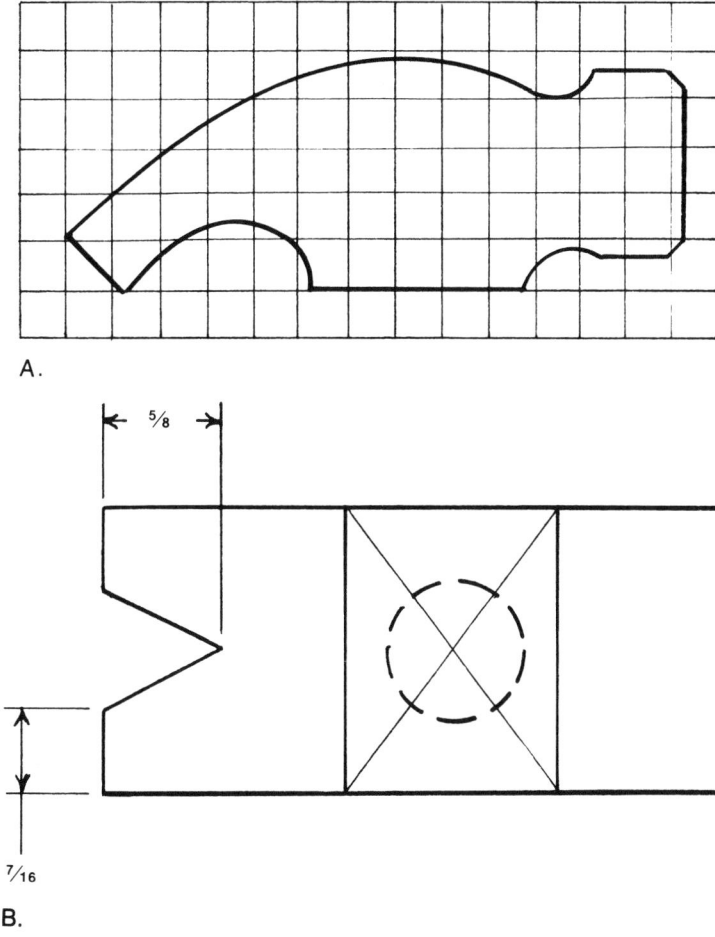

Fig. 10-14. *The claw hammerhead (A) profile; (B) top view.*

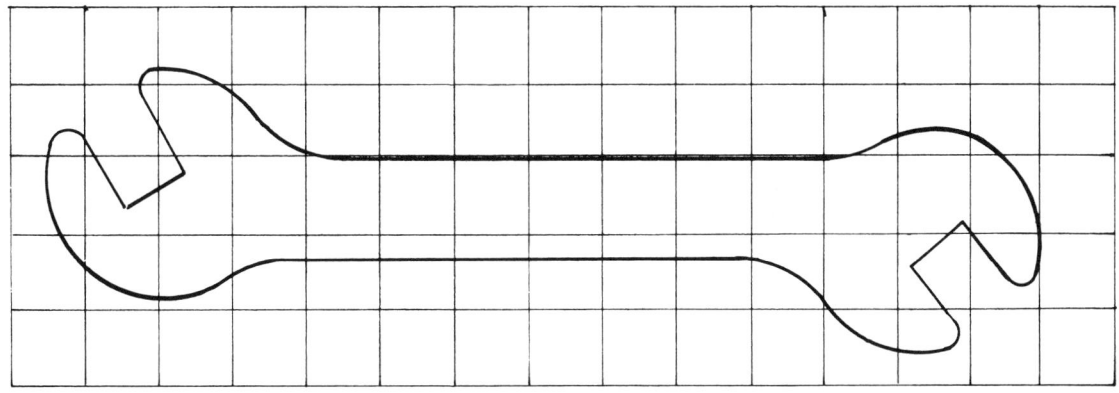

Fig. 10-15. *The shape of the open-end wrench is shown in the grid pattern.*

pattern. The grid pattern can be duplicated on heavy paper or cardboard, then traced onto the wood or drawn directly on the wood. After cutting out the wrench shape, round all sharp edges slightly to prevent any scratches.

Try Square

One of the tools often used by a woodworker is the Try Square. This toolbox should have one too.

Our Try Square is made from four ⅜-inch-thick by 1¼-inch-wide boards. Begin construction by cutting the four boards to length (Fig. 10-16). Cut two of them to a length of 4 inches (Part a), one to 3 inches (Part b), and the last to 6 inches (Part c). Assemble as shown (Fig. 10-16B).

Screwdriver

What toolbox would be complete without a screwdriver or two? This toolbox is complete! The screwdriver is made from two lengths of dowel. For the shaft of the screwdriver, use a dowel ⅜ inch in diameter and 5 inches long. For the screwdriver handle use a 3¼-inch length of 1-inch-diameter dowel. Construction begins by locating the center of one end of the 1-inch-diameter dowel. At this point, drill a ⅜-inch-diameter hole, 1 inch deep. Into the hole, glue the screwdriver shaft.

The top of the 1-inch-diameter dowel should be rounded, as actual screwdrivers are, so the sharp edges will not harm young hands. Also, in order to make the toy more realistic, file a half-round groove around the handle, near the bottom. The groove can be made with a small half-round file, or a round file.

With the screwdriver handle completely shaped and sanded smooth turn your attention to the "working end" of the screwdriver—the blade. The blade is on the end of the shank, and fits into the slot of the screw head. Since this screwdriver is not designed for actual use with a screw, the blade will not have to be shaped to an exact size.

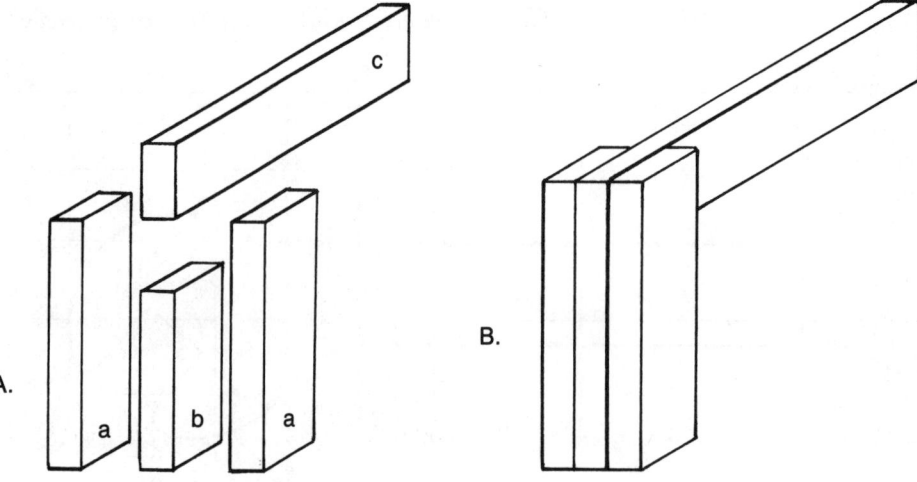

Fig. 10-16. *Assembly of the try square.*

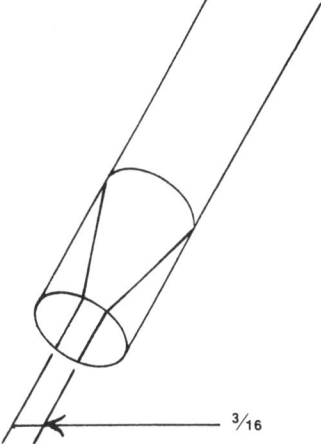

Fig. 10-17. The blade of the screwdriver is flattened on both sides.

In fact, it is better to intentionally leave the blade thick for safety's sake.

Begin by drawing the lines shown in Fig. 10-17. Remove the shaded area with a file or power sander and smooth a little more, if necessary.

Measuring Tools

The measuring instrument is one of the most vital tools found in the toolbox. The instructions that follow provide steps to make two types of measuring tools: the folding rule and the 1-foot bench rule (Fig. 10-18).

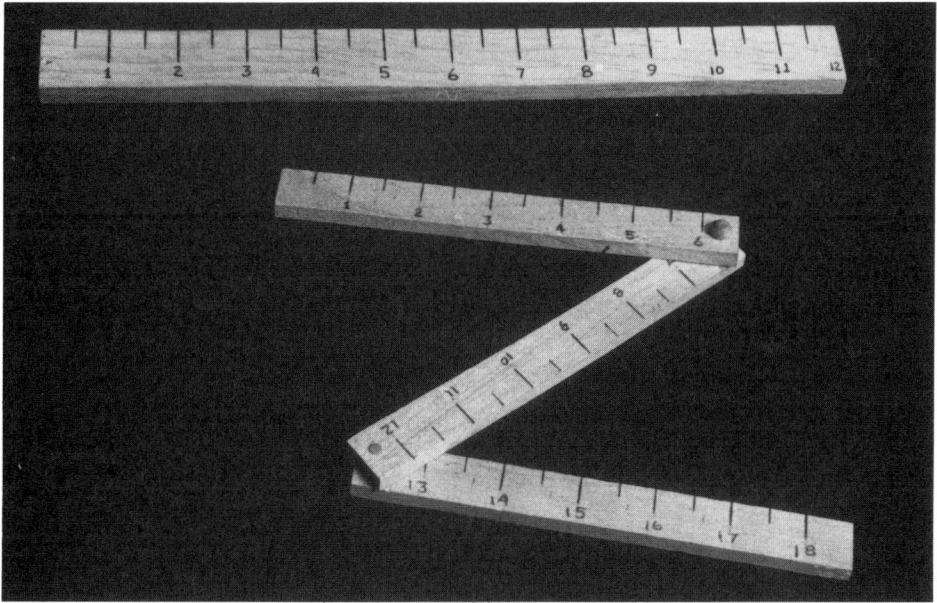

Fig. 10-18. Measuring tools are a must for the woodworker. The two shown here will be greatly appreciated by the young craftsperson.

Fig. 10-19. *The folding rule is made up of three pieces of wood each measuring ¼ inch thick, ¾ inches wide and 6½ inches long. Two of the pieces require holes drilled in their ends.*

Since the pieces for the folding rule are thin, you should use hardwood in order to make it sturdy. The three pieces should measure ¼ inch thick, ¾ inch wide, and 6½ inches long. On two of the pieces, drill a 5/16-diameter hole on one end (Fig. 10-19A). On the last stick drill two holes at the locations shown in Fig. 10-19B. (The 5/16-inch hole is for 5/16-inch axle pegs. However, you can use a 3/16-inch or 1/8-inch dowel, in which case you will have to drill the holes to the appropriate size.)

The folding rule can now be assembled, as shown in Fig. 10-20. Slip the peg through the hole of one of the two pieces with only one drilled hole. Then glue the peg into one of the holes in the piece with the two drilled holes. Remember to only get the glue in the second hole, not the first. The peg must turn freely in the first hole. The same holds true for attaching the third piece to the middle.

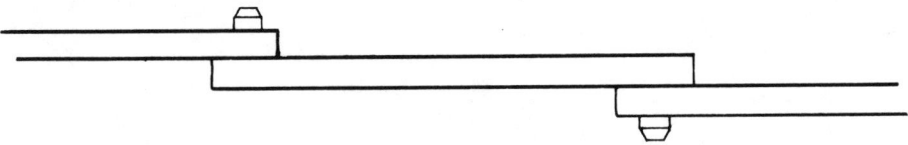

Fig. 10-20. *Assemble the three parts of the folding rule as shown.*

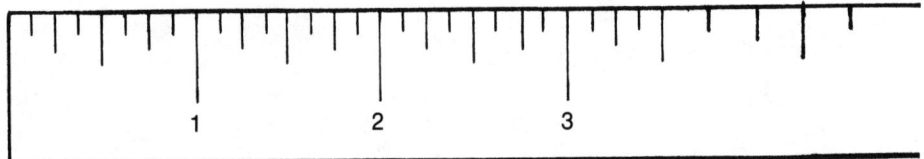

Fig. 10-21. *The increment markings of the inches can be made with a pencil, ink pen, fine point marker, or wood burner.*

When the glue has set, draw out the lines on the ruler to mark the parts of an inch (Fig. 10-21). The lines can be laid out with a pencil, but then should be darkened with a fine point marker, ink pen, or even burnt in with a wood burning tool.

For the 1-foot bench rule, use a piece of hardwood that measures 1¼ inches wide, ¼ inch thick, and 12 inches long. After a careful sanding, the parts of an inch should be marked in the same manner as for the folding rule.

Hand Drill

The Hand Drill is an action toy that resembles the actual tool. The main portion is built from an 8½-inch length of 1-inch-diameter dowel rod. Round one end of the dowel rod to remove the sharp edge. In the center of the other end drill a ⅜-inch-diameter hole to a depth of 1 inch.

There are a few more procedures to be done between the two ends, as shown in Fig. 10-22. Drill a hole for an axle peg, 3¾ inches up from the end with the ⅜-inch hole. One-half inch up from the bottom, draw a line around the dowel rod. File the lower end to resemble the shape of the hand drill chuck. Measure up from the ½ inch line 1⅛ inches. At this point, use the edge of a flat file to carve a V-shaped groove around the dowel. Glue the drill bit, which is a 4-inch length of ⅜-inch dowel rod, into the hole drilled into the bottom end of the hand drill chuck. When dry, round the lower end of the drill bit slightly to eliminate the sharp edge.

The turning hand crank is the next part to make. Cut the hand crank to a 3-inch-diameter, ⅜-inch-thick disk. In the center of the disk, drill a hole slightly larger than the hole that was drilled into the 1-inch-diameter dowel rod handle. Insert an axle peg through the disk hole and glue into the handle. This will enable the disk to turn freely on the axle peg.

The remaining step is to attach the hand crank knob to the 3-inch-diameter disk. The knob is a wood bead approximately 1 inch to 1¼ inches in diameter. The beads can be purchased from one of the toy part suppliers listed in this book, or from a craft store that sells macrame supplies. The bead can be held onto the disk by inserting an axle peg through the bead and glueing it into a hole drilled into the disk. This will allow the knob to turn while the disk is rotated.

The File

As most woodworkers are aware, there are few tools more versatile in the shaping of wood than the file. The File for this toolbox is made from three pieces of wood. The main part is ⅜ inch thick, 1 inch wide, and 11½ inches long. This part forms the file blade and part of the handle. The remainder of the handle is made from two ⅜-inch thick, 1-inch wide, by 3½-inch-long pieces of wood.

Construction of the file begins by glueing the two handle sections onto either side of the file blade (Fig. 10-23A). When dry, draw the handle shape onto the file handle (Fig. 10-23B). Then use a handsaw, jigsaw, or any other saw capable of cutting curves to shape the handle. Next, round the handle with a real file to remove the sharp edges. Further shaping and smoothing should be done with sandpaper.

To add a touch of realism to the file blade, draw lines at a 45-degree angle to the file edge (Fig. 10-24). The lines should be drawn approximately 3/16 inch a part and on

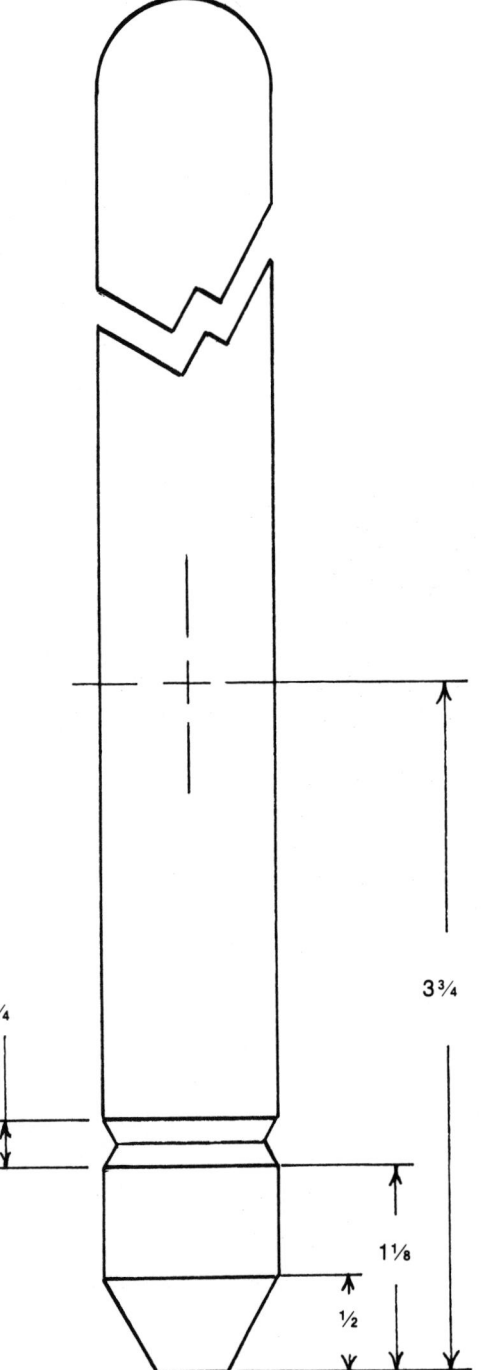

Fig. 10-22. Shape the drill body. Drill a hole at the point shown.

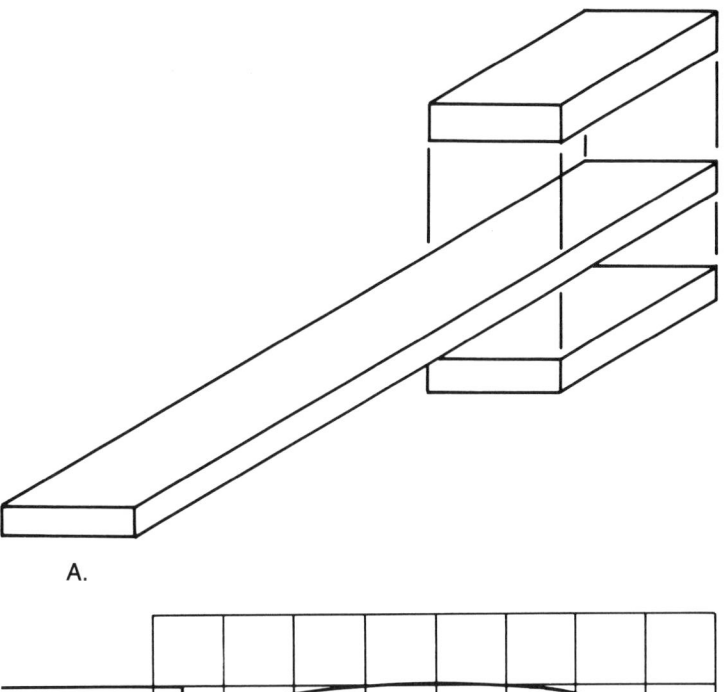

Fig. 10-23. Assemble the file as shown. When dry, shape the file handle, according to the grid pattern.

both sides of the blade. Then cut each line to a depth of 1/16 inch. These cuts will give the look and feel of a real file, but not the danger of a cutting edge.

The Saw

Almost every woodworking project involves the use of a tool that can cut wood. There is a handsaw (Fig. 10-25) in our toolbox to handle just such needs. Although the blade is constructed of wood, it can cut through the thickest, hardest wood a child's imagination can conjure up.

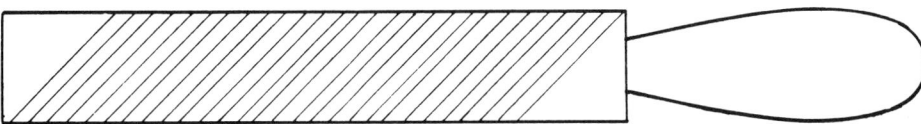

Fig. 10-24. Lines drawn at a 45-degree angle will resemble the cutting edge of a file.

215

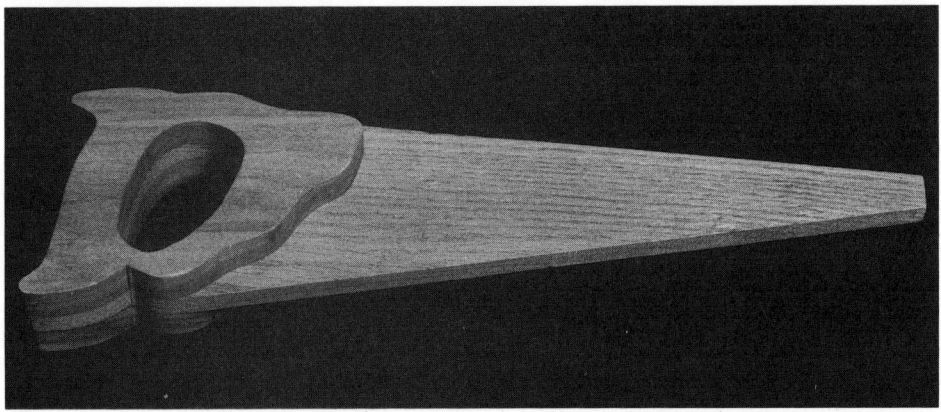

Fig. 10-25. The saw is a mainstay of the carpenter's toolbox. This saw looks great but is safe and will not damage other toys or furniture.

The Saw is made from three pieces of wood. Cut the blade from a piece ⅜ inch thick, which measures 5 inches wide and 14¼ inches long. Figure 10-26A demonstrates how the saw blade is cut. The shaded area in the drawing is material to be removed.

The two halves of the saw handle are each cut from a piece of ½-inch-thick wood that is 5 inches wide and 5½ inches long. Cut both pieces to the shape shown on the grid pattern in Fig. 10-26B. Cut the outline of the handle only. The hand hole will be cut out in a later operation. After cutting to shape, the handle halves should be filed and/or sanded, as it is much easier to perform these operations now rather than once the handles are glued in place. Then the two handle halves are glued onto the saw blade. Allow the handle halves to dry on the saw blade before proceeding further.

The part of the saw blade that extends out beyond the saw handles must be removed and made flush with the handle. The hole in the saw handle can also be cut out at this time. Cut through all three pieces of wood. After the cutting operation has been completed, the entire saw, blade, and handle, must be sanded to remove the sharp edges.

The toolbox with tools is a fun and exciting project for the craftsperson. Not all of the tools need to be built at once. You might wish to only make the toolbox and just a few tools, then add others to the collection as scrap wood or time becomes available.

BUILDING BLOCKS

Children love to stack objects one on top of another. A small child will stack cars, trucks, boxes, whatever is available. Often a child will then take pleasure in knocking them down and starting over again. With a set of building blocks (Fig. 10-27), a child can learn motor skills, proportion, size, and balance.

The building blocks in this section have been designed to be functional, easy to construct, and above all else, safe to play with. Because of the sizes, a small child is able to grasp even the largest block, yet the smallest will not fit into the mouth of the child.

Also, since the blocks are cut from common 2-by-4 lumber, the availability of the materials is not a problem, and the construction procedure is simplified. Finally, to further ensure the safety of the product, the parts are sanded smooth to prevent accidents.

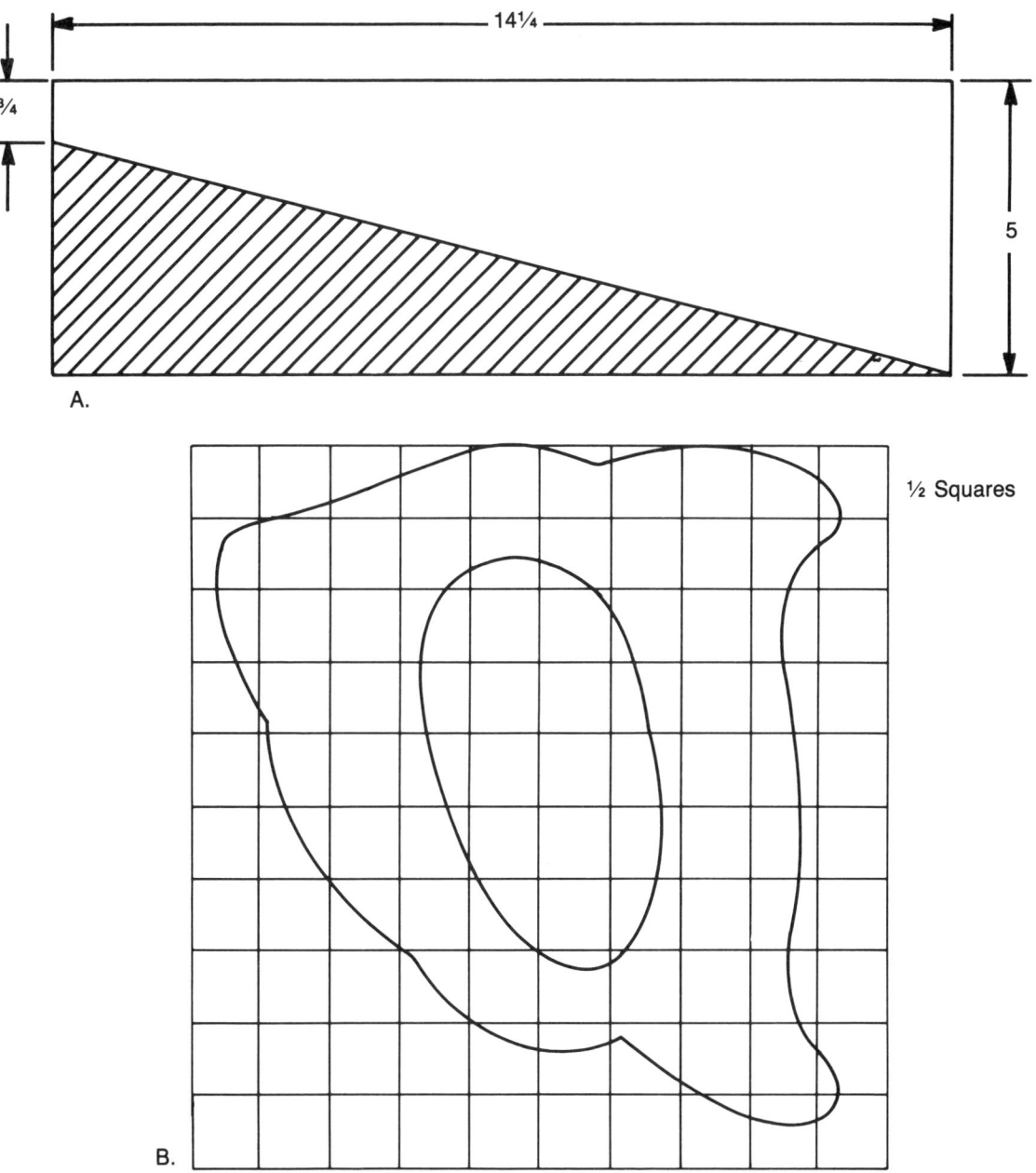

Fig. 10-26. (A) The saw blade; (B) The saw handle.

A length of 2-by-4 inch lumber, 10 feet long will be sufficient to create an average size set of building blocks. The average block set will include eighteen 2-by-4-by-5-inch blocks and ten 2-by-4-by-2½-inch blocks.

Begin by rough-cutting the pieces from the 2 by 4. Two are to be cut in half lengthwise

Fig. 10-27. Building blocks are one of the oldest and most reliable children's toy.

(Fig. 10-28A). Two more should be cut diagonally from corner to corner (Fig. 10-28B). In four of the blocks, drill a 1½-inch-diameter hole (Fig. 10-28C). Two of the blocks with the hole drilled should be cut in half across the block through the center of the hole (Fig. 10-28D).

The smaller blocks are similarly treated. Cut two of them diagonally from corner to corner and cut two more lengthwise in half. The remaining six short blocks are left as is.

By cutting the blocks in this manner, the block set will result in eight distinctly different shaped blocks. The various shapes provide more eye appeal for the child, and also gives the child more choices in selecting building materials.

The next step is one of the most important in the construction process. Sand each block thoroughly to eliminate any sharp corners, edges, or chips so that they resemble the blocks in Fig. 10-27. Well, why not?

Finally, the blocks can be painted, stained, varnished, oiled, or left natural. The natural finish is most desirable, since it does not introduce any potentially dangerous chemicals. Then just set the building blocks on the floor and watch the enthralled look on the child's face as he or she begins stacking.

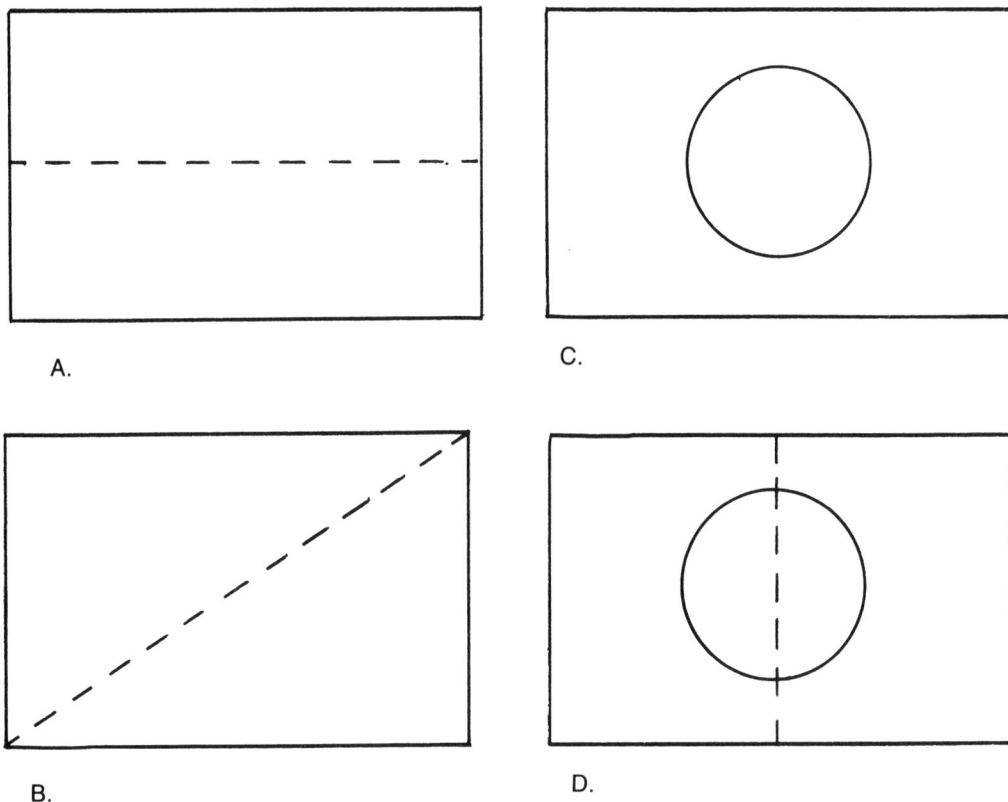

Fig. 10-28. Cut several of the larger blocks as detailed here.

SIMPLE PULL TOYS

The pull toys in this section have been designed to be cute and unique in their own simple way (Fig. 7-29). The pig, hound dog, and elephant, are all cut and painted to be viewed in profile and are permanently affixed to a wooden wagon. With a pull rope attached, they can be pulled around the house, on the sidewalk, or taken anywhere.

The directions that apply to all of the three pull toys. The size of the wagon is the same for each animal, and the construction procedure for each is essentially the same.

Begin by drawing out the animal profiles. This is done by laying out a ½-inch square grid pattern on a sheet of thick paper or cardboard. Then transfer the animal design (Fig. 10-30A, B, or C) onto the paper grid pattern. (*Note:* The animal designs shown in the crayon carriers unit can also be used.)

Cut out the outline of the animal, place it on a piece of wood (2-by-5-by-inch 6 for the elephant, 2-by-3½-by 7½-inch for the hound dog, 2 by 5 by 8-inch for the pig), and trace the outline. Use a coping saw or jigsaw to cut out the profile. Be careful to take time and follow the line accurately. This will reduce the amount of filing on the rough outline. Using a file and sandpaper, round the edges of the animal and sand the edges

Fig. 10-29. *Children enjoy pulling toys along behind them. These toys are designed for just that.*

and surfaces thoroughly, making certain there are no parts that could harm a child.

The animal figures can be finished in any of a number of methods. The eyes, ears, or mouths, can be painted onto the bare wood, then the entire area varnished. Try the varnish over the paint on a piece of scrap first to make sure the paint and varnish do not react adversely with one another. Another possibility is to paint in colors which closely resemble the animals in real life. You could also simply stain and varnish them, allowing the animal profile to tell the story.

While the animal profile is drying, it is time to build the wagon, which is built from a piece of wood ¾ inch thick, 4 inches wide, and 9 inches long. On the edges of the wagon, drill two axle holes at the locations shown in Fig. 10-31A. The diameter of each hole is determined by the axle peg you use. Repeat the drilling of these holes on the opposite edge. The wooden wheels can now be glued in place.

There are two other holes that must be drilled in the wagon. The first is a ¾-inch-diameter hole drilled ½ inch deep. Then drill a ¼-inch-diameter hole through the board at the center of the ¾-inch hole (Fig. 10-31B).

The pull toys in the photographs have round wood balls on the end of the pull rope. You can obtain the wood balls from some of the toy part suppliers listed in the Appendix, or in craft stores that sell macrame supplies. If the wood balls do not have a hole drilled through them already, drill a ¼-inch-diameter hole through the center of the ball. Then

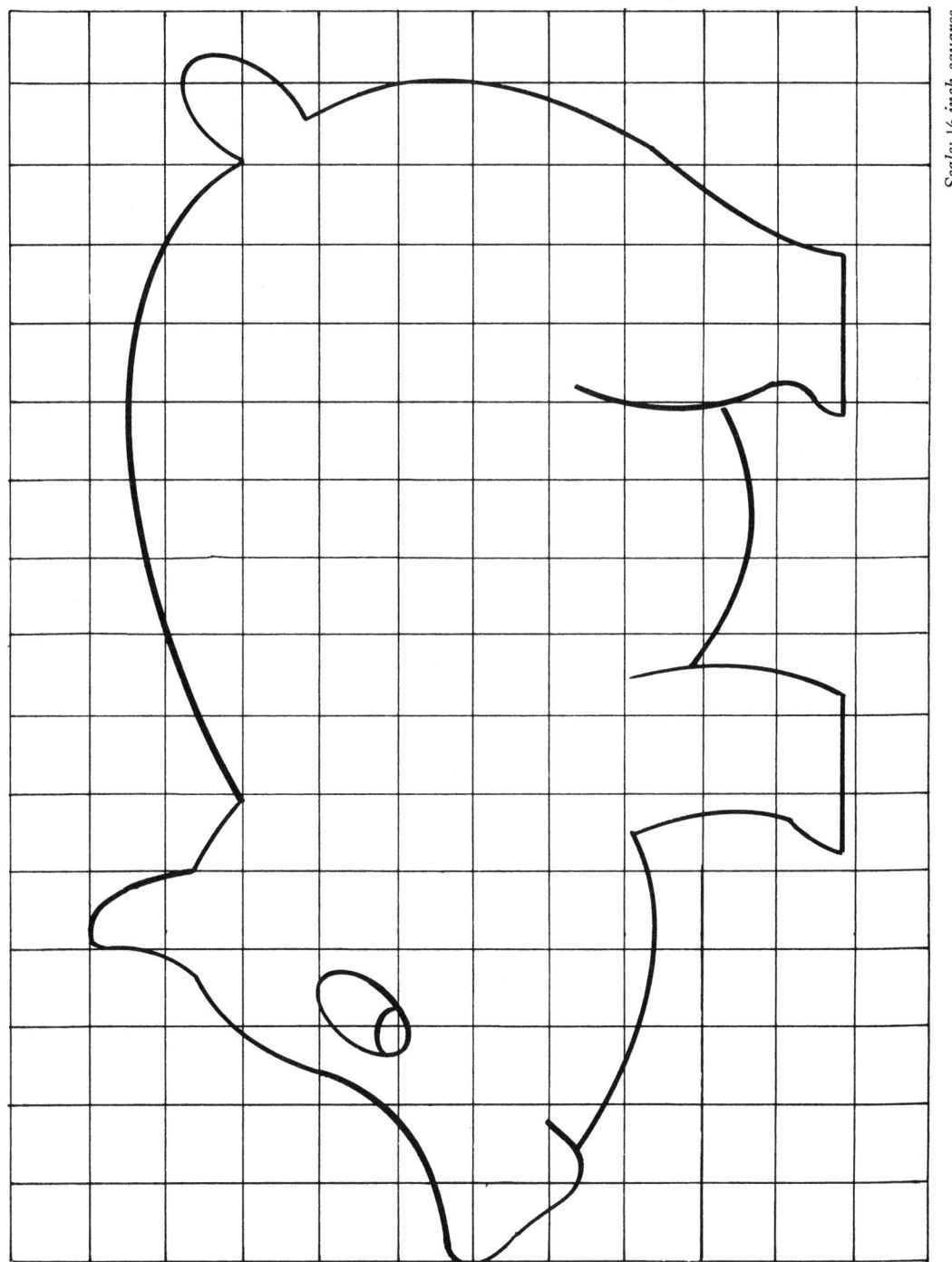

Fig. 10-30. Use the grid patterns shown here to create animal designs to decorate the pull toys. Scale: ½-inch squares

Scale: ½-inch squares

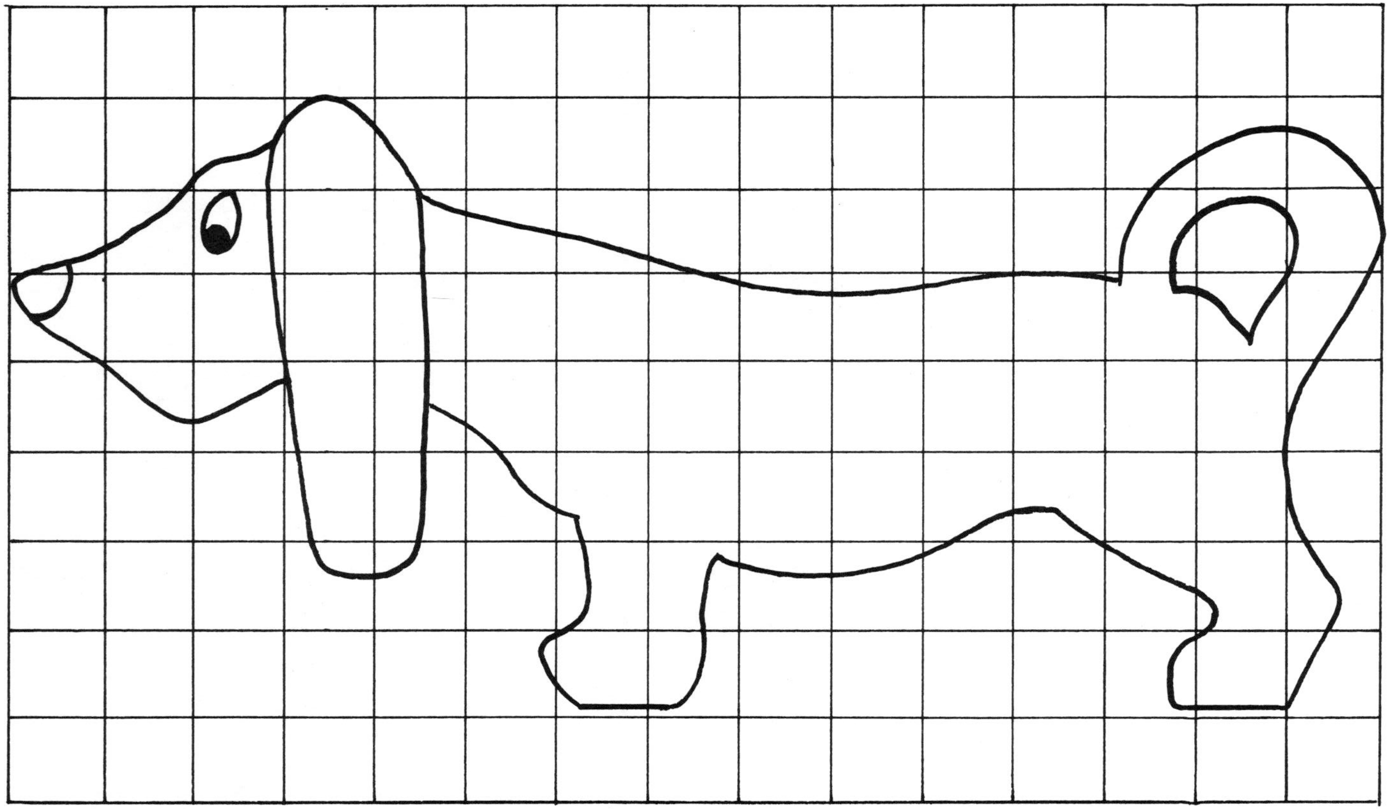

Fig. 9-14. Continued.

Scale: ½-inch squares

223

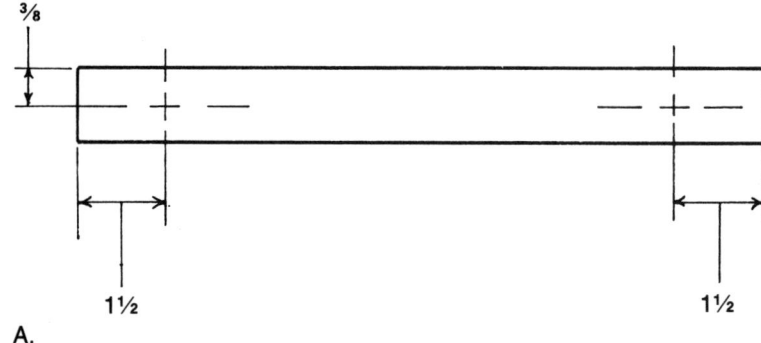

A.

B.

Fig. 10-31. *The two drawings show the locations of holes that are drilled in the edges and the top of the wagon.*

drill a ½-inch-diameter hole, centered in the ¼-inch hole, approximately ⅜ inch deep (Fig. 10-32).

The two different-size holes in the wood ball and in the wagon are drilled so that when you put a ¼-inch-diameter nylon pull rope through the wood ball, you can tie a knot, and the knot will be hidden within the hole.

Do the same on the bottom of the wagon where the knot is tied; The knot on the end of the rope will be hidden in the ½-inch-deep hole on the bottom of the wagon (See Fig. 10-33).

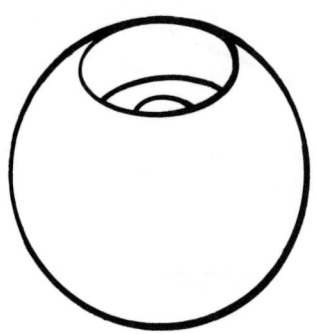

Fig. 10-32. *The wood ball used as a pull has two holes drilled into it. This allows the knot tied in the pullrope to be concealed in it.*

Fig. 10-33. Attach the ¼-inch-diameter rope to the wagon and the wood knob.

The last step is to secure the animal to the wagon. Center the animal on the wagon, then lightly trace around the feet. Then remove the animal. In the center of these two squares, and drill a ⅜-inch-diameter hole through the wagon, in the center of the two penciled squares. Likewise, you must also drill ⅜-inch holes into the animal feet that will line up exactly with the holes in the wagon. When all of the holes have been drilled, glue the animal to the wagon with two ⅜-inch dowel rods that go through the wagon and into the animal's feet. These dowels will secure the animal firmly to the wagon.

That's it. Those are the steps involved in building the simple pull toys. The toy is just that simple to build. All that remains is to add some type of finish, either paint, stain and varnish, or just varnish. Then watch the child pull the animal around room to room.

JUMPING AND PROFILE BEARS

The Profile Bear and Jumping Bear (Fig. 10-34), are both built in much the same manner. The head and torso of both animals are made from a single ¾-inch-thick board. The arms and legs are cut from ½-inch-thick wood, and are pinned in place so that they can pivot. These are two quick and easy, fun projects.

Both are begun by drawing the body and head design on a ¾-inch-thick piece of wood. Common pine works well. The body design for both bears is shown in Fig. 10-35.

First draw out a ½-inch square grid pattern on a piece of cardboard. Then draw the design, using the patterns as a guide. Then cut out the cardboard design and trace onto the ¾-inch-thick board. Next, cut out the bear design, using a coping saw, jigsaw, or scroll saw. Slow, careful cutting will result in a smoother edge, thus requiring little or no filing, and very little sanding.

The arms and legs of both bears are cut from ½-inch-thick stock, with the grain of the wood running the length of the "limb." Figure 10-36A provides a grid pattern for the right arm and leg of the Profile Bear. The grid pattern in Fig. 10-36B is for the Jumping Bear. The left leg and arm are just the same, but reversed.

As with the head and body, cut out the legs and arms carefully to avoid excessive filing and sanding. The inserting lines on the grid pattern mark the location of 5/32-inch-

Fig. 10-34. *These two bears are not just to look at, but to play with. Each has posable arms and legs.*

diameter holes that must be drilled. The next step is to drill the holes in each piece, all the way through the wood.

Temporarily assemble the bears using the axle pegs that are used on many of the automobiles and trucks in this book. There are, of course, other methods of attaching the limbs to the torso, such as glue, nails, and screws—but all of these methods are inadequate. With these other methods, the arms and legs are not allowed to move freely, or they might become loose and pose a potential health threat to their young owners.

Once you've completed the assembly inspection, take the pieces apart and sand the edges of each to remove any sharp edges. The next-to-last step is to stain, varnish, paint, or apply some form of finish to all parts. Allow the finish to dry properly according to the directions, and then assemble the bear.

To assemble the bear so that it will move properly, you must apply the glue only to the hole in the torso and not to the hole in the arm or leg. The axle peg should then slide through the limbs easily and become glued permanently into the body. While the limbs are being glued into place, occasionally move them to ensure that they still pivot.

Both of the bears are fun, easy, and fast projects to build. In addition, each is a neat, attractive sales item that is a sure hit at most craft fairs.

CLOWN DOLL

The Clown Doll (Fig. 10-37) is a bright, attractive doll that is unlike many of the dolls of today. The Clown Doll has fully jointed arms, legs, and body. The knees, elbows,

Scale: ½-inch squares

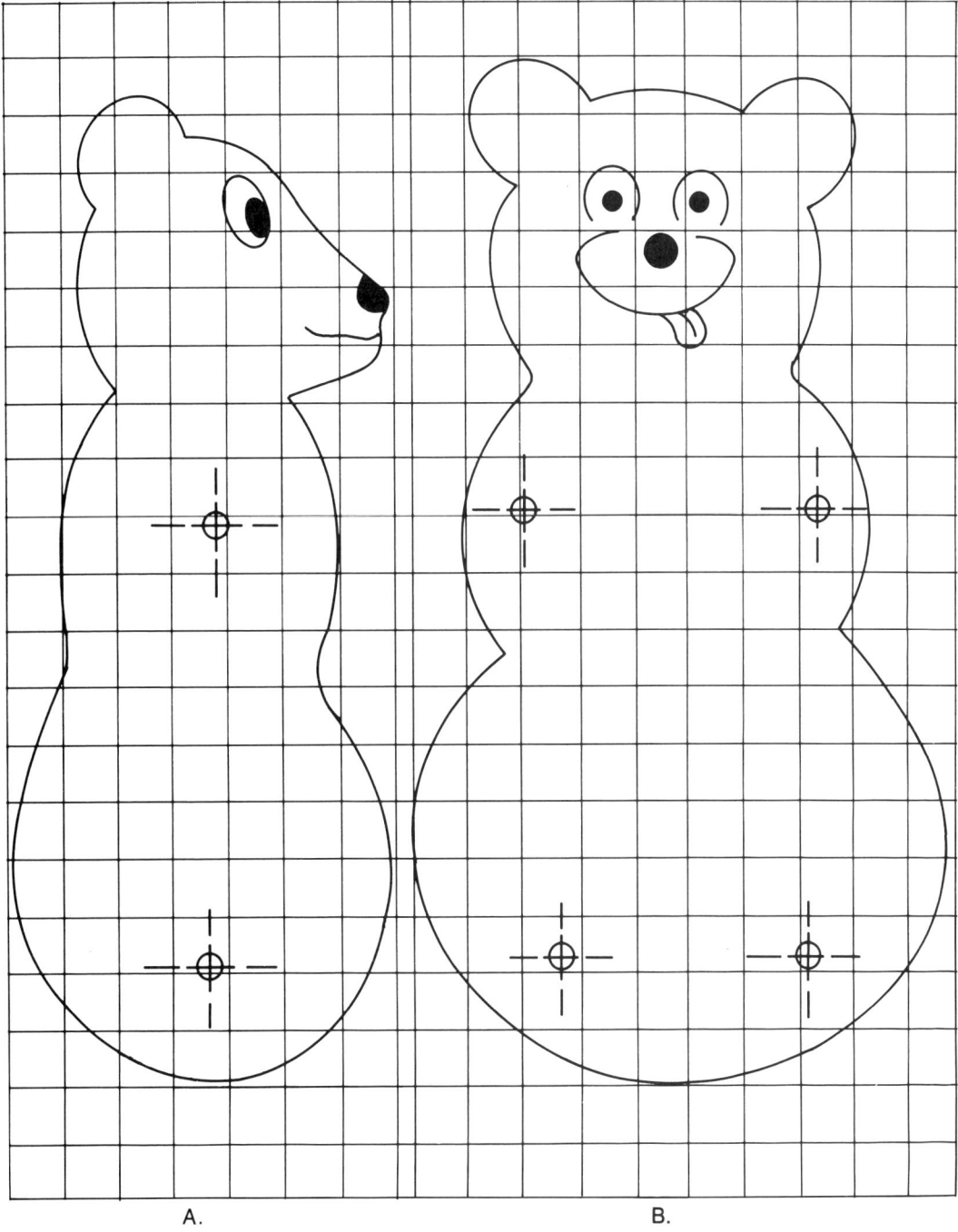

A.   B.

Fig. 10-35. *Grid patterns for the design of both bears.*

Scale: ½-inch squares

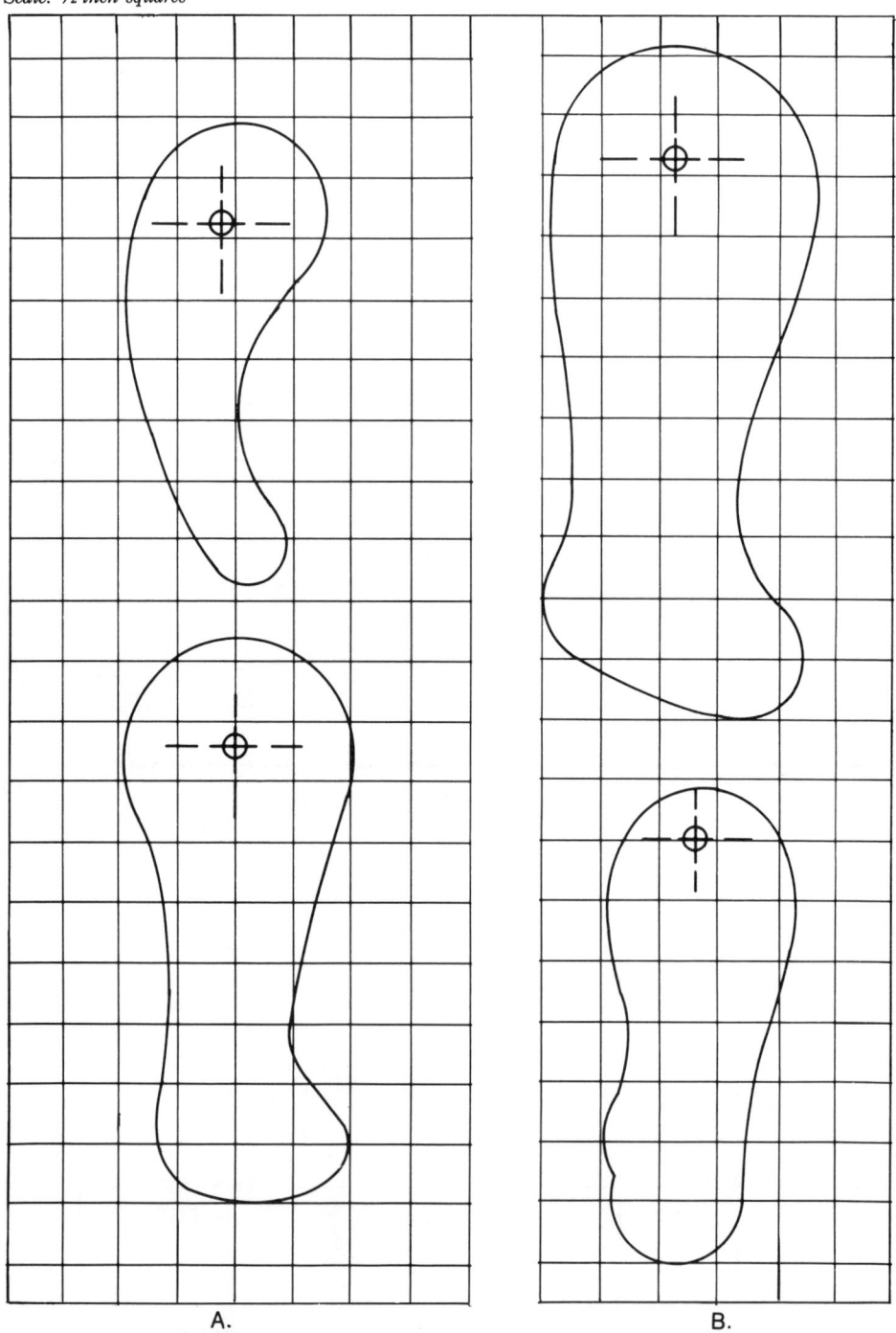

A.   B.

Fig. 10-36. *(A) The grid pattern shows the shape of the right arm and leg for the Profile Bear. The left arm and leg are identical. (B) The grid pattern for the arms and legs of the Jumping Bear.*

Fig. 10-37. The handmade, all-wood clown doll is a joy for the lucky child who receives it and a lot of fun for the craftsperson who builds it.

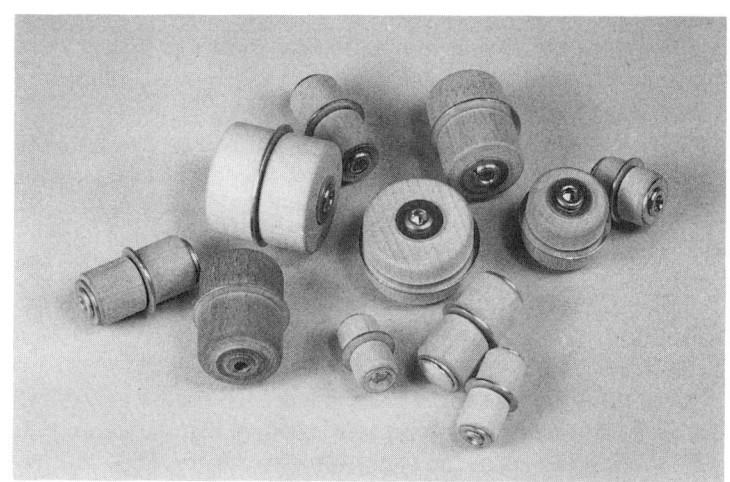

Fig. 10-38. The body (waist) and the head are assembled with swivel joints through the use of two 1/8-diameter "roto-hinges."

wrists, and ankles bend through the use of a pinned joint. The shoulders and hips also swivel with the help of roto-hinges, a new type of hinge that can be completely concealed (Fig. 10-38). The hinges can be purchased from many of the companies listed in the Appendix, or they can be obtained directly from the Roto-Hinge Company. (The address can also be found in the Appendix.) All of this jointery results in a Clown Doll that can be posed in almost any position. It's a toy that not only can be played with, but plays back.

The head is a good place to begin. It can be turned on a wood lathe, if one is available. The shape of the head is flexible—a round, cone, oval, or almost any other shape can be used. The size is also not of great importance; but a head that is about 3 inches in diameter at its widest point, and 3 inches long, is proportional to the body.

If a wood lathe is not available, many craft shops and larger lumberyards sell wood balls in various sizes. The balls are sold for many decorative purposes, but will be fine for the doll head.

The face of the clown shown in Fig. 10-37 has painted-on eyes and mouth. The small pom-pom nose and the hair can be purchased from craft stores or craft departments of larger stores. However, do not be bound by the face shown in this photograph. Use your imagination to create original designs.

In the center of the bottom of the head, drill a ½-inch-diameter hole, 1 inch deep. This hole will later be used to attach the head to the body, along with a ½-inch roto-hinge.

The torso of the Clown Doll is cut from three very similar pieces of ½-inch-thick material, each measuring 2¾ inches wide and 6⅜ inches long that will be glued together, back to front. (Refer to Fig. 10-38 to better visualize this). It is easiest to cut the shape of the three torso sections: front, middle, and back, at the same time, rather than individually. This will ensure that all parts are alike. To do this, nail the body parts together, surface to surface. Then transfer the body shape, as it is shown in Fig. 10-39, onto the top body part only. Afterwards, drill the two ³⁄₁₆-inch holes shown, and the body can be taken apart.

Once cut, separate the parts in preparation for the additional cutting to be done. Make two cuts on the bottom of the front piece, so the legs will end properly (Fig. 10-40). Cut two slots from the bottom of the middle section for the legs and two semicircles for the arms (Fig. 10-41). Cut the same size slots out of the bottom of the back piece (Fig. 10-42).

When the three pieces have been cut to their appropriate shapes, glue the three body parts together, keeping the outside edges even. Allow time for the glue to set before proceeding with the next steps.

On the top of the body, in the center of the shoulder area, drill a ½-inch-diameter hole, ½-inch deep. This hole should match with the ½-inch-diameter hole you previously drilled in the bottom of the head. The pattern in Fig. 10-39, which shows the basic outline of the body parts, also shows a dashed line across the mid-section. Cut the body in half along this line.

There are two ½-inch-diameter holes drilled into the center of the body halves, one in each half. Glue a ½-inch roto-hinge into these holes (Fig. 10-43). This will act as the doll's waist.

The arms and legs are all made in much the same way, with some slight variations. To begin, obtain a 25-inch-long piece of wood that measures ¾ inch thick and ¾ inch wide. The two forearms and two lower leg parts are identical. They measure 2½ inches

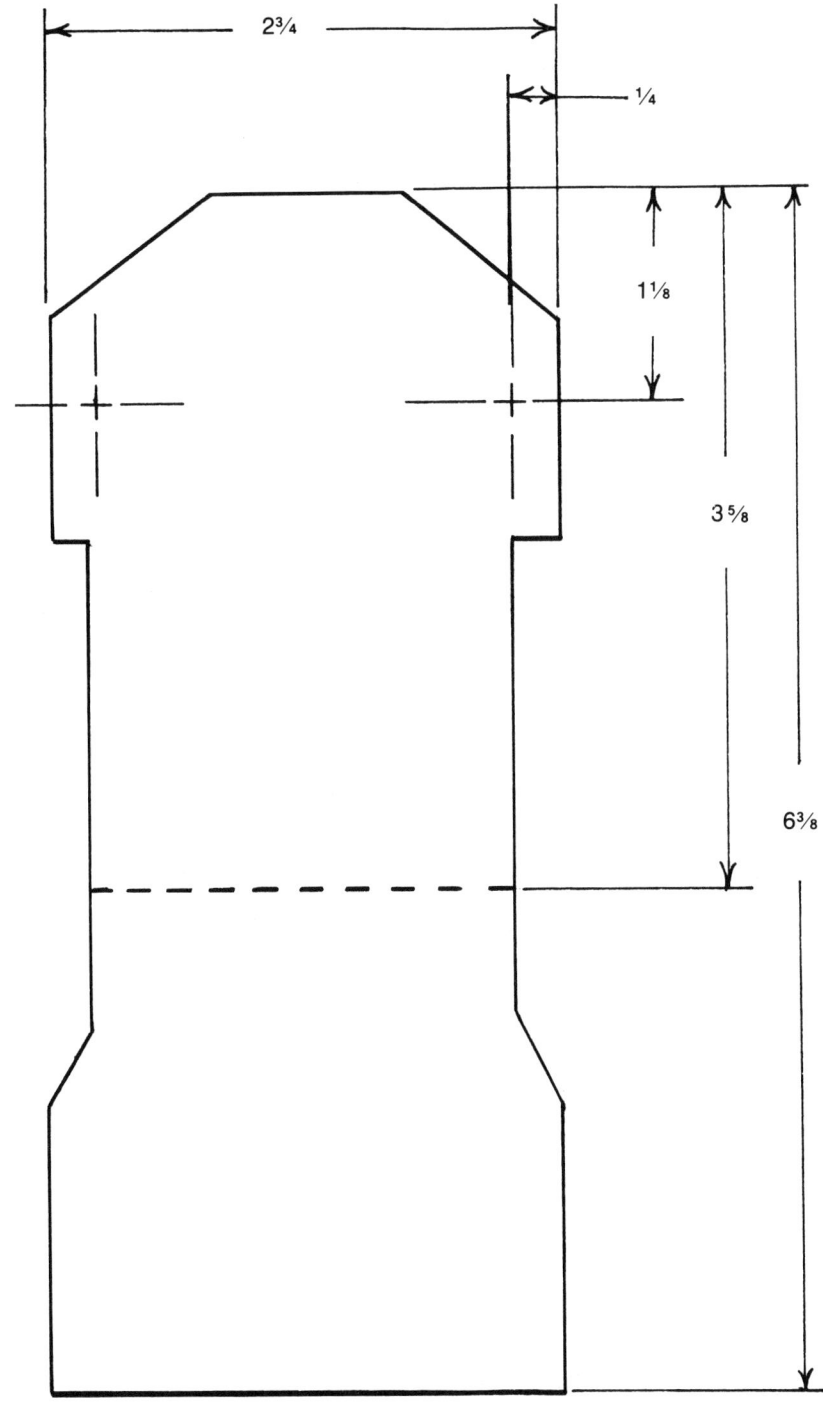

Fig. 10-39. The shape of the clown doll torso.

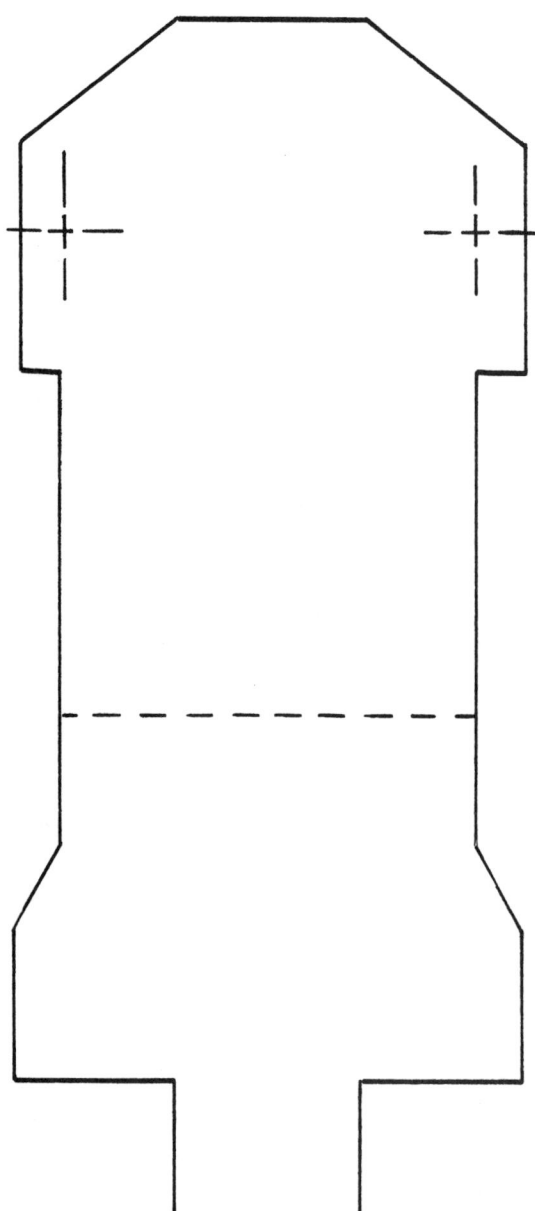

Fig. 10-40. Cut two notches out of the front piece of the torso so that the legs can bend fully.

long. Figure 10-44 illustrates how the first four parts are cut. Take care when laying out the cutting lines, and take time to cut accurately.

The four 2½-inch-long parts, as well as all of the other leg and arm parts, are rounded to a ⅜-inch radius. Also, on both ends of all of the arm and leg parts, drill 3/16-inch-diameter holes for all leg and arm parts, as shown in Fig. 10-45.

Make the two upper leg parts in the same manner as the four parts previously de-

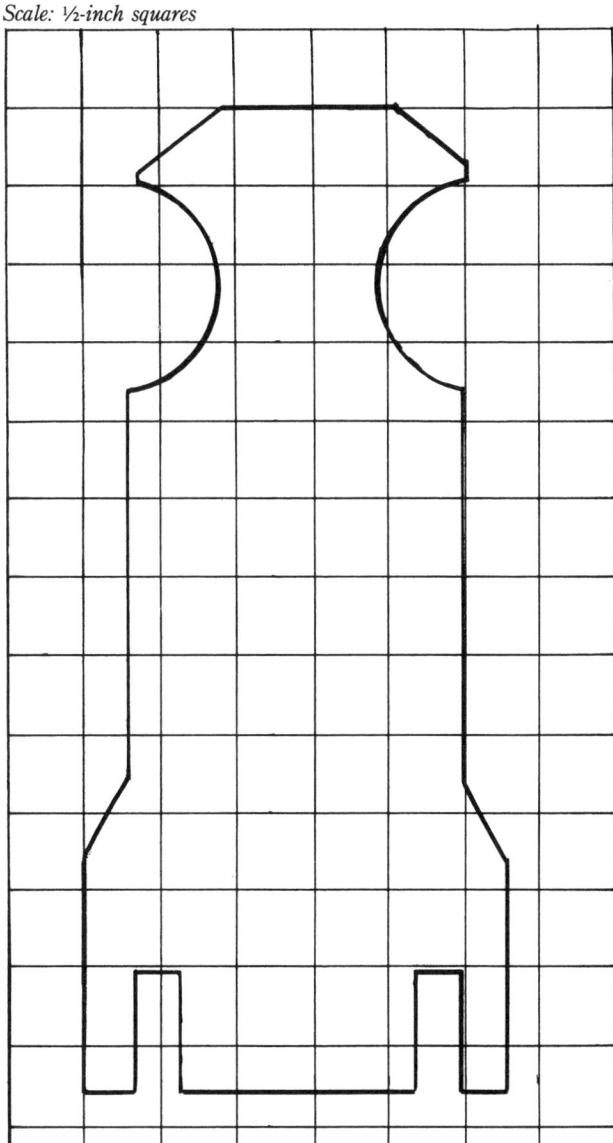

Fig. 10-41. Cut two semicircles in the middle section of the clown doll for the arms. Also cut slots for the legs.

scribed, but with a total length of 3½ inches. The radius and hole locations are the same.

The last two parts are the upper arms. These are made a bit differently. The ends are alike, with no recess cut (Fig. 10-46A). Figure 10-46B shows the layout for the second upper arm parts. Drill the holes and round the ends to a ⅜-inch radius, as was done on the other arm and leg parts.

The final construction step, prior to assembly, involves the lower part of the body. Round the front and back bottom corners of the body to a slight radius, so that the body

Scale: ½-inch squares

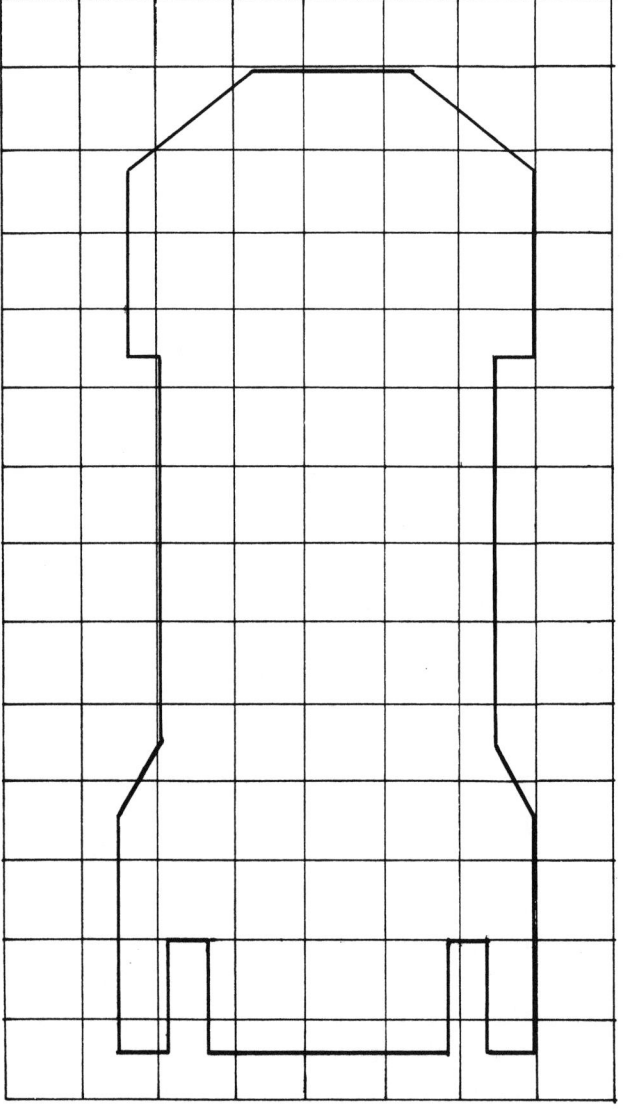

Fig. 10-42. *The back torso section has the same two leg slots as on the middle section.*

will not interfere with the movement of the legs (Fig. 10-47). Also drill two 3/16-inch-diameter holes into the sides of the lower body. These holes will be used to pin the legs into place.

The arms and legs can now be tested to ensure that they fit properly. It might be necessary to sand or file some parts so that they move freely. Pin the joints together by using small axle pegs or 3/16-inch-diameter dowel rods. Glue the dowels into the 3/16-inch holes, taking care to apply glue only in the holes of the arm and leg part. The matching part must be able to move freely. The photograph in Fig. 10-48 shows the legs and arms attached to the body.

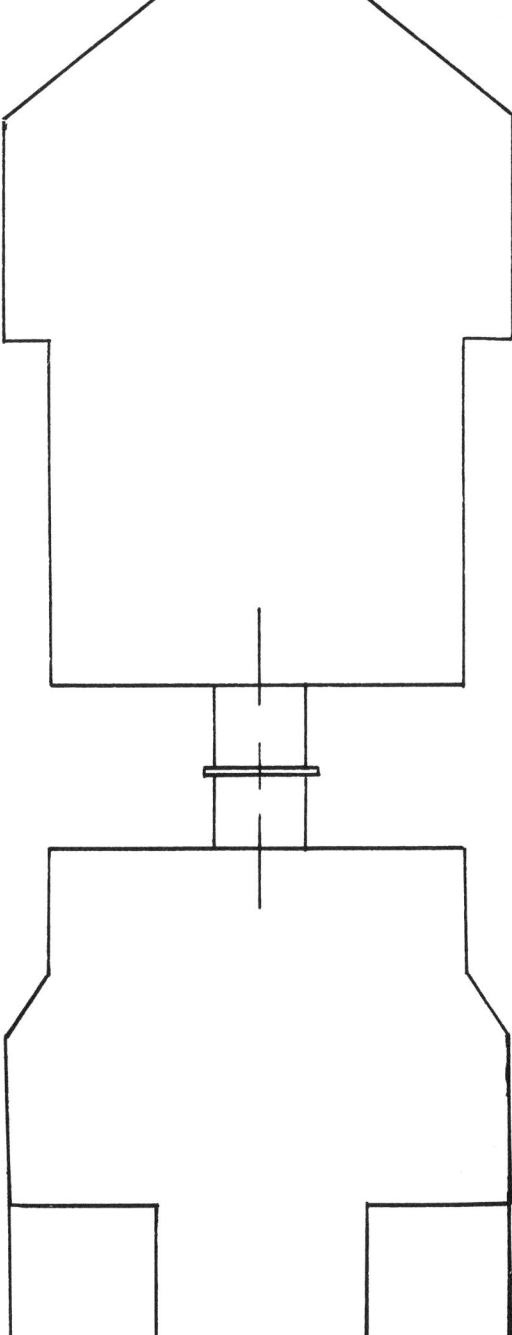

Fig. 10-43. Cut in half the glued-together body torso along the dashed line, then reassemble by glueing a ½-inch "roto-hinge" between the two holes.

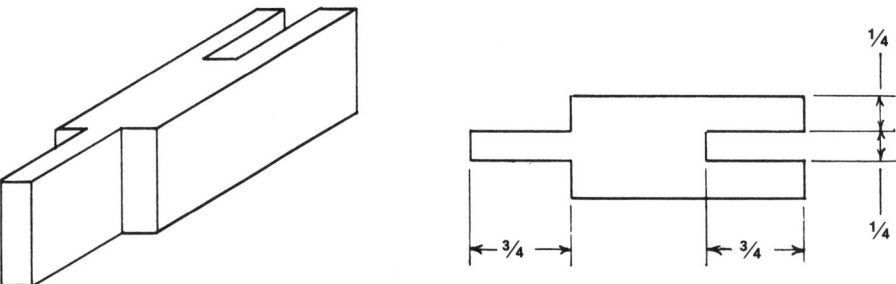

Fig. 10-44. Shape the two forearm and two lower leg parts to the specifications.

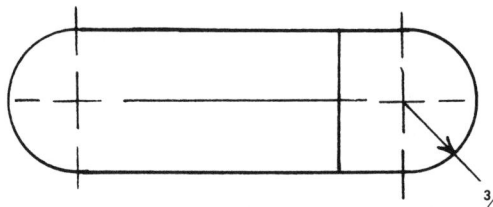

Fig. 10-45. Round the ends of the arm and leg parts to a 3/8-inch radius. Drill at points indicated.

The remaining parts to be made are the hands and feet. The hands are made as if they have on mittens, for ease of cutting. Cut each hand from a ¾-inch-thick, 1⅝-inch-wide, 2⅜-inch-long piece of wood. The shape of the hand is shown on the grid pattern in Fig. 10-49A. Notice that there is a ¼-inch-wide recess cut on the end of the hand. Also drill the 3/16-inch hole, at the point indicated in the drawing.

Figure 10-49B shows the shape of the foot. Notice that the foot has a ¼-inch-thick

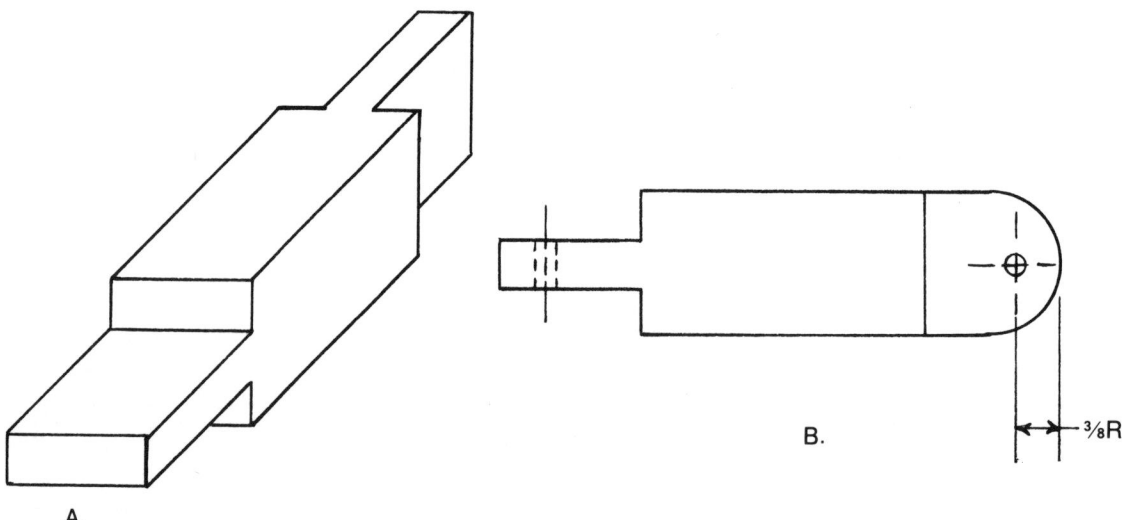

Fig. 10-46. (A) The upper arm parts of the clown doll are made somewhat differently than the other arm parts, in that neither end has a recess. (B) Drill the hole at the point indicated.

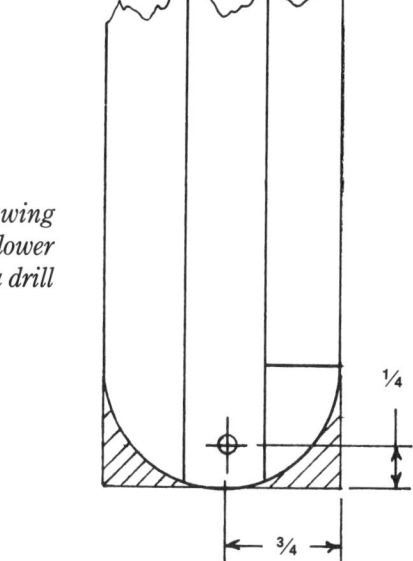

Fig. 10-47. This drawing shows a side view of the lower torso, and the position of a drill hole.

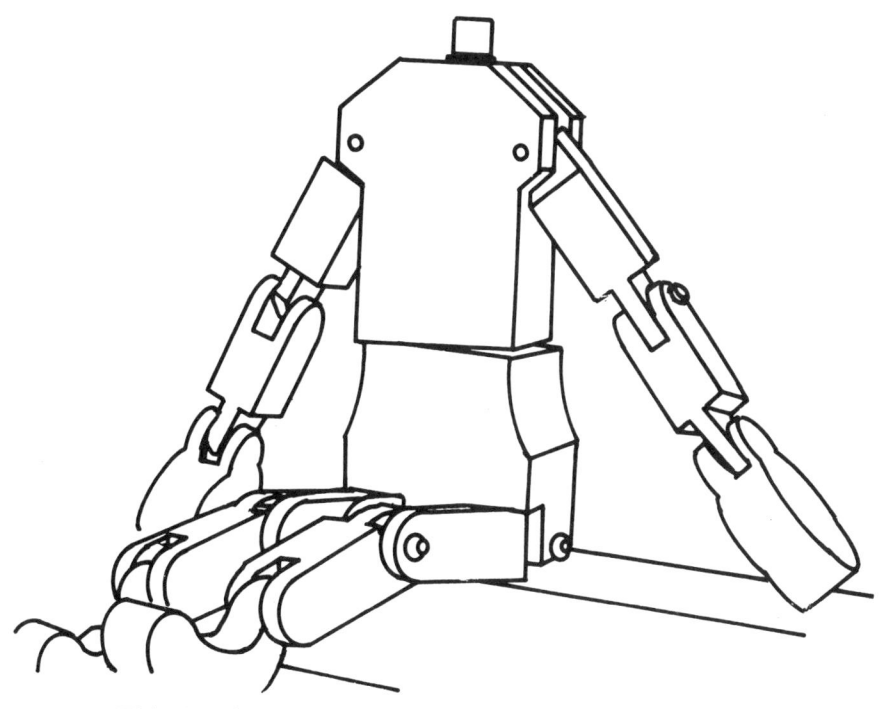

Fig. 10-48. This drawing shows the clown doll with the arms and legs attached to the body.

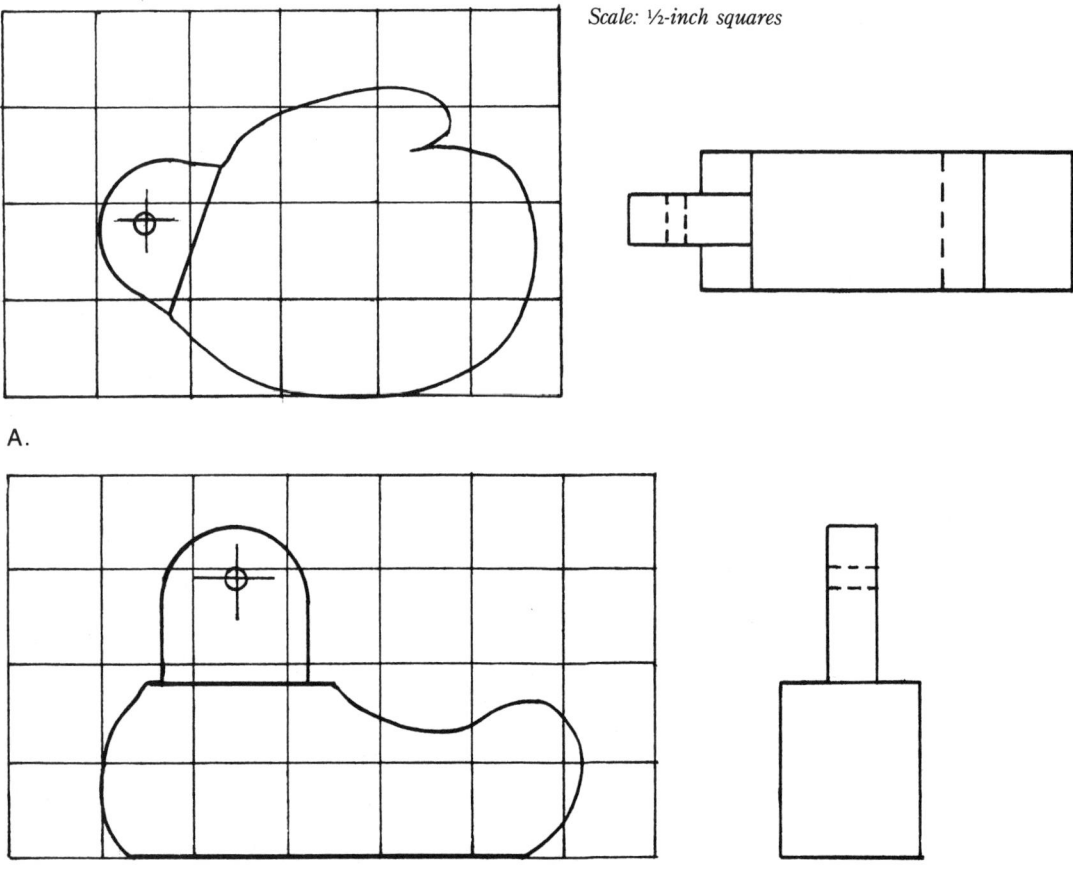

Fig. 10-49. *The hands and feet should be drawn on a ½-inch-square grid pattern.*

top that fits into the recess in the lower leg. Drill a 3/16-inch-diameter hole in the foot, where shown.

I advise that the hands and feet *Not* be glued into position just yet. For that matter, the head, if not yet glued on, should not be glued into position either. The reason is that it will be easier for the seamstress to fit clothes on the clown if they are not yet attached.

When the clown is dressed, the head, hands, and feet can be permanently attached to the rest of the body. The directions for the clown clothes are not provided in this book. The clothing is left up to your discretion.

The Clown Doll is a challenge to make because of all the moving parts involved; but it is not beyond the reach of most amateur woodworkers.

SANDWICH STACKING TOY

Younger children derive much pleasure from stacking objects one on top of the other. This is not only a great way for children to pass time and occupy themselves, but

Fig. 10-50. Making a sandwich is fun when it's with this stacking toy.

it teaches them hand-eye coordination. The Build-a-Sandwich Stacking Toy (Fig. 10-50) has been designed to be of a familiar shape to attract and hold the child's interest, while also assisting the child's mind in learning.

Use two pieces of wood that measure ⅝ inch thick (¾ inch can also be used), 4¼ inches wide, and 4½ inches long, to form the two slices of bread. Figure 10-51 shows the outline of the slice of bread. You may use the slice of bread in the grid pattern or simply trace an actual slice of bread.

Draw the outline onto the ⅝-inch-thick boards, then cut them out. File and sand the slices of bread as necessary. On one slice, drill a ¾-inch-diameter hole at the center point. Drill a ⅞-inch-diameter hole on the other slice.

Next to make is the meat. Cut the meat from a ⅛-inch-thick piece of material. Masonite is a good choice for this project, since it is readily available, comes in ⅛-inch thickness, and is brown in color. Cut the ⅛ inch-thick "meat" into a round slice that is 4½ inches in diameter. In the exact center, drill a ⅞-inch-diameter hole.

At this point the sandwich contains bread and meat. Now for a piece of lettuce. Cut the lettuce from a piece of ⅛-inch-thick material that is 5 inches wide and 5 inches long. The edges of the lettuce should be ragged to resemble a piece that has been torn from a head of lettuce. Figure 10-52 shows what a piece of lettuce might look like. Finally, drill a ⅞-inch-diameter hole in the approximate center of the lettuce.

What next? A tomato would certainly add a little flavor to our sandwich. Make the tomato from a ¼-inch-thick piece of wood that is 4 inches in diameter. Just as you did with the slice of meat, drill a ⅞-inch-diameter hole in the center of the tomato.

How about a slice of Swiss cheese (Fig. 10-53)? Use a piece of ⅛-inch-thick by 4¾-inch-wide by 4¾-inch-long material for our cheese. First drill a ⅞-inch hole in the

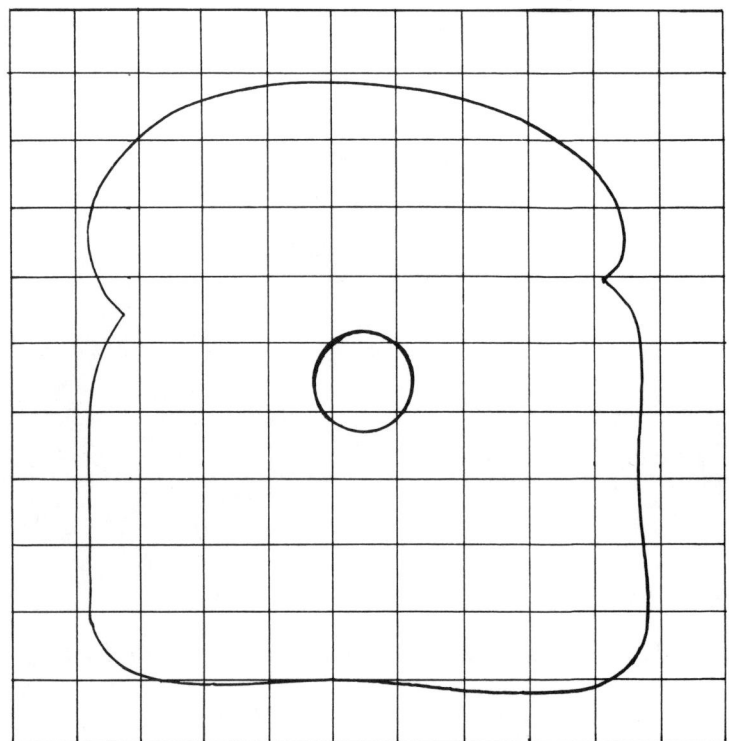

Fig. 10-51. *The ½-inch grid pattern shows the shape of the piece of bread. The shape may be transferred onto the wood or a piece of real bread can be traced.*

Fig. 10-52. *A piece of lettuce will add a bit of fiber to the sandwich.*

approximate center; then to make it look real, drill several different diameter holes randomly throughout the slice.

All of the parts have now been assembled to create a sandwich that can match even the heartiest of appetites. To heighten the realism further, and to make it more eye-

Fig. 10-53. Add swiss cheese for color and "flavor."

catching to the child, paint the parts to resemble the contents of a real sandwich. But remember: Child-safe paint *must* be used.

Paint the bread beige with brown edges. You can leave the meat as is, if it was made from masonite, or paint a reddish-brown color. The lettuce, of course, should be painted green, and the tomato, a nice, fresh red color. Finally, paint the cheese light yellow.

After allowing ample time for the paint to dry, prepare the parts for assembly. Begin by cutting a 4-inch length of ¾-inch diameter dowel. The dowel should be rounded on one end to eliminate sharp edges. Glue the end of the dowel into the slice of bread that has the hole in the center. Once the glue has set, you may give the toy to the child. Show the child how the parts go together. Then take them apart and watch the child try to assemble the sandwich.

TOOTHBRUSH TUGBOAT

All children must exercise proper dental hygiene. But most parents will testify that sometimes small children are forgetful, and fail to brush. If a child has a Toothbrush Tugboat (Fig. 10-54) to hold his or her toothbrush, however, it might help to remind the child to brush. The Toothbrush Tugboat is an attractive attention-getting project that, by its presence, reinforces the idea of brushing teeth often.

The Toothbrush Tugboat can be cut from a 8⅛-inch-long piece of 2 by 4 that is free of knots and other defects. The two surfaces of the 2 by 4 should be sanded to a smooth, clean finish.

Next, draw the outline of the tugboat onto one side of the 2 by 4 (Fig. 10-55). If this is a project that you intend to build in multiples for craft shows or stores, you should make a templet out of ⅛-inch to ¼-inch hardboard.

The cutting of the tugboat shape is done most easily with a ower tool such as a scroll saw, jigsaw, or band saw; but a hand-operated coping saw can also be used. After completing the cutting, sand the cut edges of the tugboat shape to a smooth finish. Remember that careful cutting will reduce the amount of filing and sanding. While sanding, round the edges slightly to prevent scratches.

Next, drill four ½-inch-diameter holes for the toothbrush holder as shown in Fig. 10-56. Drill the holes all the way through the tugboat, so that any water that might be

Fig. 10-54. What could be better than a tugboat in the bathroom to hold the toothbrushes?

on the toothbrush will run down the brush and not get trapped in the hole. Trapped water could cause the wood to decay.

There are a few other holes that need to be drilled. First, drill a ⅜-inch-diameter hole in the pilot house on the top of the boat. Below that, drill three ⅜-inch portholes in the cabin. The exact locations of these holes are shown on the grid pattern in Fig. 10-55.

The Toothbrush Tugboat shown in the photograph has had two 1-inch-diameter wood wheels attached to the front of the tug. Tires are attached to real tugs to prevent scratches on the large ships they push around.

The type of finish you apply to the Toothbrush Tugboat should be resistant to water. Since it will be kept in the bathroom, the tug will be subjected to more moisture. Coat the entire project with a good coat of enamel paint or varnish, including the bottom and inside of the holes. Then set the tug on the back of the toilet tank, or on the vanity, and watch. Chances are, it will attract the child's attention, and he or she will begin to brush more often.

SHAPE PUZZLE

This child's toy, the Shape Puzzle, has two advantages. The first is that children love to play with puzzles, and the second is that the play is very educational, because it assists children with the development of a good sense of shape and space relationships.

This project is made from two pieces of ¼-inch-thick hardboard (or any wood that is ¼ inch thick) and six small pieces of ¼-inch scrap material. The width of the pieces

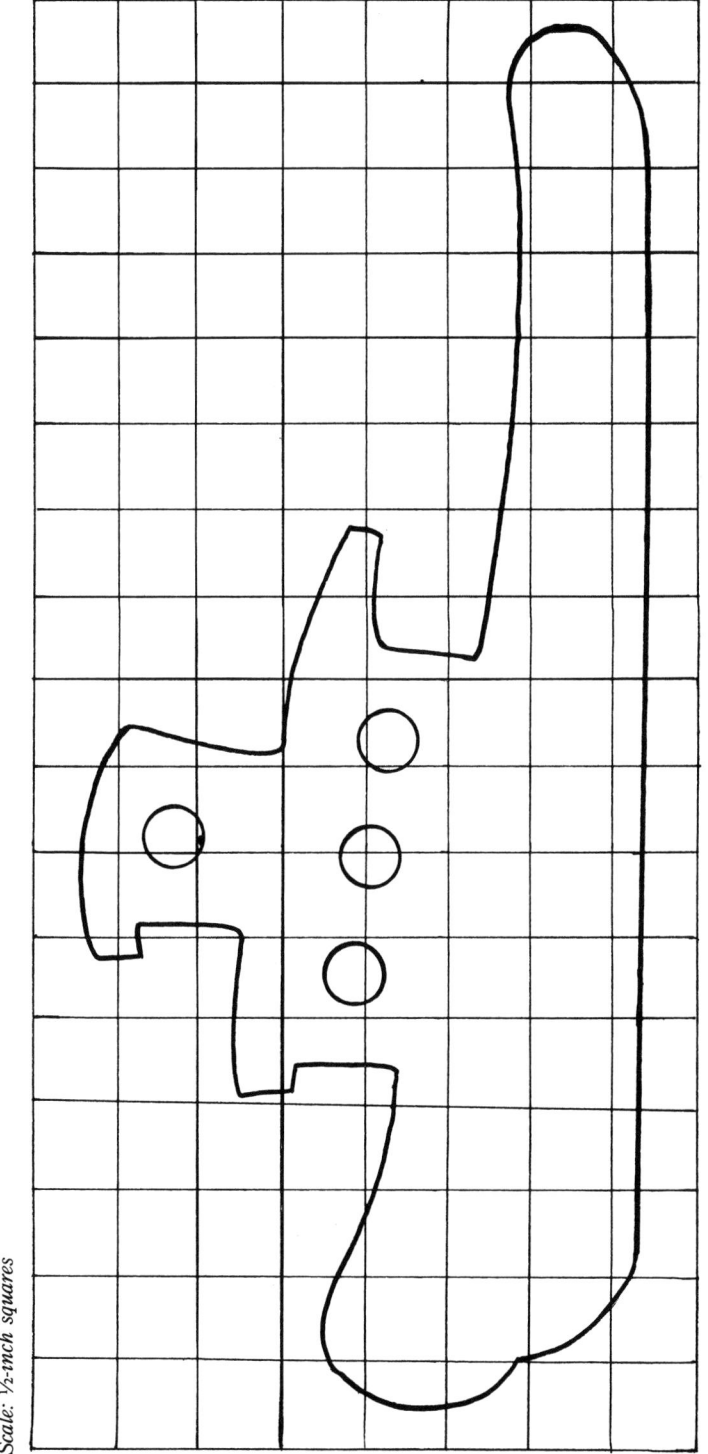

Fig. 10-55. The outline of the toothbrush tugboat, drawn on a grid pattern.

should be 9 inches, and the length 11 inches. On one of the pieces, draw the shapes, as shown in Fig. 10-57.

Once drawn, carefully cut the shapes out of the background. This piece will become the background for the puzzle. The puzzle shapes are also cut from ¼-inch-thick material, to the size and shape that will fit into the shape holes. When cutting both the background and the shapes, remember that careful cutting will reduce, if not eliminate, the need for sanding.

After cutting and sanding, glue the puzzle background onto the second 9-by-11-by ¼-inch piece. Be careful not to allow glue to seep into the shape openings.

After the glue has had sufficient time to dry, lightly sand the edges of the two puzzle parts. Round the corners slightly to remove the potential of danger to the youngsters (Fig. 10-58).

The next step is to either stain, varnish, or paint the shape pieces and the background. *Hint:* Brightly painted puzzle shapes, with a contrasting or complementary color background, will tend to be more attractive to youngsters.

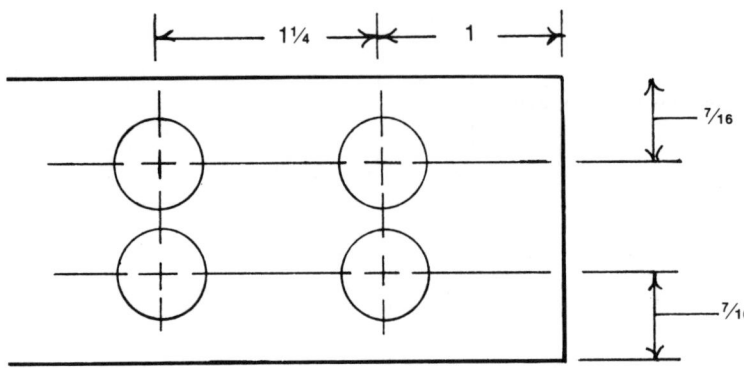

Fig. 10-56. *The tugboat when viewed from the top, shows the locations of the four ½-inch-diameter holes.*

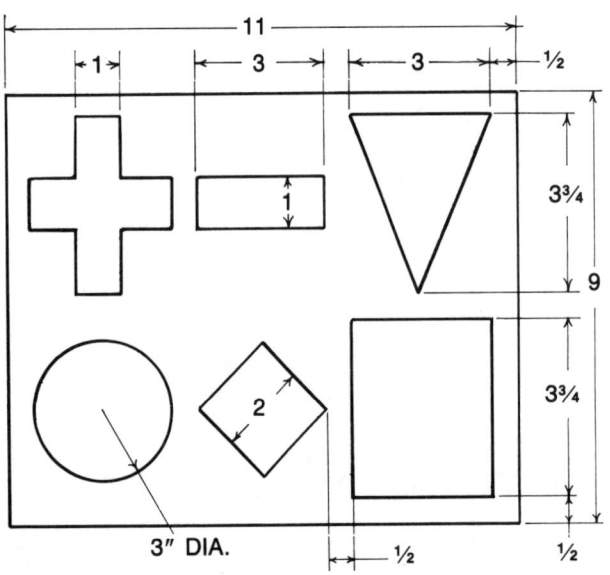

Fig. 10-57. *This drawing shows the size and shape of each puzzle piece.*

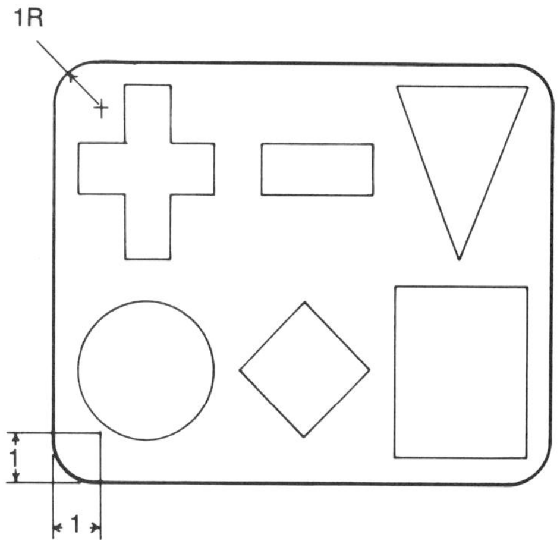

Fig. 10-58. *Round the corners of the shape puzzle slightly to prevent scratches caused by sharp edges.*

When dry, drill a hole in the center of each puzzle part. The diameter of the hole is determined by the size axle peg that you use as handles for the puzzle shape parts. Once drilled, the axle pegs can be glued permanently into the parts.

That's it! It's just that easy to build a child's puzzle. Though the puzzle shown in the instructions has parts that are cut into familiar shapes, any shapes may be used. Look through children's coloring books. They are a good source of ideas.

PASSENGER SHIP

The world of passenger ships crossing the oceans has all but disappeared. But, the ships can still be found cruising the warm waters of the Carribean, stopping at such ports of call as St. Thomas, Nassau, and San Juan. The Passenger Ship described in this section (Fig. 10-59) can cruise to these ports or be carried on the waves of a child's imagination to other exotic islands, maybe even some with buried pirate treasures.

The Passenger Ship is built from small pieces of wood, most of which can probably be found in the scrap barrel of the wood shop. Begin by cutting all of the pieces to size. The hull is a 10-inch length of 2-by-4 material. The lower deck cabin is ¾-inch-thick wood cut to 2¼ inches wide and 7 inches long. The upper deck cabin structure is ¾-inch-thick wood cut to 1¾ inches wide and 5 inches long.

The two remaining pieces to make are the wheel house, which should measure ¾ inch thick, 1½ inches wide, and 1¾ inches long, and the smokestack, which is 2¼ inch length of 1-inch-diameter dowel.

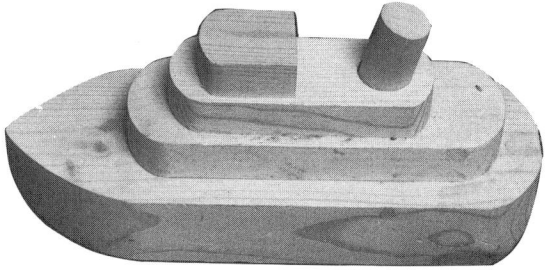

Fig. 10-59. *The passenger ship is an all-time favorite toy of most children.*

Scale: ½-inch squares

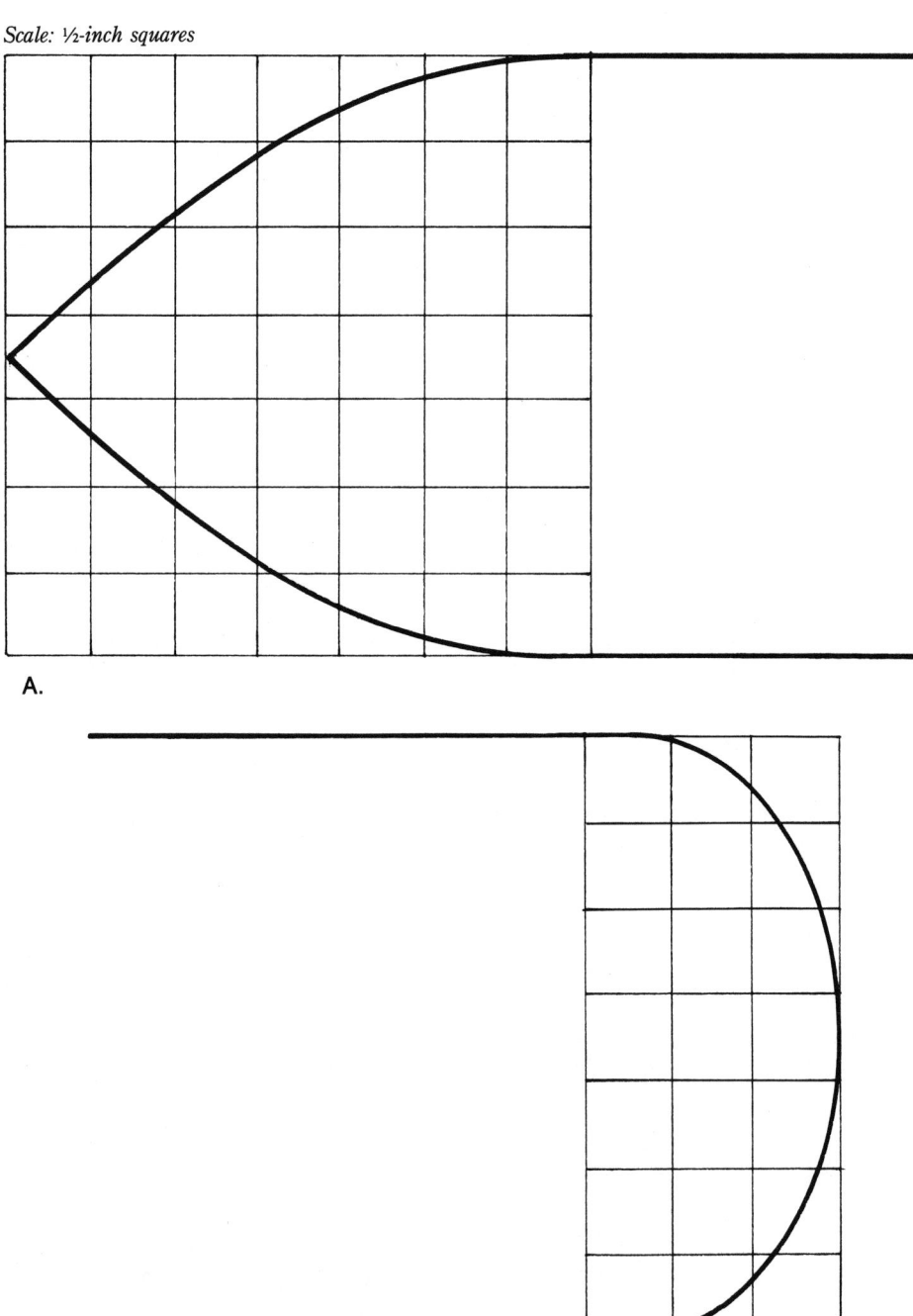

Fig. 10-60. Shape the ship's hull, (viewed from above) as shown. (A) The bow of the ship; (B) the stern.

Scale: ½-inch squares

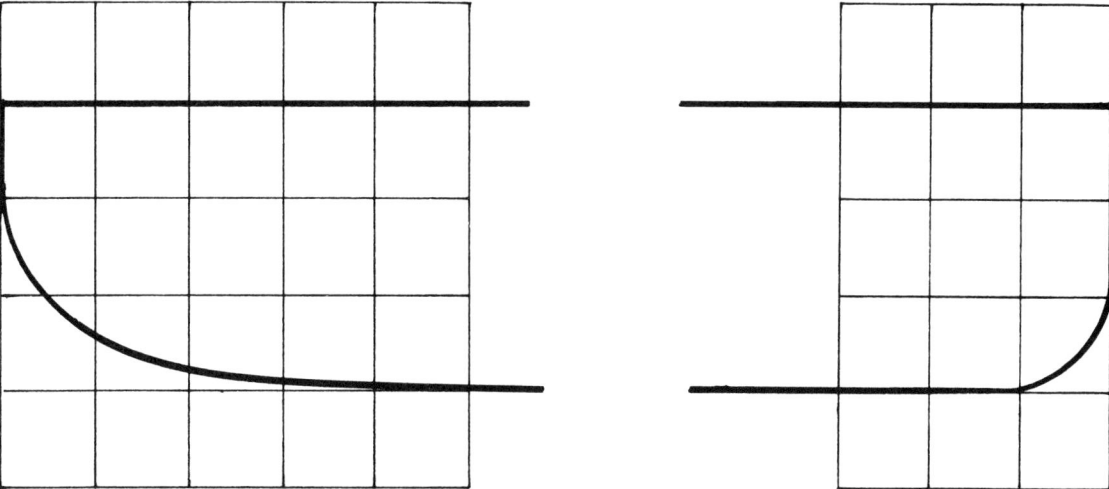

Fig. 10-61. *The side view of the hull.*

Now that all pieces have been cut to their rough size, you must shape them before glueing them in place. First, shape the bow and stern, according to the grid drawings Fig. 10-60. Next, cut the shape and file and sand until smooth. The grid pattern in Fig. 10-61 graphically illustrates the profile of the bow and stern of the Passenger Ship. Again, after drawing the design on the wood, cut and sand the hull.

Shape the two deck cabin structures, both upper and lower, in much the same manner. Round the front and rear each. Then glue the upper deck cabin structure to the lower section, centered between the sides and ¾ inch back from the front.

Next, drill a 1-inch-diameter hole, ¾ inch deep into the upper deck cabin at the approximate point shown in Fig. 10-59. Glue the smokestack into the hole.

Figure 10-59 also shows the location for the wheel house. Before glueing the wheel house onto the upper deck, slightly round the front edge of the wheel house, as you did on the cabin structures.

The last step is to glue the cabin deck assembly onto the ship hull. Be sure to glue it so that it is centered between the sides of the hull and so the front end of the lower cabin structure is ¼ inch back from the forward point of the hull.

The Passenger Ship is an especially practical project since it requires only small pieces of scrapwood. In addition, you can build the ship in a single evening. Yet, the child who receives the ship will cherish it and travel thousands of imaginary miles.

LIST 10-1. REQUIRED MATERIALS

Shape Box

2	Sides	– ¾ × 3 × 9
2	Ends	– ¾ × 3½ × 5½
1	Bottom	– ¾ × 3½ × 7½
1	Handle	– ¾-inch dowel 9¼ inches long
16	Dowels	– ⅜-inch diameter × 1½ long
1	Round Shape	– ¾ × 3
1	Square	– ¾ × ¾ × 3
1	Rectangle	– ¾ × 1⅞ × 3
1	Diamond	– ¾ × ¾ × 3
1	Triangle	– ¾ × ¾ × 3
1	Obtuse Triangle	– ¾ × 1⅞ × 3
1	"L" Shape	– ¾ × ¾ × 3
		– ¾ × 1¾ × 3
1	Upside Down "T" Shape	– ¾ × ¾ × 3
		– ¾ × 1¾ × 3

Tool Box

2	Ends	– ¾ × 5½ × 6
2	Sides	– ¾ × 3½ × 17⅜
14	Dowels	– ⅜-×-2-inches long
1	Bottom	– ¾ × 5½ × 16
1	Handle	– ¾ dowel × 17 × 12

Tools

Mallet
- 1 – Head – 1¼-inch dowel × 3
- 1 – Handle – ¾-inch dowel × 6½

Hammer
- 1 – Head – 1½ × 1¼ × 3½
- 1 – Handle – ¾ × 6½

Open End Wrench
- 1 – Open-End Wrench – ⅜ × 1½ × 7

Try Square
- 2 – Handle – ⅜ × 1¼ × 4
- 1 – Handle Insert – ⅜ × 1¼ × 3
- 1 – Blade – ⅜ × 1¼ × 6

Screwdriver
- 1 – Handle – 1-inch dowel × 3¼
- 1 – Shaft – ⅜-inch dowel × 5

Folding Rule
- 3 – Rule Parts – ¼ × ¾ × 6½
- 2 – Axle Pegs – Small Size

Bench Rule
   1 – Blade   – ¼ × 1 × 12

Hand Drill
   1 – Drill Body   – 1-inch-diameter dowel × 8½ inches long
   1 – Turn Crank   – ⅜ inch thick × 3 inches diameter
   1 – Crank Knob   – 1- to 1¼-inch-diameter ball
   1 – Drill Bit   – ⅜-inch-diameter dowel × 5 inches long
   2 – Axle Pegs   – Large Size

File
   1 – File Blade   – ⅜ × 1 × 11½
   2 – Handle Parts   – ⅜ × 1 × 3½

Saw
   1 – Saw Blade   – ⅜ × 5 × 14¼
   2 – Handle Halves   – ½ × 5 × 5½

Building Blocks
  18 – Large Blocks   – 2 × 4 × 5
  10 – Smaller Blocks   – 2 × 4 × 2½

Pull Toys
   1 – Elephant   – 2 × 5 × 6
   1 – Hound Dog   – 2 × 3½ × 7½
   1 – Pig   – 2 × 5 × 8
   1 – Wagon   – ¾ × 4 × 9
   1 – Wood ball   – 1¼ inch diameter
   1 – Rope   – ¼ inches diameter
   4 – Wheels   – 1½ to 2½ inches diameter
   4 – Axle Pegs   – Sized to fit wheels
   2 – Dowels   – ⅜ inch diameter

Jumping and Profile Bears
   1 – Jumping Bear Body
   2 – Arms
   2 – Legs
   4 – Axle Pegs   – Small Size
   1 – Profile Bear Body
   2 – Arms
   2 – Legs
   4 – Axle Pegs   – Small Size

Clown Doll

1 -	Head	- Approximately 3 inches Round
3 -	Body Sections	- ½ × 2¾ × 6⅜
2 -	"Roto-Hinges"	- ½-inch diameter
2 -	Forearms	- ¾ × ¾ × 2½
2 -	Lower Legs	- ¾ × ¾ × 2½
2 -	Upper Legs	- ¾ × ¾ × 3½
2 -	Upper Arms	- ¾ × ¾ 3
12 -	Axle Pegs	- Small Size
2 -	Feet	- ¾ × 1¾ × 2⅝
2 -	Hands	- ¾ × 1⅝ × 2⅜

Sandwich Stacking Toy

2 -	Pieces of bread	- ⅝ × 4¼ × 4½
1 -	Slice of Meat	- ⅛ inch thick × 4½ diameter
1 -	Slice of Lettuce	- ⅛ × 5 × 5
1 -	Tomato Slice	- ¼ inch thick × 4 inches diameter
1 -	Slice of Swiss Cheese	- ⅛ × 4¾ × 4¾
1 -	Dowel	- ¾ inch diameter × 4 inches long

Tugboat Toothbrush Holder

1 -	Tugboat	- 2 × 4 × 8⅛
2 -	Wheels	- 1 inch diameter
2 -	Axle Pegs	- Small Size

Shape Puzzle

1 -	Puzzle Background	- ¼ × 9 × 11
1 -	Shape Foreground	- ¼ × 9 × 11
6 -	Puzzle Pieces	- 2/4 ×

Passenger Ship

1 -	Hull	- 2 × 4 × 10
1 -	Lower Cabin Deck Structure	- ¾ × 2¼ × 7
1 -	Upper Cabin Deck Structure	- ¾ × 1¾ × 5
1 -	Wheel House	- ¾ × 1½ × 1¾
1 -	Smokestack	- 1-inch diameter × 2¼ inches long

Section IV

Kids' Furniture

The projects in this section are not only fun to build—they're practical, too. As many parents are aware, children do not always pick up after themselves. Furniture like the Corner Shelf, Toy Box, and the Clothes Pole just might encourage children to keep their rooms neater and better organized.

11
CHAPTER

Room Organizers

Let's be serious for a moment. Do you find that in your children's bedrooms there always seems to be clothes lying around? All is not lost, however. The Child-Size Clothes Pole just could be the solution to the problem.

CHILD-SIZE CLOTHES POLE

Most of materials needed for the clothes pole can be easily found at any lumberyard. The only parts that you might not find locally are the shaker pegs and finial; but these are common items sold through woodworking mail-order supply companies. The Appendix of this book lists many fine mail-order companies.

Carefully select a 5-foot-long piece of 2 by 2 (actual measurement of a 2 by 2 is 1½ inches by 1½ inches). Look for wood that is free from loose or large knots, warping, splits, or crooked grain. Also purchase a 4-foot-long piece of 2 by 4 to be used later for the four base parts.

Begin by drawing two diagonal lines from corner to corner on the top end of the 2 by 4. Where the two lines cross, drill a 1-inch-deep hole (Fig. 11-1A). The diameter of the hole will depend on the size of the finial you use. Also on the top end, round the upper corners slightly (Fig. 11-1B). Then measure down 2 inches along one side and make a light mark. Repeat on the opposite side.

On the other two sides, measure down 5 inches and again make a light mark (Fig. 11-2). At these four marks, drill a ½-inch hole centered in the board. These holes are for four shaker pegs to be installed later.

If you wish you can install another set of shaker pegs about midway down the center pole. This will allow more clothes to be hung up, and provides easy access to younger children who might be too short to reach the upper pegs.

Now sand the pole so that all dangers from splinters are removed. Also, round the corners slightly to prevent scratches. You can sand round with paper and a file or with a router to create a decorative edge. The choice is yours.

The base is made of four pieces of 2-by-4-inch material, each measuring 10 inches long. To add a bit of style to the legs, cut an angle on the front top edge of each leg and a recess on the bottom. The exact size, location, and shape of these cutouts is shown in Fig. 11-3A.

Next, drill three holes in each leg at the locations illustrated in Fig. 11-3B. First,

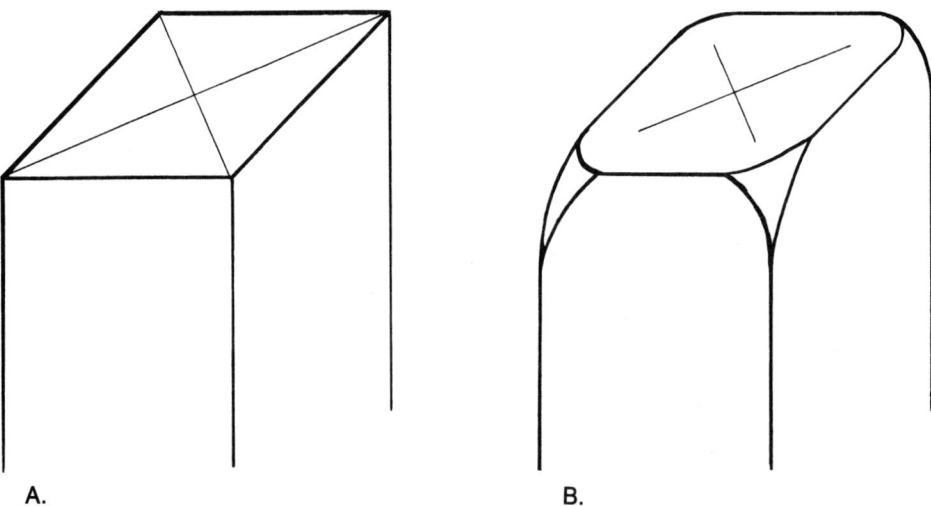

Fig. 11-1. Drill a hole in the center of the top end of the clothes pole. (A) To find the center, draw two diagonal lines from corner to corner. (B) Round the upper corners slightly.

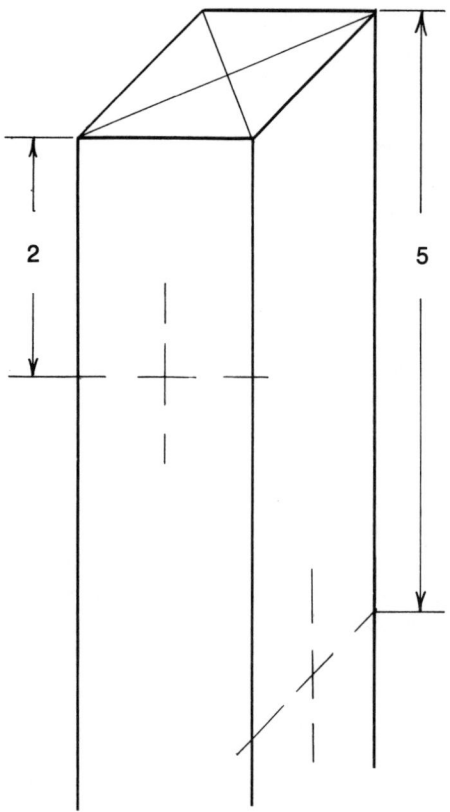

Fig. 11-2. This drawing illustrates the locations of the coat pegs.

254

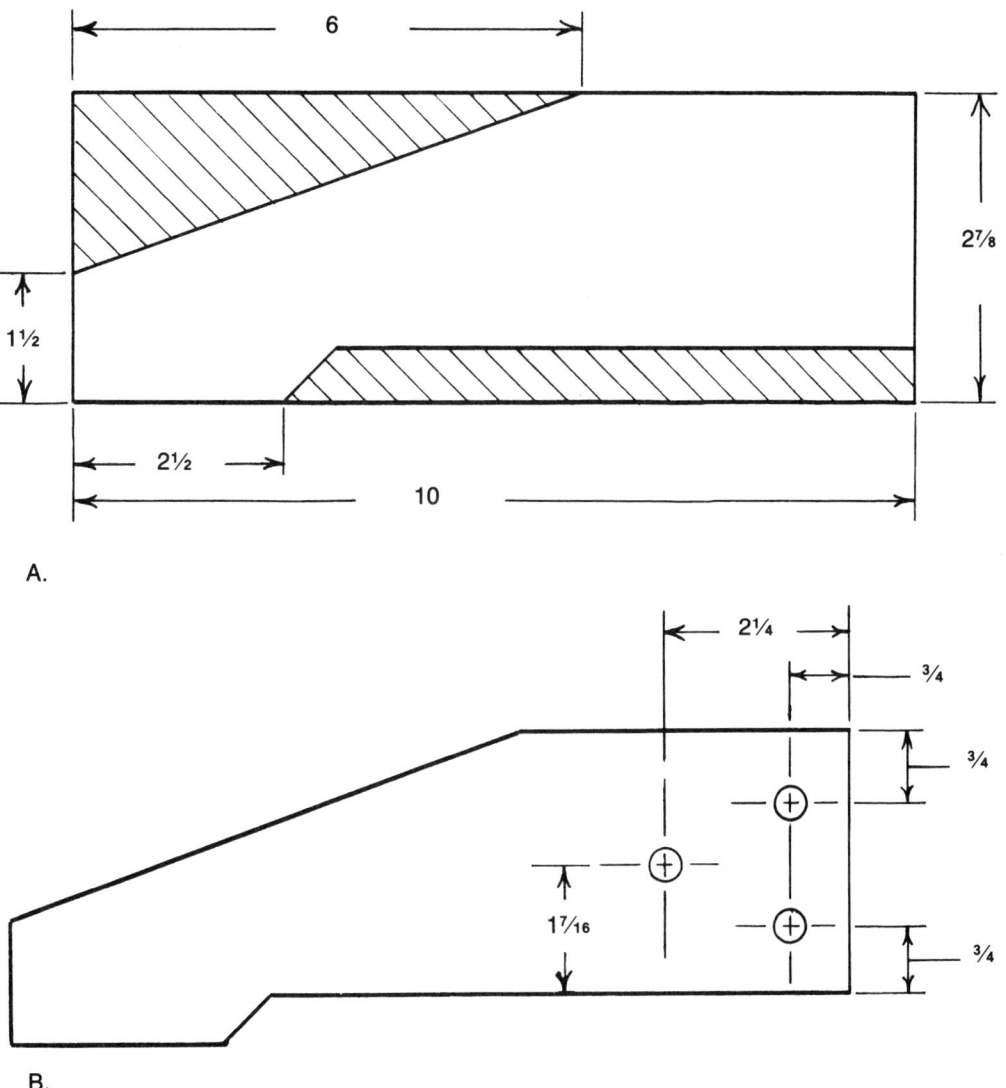

Fig. 11-3. (A) Shape the four legs of the clothes pole as shown; (B) also shown are the locations for the screw holes.

drill a pilot hole about 3/16 inch at the three spots on each leg. Then drill a 1/2-inch-diameter hole, 3/8 inch deep at the same location as the 3/16-inch holes. The larger holes are drilled so the head of the screw will fit below the surface of the wood and so that the 1/2-inch-diameter furniture button will fit into the hole covering the screw head.

When the rough construction has been completed, and all parts thoroughly sanded, it is time to assemble the clothes pole. Begin by glueing the finial in the top hole of the center pole. Next, glue the shaker pegs into position. Use a small artist's paintbrush or toothpick to lightly coat the inside surface of the hole. Then lightly tap the shaker peg into the hole.

If the peg will not go in all the way, don't force it. That will only result in a broken peg. Try to remove the peg and clean the excess glue from the hole, which may be preventing the seating.

Now glue and then screw the legs into place. First lay one of the legs on the bottom

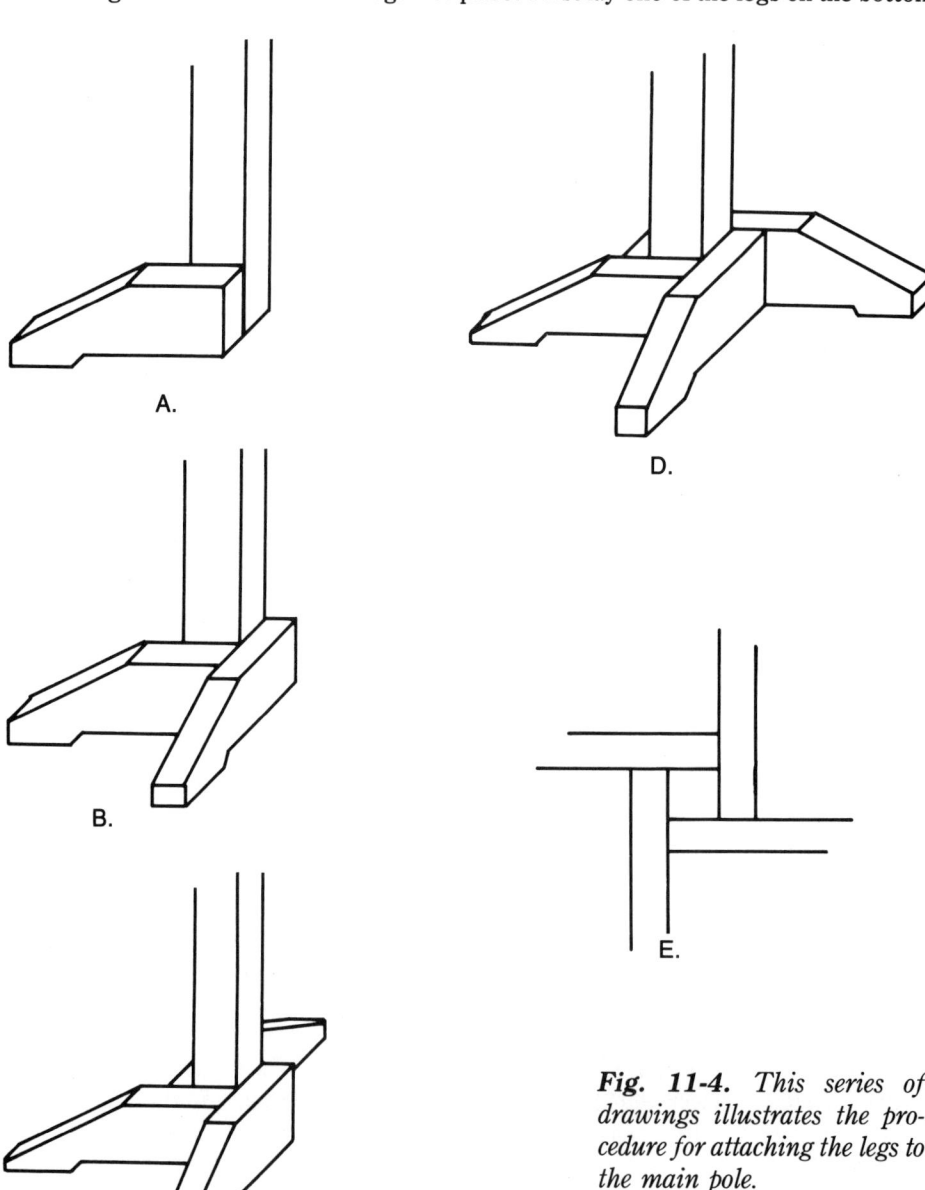

Fig. 11-4. This series of drawings illustrates the procedure for attaching the legs to the main pole.

of the center pole, keeping the leg flush with the bottom and side (Fig. 11-4A). Then glue and screw the next leg into the center pole and into the end of the first leg (Fig. 11-4B). Next glue and screw the third leg onto the side of the center pole, opposite the second leg (Fig. 11-4C). Glue and screw the final leg in place on the remaining side, as shown in Fig. 11-4D. Figure 11-4E shows what the completed leg and center pole assembly looks like from the bottom. When all of the legs have been installed, glue ½-inch-diameter plugs or furniture buttons in the holes to hide the screw heads.

The Child-Size Clothes Pole is an inexpensive project that results in an attractive and functional piece of furniture. Although the height of the clothes pole has been designed for children over the age of six, the center pole may be increased or decreased in size to suit the child. If increased in height, it could also be used by adults.

PERSONALIZED COATRACKS

Children enjoy seeing their name printed on various items. This accounts for the continued success of personalized lunch bags, pencils, plates, jewelry, pennants, and so on. For this reason, I've included personalized name coatracks in this group of projects.

The two coatracks are similar in that they are personalized with the child's name and utilize shaker-style pegs for hanging coats. The first (Fig. 11-5) is cut from a single piece of wood. The letters of the name are perched on top of the coat hanger base. The second coatrack (Fig. 11-6) is composed of large letters all cut into a single piece of wood. The shaker pegs are then attached directly to the letters.

The piece of wood that is used for the first rack is ¾ inch thick, 5 inches wide, and 19 inches long. The 19-inch length will provide enough room on the coatrack for a name of seven letters. If more letters are needed, increase the length 2 inches for

Fig. 11-5. *The first style of coatrack.*

Fig. 11-6. The second style of coatrack.

each letter and ½ inch for each space between letters. However, if the name is short, the coatrack should not be shortened. Simply center the name in the middle of the board.

Begin the layout by drawing a line 2 inches up from the bottom edge. The top portion above the line will be the name area. The lower area is for the coatrack. The letters shown in Fig. 11-7 provide you with a sample of the type of letters. They are the same style for both coatracks, although the letters will be larger for the second coatrack. Transfer the letters from the sample pattern to thick paper or cardboard. Then trace them directly onto the board, allowing a ½-inch space between each letter.

When the final layout has been completed, it is time to cut out the name. The jigsaw is best for this, but a motorized, hand-held scroll saw will also work. (A coping saw may be used, but it will take a considerable amount of time.) Cut carefully, in order to keep sanding to a minimum. Still, some sanding of the edges of the letters will be necessary.

The final steps in construction include locating and drilling holes for the coatrack pegs, and minor shaping of the lower part of the board. Figure 11-8 shows the locations of the coat pegs on a rack that is the same length described in this section. If you must lengthen the basic coatrack for a longer name, alter the peg layout accordingly.

At each point where a peg must be installed, drill a hole (usually ½ inch diameter). Do not glue the pegs into place until the coatrack board and pegs are sanded, stained, and varnished.

The second coatrack is built from a ¾-inch-thick piece of wood that measures 5 inches wide. The exact length of the board needed is determined by the number of letters in the name. Each letter is 3¼ inches wide. Therefore, to find the length, multiply the number of letters in the name by the 3¼ inch measurement.

Begin by transferring the letters needed from the sample letters in Fig. 11-9 onto

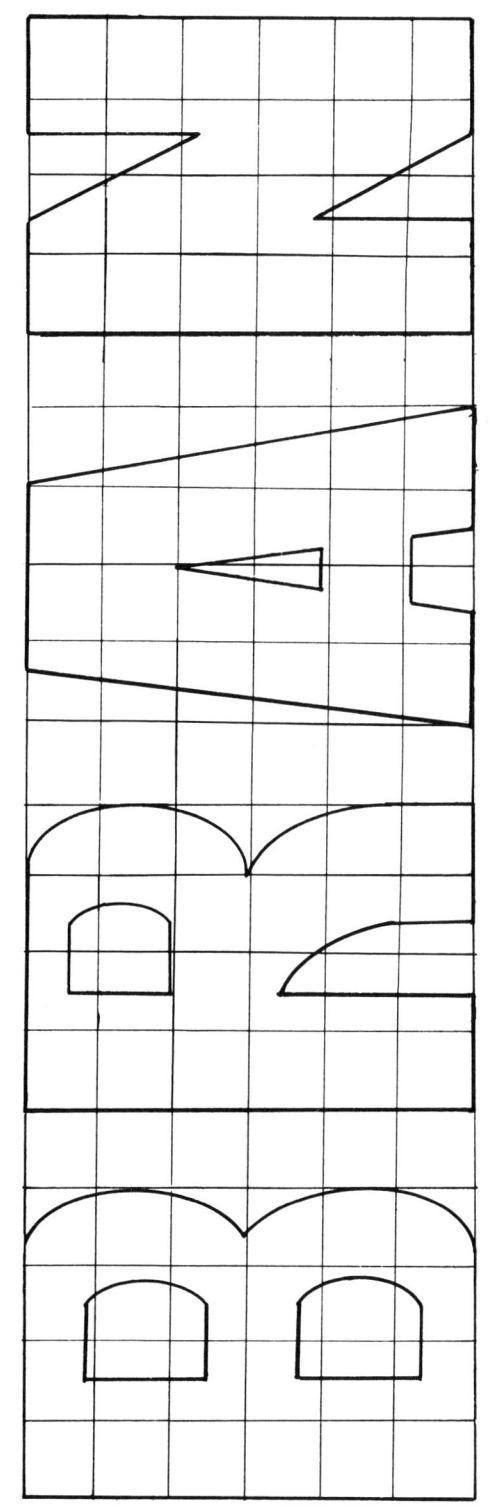

Fig. 11-7. A grid pattern of sample letters.

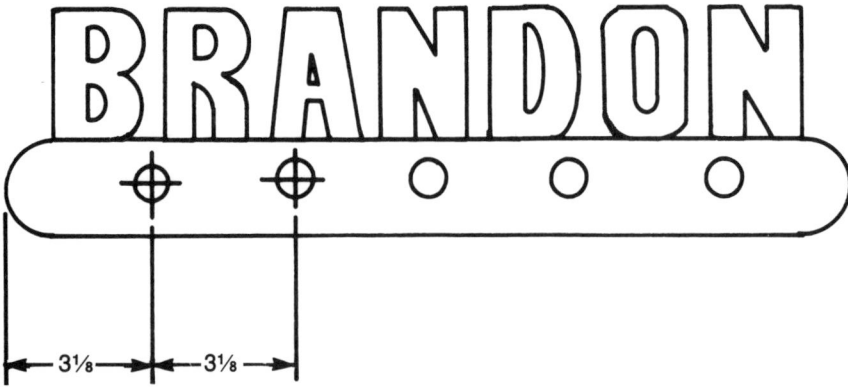

Fig. 11-8. *If the coatrack is made to the same length as described in the text, this illustration shows the location for drilling the coat peg holes.*

a piece of heavy paper or cardboard. Then, after cutting out the letters, trace them onto the board.

Prior to cutting out the shape of the letters, cut a 3/16-inch-deep kerf, the width of the saw blade, across the board where two letters join (refer to Fig. 11-6). This can be done most easily with a table saw or radial-arm saw; but a handsaw or hand-held circular saw can also be used. These cuts provide a separation between the letters, making the name easier to read.

The next step is to cut out the outline of each letter. Do not cut between the letters where the saw kerf has just been cut. Where it is necessary to make interior cuts, such as the inside of the "A" in the example, first drill a hole in the waste material, then cut away the waste.

The edges of the letters might require some sanding. Check over each letter carefully and sand where necessary. The surface of the coatrack can be sanded at this time too.

The final step is to locate and drill the coat peg holes. The pegs usually require a ½-inch-diameter hole; but check the pegs you are using. The peg hole locations must be determined for each coatrack individually. Each is different in terms of length and how the letters are joined together.

After sanding and drilling the peg holes, it is time to apply a finish to the project. The finish can be either paint, stain and varnish, or just varnish. It's up to you.

The two personalized coatracks that are described in this chapter have been designed to prove an attractive, yet functional, location to hang up the children's clothes and help keep the bedroom tidy.

WALL SHELF UNIT

There always seems to be a shortage of storage space in a child's room. To alleviate this problem, a well-designed, well-built shelf unit is the answer. The shelf presented here meets this criteria. It is simple in construction, pleasing in appearance, and very functional (see Fig. 11-12).

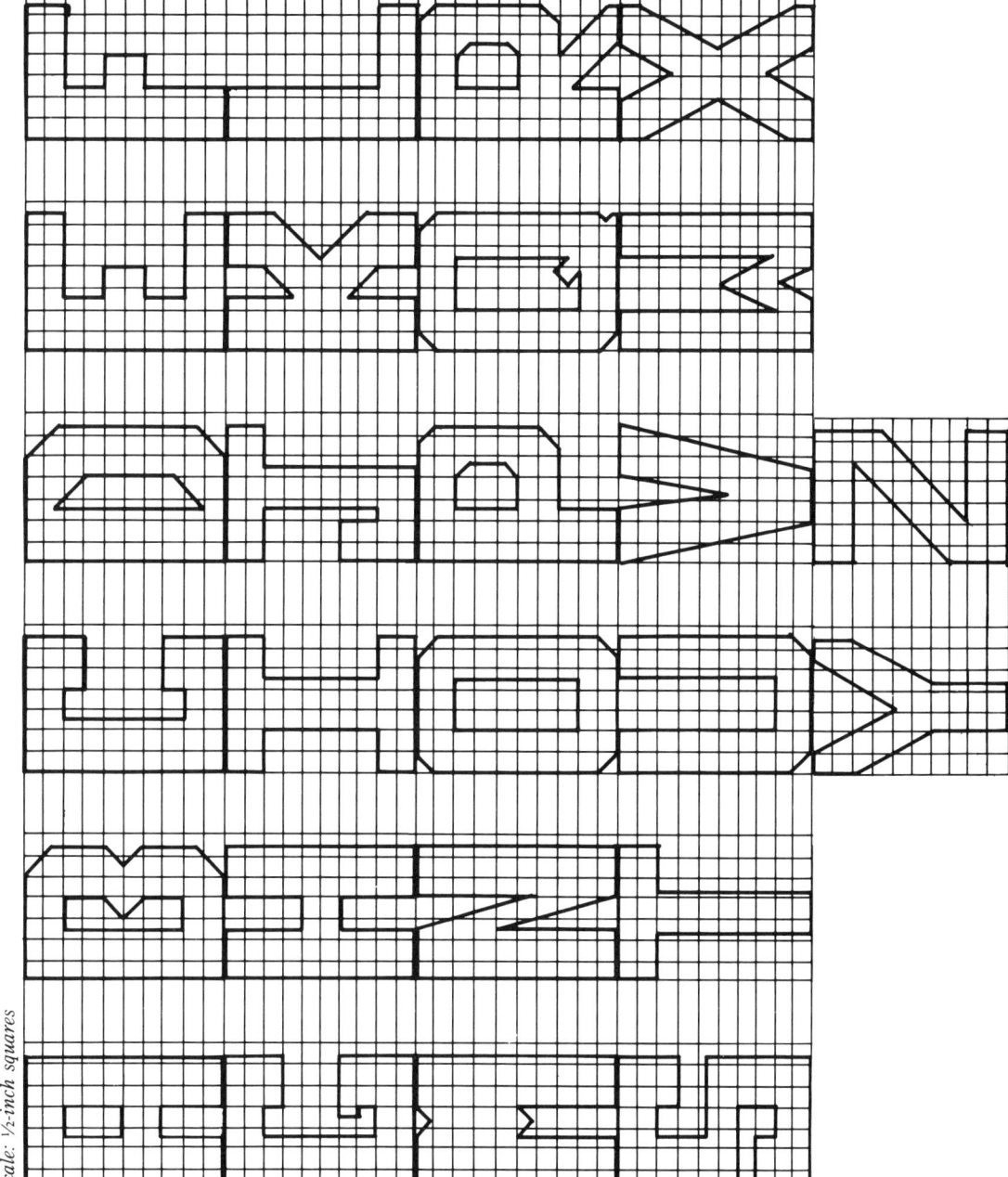

Scale: ½-inch squares

Fig. 11-9. Sample letters.

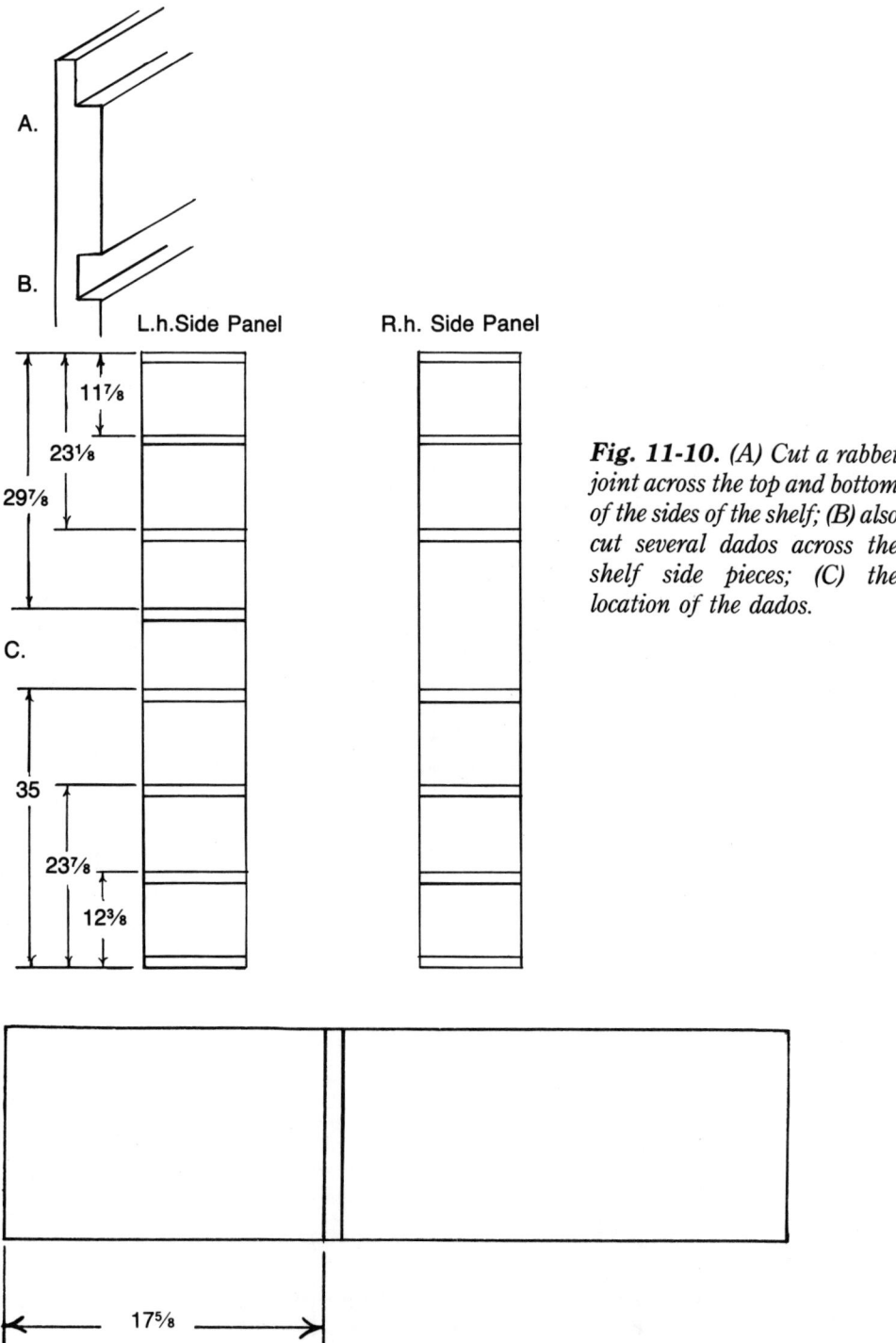

Fig. 11-10. *(A) Cut a rabbet joint across the top and bottom of the sides of the shelf; (B) also cut several dados across the shelf side pieces; (C) the location of the dados.*

Fig. 11-11. *Cut a dado across two of the shelves.*

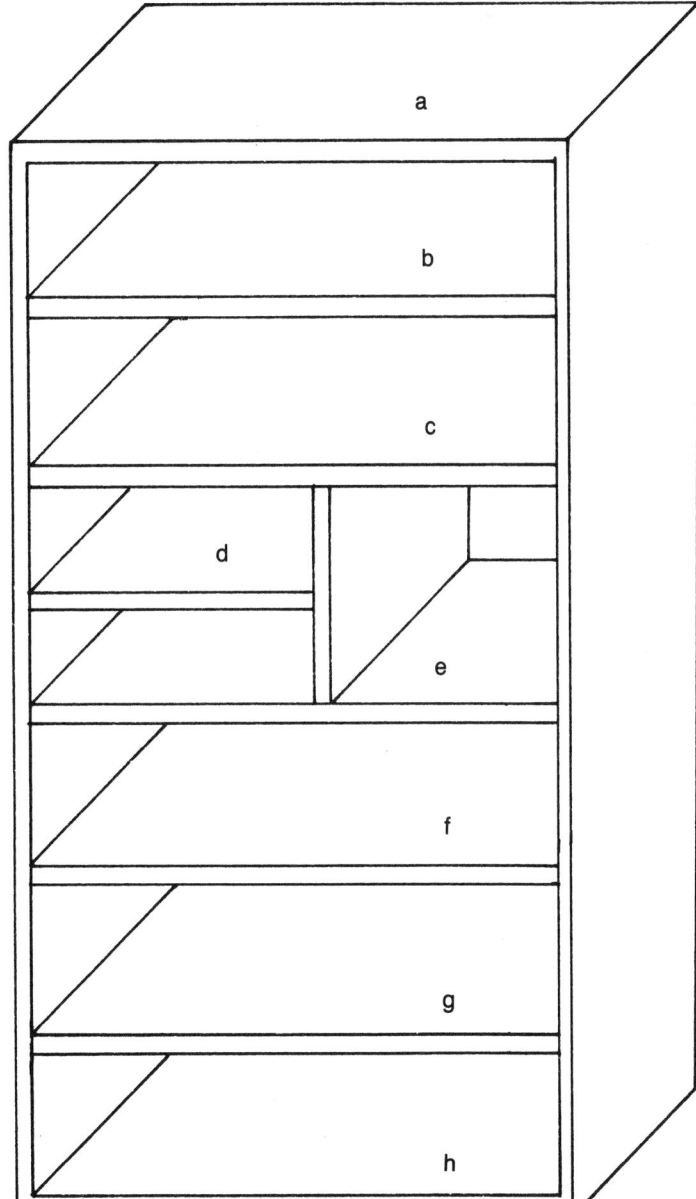

Fig. 11-12. *A short shelf fits between shelves c and e.*

The 9¼-inch full-length shelves, though permanently secured, can be placed at almost any height within the shelf unit during construction. This allows you to personalize and customize the shelf unit to meet any particular needs. The shorter shelves have been designed to hold 8-track or cassette tapes, while the taller half shelf is the perfect size to store record albums.

The shelf unit is built entirely from materials that can be purchased from local lumberyards. Three boards, which are ¾ inch thick, 10 inches wide, and 144 inches long, will provide enough material for the sides and shelves.

Begin by cutting the two side pieces to a length of 72 inches. On these two parts, cut a rabbet joint on the top and bottom ends. The rabbet should be ⅜ inch deep and ¾ inch wide (Fig. 11-10A). Then cut several ¼-inch-wide, ⅜-inch-deep dados across the boards of the side pieces (Fig. 11-10B). The locations of these dados are shown in Fig. 11-10C.

Also cut a 13¾-inch length of wood that is the same width as the sides. This board should also have a ¾-inch-wide by ⅜-inch-deep dado cut across it. The board will be used as a vertical divider between two of the shelves (c and e in Fig. 11-12).

The shelves consist of seven boards that measure ¾ inch thick, the same 9¼-inch width as the sides, and a length of 36 inches. Five of the shelves need only be sanded smooth in preparation for assembly. On two of the shelves, cut a ⅜-inch-deep-by-¾-inch-wide dado cut across the width. The location of the dado should be 17⅝ inches from the left end (Fig. 11-11).

There is one short shelf that is only half the length of the others. It is the same thickness and width as the others, but its length is only 18 inches. Fit this shelf between shelves c and e, as shown in Fig. 11-12.

Assembling the shelf unit primarily involves fitting each shelf into its respective dados. Be sure that the shelves fit snugly, but are not so tight as to require a mallet to force them into position. If you find that all parts fit properly, you can begin the final assembly.

First glue and clamp the entire shelf unit together. In the event that long enough clamps are not available, you can glue the shelves and then hold them in place with several 1¼-inch-long finish nails or 1½-inch-long number 8 wood screws.

Although the instructions presented here might appear a bit brief in relation to the large size of the project, this project really is simple to build. Yet, in its simplicity rests its uniqueness. It is designed to serve a purpose as a piece of functional furniture in the child's bedroom or playroom.

CORNER SHELF

The Corner Shelf Unit is another in a series of projects in this book which have been designed to help keep the kid's bedroom or play area neat. A corner shelf should be selected for rooms that do not have much free wall space where a conventional wall or floor shelf would normally be used. This type of shelf does not take up much room and is set in the corner between two walls where there is generally nothing in its way.

The instructions which follow are for a four shelf unit, with the shelves 10 inches apart. The distance between the shelves and the number of shelves in the unit may be increased or decreased to any specifications. Possibly you need a floor-to-ceiling corner unit for one particular room and a small two or three shelf unit with close shelves for another room. The plans are flexible enough to allow for individual requirements.

Cut the four shelves from individual squares of wood that measure ¾ inch thick, 7 inches wide, and 7 inches long. Set a compass to draw a 7-inch radius, then place the compass point at the corner of one of the 7-by-7 square pieces and draw the arc as shown in Fig. 11-13A. Repeat this process on all of the shelves, then cut away the excess material.

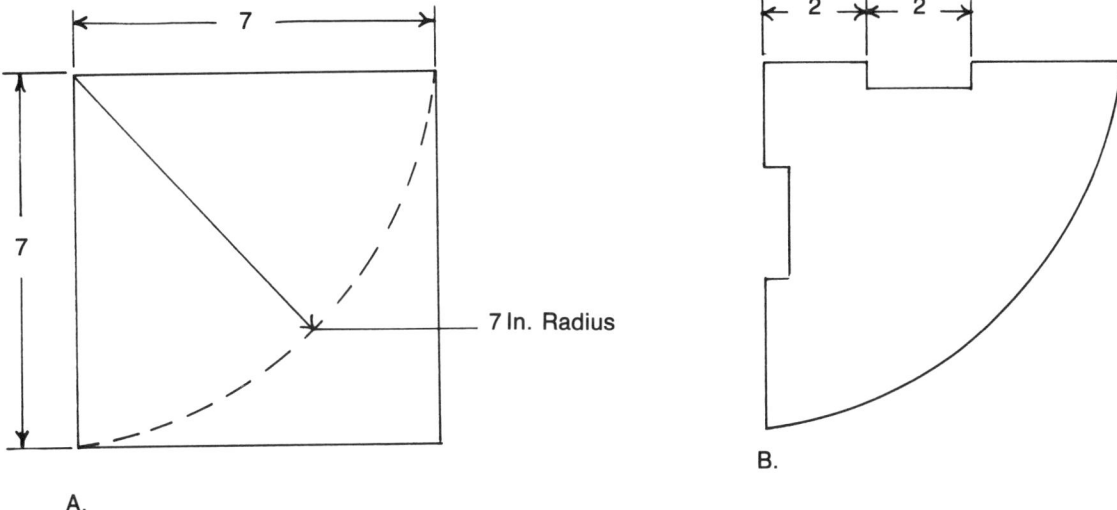

Fig. 11-13. *(A) Cut a 7-inch-radius curve on the front edge of the shelves. (B) Cut two rectangular slots into the straight sides of the shelf.*

While the saw is still out, cut two rectangular cuts on the sides of the shelves (Fig. 11-13B). They are there so that two upright supports can be attached to the shelves and hold them in place. The size of the rectangular recesses is ½ inch wide by 2 inches long.

Before proceeding any further, you might consider routing the front, curved edge of the shelves with a decorative bit to add to the professional appearance of the project.

The Corner Shelf that I built has the shelves positioned 10 inches apart. This will result in a shelf unit that is 33 inches long. This size has been selected after deciding what items will be placed on which shelf.

As stated earlier, alterations in height can easily be done. You need only increase or decrease the length of the two upright supports. Presently the supports are at a length of 33 inches with a thickness of ½ inch and width of 2 inches.

When cut, the 2-inch-wide upright supports should fit snugly into the rectangular cutouts in the shelves. Test fit them to be sure of the fit. Place the shelves with one on the top, one on the bottom, and the other two shelves 10 inches away from those on the top and bottom.

If the trial assembly is satisfactory, the next step is to sand the entire project to create a smooth, flawless shelf unit. Then final assembly takes place.

Assemble the shelf unit by using a good grade of wood glue and 16 four-penny finish nails. Begin by placing the two upright supports in position on the shelves, then glueing and nailing them with two 4d nails (Fig. 11-14). Then nail the next shelf into place similarly, 10 inches down from the first. Repeat this process until all shelves have been permanently secured to the uprights. Allow the unit to thoroughly dry before proceeding to stain, varnish, or paint.

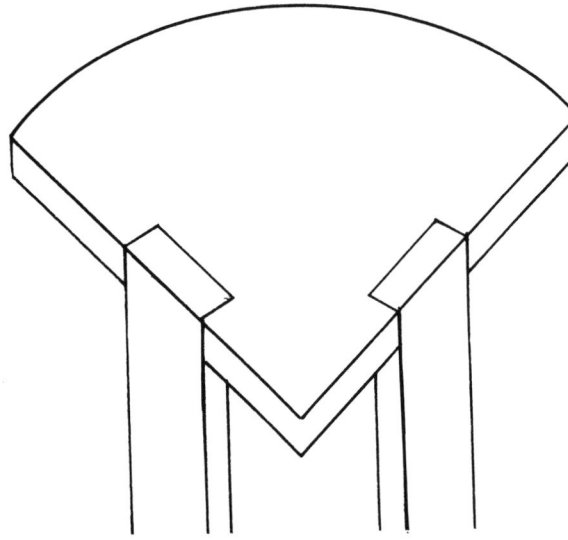

Fig. 11-14. *Glue and nail the upright supports into the rectangular cutouts in the shelves.*

The corner shelf unit is an easy-to-build, inexpensive project that can be used in most homes. The project does not have to be for the child's room alone. The shelf will function beautifully in the living room or dining room to display collectibles.

BASEBALL BAT COATRACK

The Baseball Bat Coatrack shown in Fig. 11-15 is another example of an inexpensive, easy-to-build project that can be hung in the kid's room, family room, or den, to help keep the room neat. Its unique design makes it a favorite with kids and adult baseball fans.

The inexpensive material consists of a 6-inch-wide, ¾-inch-thick board, 7 preturned coatrack pegs, and a baseball bat. The bat must be wood, whether new or used, flawless or cracked. (Finally a use for a cracked baseball bat!) These materials and some glue, stain, varnish, and a couple of screws are all you need to build this project.

Begin by cutting the baseball bat in half lengthwise. You can do this most easily on a bandsaw, but a scroll saw or handsaw will work, too. (Do not attempt to make this cut on a table saw, radial-arm saw, or with a hand-held circular saw. This would be much too dangerous.) When cutting, keep the bat trademark (the Louisville Slugger logo shown in the photograph) on the front. Do not cut through it. If the cut surface of the bat is rough or has many high or low spots, take time to sand or file it smooth. This will allow the bat to lie evenly against the backboard.

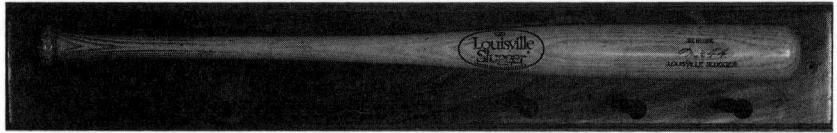

Fig. 11-15. *The Baseball Bat Coatrack is a unique rack with the sportsperson in mind. It is inexpensive, easy to build, and a very popular gift.*

The backboard of the coatrack is made from a 6-inch-wide rectangular board. I cannot give an exact length because lengths of bats vary. To determine the backboard length, measure the length of the bat, then add 4 inches.

The two edges and ends of the coatrack in the photograph have been routed to produce an attractive, professional-appearing edge. This is an option, however. The coatrack will function fine without the routing.

After routing or sanding the edges and ends, drill the peg holes. Since the backboard length will vary, I cannot provide dimensions for the spacing between pegs. However, the following steps will assist in finding the locations regardless of the length.

Step 1.

Begin by measuring the total length of the backboard. We'll call this measurement "W." Divide measurement "W" by two to arrive at measurement "X." Measure in from one end "X" inches. This will provide the location of the center peg (peg number 4 in the photograph).

Step 2.

Next, divide measurement "X" by two to arrive at dimension "Y." By measuring "Y" inches from the left and right of the center peg, you can find the location of pegs number 2 and 6.

Step 3.

This next operation is similar to the others. Divide dimension "Y" in half (measurement "Z"). By measuring "Z" inches either side of peg hole location numbers 2, 4, and 6, you can find the remaining peg holes.

Step 4.

The final step is to measure up from the bottom edge 1⅜ inches to find how far up the holes are drilled. Drill the holes. The diameter of the holes is determined by the size of the coatrack peg being used.

The coatrack shown in the photograph has two 3/16-inch-diameter holes drilled through the backboard. The holes drilled at either end (Fig. 11-15 shows the location) of the board are so that the coatrack can be mounted on the wall. Furniture buttons may be used to hide the screw holes.

If you use buttons, you must drill a hole ¼ inch deep and the diameter of the furniture button (usually ½ inch, but check the button being used). Drill this hole at the two 3/16-inch hole locations. Do not glue the button in the hole until the coatrack is mounted on the wall.

At this point, give the backboard a final sanding in preparation for staining. The stain used can be of any color; but I suggest that the stain be a contrasting color to the bat. (Remember to stain the furniture buttons also.) Stain the backboard and allow it to dry.

The next step is to mount the bat onto the backboard. Because of the weight and density of wood used in baseball bats, they present a small problem in securing the bat to the backboard. Glue alone cannot hold the bat on, because the weight might cause it to break away. You must use wood screws along with the glue.

Because the bat is made of dense hardwood, however, you might find it difficult to turn screws into it. To alleviate the trouble, first drill a small pilot hole into the bat. Then put some bar soap (the type used in the bathroom) on the screws. The soap will act as a lubricant, allowing the screw to turn in more easily. The bat should be located 2 inches in from the ends and centered between the top of the backboard and the coatrack pegs. When the exact location is determined, drill the small hole through the backboard so that they will enter a point in the bat where it is thick. Turning a screw into the bat where it is thin, might cause it to crack or splinter.

With the coatrack pegs glued in place, the bat securely held onto the backboard, and the mounting holes drilled, the project is ready for a coat of varnish. Do not varnish the coatrack with the furniture buttons in place (if used) or the buttons will be impossible to remove without damage. Also be careful the mounting holes and button holes do not become clogged with varnish.

The Baseball Bat Coatrack is a project that is easy to build, with a result that is both functional and attractive. The project here, though presented in a book of children's projects, is also a favorite for adults. It is a great gift for the kids' little league coach; or with a brass name plate available at trophy dealers, the coatrack becomes an inexpensive trophy for an outstanding softball player or baseball player.

BASEBALL EQUIPMENT RACK

The following project provides a convenient storage place for baseball equipment like the bat, ball, mitt, hat, and jacket (Fig. 11-16). The Baseball Equipment Rack entails little investment of time to complete. The entire project consists of only five parts, the back, bat and ball rack, and three pegs.

Cut the back from a board that is ¾ inch thick, 5 inches wide, and 29½ inches long. This is the major portion of the project, and the one that is the most visible. The back should be made from a piece of wood free from defects that might detract from the appearance of the project.

Sand the front surface of the back to remove any marks left from the lumber mill, or any minor defects. Once sanded, the next step is to rout a decorative edge along the ends and edges of the front surface. The bit used can be very ornate or a simple rounding-over bit. The choice is entirely up to you. If no router is available, you can round the edges and ends by using a file and sanding it smooth.

The next part to make is the ball and bat rack. It is made from a ¾-inch-thick piece of wood, 3 inches in width and 6½ inches long. First, bore two 1½-inch-diameter holes into the board, 2 inches in from the left end, 1½ inches in from the right end, and centered 1½ inches in from the front and back edges (Fig. 11-17). The 1½-inch-diameter hole size should be large enough to hold most bats, though if it is too small or large, you will have to adjust it accordingly.

Routing may be done on the ball and bat rack portion, on both ends, and the front edge. This is again an option, not a necessity. The router bit, if used, should be the same as the one used on the backboard.

Be sure that one of the holes previously cut into the ball and bat rack has an access hole cut out to allow the bat to be slipped in and out. The access hole is cut slightly larger than the bat handle (Fig. 11-18). An average size for the access cut seems to

Fig. 11-16. Baseball Equipment Rack is an excellent way to keep all of the child's baseball gear in one place.

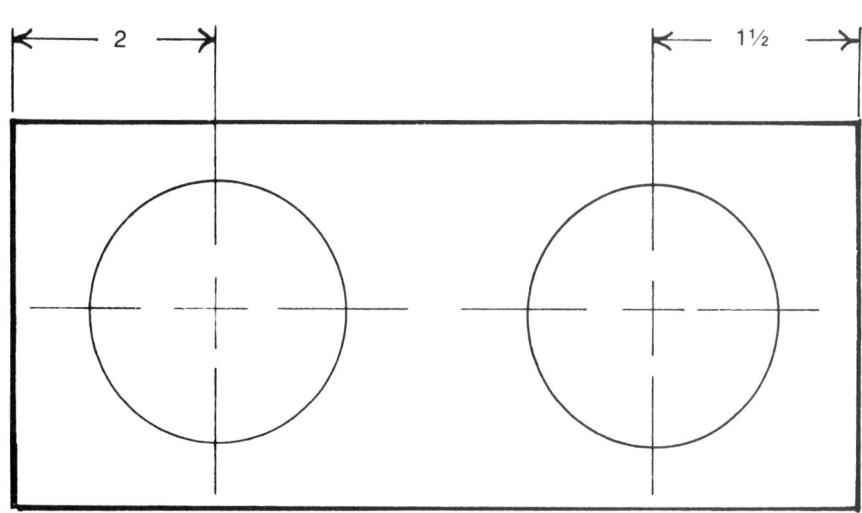

Fig. 11-17. Bore two ½-inch-diameter holes into the board.

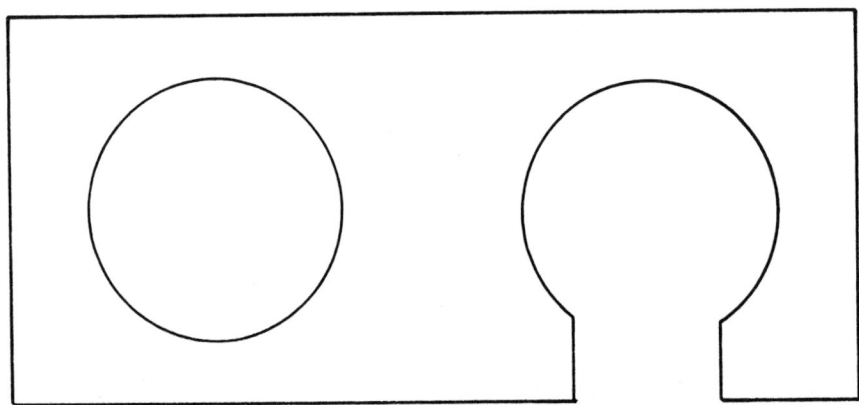

Fig. 11-18. Cut an access notch in one of the holes in the bat and ball rack for the bat.

be 1 inch, but measure for the specific bat to determine the proper size.

Turn your attention back to the back once again. Measure and lay out the dimensions as shown in Fig. 11-19. Beginning from the left end, measure in 4 inches and make a slight vertical pencil line across the board. From there, measure over 6 inches, make another vertical line. Continue this all the way across the board to find the locations of the remaining points.

Next, measure up from the bottom edge 2½ inches. At this point, draw a horizontal line across the length of the board. Where the vertical and horizontal lines meet, mark the location of the holes to be drilled.

The first hole from the left side is ½ inch in diameter. Drill the next two holes from the left to ⅛ inch in diameter. The last two holes from the left should be ½ inch in diameter. (Later you will glue coatrack pegs into the ½-inch-diameter holes, and glue and screw the ball and bat rack onto the project back through the ⅛-inch holes.) Next, drill two ⅛-inch pilot holes into the rear edge of the ball and bat rack, 1 inch in from each end (Fig. 11-20). The diameter of the pilot holes is ⅛ inch.

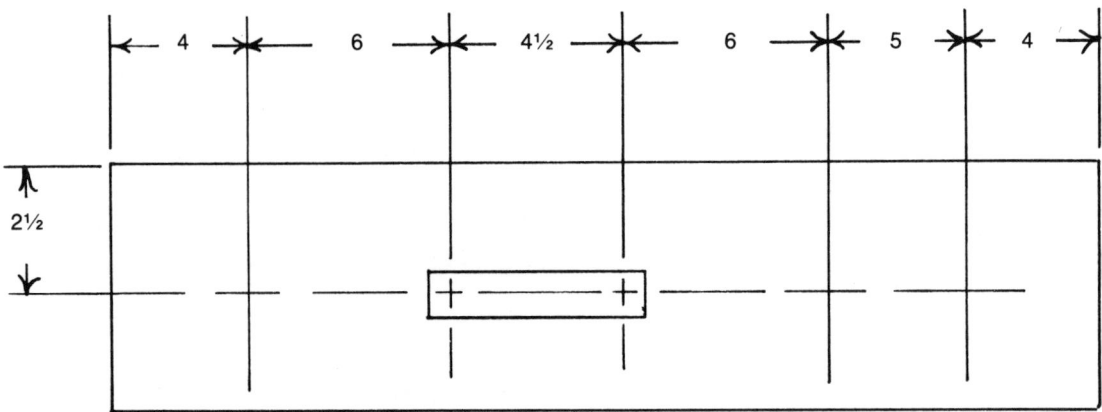

Fig. 11-19. Drill a series of holes in the project back.

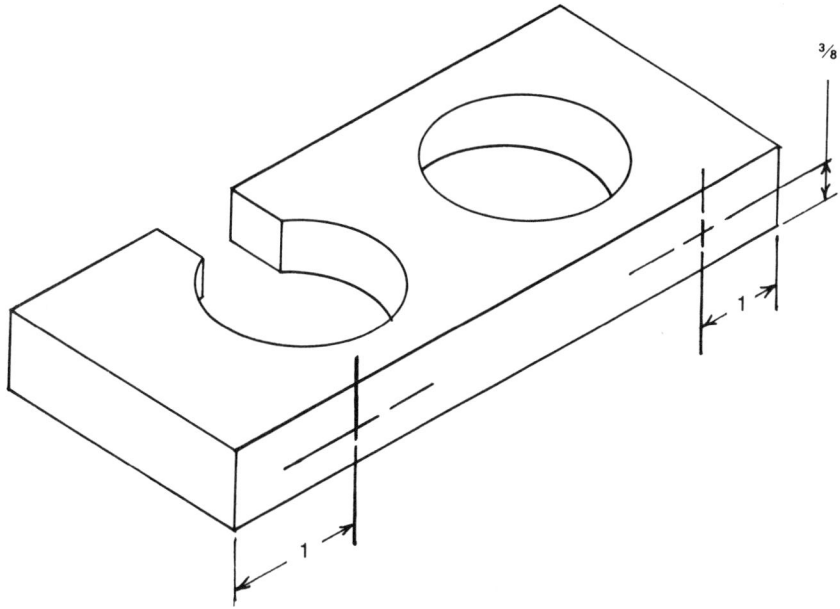

Fig. 11-20. *Drill two pilot holes into the rear edge of the bat and ball rack. This is where the rack will be screwed and glued to the project back.*

All of the pieces of the Baseball Equipment Rack have now been cut to size and shape. Sand each piece, including the coat pegs, to remove any splinters.

To assemble the Baseball Equipment Rack, glue the coat pegs into the ½-inch-diameter holes. Then, from the back, screw two 1½-inch-long number 8 flathead wood screws into the ⅛-inch pilot holes.

The only remaining steps are to paint, stain, and/or varnish, and then mount it on the wall. When finished, the Baseball Equipment Rack will provide budding Hank Aarons or Al Kalines with a place to keep all of their baseball gear.

This project need not be limited to children. How about all of those overgrown kids involved in softball leagues? This project could be awarded as a trophy for ball players. With the addition of an engraved brass plate for a personalized trophy, this project could make a great trophy—one that will not just sit around on a bookshelf collecting dust.

LIST 11-1. REQUIRED MATERIALS

Clothes Pole

1	Pole Upright	– 1½ × 1½ × 54
4	Shaker Pegs	– Standard Size
4	Clothes Pole Legs	– 1½ × 3½ × 10
1	Finial	
8	Furniture Buttons	– ½-inch diameter
8	Wood Screws	– 1¾, no. 8

Personalized Coatracks

COATRACK "A"
- 1 – Rack Back — ¾ × 5 × 19
- 5 – Shaker Pegs — Standard Size

COATRACK "B"
- 1 – Rack Back — ¾ × 5 × Allow 3¼ inches in length for each letter
- ? – Shaker Pegs — Standard Size (The amount of shaker pegs is at the discretion of the craftsperson.)

Wall Shelf
- 2 – Sides — ¾ × 9¼ × 72
- 7 – Shelves — ¾ × 9¼ × 36
- 1 – Short Shelf — ¾ × 9¼ × 18
- 1 – Vertical Divider — ¾ × 9¼ × ? (Height depend on the amount of space you allow between shelves.)

Corner Shelf
- 4 – Shelves — ¾ × 7 × 7
- 2 – Shelf Supports — ½ × 2 × 33

Baseball Bat Coatrack
- 1 – Backboard — ¾ × 6 × ? (Length depends on the length of the bat.)
- 1 – Baseball Bat — Any Size
- 7 – Shaker Pegs — Standard Size

Baseball Equipment Rack
- 1 – Backboard — ¾ × 5 × 29½
- 1 – Bat and Ball Rack — 3 × 3 × 6½
- 3 – Shaker Pegs — Standard Size
- 2 – Screws, Flathead — 1½, no. 8

12
CHAPTER

More For The Kids' Rooms

Every child needs a place to keep cherished toys safe and out of the way. The toy box described here will satisfy these requirements and do it in a stylish, easy-to-build way (Fig. 12-1).

TOY BOX

You can build the toy box from materials commonly found at the local lumberyard. The two sides, top, front, and back, are all made from ¾-inch-thick pine which is 3½ inches wide. Six 10-foot-long pieces will build everything except the bottom of the box, which is built from ½-inch plywood.

Begin construction by cutting five lengths of wood, each measuring 3½ inches wide by 17½ inches long. These five will form one side. Lay them on a flat surface with the ends lined up, as shown in Fig. 12-2A. Use a carpenter's square to ensure the squareness of the side panel.

Fig. 12-1. *The traditional place to store children's toys is the toy box. This toy box has been designed with strength and function in mind.*

273

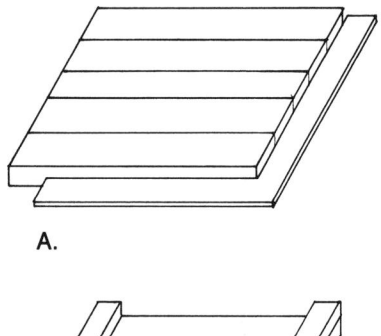
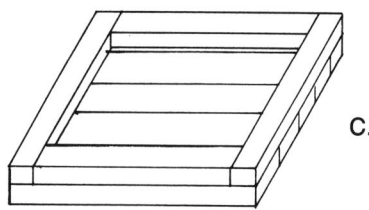

Fig. 12-2. (A) Use a carpenter's square to ensure the ends of the boards are squared. (B) Nail the two trim side pieces onto the side boards. (C) Nail and glue the top and bottom side trim pieces to the sides.

Next, cut two side trim pieces, each ½ inch thick, 1½ inches wide, and 14½ inches long. Lay the two pieces on top of the side panel, at a 90-degree angle to the boards. Glue and nail these into position with 1-inch-long finish nails (Fig. 12-2B).

Now cut the upper and lower side trim pieces so that they measure ½ inch thick, 1½ inches wide, and 17½ inches long (Fig. 12-2C). Glue and nail into place. Repeat this process to make the other side panel.

Next, cut the ten pieces of wood used for the front and back of the toy box to ¾ inch thick, 3½ inches wide, and 24 inches long. (The instructions provide the necessary information for building a toy box which is 24 inches long. If you want a longer toy box, simply increase the length of the front, rear, and top boards.)

Once cut, glue and nail the front and rear boards onto the edges of the side panels.

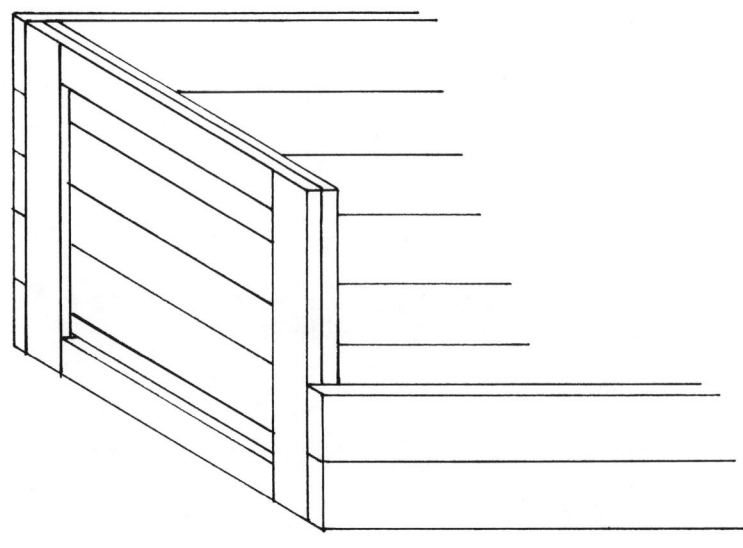

Fig. 12-3. Glue and nail the front and back boards onto the sides.

Begin nailing them on the bottom, progressing toward the top (Fig. 12-3). Make sure that the end of each front and rear board is flush with the surface of the sides.

Next to build is the top, which is made of 3½-inch-wide boards, ¾ inch thick, and 24 inches long. First glue six of these pieces edge to edge to make a panel ¾ inch thick, 21 inches wide, and 24 inches long. Then cut down the width to 19¼ inches.

Now cut a 2-inch-wide strip off the top (Fig. 12-4A). Then glue and nail this piece onto the back edge of the toy box top (Fig. 12-4B).

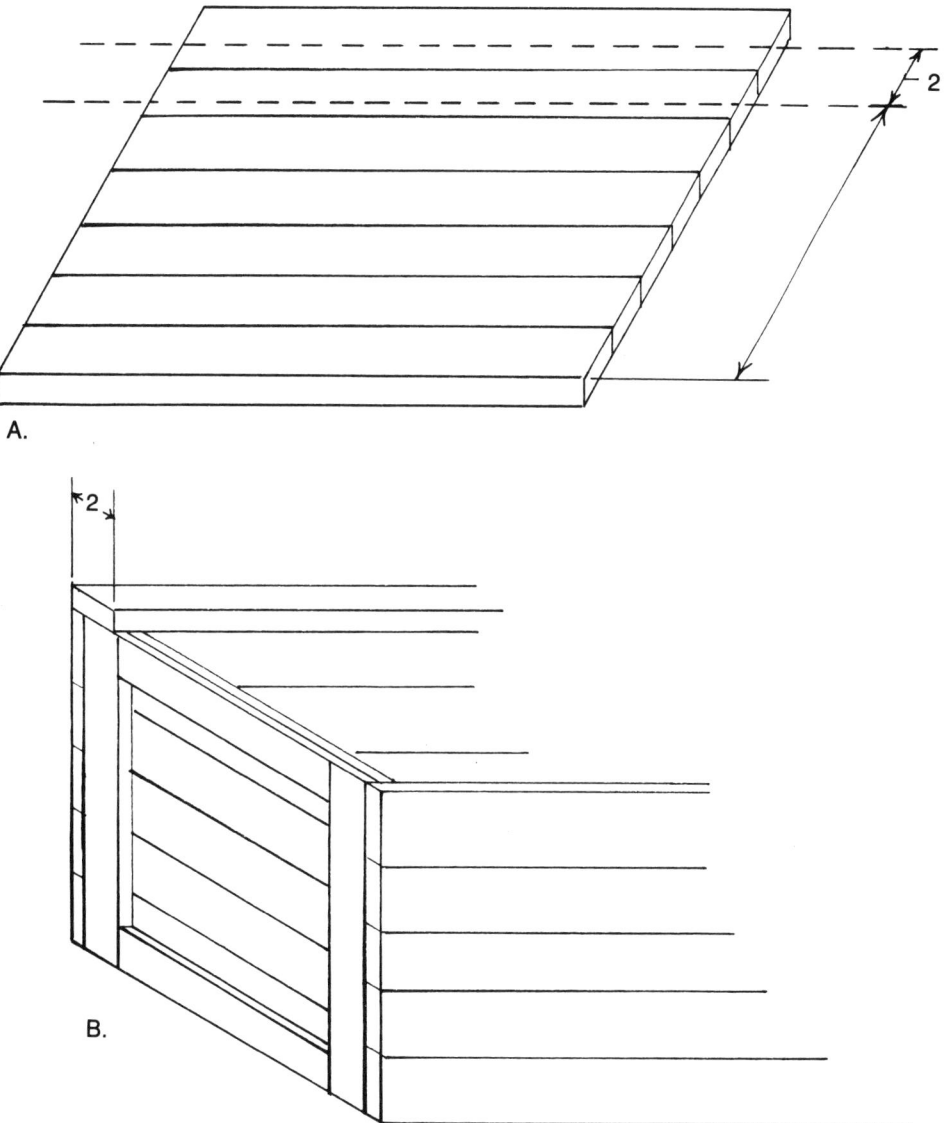

Fig. 12-4. *(A) Cut a 2-inch wide strip off the top panel. (B) Nail the strip onto the top of the toy box.*

Now the opening top can be installed. The toy box in the photograph has the top held in place by two 3-inch strap hinges. I selected this type of hinge because it is durable.

Next cut the bottom from any type of panel stock—plywood, particle board, or hardboard—which is ½ or ⅝ of an inch thick. This thickness is necessary to support the weight of all toys in the box.

The toy box bottom will fit between the sides and front and back. The size of the bottom panel should be 17½ inches wide by 21½ inches long. Check the fit of the bottom in the toy box by sliding it into the box from the bottom. If the fit is correct, leave it in the box, then glue and nail two ¾-inch-thick, ¾-inch-wide, 1-foot-long glue blocks on the box sides. Then glue and nail two 18-inch-long glue blocks along the sides, allowing the bottom to rest on the glue blocks (Fig. 12-5).

The only work that remains is to sand and finish the surfaces. Much care should be taken during the sanding operation for two reasons. First, the entire project should be sanded to remove any surface defects for the sake of appearance. Second, sanding should eliminate any possibility of scratches or slivers harming the youngsters.

The finish to be applied is entirely your choice. The toy box can be stained then varnished, or just varnished. The box can also be painted to match or contrast the colors in the child's room and then stenciled with designs and pictures of animals and toys.

When all steps are completed, the toy box is ready for use. There is, however, one more piece of hardware that should be applied to the toy box for safety's sake: two lid top clamps. These clamps are designed to hold the lid in an open position, thus eliminating the chance of the lid slamming down on little fingers or heads.

PAINTING EASEL

It is very important for a child to express his or her artistic creativity from an early age by coloring with crayons, building with blocks, or simply drawing pictures. A painting

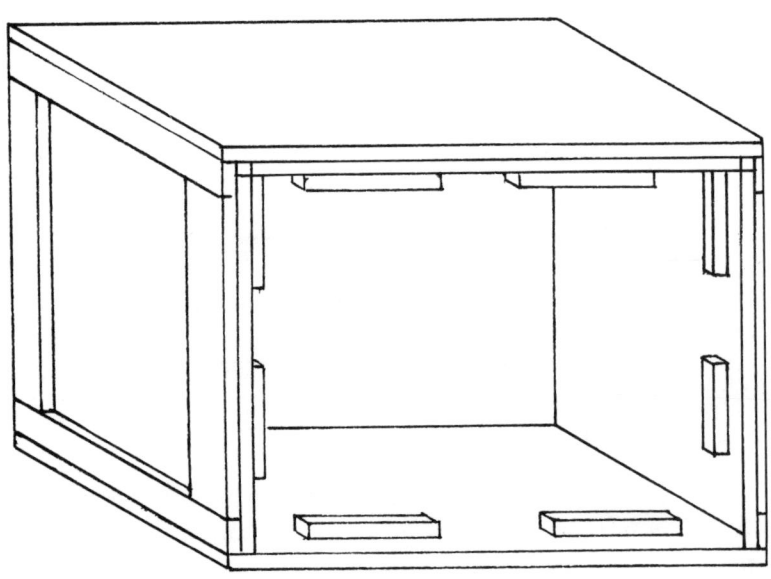

Fig. 12-5. The bottom of the toy box is held in place by four ¾-by-¾-inch glue blocks.

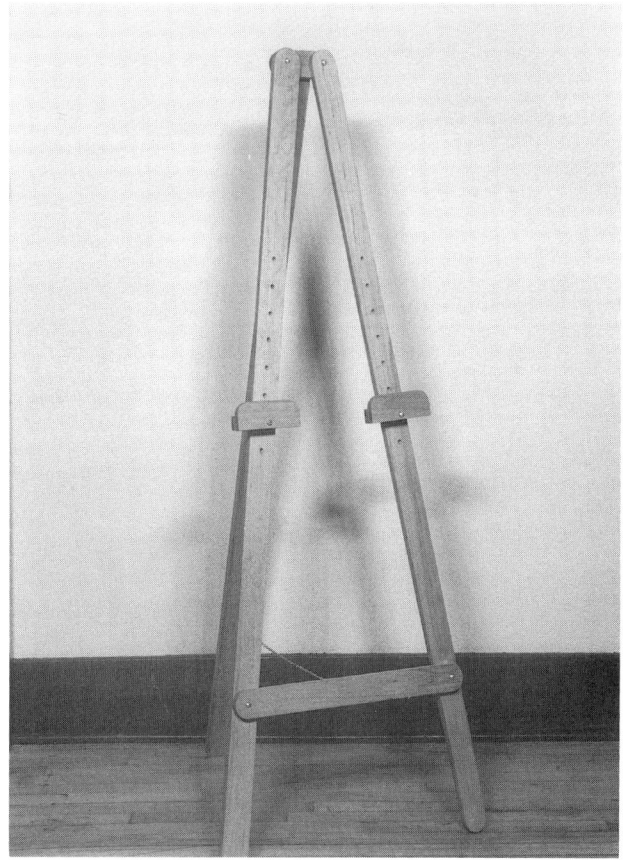

Fig. 12-6. *The paint easel takes the pain out of painting and allows the child's creative juices to flow.*

easel will assist in the child's artistic pursuits (Fig. 12-6).

The easel is made from several lengths of 2-inch-wide wood. The wood may be either hard or soft, but it should have a relatively straight grain and be free from warps or twisting.

Cut two lengths of the 2-inch-wide boards to 60 inches. Then drill several 5/16-inch-diameter holes in these two boards (Fig. 12-7). Notice that the series of holes drilled in the upper end of the boards are drilled at 2-inch intervals.

Round the top and bottom of the two boards to a 1-inch radius by cutting then sanding. Now sand smooth all edges and surfaces on both boards.

The next piece to make is the short, 2-inch-wide, top-horizontal spreader. The spreader (Fig. 12-8) should be 5 inches long, with the two ends rounded to a radius of 1 inch. Drill two 5/16-inch-diameter holes in the spreader at the points indicated. Then sand all surfaces and edges and attach the spreader to the top ends of the two 60-inch-long pieces with two 2-inch-long, 1/4-inch stove bolts. Be sure to use two flat washers and lock nuts on the back of the two bolts.

Next cut the back leg to a width of 2 inches and a length of 60 inches. This piece differs from the other two long front legs in that only one end, the bottom, should be rounded.

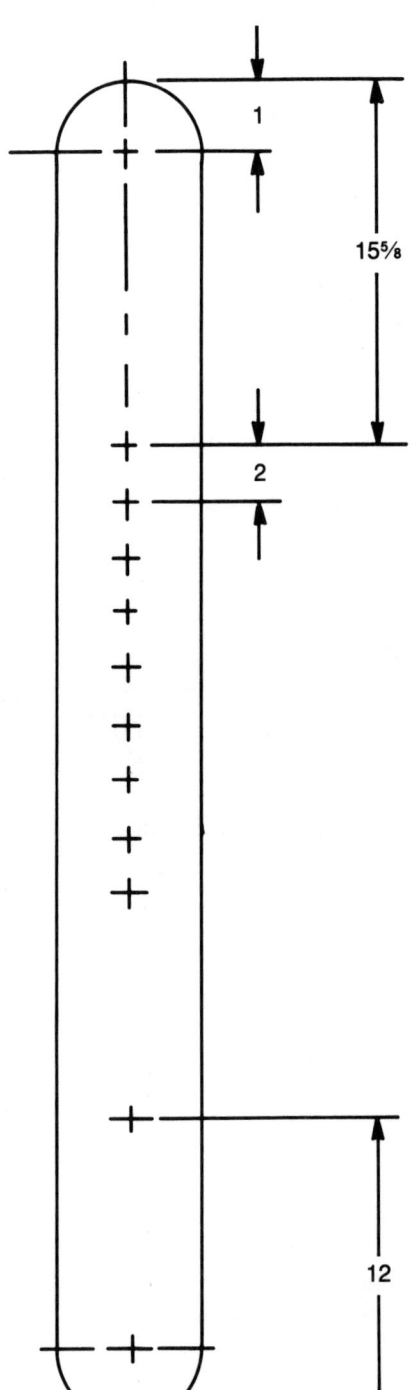

Fig. 12-7. Drill a series of adjoining holes into the two front easel uprights.

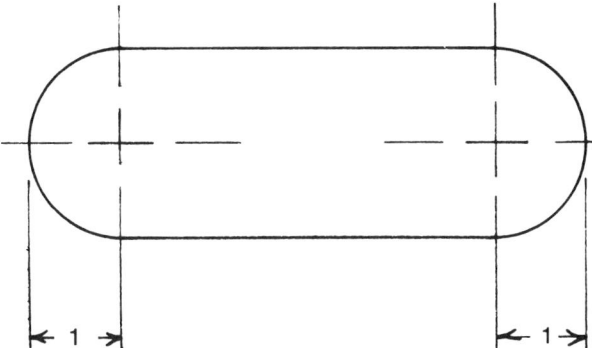

Fig. 12-8. Drill two 5/16-inch-diameter holes in the top spreader, 1 inch in from each side.

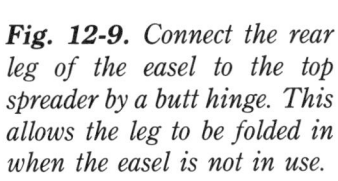

Fig. 12-9. Connect the rear leg of the easel to the top spreader by a butt hinge. This allows the leg to be folded in when the easel is not in use.

On the top squared end of the back leg, screw a 2-inch butt hinge into place (Fig. 12-9). Then screw the other end of the hinge into the center of the back of the horizontal spreader.

Now install a two-inch-wide, 19-inch-long horizontal spreader between the two front legs, 12 inches up from the bottom. Drill two ¼-inch-diameter holes through the lower horizontal spreader (Fig. 12-10). After sanding the spreader screw it to the two front

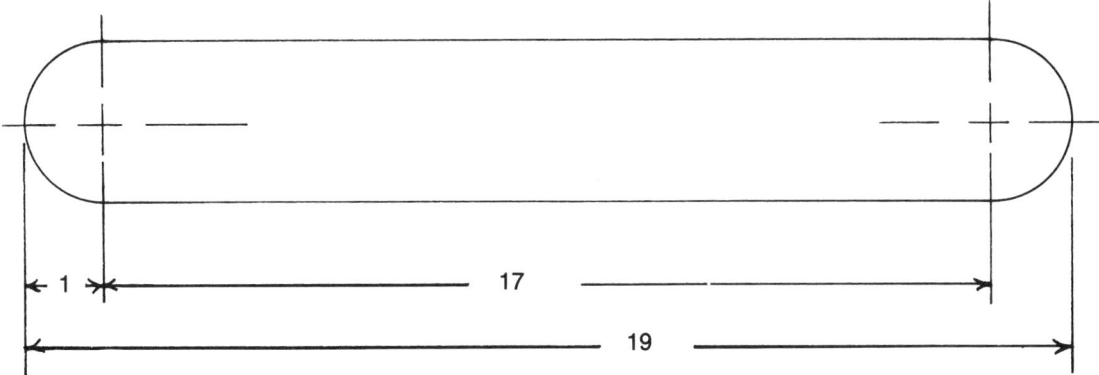

Fig. 12-10. Drill two ¼-inch-diameter holes 1 inch from each end of the horizontal spreader.

legs at the holes that were drilled 12 inches up from the bottom.

The easel in the photograph has been designed to be folded up when not in use. To accomplish this, screw one end of the lower horizontal spreader to the leg with a 1¾-inch-long stove bolt, flat washer, and lock nut. Then attach the opposite end to the other leg with a 1¾-inch-long stove bolt, flat washer, and wing nut.

Now the front and back legs are built and assembled; but there is nothing in their construction to keep them from spreading apart. For this reason, attach a 20-inch length of light chain from the rear leg, about 12 inches up from the bottom end. Attach the other end of the chain to the center of the lower horizontal spreader. The chain can be attached to the wood parts with small screws or screw eyes.

The final parts to be made for the easel are the two supports that will hold the canvas. Make each support from a 2-inch-wide, ¾-inch-thick, 5-inch-long piece of wood. Behind this part, glue a ¾-inch-thick, 1-inch-wide, 5-inch-long board (Fig. 12-11). Then drill a 5/16-inch-diameter hole through both pieces of the supports, ¾ inch up from the bottom edge and centered.

After sanding the supports, screw them into one of the series of holes that are 2 inches apart on the front legs. Use 2½-inch-long, ¼-inch-diameter stove bolts, along with washers and wing nuts. Now the supports can be raised or lowered easily to accommodate almost any size canvas.

Artists, both young and old, will appreciate this painting easel. It can be lowered for small children, and gradually raised as they grow. In fact, because it is adjustable, the easel can be used by adults, as well.

CHILD-SIZE WORKBENCH

Children need an area where they can build fantastic creations and store their tools—a place that is their own. The following is a very sturdy workbench—one that is sized just right for a child (Fig. 12-12).

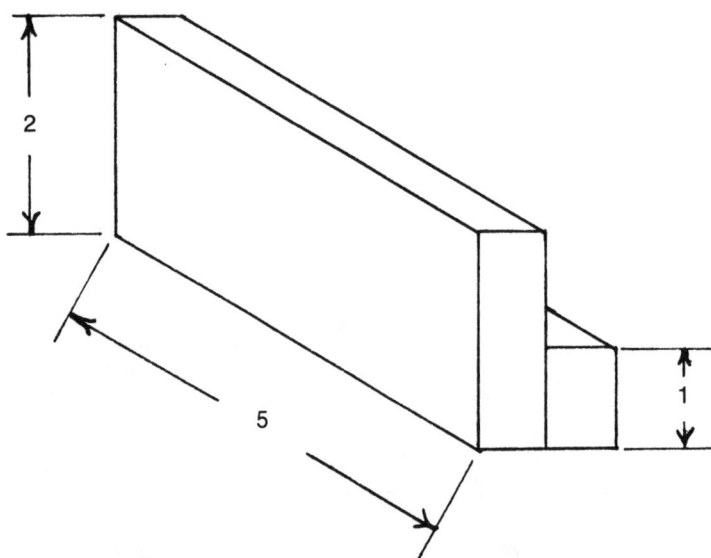

Fig. 12-11. The two supports that hold the paint canvas are made up of two ¾-inch-thick pieces.

Fig. 12-12. *A child enjoys working with tools so a child-size workbench will be a welcome addition to the playroom, shop or garage.*

The materials for the workbench are all readily available from local sources. The 2-by-4 lumber may be of the less expensive construction grade, providing it is free from loose knots, splits, or any other defects that might cause injury.

Cut three of the 2 by 4's to a length of 8 feet, and one to 10 feet. The bench top and lower shelf can be made from either ½-inch- or ⅝-inch-thick plywood, particle board, or any type of board that is the proper thickness. Cut the remaining piece of lumber to 8 feet long, 1 inch thick, and 4 inches wide.

After selecting all of the materials listed at the end of this chapter, you can begin

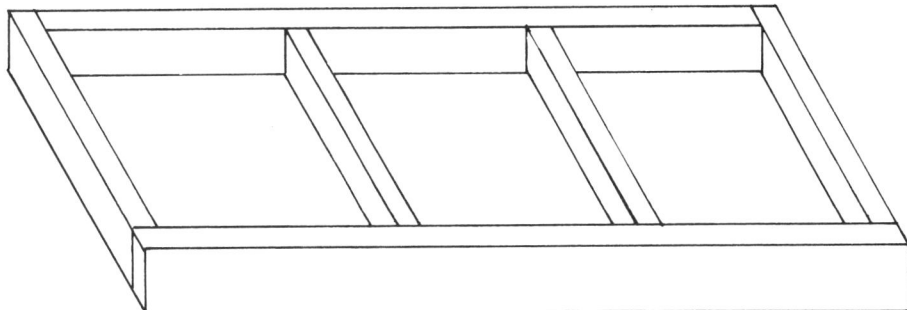

Fig. 12-13. *This drawing illustrates the manner the 2 by 4 frame of the workbench is assembled.*

building the bench top frame. Cut the front and sides of the bench top frame from one of the 8-foot-long 2 by 4's. The front should be 48 inches long, and the other two sides 16½ inches long.

From another 8-foot 2 by 4, cut the back to a length of 45 inches. Cut two 15-inch-long pieces from the same 2 by 4 to lend support to the bench top.

Assemble the bench top frame with 16-penny box nails. I prefer box nails over common ones because they are thinner in diameter and less apt to split the ends of the 2 by 4's. (If splitting becomes a problem even with the box nails, first drill a small hole, then drive the nail into it.

Before assembling the frame, view the illustration in Fig. 12-13. First, nail the 48-inch-long front piece to the two 16½-inch-long side pieces. Then nail the 45-inch-long back between the sides and the 15-inch-long bench supports between the front and back. The center of the first supports should be 16 inches from the outside end, and the second support centered at the 32-inch mark.

When the bench top frame is built, the top can be added. Nail, glue, or screw the plywood or particle board onto the top surface of the bench frame.

Next, cut four 29-inch legs from the 10-foot 2 by 4. Measure these carefully, so that they are all cut to the same length. Then nail the legs into the corners of the workbench, driving the nails in from the sides and the front or back. Each leg must be

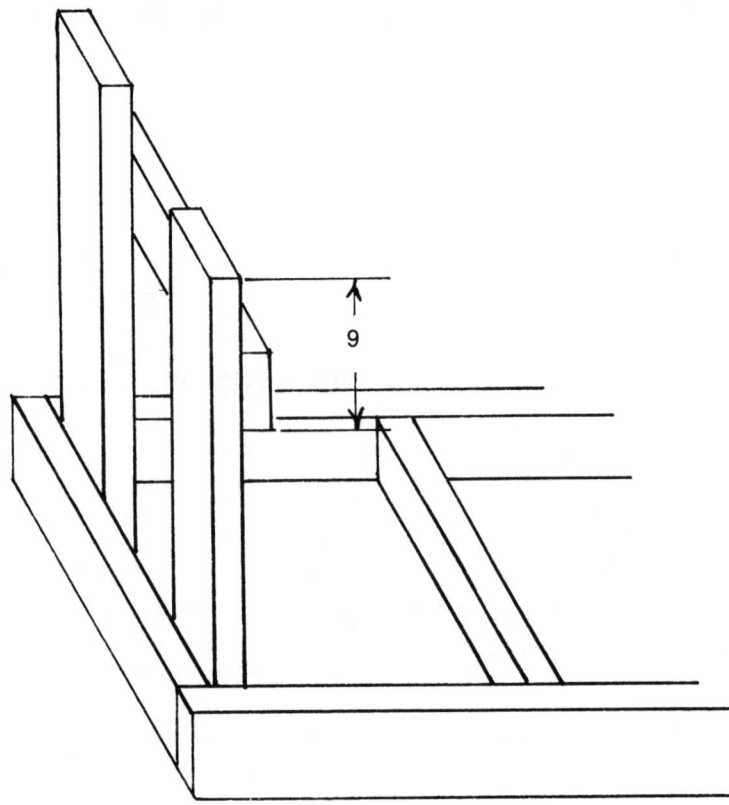

Fig. 12-14. Nail the legs into the corners of the bench top frame; then nail the 2-by-4 horizontal leg braces into place, 9 inches from the bottom of the leg.

nailed in place from two different directions to ensure the legs will be firmly attached to the bench top.

Cut the two horizontal leg braces, which measure 15 inches in length, from the remaining 8-foot 2 by 4. Nail these to the legs, 9 inches up from the end of the legs (Fig. 12-14). Cut the lateral support to 39 inches from the remaining 2-by-4-inch material. Nail the lateral support between the two horizontal leg braces, centered between the legs.

Cut the lower shelf from the second piece of ½-inch-thick plywood or particle board. All that is necessary to fit the lower shelf into position is to cut a 3-by-3½-inch rectangle out of each corner (Fig. 12-15).

The workbench top, as designed, has a 1-by-4-by-48-inch ledge running the length of the back. The ledge is there to prevent tools from rolling off the back of the bench. To hold the ledge in place, nail three 1-by-4-by-6-inch boards into the rear 2 by 4 of the bench, one in the center, the other two 8 inches in from both sides. Next, nail the back ledge to the back supports with smaller 4-penny nails.

The instructions for the child-sized workbench are only basic—you can alter its length, width, and height or, perhaps adapt the back ledge to become a tool holder. In addition, the workbench can be painted, varnished, or left natural. The choice is up to you.

BALANCE BEAM

A child's physical development should not be left to chance. One important physical lesson is that of balance. An excellent way for a child to learn this skill, while having fun, is to use a Balance Beam.

The Balance Beam described in this section is very simple to build, using easily obtainable materials. The only wood needed is a straight, knot-free, 10-foot length of 2 by 4. To begin, cut two 12-inch pieces from the 10-foot length. Then set the remaining 8 feet aside for later use.

Fig. 12-15. Cut the corners of the lower shelf of the workbench as shown.

First, cut two floor supports from the two 12-inch pieces (Fig. 12-16A). Measure along the top surface 5¼ inches, and make a mark. From that mark, measure over another 1½ inches, and again make a mark. Then measure across the surface of the board 2¾ inches down from the two marks previously made on the top. Remove the area between these two lines with a handsaw or power saw.

Next, measure in 4½ inches from both sides along the top edge, and 1½ inches up from the bottom on the ends, as shown in Fig. 12-16B. Draw a diagonal line between the two marks, and remove the material above it. When the cutting process has been completed, thoroughly sand the floor supports, taking time to round the corners.

The last step in making the floor supports for the indoor Balance Beam is to drill a ⅛-inch-diameter hole through the center of the bottom of the 1½-by-2¾-inch cutout. The hole will later be used to attach the floor supports to the beam.

As previously mentioned, the beam is made from the 8-foot-long 2 by 4. On the top of the beam, round the sharp corners slightly. This is done to help prevent accidents that might result if the child should fall and hit the end of the beam.

After sanding, screw the floor supports into position on the balance beam, using

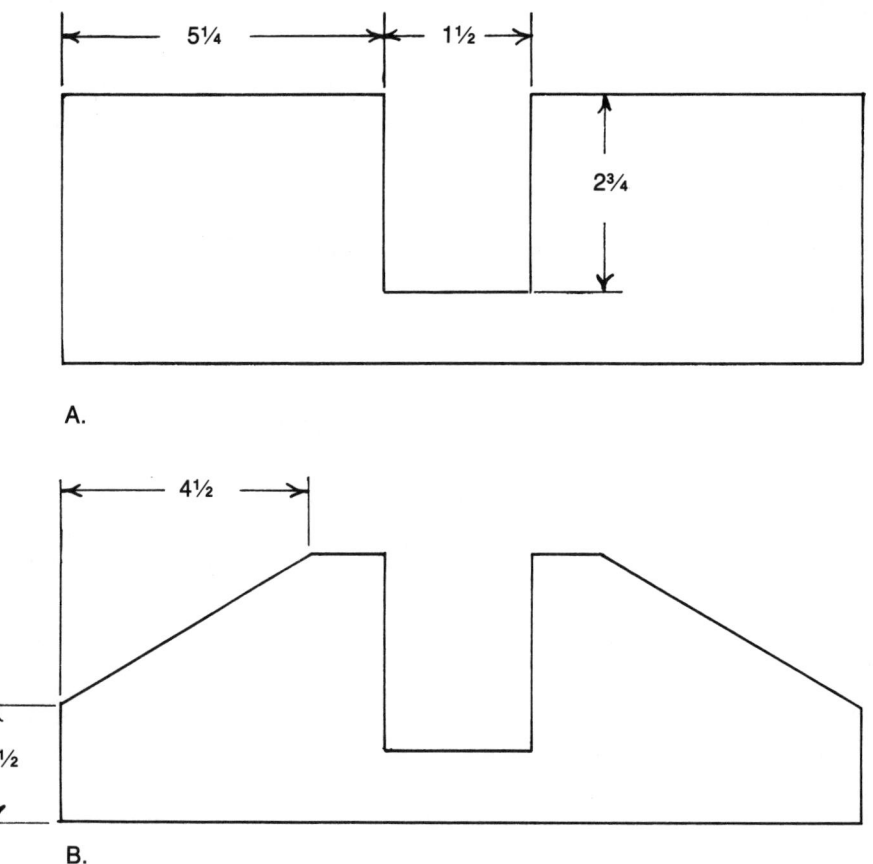

Fig. 12-16. *The two drawings show the method by which the floor supports are cut.*

two 1½-inch-long, number 8 wood screws. Place the floor supports about 1 foot from each end, and turn the screw into the beam from the bottom of the support. Be sure the screw head is turned in flush or slightly below the surface of the wood.

The indoor Balance Beam can be painted, varnished, or left natural. One additional improvement that might be made to the indoor Balance Beam is to apply a layer of scrap carpeting to the bottom of the floor supports. This will eliminate scratches on tile floors. It will also help to keep the beam from sliding on uncarpeted surfaces.

CHILD'S STOOL

Every child needs a stool for a variety of reasons (Fig. 12-17). It can be used to reach a wall phone or light switch, to watch dinner being prepared on the kitchen counter, or simply to get things that are out of reach.

The stool described in this chapter has been designed with safety and strength as two of its most important considerations. The top is wide enough to provide a good foothold, reducing the possibility of accidental slips. The legs lean toward the outer ends of the seat, improving the stool's stability. To further strengthen the stool, a support is glued and screwed between the legs. This is an inexpensive project, and one that will stand up to much use and abuse.

Construction begins by cutting the top to size. It should measure ¾ inch thick, 8 inches wide, and 13 inches long. Round the corners of the top to a 1½-inch radius (Fig. 12-18). Also round the edges of the top with either a file or router.

Cut both legs of the stool from wood that is the same thickness and width as the top but that is only 7 inches long. The legs should have a slight taper along their sides (Fig. 12-19). Also shown in the illustration is the location of two ⅛-inch holes, and the size and shape of the decorative cutout on the bottom.

The legs are not attached to the bottom of the top piece at a 90-degree angle. Rath-

Fig. 12-17. Every child needs a stool to climb on, maybe to reach a wall switch, a favorite toy on a shelf, or to brush their teeth. This stool is a fun, functional project.

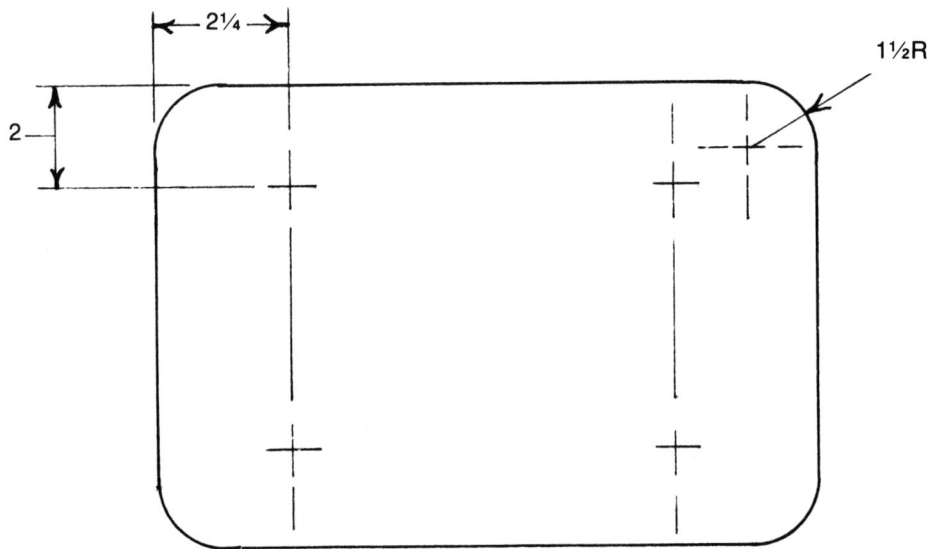

Fig. 12-18. Round the corners of the stool top to prevent the chances of sharp corners scratching youngsters.

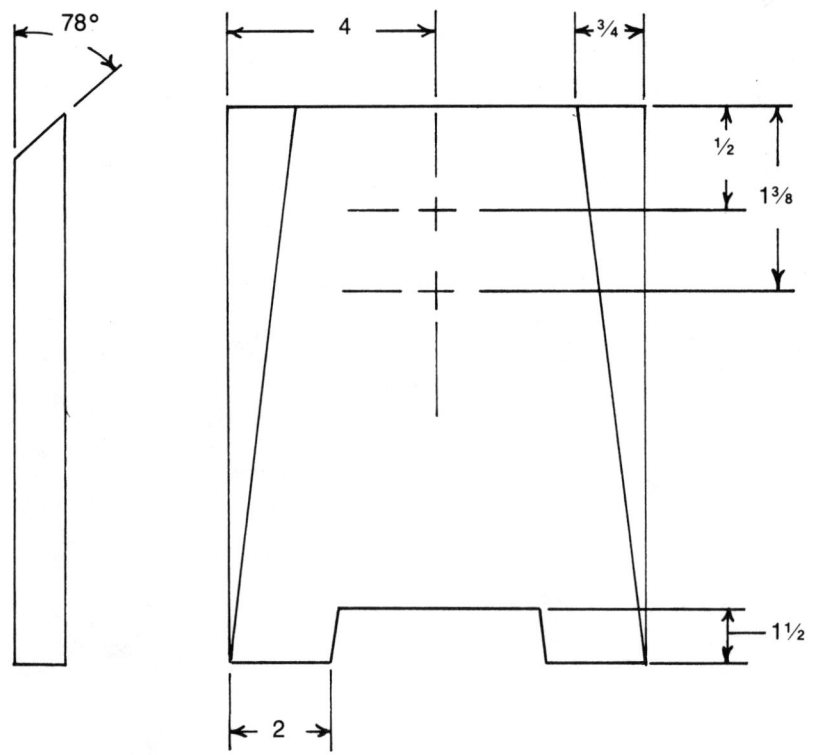

Fig. 12-19. The legs of the stool are tapered on both sides with decorative cutouts on the bottom of each.

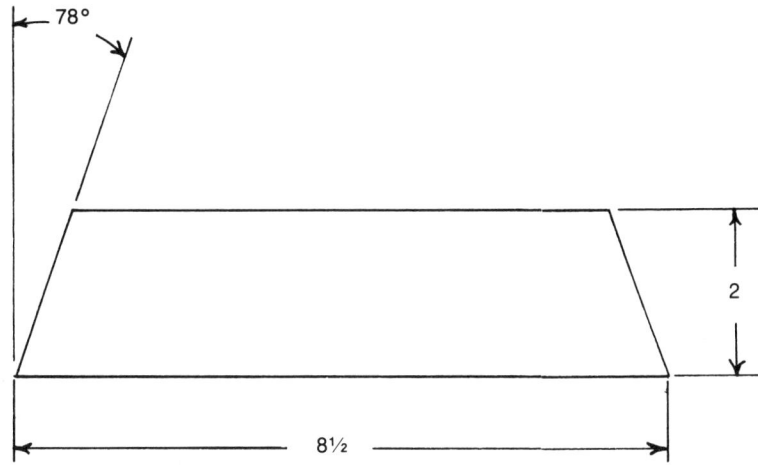

Fig. 12-20. *Cut the ends of the leg support at a 78-degree angle.*

er, they are attached at a slight angle, leaning outward, to provide more stability. To achieve this, cut the top end of the leg to a 78-degree angle, as shown in Fig. 12-19.

The last part of the Child's Stool to make is the leg support. The leg support (Fig. 12-20) is an 8½-inch length of 2-inch-wide and ¾-inch-thick wood. Be sure to use the same type of wood for the support that you used for the rest of the stool. Cut the ends of the support at a 78-degree angle.

To assemble the legs and the leg support, turn two 1½-inch-long, number 6 flathead wood screws through the ⅛-inch-diameter holes drilled through the legs, and into the angled ends of the leg supports. The final assembly of the legs is shown in Fig. 12-21.

Drill four ⅛-inch holes into the stool top, at the points indicated in Fig. 12-18. Then screw four 1¼-inch-long, number 6 flathead wood screws through the top into the leg

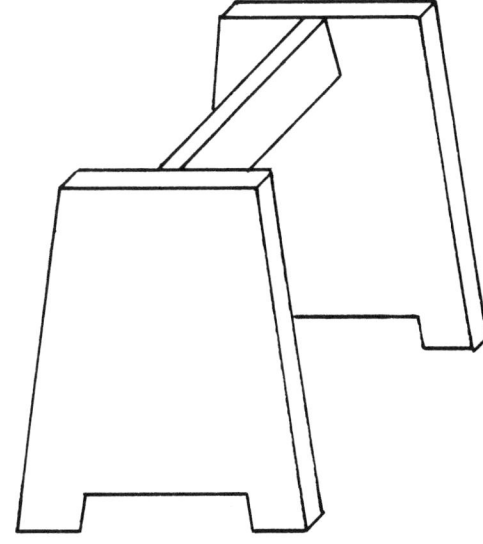

Fig. 12-21. *The leg support holds the two legs at an angle.*

assembly. The screws should be countersunk so that the screw head is either flush with the stool top or recessed below the surface and covered with wood plugs or furniture buttons. Use ⅜-inch furniture buttons.

The entire stool could be painted, or stained and/or varnished. To add a personalized touch, paint the child's name on the stool top or stencil the top with a cheerful design.

LIST 12-1. REQUIRED MATERIALS

Toy Box

10	Sides	¾ × 3½ × 17½
10	Front and Back	¾ × 3½ × 24
6	Top	¾ × 3½ × 10¼
1	Bottom	½ × 17½ × 21½
4	Upper and Lower Side Trim	½ × 1½ × 17½
4	Side Trim	½ × 1½ × 14½
2	Glue Blocks	¾ × ¾ × 12
2	Glue Blocks	¾ × ¾ × 18

Easel

2	Front legs	¾ × 2 × 60
1	Rear Leg	¾ × 2 × 60
1	Top Spreader	¾ × 2 × 5
1	Bottom Spreader	¾ × 2 × 19
2	Canvas Supports	¾ × 2 × 5
2	Canvas Support Backs	¾ × 1 × 5
2	Screw Eyes	⅝ inch
1	Light Chain	20 inches long
4	Stove Bolts	¼ × 1¾
2	Stove Bolts	¼ × 2½
6	Flat Washers	5/16
3	Lock Nuts	¼
3	Wing Nuts	¼

Child-Size Workbench

1	Bench Top Frame Front	2 × 4 × 48
2	Bench Top Frame Sides	2 × 4 × 16½
1	Bench Top Frame Back	2 × 4 × 45
2	Bench Top Frame Supports	2 × 4 × 15
4	Legs	2 × 4 × 29
2	Horizontal Leg Braces	2 × 4 × 15
1	Lateral Support	2 × 4 × 39
1	Bench Top	½ × 18 × 48
1	Bottom Shelf	½ × 15 × 48
1	Ledge	1 × 4 × 48
3	Back Ledge Supports	1 × 4 × 6

Indoor Balance Beam

2 – Floor Supports — 2 × 4 × 12
1 – Beam — 2 × 4 × 8

Child's Stool

1 – Top — ¾ × 8 × 13
2 – Legs — ¾ × 8 × 7
1 – Support — ¾ × 2 × 8½

Appendix

Toy Making Suppliers

Today's toymaker has many advantages over the craftsperson of the past. The tools used today are more efficient and more durable. Woodworking machines are now within the price range of the home craftsperson. This Appendix offers you yet another of today's advantages: a list of mail-order companies that sell plans and materials specifically for toy builders.

These fine companies all advertise periodically in woodworking-related magazines, but they are brought together here in alphabetical order. Each entry contains the mailing address and a brief description of the merchandise which they sell. Some also provide their phone number's.

Albert Constantine And Son, Inc.
2050 Eastchester Road
Bronx, New York 10461
Phone: (212) 792-1600

The Constantine catalog has long been a mainstay in the mail-order business for the woodworker. For the toymaker, they offer a wide range of toy, game, and children's furniture plans, including some wood toy kits. In addition, they offer the toymaker wood wheels (1 to 2¾ inches in diameter), train parts, axle pegs, a fine selection of hardwoods and veneers, toy-making books, balls, spindles, dollhouse furniture and supplies, plus a wide range of general woodworking supplies.

Anderson's Patterns in Wood
6715 Chicago So.
Richfield, MN 55423

Anderson's offers plans for cars, trucks, construction vehicles, boats, pull toys, and trains. Also available are plans for over 148 Christmas tree ornaments. Send $1 for a photo-brochure and one free plan (refundable with first order).

Armor Products
96 East Industry Court
Box 290
Deer Park, NY 11729
Phone: (516) 667-3328

Car, truck, construction vehicles, boat puzzles, trains, and rocking horse plans are available from Armor. Also sold from this company, which has been serving the woodworker for over 20 years, are wood wheels, train parts, axle pegs, and wood people. In addition, Armor sells, a fine line of hardware and supplies for the woodworker.

Bob Morgan Woodworking Supplies
1123 Bardstown Road
Louisville, KY 40204
Phone: (502) 456-2545

This company sells a wide variety of products directed toward the toymaker. Plans from cars and trucks to dollhouses and dollhouse furniture are available. Also sold by Bob Morgan are wood wheels, train parts, axle pegs, hardwood, shaker pegs, toy books, wood people, and furniture buttons. Of general interest to the woodworker, Morgan Woodworking Supplies carries a line of chair cane, rush, veneers, candle cups, and inlays, just to name a few items.

Brown Wood Products
Box 8246
Northfield, IL 60093
Phone: (312) 446-5200

Brown Wood Products sells a line of wood accessories especially designed for the toymaker. A sampling of their inventory includes wood wheels, train parts, axle pegs, shaker pegs, furniture buttons, wood balls, spindles, and wood people.

Cherry Tree Toys, Inc.
P.O. Box 369
Belmont, OH 43718
Phone: (614) 484-1746

A full-color catalog is available for $1. Included in the catalog are over 125 wood-turned parts for toy making and woodworking. They offer over 30 toy kits for a wide variety of skill levels. Plans for all kits are available from Cherry Tree. Of interest to the toymaker building in mass quantities, Cherry Tree offers bulk prices for all items in their catalog.

Clayt's Wooden Toy Plans
601 Oak Terr.
Jupiter, FL 33458

Clayton and Arlene McLaughlin have written a fine book that contains general information of interest to the toymaker, as well as detailed plans for 18 great wood toys.

Craft Patterns
2200 Dean Street
St. Charles, IL 60174
Phone: (312) 584-9600

Craft Patterns sells a catalog of hundreds of plans for the home woodworker. Those plans of special interest to the toymaker are pull toys, rocking horses, toy boxes, child-sized furniture, dollhouses, and dollhouse furniture. Craft Patterns also offers wood and rubber wheels, train parts, axle pegs, hardware, and dollhouse furniture and supplies.

Craft Plans Co.
21801 Industrial Boulevard
Rogers, MN 35374

Craft Plans offers a large selection of plans for furniture, looms, spinning wheels, clocks, dollhouses, cradles, toys, alphabets, birdhouses, weather vanes, kites, and more. (Include 50¢ for catalog.)

Cryder Creek Wood Shoppe, Inc.
101 Commercial Avenue
P.O. Box 19
Whitesville, NY 14897
Phone: (607) 356-3303

Cryder Creek specialized in hardwood-turning supplies, including large diameter dowels, preturned spindles, wood wheels, axle pegs, shaker pegs, wood turned balls, and a fine line of woodworking tools.

D & E Crafts
6118 N. Coast Hwy.
P.O. Box 647
Newport, OR 97365

Dick and Elaine Crandall have designed over 15 toy plans, with more to come in the future. The toys have been designed to be exceptionally sturdy and free from small loose parts. The plans range from a 46-inch-long train and several trucks, to a rocking horse and child-size table and chairs.

Design Group
P.O. Box 514
Miller Place, NY 11764

The Design Group offers for sale a large choice of plans for toys, children's and full-size furniture, birdhouses, and Christmas decorations, just to name a few. All blueprint patterns are full-size outline drawings. There is never a need to enlarge or reduce any part, simply "trace and create." Also offered by this company are four sizes of birch hardwood wheels.

Dutchman's Sawmill
P.O. Box 5381
Phoenix, AZ 85010

The people at the Dutchman's Sawmill provide full-size plans (when the project is not of extreme size) for many wood toy projects. Examples of their toys include cars and trucks, construction vehicles, trains, airplanes, and even an aircraft carrier and destroyer with movable gun turrets. Outside the toy catagories, they offer plans for such items as shelves, magazine stands, tables, gun racks, plant stands, a patio cart, and a porch swing.

Educational Lumber Co., Inc.
P.O. Box 5373
Ashville, NC 28813
Phone: (704) 255-8765

The Educational Lumber Co., Inc. supplies a fine selection of hardwoods and softwoods, veneers, turning squares, project and instructional books, and plywood to both large manufacturers and the home craftsperson.

Elf Creek Wood & Toy Company
1125 N.W. Overlook Ct.
P.O. Box 572
Gresham, OR 97030
Phone: (503) 661-4154

The toymakers of Elf Creek turn out a fine selection of wood toys. The toys range from colorful baby rattles, cars, trucks, and puzzles, to the unique, such as the rocking pig bank, and the mycrodome, a geodesic-shaped play structure. Write for their brochure, complete with photographs of their projects.

Franks Plan Service
1202 South Second St.
Boonville, MS 38829

Franks is a small family business that has developed over 100 original toy plans. The designs have been developed using "shopsmith" equipment, although they can be adapted to any tools. The plans are all full-size with step-by-step instruction, and even a list of needed tools.

General Woodcraft, Inc.
100 Blinman Street
New London, CT 06320-1029
Phone: (203) 442-5301

General Woodcraft sells a fine selection of hardwoods and softwoods. Along with their product line, they also offer a planing and milling of lumber. Many of the wood types are available in thicknesses of ½ to 4 inches. Write for a brochure and price list.

Hawk Craft
P.O. Box 875
Chariton, IA 50049

Hawk Craft will send a copy of their catalog for $1. The catalog is well worth seeing, for the plans they offer are some of the most detailed available. The resulting vehicles, photographed in the catalog, are beautiful gifts to adorn adult office desks or book shelves in the most elegant study.

Hayes Patterns
6 Willow Street
Woburn, MA 01801

Hayes Patterns are full-size plans that just require tracing and cutting the shape. Their product selection ranges from cars and trucks to games and puzzles, lawn ornaments, furniture, and wood carving designs. A catalog can be purchased from them for 25¢. The cost is refundable with the first order.

Impressions
R.R. 2, Box 463
Ferdinand, IN 47532

This company offers a fine line of child-size and full-size furniture plans. The plans are very clear and easy to read. Additional information can be obtained by writing Impressions at the above address.

John Lewman, Toymaker
4954 N. Revere
Parkville, MO 64152
Phone: (816) 587-0119

John Lewman sells a fantastic line of toy plans. You name it, it's included—airplanes, dump trucks, trains, cars, doll cradles, dollhouses, telephones, boats, tanks, wood people, stake trucks, flatbed trucks, child-size complete kitchens, ride-on stutz bearcats, pull toys, a complete farm set, and many more. This is just a partial list. Write to John Lewman at the above address for a copy of his latest, uniquely illustrated catalog.

K & K Wood Crafters
RD 4, Box 270A
Scotia, NY 12302

The folks at K & K Wood Crafters will be glad to send you a brochure of their offerings—a catalog full of wood parts that can be used in toy production—if you send them your name, address, and the return postage. An example of their wares includes a nice selection of hardwood wheels, screwhole buttons, wood balls, wood rings, four types of train boilers, four sizes of train smokestacks, wood barrels, drums, milk cans, people, and much more. Another item they sell is a unique wooden cam mechanism that is used for pull toys that have a wobble or hopping action.

K & K boasts that they sell the finest products available and back them up with a 100-percent money-back guarantee. Also, they offer quantity prices for the craftsperson producing wood toys in mass. The more purchased, the lower the cost per unit.

Kaymar Wood Products, Inc.
4603 35th S.W.
Seattle, WA 98126
Phone: (206) 932-3584

Kaymar Wood Products offers over 70 different kinds of lumber ranging from domestics to the exotics. Send for their free price list at the above address. They will be more than glad to mail-order hardwoods anywhere. Speciality mill work is available on request.

L L Enterprises
P.O. Box 35203
Phoenix, AZ 85069

The L L Enterprises catalog, available for $1, contains a great amount of plans of general interest to the woodworker. For the toymaker, there are plans for rocking horses, toy boxes, and child-size tables and chairs.

Meisel Hardware Specialties
P.O. Box 258
Mound, MN 55364
Phone: (612) 472-5544

The discount catalog offered by Meisel Hardware is available to woodworkers by writing them at the address above. The merchandise includes some of the hard-to-find parts woodworkers always seem to need. For the toymaker, they offer a fine selection of toy plans and kits. Many of their plans are for projects not found at any other suppliers, such as a wood truck, cribbage board, or a battleship cribbage board. They also sell a complete line of supplies for toy making. Their wood wheels range in size from ¾ inch to 2 inches in diameter. Cargo for the wood vehicles include oil drums, milk cans, pickle barrels, wood people, and smokestacks, just to list a few. This is a catalog every woodworker should have in his or her reference library.

Native American Hardwoods, Ltd.
RD 1, Box 6484
West Valley, NY 14171
Phone: (716) 942-6631

The Native American Hardwood company sells a great selection of hardwoods in quantities to suit the home woodworker. In addition to lumber, they offer the service of planing it to any thickness. Some rare, hard-to-find wood items, which are made available to the craftsperson through this company's catalog, include heavy basswood for carving, spalted blocks, hardwood turning squares, extra-wide lumber, flitch-sawn slabs, hardwood flooring, paneling, and trim.

Noble Toy Company
Box 732
Manchester, MA 01944

Chris Noble has turned out beautifully crafted car and truck kits and finished products. His vehicles are both great toys and collectible items. The Noble Toy Company also offers wood wheels and axle pegs. Write for a brochure to the above address.

Patterson Enterprises
Box 1390
Apopka, FL 32704

Write for information about Patterson's latest catalog, "The Poor Man's Catalog," with 300 ways to beat inflation. Among many other things, the catalog offers plans for cars, trucks, construction vehicles, boats, pull toys, bucking broncos, musical instruments, child-size furniture, dolls, boomerangs, action toys, cradles, sleds, and much, much more. This is definitely one of America's most unique catalogs.

Play For Growth
Miller Falls, MA 01349
Phone: (413) 659-2211

Toys are not only for entertaining youngsters; they are also designed to assist in the development of the child's motor skills and education. The Play For Growth company offers parents a great selection of carefully selected educational and fun toys.

Roto-Hinge
P.O. Box 55
Bloomington, IN 47401

Roto-Hinge Company offers a fine piece of hardware for the woodworking craftsperson. The Roto-Hinge is a concealed swivel hinge that can be utilized in a variety of ways. The hinge was used twice in the clown doll in Chapter 10, as the swivel between the head and shoulders and also on the waist. The Roto-Hinge is also used extensively in folding wood furniture. Write for information on the hinges and furniture plans.

Sun Designs
P.O. Box 206
Delafield, WI 53018
Phone: (414) 567-4255

The Strombecks of Sun Designs have designed some beautiful wood toys. They sell plans for many toys, including a complete marina, town, sailboats, power boats, ferris wheel, rocking horse, banks, a fantastic doll buggy, wagon, construction vehicles, trucks, and a large selection of puzzles.

The plans are well-drawn, full-size drawings, with complete material lists and clear, concise instructions. To complement the plans, Sun Design offers a very well-put-together book describing their projects. The projects are illustrated with color photographs. Also included is an entertaining child's story, telling how the Strombecks have been assisted in their toy making endeavors by the Stroms, a group of 18-inch-tall toymakers.

T.J.'s Craftshop
Box 5074
Athens, GA 30604

The people at T.J.'s Craftshop have designed a fine selection of classic wood cars and trucks. They sell the plans for these vehicles, which are great play toys and also of fine enough design to grace a desk or fireplace mantle.

The same vehicles are also available from T.J.'s Craftshop in kit form. The kits contain all of the thirty or more pieces to completely build the vehicles. All that the craftsperson is required to buy is the glue.

Taylor Products
4949 W. Saint Charles Avenue
Lake Charles, LA 70605

Car, truck, airplane, and train plans are available from Taylor Products. The plans are designed so that only common sizes of lumber are needed. The wood will not need to be planed to specific thicknesses. Also, all the projects can be made with either power tools or hand tools. Write the people at Taylor Products for a copy of their brochure at the above address.

Timber's Country Store
2907 Lake Forest Road
Carnelian Bay, CA 95711
Phone: 1-800-824-5897

This company provides the toy making craftsperson with one-stop shopping service. They sell hundreds of woodworking patterns, instruction books, unique wood projects, and almost anything a toymaker needs, including a 24-hour ordering service. A copy of the Timbers Country Store catalog can be obtained by writing or calling them at the above address.

Tot Toys
3056 Oneida Street
Sauquoit, NY 13456

Brad Smith and the people of Tot Toys have produced kits and plans for over thirty original designs. They are especially helpful for teachers, camp counselors, and scout troops by offering kits complete with lesson plans and quizzes. They are even prepared to custom design a toy for your particular needs.

Tot Toys sells plans and kits for cars, trucks, pull toys, games, puzzles, and trains. In addition, they sell four sizes of wood wheels, axle pegs, hardwood, softwood, shaker pegs, balls, and wood people. For more information, contact Tot Toys at the above address.

Toy Designs
Box 441
Newton, IA 50208

The toy designers at Toy Designs have worked long and hard hours to produce the over 80 vehicle plans and kits. (The kits are not the wooden pieces, but rather the accessories used with the vehicle). The projects have all been engineered to ensure safety, sturdiness, and ease of construction. The plans are all drawn full-size with general instructions and a list required of materials. The people at Toy Designs also sell toymaking supplies such as wood wheels, train parts, axle pegs, shaker pegs, furniture buttons, dowels, and wood people.

Toymakers Supply Company
2907 Lake Forest Road
Tahoe City, CA 95730
Phone: (916) 583-1555

The Toymakers Supply Company has been in the business of publishing wood toy patterns and supplying wood toy parts longer than anyone else in the industry. This has enabled them to develop the largest variety of wood project patterns available.

The wood toy parts—wheels, toy train smokestacks, axle pegs, etc.—used in the photographed projects in this book have been supplied by the Toymakers Supply Company. Their catalog lists these parts, and almost anything else the toy-making woodworker will need.

Toys & Joys
Box 628
Lynden, WA 98264

Toys & Joys is a mail-order company that specializes in selling quality patterns and parts for the woodworker involved in toy making. They also offer a good variety of toy-making materials such as wheels, axle pegs, spindles, and wood people.

Woodcraft Supply Corporation
41 Atlantic Avenue
Woburn, MA 01888
Phone: (617) 935-5860

The Woodcraft Supply Corporation, established in 1928, is a mail-order company that specializes in the selling of domestic and imported woodworking hand tools and supplies, including books, finishes, carving tools, clamps, hardware, benches, turning equipment, sharpening stones, drills, saws, and marking tools. Products of particular interest to the toymaker are shaker pegs, wood wheels, axle pegs, wood people, knife kits, and a rocking horse kit.

Woods By Jeff
6 Depot Street
South Grafton, MA 01560

Jeff produces a variety of toys and other wood projects that are sold as finished products only. They include dominoes, pull toys, airplanes, a train, and a message center, to name just a few.

The Woodworkers' Store
21801 Industrial Boulevard
Rogers, MN 55374
Phone: (612) 428-4101

The Woodworkers' Store has a 112-page catalog of tools, plans, kits, and many hard-to-find items of interest to the woodworker. A copy of their catalog may be obtained for $1. With over 30 years in the business, they have developed a fine selection. The Woodworkers' Store is opening retail stores in Minneapolis, Seattle, Denver, Boston, Columbus, Ohio, and San Diego.

Woody's
55378 Mayflower Road
South Bend, IN 46628

Woody's sells a fine selection of wood toy plans. The product line includes such items as a toy tractor and wagon, a heavy-duty child-size wagon, and several different car and truck designs. Write to Woody's to inquire about plans and prices.

Index

35mm camera, 157

A

abrasives, 5
adhesives, 11
airplanes and flying toys, 110-150
   helicopter, 114
   interstellar fighter, 115
   Orican shuttle, 123
   personnel transporter, 126
   Piper Cub, 110
   planetary landing vessel, 133
   planetary mobile unit (PMU), 138
   space shuttle, 123
   Venusian star cruiser, 144
assembly, toys, 10
axle pegs, 10
axles, general design and manufacture of, 9-10

B

balance beam, 283
band saws, 4
baseball bat coatrack, 266
baseball equipment rack, 268
bass boat, 187
bed, doll, 164
blind dowel, 11
blocks, 216
boat
   bass, 187
   Great Lakes freighter, 191
   passenger ship, 245
   tanker, 191
   tug, toothbrush holder, 241
box car, 171
box trailer, 52
bug keeper, 156
building blocks, 216
bulldozer, 62
   creeper unit for, 61

C

cab, large truck, 36
caboose, 172
camera, 157
cars, 26-35
   cutout, 89-109
   import, 26
   Indy-style racer, 30
   sedan, 26

sports car, 26
station wagon, 26
cement mixer, 55
child's stool, 285
child-size clothes pole, 253
child-size workbench, 280
circle cutter, 7, 8
clamps, 5
clawhammer, infant and toddler toys, 208
clipboard, 161
clothes pole, 253
clown doll, 226
coal car, 171
coatracks
   baseball bat, 266
   personalized, 257
compass, 7
construction vehicles, 61-85
   bulldozer, 61, 62
   crane shovel, 65
   creeper unit, 61
   grader, 77
   pay loader, 71
   shovel, 61, 65
   truck-mounted shovel, 79
coping saws, 3
corner shelf, 264
coupling for train, 90
cradle, doll, 151
krayon keeper, 160
creature keeper, 156
creeper unit, 61
crosscut saws, 3
cutoff saws, 4
cutout toys, 89-109

D

delivery van, 24
doll bed, 164
doll cradle, 151
doll high chair, 178
dowels, 9, 11
   joining boards with, 12, 13
drilling tools, 4
   circle and hole cutter for, 7
dump truck, 44

E

easel, 276
engine, train, 169

equipment rack, baseball, 268
eye protection, 3

F

file, infant and toddler toys, 213
finishing materials, 12
flat car, train, 172
flatbed trailer, 51
flatbed trucks, 42
fleet vehicles, 15-85
fly cutter, 7, 8
flying toys, 110-150
freighter boat, 191
fuel tanks, semi-truck, 47

G

gas hauler, 54
glues, 11
grader, 77

H

hand drill, infant and toddler toys, 213
helicopter, 114
high chair, doll, 178
hole cutter, 7, 8
hood, large truck, 37
hydroplane, 183

I

import car, 26
Indy-style racer, 30
infant and toddler toys, 199-250
   building blocks, 216
   clown doll, 226
   jumping bear, 225
   passenger ship, 245
   profile bear, 225
   sandwich stacking toy, 238
   shape box, 199
   shape puzzle, 242
   simple pull toys, 219
   toolbox and tools, 204
   toothbrush tugboat, 241
interstellar fighter, 115

J

joints, 11
jumping bear, 225

K

kids' furniture, 251-289
   miscellaneous pieces, 273-289
   room organizers, 253-272

L

lap board, 161
large trucks, 36-60
  cab for, 36
  cement mixer, 55
  dump, 44
  flatbed truck, 42
  gas hauler, 54
  hood for, 37
  log hauler, 43
  lumber hauler, 43
  milk hauler, 54
  semi, 47
  tankers, 54
light duty trucks, 17-25
  delivery van, 24
  mini motor home, 23, 23
  pickup, 17
log hauler truck, 43
lumber truck, 43

M

mallet, infant and toddler toys, 208
measuring tools, infant and toddler toys, 211
milk hauler, 54
miscellaneous furnishings, 273-289
  balance beam, 283
  child's stool, 285
  child-size workbench, 280
  painting easel, 276
  toy box, 273

N

name train, 173

O

"Old 99" toy train, 167
Orican shuttle, 123

P

paint, 12, 13
painting easel, 276
passenger car, train, 172
passenger ship, 245
pay loader, 71
penetrating oil finish, 14
personalized coatracks, 257
personnel flying transporter, 126
pickup truck, 17-22
Piper Cub airplane, 110
planetary landing vessel, 133
planetary mobile unit (PMU), 138
potpourri projects, 151-198
  35mm camera, 157
  bass boat, 187
  clipboard, 161
  krayon keeper, 160
  creature keeper, 156
  doll bed, 164
  doll cradle, 151
  doll high chair, 178
  Great Lakes freighter, 191
  hydroplane, 183
  lap board, 161
  name train, 173
  stilts, 176
  tictactoe, 174
  toy train, 167
power saws, 4
profile bear, 225
pull toy, 219
puzzle, shape, 242

R

radial arm saws, 4
rasps, 4
ripsaws, 3
room organizers, 253-272
  baseball bat coatrack, 266
  baseball equipment rack, 268
  child-size clothes pole, 253
  corner shelf, 264
  personalized coatracks, 257
  wall shelf unit, 260

S

safety, 3
sandpaper, 5
sandwich stacking toy, 238
saw, infant and toddler toys, 215
saws, 3
  power, 4
screwdriver, infant and toddler toys, 210
scroll saws, 3

sedan, 26
semi-truck, 47
  box trailer for, 52
  flatbed trailer for, 51
  fuel tanks for, 47
  sleeping cab for, 47
  trailer for, 49
shape box, 199
shape puzzle, 242
shaping tools, 4
shelves
  corner, 264
  wall unit, 260
shovel, creeper unit for, 61
sleeping cab, semi-truck, 47
space shuttle, 123
sports car, 26
stacking toy, 238
stain, 13, 14
star cruiser, 144
station wagon, 26
steam shovel, 65
stilts, 176
stool, 285
suppliers, 293-302

T

tictactoe game, 174
tanker boat, 191
tanker car, train, 172
tanker trucks, 54
toolbox and tools
  clawhammer for, 208
  file for, 213
  hand drill for, 213
  infant and toddler toys, 204
  mallet for, 208
  measuring tools for, 211
  saw for, 215
  screwdriver for, 210
  try square for, 210
  wrench for, 208
tools, 3-5
toothbrush holder, tugboat, 241
toy box, 273
toy box stuffers, 87-250
  airplanes and flying toys, 110-150
  infant and toddler toys for, 199-250
  potpourri projects for, 151-198
toy making, 1-14
  assembly steps in, 10-11
  design tips for, 6-14
  finishing materials in, 12
  suppliers for, 293-302
toy train, 167
trailer
  box, 52
  flatbed, 51
  semi-truck, 49
train, 167
  box car for, 171
  caboose, 172
  coal car for, 171
  coupling for, 90
  cutout, 89-109
  engine for, 169
  flat car, 172
  name, 173
  passenger car for, 172
  tanker car, 172
truck-mounted shovel, 79
trucks
  cement mixer, 55
  cutout, 89-109
  delivery van, 24
  dump, 44
  flatbed, 42
  gas hauler, 54
  large, 36-60
  light duty, 17-25
  log hauler, 43
  lumber, 43
  milk hauler, 54
  pickup, 17
  semi, 47
  shovel mounted on, 79
try square, infant and toddler toys, 210
tugboat toothbrush holder, 241

V

varnish, 14
vehicle fleet, 15-85
  construction vehicles in, 61-85
  light duty trucks in, 17-25
Venusian star cruiser, 144

W

wall shelf unit, 260
workbench, child-size, 280
wrench, infant and toddler toys, 208
wheels, general design and manufacture of, 6-8

Other Bestsellers from TAB

☐ **ENCYCLOPAEDIA OF MILITARY MODELS 1/72 SCALE**—Claude Boileau, Huynh-Dinh Khuong, and Thomas A. Young

A complete guide to all 1/72 scale military models produced worldwide! Brief histories accompany full-color illustrations of kits and kitboxes manufactured at 1/72 scale throughout the world. Concise critiques evaluate the type and quality of kit materials and the accuracy of detail replicated in finished models. Model manufacturers (including addresses) comprise the entire second portion of the book. All the models ever made by these companies are listed. 204 pp., illustrated in four-color, hardcover.
Paper $22.95   **Hard $28.95**
Book No. 22383

☐ **MAKING ANTIQUE FURNITURE**—Edited by Vic Taylor

A collection of some of the finest furniture ever made is found within the pages of this project book designed for the intermediate- to advanced-level craftsman. Reproducing European period furniture pieces such as a Windsor chair, a Jacobean box stool, a Regency table, a Sheraton writing desk, a Lyre-end occasional table, and many traditional furnishings is sure to provide you with pleasure and satisfaction. Forty projects include materials lists and step-by-step instructions. 160 pp., fully illustrated, 8½ " × 11"
Paper $19.95   **Hard $25.95**
Book No. 3056

☐ **COUNTRY FURNITURE—114 Traditional Projects**—Percy W. Blandford

Show off a house full of beautiful country furniture—you created! There is an undeniable attraction about handmade furniture. Whether the craftsman is an amateur or professional, individually made furniture carries on the tradition of the first settlers and their ancestors. Blandford captures the rustic flavor in these traditional projects—and shows how you can too! Projects range from simple boxes to more elaborate cabinets and cupboards. 260 pp., 246 illus.
Paper $19.95   **Hard $24.95**
Book No. 2944

☐ **WOODWORKER'S 30 BEST PROJECTS**—Editors of *Woodworker* Magazine

A collection of some of the finest furniture ever made can be found within the pages of this project book. Designed for the woodworker who has already mastered the basics, the projects presented in this book are for the intermediate- to advanced-level craftsman. Each furniture project comes complete with detailed instructions, a materials list, exploded views of working diagrams, a series of step-by-step, black-and-white photos, and a photograph of the finished piece. 224 pp., 300 illus.
Paper $18.95   **Hard $23.95**
Book No. 3021

☐ **DESIGNING AND BUILDING COLONIAL AND EARLY AMERICAN FURNITURE, WITH 47 PROJECTS**—2nd Edition—Percy W. Blandford

Original designs that allow plenty of room for creativity! This volume captures the spirit and challenge of authentic Early American and Colonial craftsmanship. Blandford, an internationally recognized expert in the field, provides first-rate illustrations and simple instructions on the art of reproducing fine furniture. Every project in this volume is an exquisite reproduction of centuries-old originals: drop-leaf tables, peasant chairs, swivel-top tables, firehouse armchair, ladderback chairs, tilt-top box tables, hexagonal candle stands, trestle dining tables, wagon seat benches, jackstands, dry sinks, love seats, and Welsh dressers. 192 pp., 188 illus.
Paper $15.95   **Hard $21.95**
Book No. 3014

☐ **33 USEFUL PROJECTS FOR THE WOODWORKER**—Editors of *School Shop* Magazine

A wealth of information for beginning and advanced hobbyists . . . tools, techniques, and dozens of exciting projects. Here's a handbook that deserves a permanent spot on every woodworker's tool bench. Packed with show-how illustrations and material lists, this invaluable guide provides you with a wide variety of useful, and fun-to-make woodworking projects: a spice rack, a wall clock, a plant stand, a cutting board, a wooden chest, a magazine rack, a serving cart, a child's playhouse, and more! 160 pp., 122 illus.
Paper $10.95   **Hard $12.95**
Book No. 2783

Other Bestsellers from TAB

☐ **THE FRUGAL WOODWORKER**—Rick Liftig

Who says you need an elaborate workshop to fully enjoy your woodworking hobby? And who says you have to spend a small fortune on expensive materials to produce pro-quality furniture? *Certainly not Rick Liftig!* And neither will you after you get a look at the expert advice, money-saving tips, and practical low-cost projects included in this exciting new woodworking guide. You'll find invaluable advice on where and how to acquire wood at bargain prices, even for free! 240 pp., 188 illus.
Paper $10.95   Hard $12.95
Book No. 2702

☐ **A MASTER CARVER'S LEGACY—essentials of wood carving techniques**—Brieuc Bouché

Expert guidance on the basics of wood carving from a master craftsman with over 50 years experience. All the techniques for making a whole range of woodcarved items are included. You'll learn how-to's for basic chip carving, the basic rose, cutting of twinings, a classic acanthus leaf, and a simple carving in the round. In no time at all you will be making many of the projects featured. 176 pp., 135 illus., 8½ ″ × 11″.
Paper $17.95   Hard $24.95
Book No. 2629

Send $1 for the new TAB Catalog describing over 1300 titles currently in print and receive a coupon worth $1 off on your next purchase from TAB.

(In PA, NY, and ME add applicable sales tax. Orders subject to credit approval. Orders outside U.S. must be prepaid with international money orders in U.S. dollars.)
*Prices subject to change without notice.

To purchase these or any other books from TAB, visit your local bookstore, return this coupon, or call toll-free 1-800-233-1128 (In PA and AK call 1-717-794-2191).

Product No.	Hard or Paper	Title	Quantity	Price

☐ Check or money order enclosed made payable to TAB BOOKS Inc.
Charge my   ☐ VISA   ☐ MasterCard   ☐ American Express

Acct. No. _____ Exp. _____

Signature _____

Please Print
Name _____

Company _____

Address _____

City _____

State _____ Zip _____

Subtotal
Postage/Handling
($5.00 outside U.S.A. and Canada) $2.50
In PA, NY, and ME add applicable sales tax
TOTAL

Mail coupon to:
TAB BOOKS Inc.
Blue Ridge Summit
PA 17294-0840   BC